AREA HANDBOOK

for the

MALAGASY REPUBLIC

Co-Authors
Harold D. Nelson

Margarita Dobert
Gordon C. McDonald
James Mc Laughlin
Barbara Marvin
Philip W. Moeller

309.108
A 678
Pam 550-163
1973
71479

DT
469
M26
N4

First Edition
Research completed October 1972
Published 1973

Library of Congress Catalog Card Number: 73-600012

For sale by the Superintendent of Documents,
U.S. Government Printing Office, Washington, D. C. 20402
Price $3.85 domestic postpaid or $3.50 GPO Bookstore

FOREWORD

This volume is one of a series of handbooks prepared by Foreign Area Studies (FAS) of The American University, designed to be useful to military and other personnel who need a convenient compilation of basic facts about the social, economic, political, and military institutions and practices of various countries. The emphasis is on objective description of the nation's present society and the kinds of possible or probable changes that might be expected in the future. The handbook seeks to present as full and as balanced an integrated exposition as limitations on space and research time permit. It was compiled from information available in openly published material. An extensive bibliography is provided to permit recourse to other published sources for more detailed information. There has been no attempt to express any specific point of view or to make policy recommendations. The contents of the handbook represent the work of the authors and FAS and do not represent the official view of the United States government.

An effort has been made to make the handbook as comprehensive as possible. It can be expected, however, that the material, interpretations, and conclusions are subject to modification in the light of new information and developments. Such corrections, additions, and suggestions for factual, interpretive, or other change as readers may have will be welcomed for use in future revisions. Comments may be addressed to:

The Director
Foreign Area Studies
The American University
5010 Wisconsin Avenue, N.W.
Washington, D. C. 20016

PREFACE

Few recent works offering a comprehensive explanation of the various elements of Malagasy society have been published in the English language. *The Area Handbook for the Malagasy Republic*, therefore, seeks to provide a compact and objective exposition and analysis of the country's dominant social, political, and economic aspects. It is designed to give the reader an understanding of the forces operating within a developing country, which is regarded by France and various other nations of the world as an area of some strategic importance in the southwestern Indian Ocean. There remain, however, a number of gaps in certain information to which attention has been called. In producing the handbook, difficulties were encountered regarding the highly contradictory nature of numerous published source materials. The authors have attempted to exercise reasonable judgment in dealing with these contradictions. Moreover, before work on the handbook was completed, the Malagasy government collapsed, and power was given to a military regime. Many of the reform measures being initiated by the new government had not been sufficiently clarified to permit detailed treatment by the authors.

There are some misconceptions regarding the correct name of the country that serves as the subject of this handbook. Before independence in 1960 it was known as Madagascar; after achieving sovereignty its name became the Malagasy Republic. Nonetheless, since 1960 both names have been officially correct. The longer form is a more precise political designation, as the republic consists of the large island of Madagascar and numerous small offshore island dependencies. Because most of the people live on the larger landmass, however, Madagascar remains the officially accepted short-form designation. Throughout this handbook the two names are used interchangeably, except in specific references to the Malagasy polity.

Similar misunderstanding is associated with use of the term *Malagasy*. As a noun, it denotes only the local people and their language. Its use in describing the country is correct only in adjectival form, as in Malagasy Republic.

The spelling of place names generally follows those established by the United States Board on Geographical Names in its latest available gazetteer, published in 1955. The spelling of other proper names conforms to current usage in the country or to the most authoritative available source. Currency conversion factors appear in the Glossary, which is included as an appendix for the reader's convenience.

COUNTRY SUMMARY

1. COUNTRY: Long form, Malagasy Republic; short form, Madagascar. Former French colony and later an autonomous member of French Community; date of independence, June 26, 1960. Capital, Tananarive.

2. SIZE: 228,000 square miles.

3. TOPOGRAPHY: Fourth largest island in the world (after Greenland, New Guinea, and Borneo), plus small offshore islands and reefs; smooth coastlines marked by near absence of bays or natural harbors except for estuaries in northwest. Coastal plains, narrow in east and broad in west, rise to central plateaus and highlands, averaging 4,000 to 5,000 feet elevation, with many small valleys separated by rolling hills; some peaks above 8,000 feet.

4. CLIMATE: Tropical marine over much of island. East coast and eastern mountain slopes, directly influenced by trade winds, are wet all year; western slopes have short dry season in north, progressively longer dry season in west-central areas, and near desert conditions in southwest. Central Highlands are relatively comfortable with short dry season, lower average humidity, and lower temperature maximums than those prevailing on coastal plains.

5. POPULATION: Estimated at 7.6 million in 1972; growth rate averaged about 2.1 percent. Rural densities greatest on the narrow eastern coastal plains and in Central Highlands. Western half is sparsely populated; densities increase somewhat along north-western coast. Tananarive, capital city in highlands area (with 375,000 people in 1972), was six times the size of any other town. Eighteen identifiable ethnic groups of mixed Asian and African origins; all share similar cultural traditions, Social and political rivalries exist between highland people—especially Merina—and others, who are collectively referred to as *côtiers* (see Glossary).

6. LANGUAGES: Official languages are Malagasy and French; somewhat different but mutually understandable dialects of Malagasy are spoken in different parts of the country.

7. RELIGION: About one-third of population are Christians, divided almost evenly between Roman Catholics and Protestants; small Muslim element; rest of population adheres to indigenous beliefs and practices in which ancestor cult is primary feature.

8. EDUCATION: In 1970 about 50 percent of all children between ages of six and twelve were attending school; 35 percent of second-ary students were enrolled in public institutions. Educational advancement limited by teacher shortage and insufficient facilities. Increasing number of graduates from University of Madagascar and

French colleges and universities. Literacy rate estimated at between 30 and 40 percent for entire population; lowest rate in rural côtier areas.

9. HEALTH: Fairly high incidence of disease reflects nutritionally inadequate diet and insufficient medical care and sanitation practices. Malaria, schistosomiasis, and tuberculosis particularly prevalent; other diseases include leprosy, bubonic plague, diphtheria, typhoid, venereal infections, tetanus, hepatitis, and gastroenteric parasites. Health services capable of coping with major epidemics and providing limited modern medical care in parts of country, particularly Central Highlands.

10. GOVERNMENT: Until May 1972 country had strong presidential form of government. President was head of state and head of government, assisted by Council of Ministers (cabinet), responsible to bicameral legislature. After declaration of state of national emergency in May 1972, government was dissolved, Parliament was suspended, and new prime minister was designated as head of government. Reformed cabinet consisted of five military officers and five civilians; new government ruled by decree. In national referendum of October 8, 1972, prime minister was granted further authority as head of state. Major regional division consisted of six provinces. All administrative functions were directed from Tananarive through civil servants appointed by national government, although each province had quasi-legislative body (Provincial Council), which was responsible for some local matters. Provinces further divided into subprefectures, administrative districts, and cantons.

11. JUSTICE: Court system and legal codes based primarily on French colonial codes and practices, secondarily on historic codes of early Merina kingdom. Law applied by courts according to these fixed codes without consideration of judicial precedent. Four levels of courts: at lowest level, tribunals headed by subprefects; judges headed tribunals of first instance at provincial level; Court of Appeals (highest court with appellate jurisdiction); Supreme Court. Judiciary free of executive interference since independence.

12. ECONOMY: Small-scale cultivation predominates, chiefly rice for subsistence, but also range of more than eight export crops. Large sector of commerce and services takes nearly half of national income. Small industrial sector processes farm products, which are beginning to replace imports. Economy remains dependent on French aid; industry and commerce dominated by French firms and Asian entrepreneurs. National development plans: First Five-Year Plan 1964-68; Program of Major Operations 1968-69; and Second Three-Year Plan 1972-74. Development plans seek to boost rice, beef, export crop production; to exploit some minerals; to develop

processing industries to reduce consumer imports; and to raise Malagasy participation in commerce, management, and work requiring skilled labor.

13. PRINCIPAL EXPORTS: Coffee, vanilla, specialty rice, sugar, cloves, live cattle, beef, sisal, lima beans, tobacco, essential oils for perfumery, pepper, tung oil, chromite, and graphite.

14. PRINCIPAL IMPORTS: Machinery and equipment, vehicles, textiles and clothing, chemicals, intermediate products for industry, crude petroleum, and rice.

15. CURRENCY: Monetary unit is Malagasy franc (FMG), divided into 100 centimes; FMG256 equaled US$1 in 1972.

16. COMMUNICATIONS: Rapid, reliable air postal service; five telephone exchanges; satellite telecommunications link with France. Government-owned and -operated domestic radio broadcasting reaches major population concentrations; booster transmitters planned. Television reception limited to Tananarive area. Seven major daily newspapers, most in Malagasy language; large number of less frequent periodicals.

17. RAILROADS: High-cost 530-mile railroad connects capital with eastern port of Tamatave, Andriamena chromite mine, and Alaotra rice-growing center; second railroad of 110 miles between Fianarantsoa and eastern port of Manakara.

18. INLAND WATERWAYS: The 400-mile Pangalanes Canal paralleling east coast handles small boats.

19. PORTS: Twenty-three ports, mostly small, serve domestic and international trade. Most foreign trade is processed through larger ports of Tamatave, Diégo-Suarez, Majunga, and Tulear. Plans to develop major tanker port and drydock at Narinda await financing decision.

20. ROADS: Sparse network of about 20,000 miles of roads and improved trails; not more than one-third are capable of all-weather use. About 1,850 miles of hard-surfaced roads; primary routes link Central Highlands with east coast and Tananarive with north-western port of Majunga. Connections with south consist mainly of trails.

21. CIVIL AVIATION: Well-developed internal network of airports served by Air Madagascar; requires government subsidy. International service by Malagasy and foreign carriers.

22. INTERNATIONAL MEMBERSHIPS AND AGREEMENTS: Member of United Nations and its specialized agencies; Organization of African Unity (OAU); Common Organization of African and Malagasy States and Mauritius (Organisation Commune Africaine, Malgache, et Mauritien—OCAMM). In 1972 majority of bilateral aid and trade agreements were with France; others concluded with

Federal Republic of Germany (West Germany), Republic of China (Nationalist China), Italy, Israel, and United States. Economic ties being negotiated with Soviet Union.

23. SECURITY FORCES: Military establishment of approximately 4,000 men, mostly army ground troops; air element and navy being developed around training groups of about 200 men each. Most military equipment, instructors, and technical support supplied by France. Paramilitary forces include National Gendarmerie (approximately 4,000 men) and Civic Service (about 1,500 men), which provides potential reserve for security units. Local civil police forces estimated at more than 3,000 men.

MALAGASY REPUBLIC

TABLE OF CONTENTS

LIST OF ILLUSTRATIONS

LIST OF TABLES

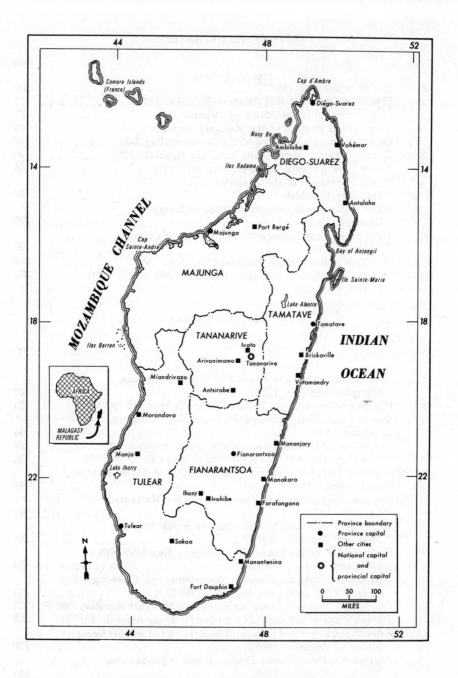

Figure 1. The Malagasy Republic

SECTION I. SOCIAL

CHAPTER 1
GENERAL CHARACTER OF THE SOCIETY

The Malagasy Republic joined the family of sovereign states in 1960 after sixty-four years of French colonial rule. Its economy was agrarian and alien-dominated, and its fledgling government was a presidential form in which the head of state and his cabinet were responsible to a popularly elected legislature. At independence President Philibert Tsiranana and his colleagues, following an avowed course of pragmatic socialism, dedicated themselves to the achievement of three major goals: the achievement of national unity within a population divided by ethnic and regional rivalry; the attainment of economic development and diversification; and the establishment of democratic government. In 1972 the first two of these goals remained elusive. Achievement of the third goal was limited in scope. Its meaning was not clear after the collapse of the Tsiranana government in May of that year and the accession to power of the army chief of staff, General Gabriel Ramanantsoa.

The Malagasy Republic occupies a unique position among the developing nations that are generally associated with the African area. Located in the Indian Ocean off Africa's southeastern coast, the island republic is separated from its nearest continental neighbor, about 250 miles away, by the Mozambique Channel. The country consists of Madagascar—the world's fourth largest island after Greenland, New Guinea, and Borneo—and a number of tiny offshore island dependencies (see fig. 1). Its area totals approximately 228,000 square miles. Spanning about fourteen degrees of latitude, Madagascar provides important regional contrasts in topography and climate (see ch. 3).

To the outside observer the country long has been surrounded by an air of mystery, which is created in part by its geographic isolation, its exotic flora and fauna, and its unique climatic patterns. For the most part, however, this inexplicable quality has arisen from unanswered questions regarding the diverse origins of the Malagasy people (see ch. 2). It is generally accepted that the country's inhabitants basically are the descendants of early Asian and African settlers. Still largely unanswered, however, are questions concerning the manner in which the original Asian immigrants reached the island over 2,000 years ago and the circumstances that led both the Asian and the African settlers to migrate from their homelands.

A progressive process of integration has resulted in a generally common culture, which is evident in the widespread mixture of

1

customs imparted by the population's diverse origins. From the Far East have come such features as the dietary preeminence of rice, which is grown—as in Asia—in terraced plots; use of the outrigger canoe; and the prominent role of ancestor adulation (see ch. 5). From Africa have come such cultural characteristics as belief in witchcraft, the growing of millet, and an emotional attachment to cattle. The degree of cultural integration, however, is more readily apparent in the Malagasy language. Derived from the Malayo-Polynesian family of languages, Malagasy also reflects African influences and borrowings from Arabic, Sanskrit, and the languages of European cultures. Somewhat different but mutually understandable dialects of Malagasy are spoken and understood throughout the island.

Madagascar is the home of more than 7 million people, including small numbers of immigrants from the nearby Comoro Islands and Réunion, plus other minority groups of French, Indians, and Chinese. In the early 1970s the population was increasing at the rate of about 2.1 percent annually. The Malagasy people are generally divided into eighteen ethnic groups, each of which traditionally has considered itself distinct because of its different history (see ch. 4).

Until the beginning of the twentieth century these groups were largely isolated from one another, developing independently in regional groupings. The interior of the island—the ecologically favored Central Highlands—is the domain of the largest group, the Merina, but some parts are inhabited by other peoples, notably the Betsileo. Traditional ethnic homelands persist to some degree in modern times, although internal migrations, caused mainly by economic necessity, have led to a certain amount of ethnic fusion. No part of the country has remained ethnically unmixed, but the Asian influence is most pronounced in the Central Highlands among the Merina and the Betsileo.

In 1972 approximately 86 percent of the population consisted of rural inhabitants, who derived a living from agricultural activities. The rest lived in towns and worked in manufacturing industries, in commerce, or for the various levels of government. Areas of greatest population density were the Central Highlands, the eastern coastal plain, and the far north. Even in these areas most of the cities and towns were relatively small. The largest city, the national capital of Tananarive, had an estimated population of 375,000.

Malagasy social structure is based on groups defined by common descent and residence and ranked according to social importance (see ch. 5). Traditionally, social organization is seen almost everywhere in terms of the family or the larger kin group, but genealogies seldom are traced farther than the grandfather of the group's oldest living member. Ancestors are regarded as the invisible roots of the family tree and thus are considered a vital part of society. Elaborate burial rites attest to their revered place. Among both urban and rural peoples, kin-group solidarity remains the primary social value and finds expression in the commonly practiced system of mutual assistance. Gradual change within the social order is occurring largely in the cities as a result of interaction among unrelated people who have left their homeland areas to seek opportunities within the modern sector of the economy. Here new classes based on wealth and individual achievement have formed. Nonetheless traditional concepts, such as an emphasis on inherited rank and reverence for the dead, are still shared as ideals that link otherwise diverse people.

Religious practices range from organized Christianity to complex traditional beliefs in which dead ancestors are believed to intercede between their living descendants and a universal deity and to have continuing influence over these descendants. Christianity, which first was introduced in the early nineteenth century, has been accepted by roughly one-third of the population. Christians are divided almost evenly between Roman Catholics and Protestants.

Living conditions vary considerably between rural and urban environments and among different regions of the country, chiefly because of marked disparities in income levels (see ch. 6). In 1971 the average per capita income for the entire country was estimated to vary from the equivalent of US$95 to US$120. Roughly half of all personal incomes are classified as nonmonetary; included in this category are goods and food produced by the family who consumes or barters them. Most Malagasy lead frugal lives as subsistence-level agriculturalists. Only in the larger urban centers such as Tananarive are there people having enough money to aspire to consumer durables and higher education, neither of which is cheaply acquired.

A generally high incidence of disease is attributable to diets low in nutritional value, insufficient modern medical care, low standards of sanitation in areas outside the major cities, and ecological conditions that are sometimes difficult. Most of the modern medical facilities are found only in the cities. Large numbers of rural inhabitants rely on traditional diagnosis and treatment in times of illness.

Tananarive Province, traditional homeland of the Merina, is the richest sector of the country. Greater school attendance, higher literacy rates, better diets and housing, and more health facilities provide a marked contrast to conditions in Tulear Province in the south, the country's poorest area. Here most people subsist under difficult conditions, primarily as pastoralists. Conditions in other areas vary between these extremes.

Despite a culture shared to a greater or lesser extent by most Malagasy, a serious cleavage has long existed within the society. This schism, which has been the major reason for the country's lack of national unity, has been created by longstanding ethnic rivalry between the Merina and most of the other surrounding peoples, who often are referred to collectively as côtiers (see Glossary). The animosity began in the late eighteenth century when the Merina succeeded in establishing hegemony over the major part of the island. For nearly a century before the French gained control of Madagascar in the late 1890s, the Merina monarchy was able to exploit the mutually competitive interests of the French and the British to maintain its position of authority over the Malagasy people (see ch. 2). In the process of accepting British assistance during the mid-1800s, the Malagasy queen and her court were converted to Protestant Christianity and in turn made it the official state religion.

When the French established complete control over Madagascar in 1896, the Merina monarchy was abolished, and colonial rule was superimposed on the semimodernized Merina state. Under the French the Merina strengthened their already pronounced educational and economic advantages. Although the French brought relative stability to the island, the Merina continued to harbor a strong resentment against the colonialists, a feeling that was exacerbated by the introduction of Roman Catholicism among the côtiers by French missionaries. Throughout the long period of colonial rule, the côtiers sought equality with the Merina. In the move toward independence in the late 1950s both factions were prominent but, when national sovereignty was achieved in 1960, the côtier majority gained political control of the country.

For the first decade of Malagasy independence the country functioned under a constitution modeled after that of the Fifth French Republic of Charles de Gaulle (see ch. 8). A strong central government led by Tsiranana, a côtier, proceeded on a course of national development ever mindful of the cleavage between the highlanders and the côtiers. During the period several competing political parties were active, running the ideological gamut from conservative to communist (see ch. 9). Only one—the Social Democratic Party (Parti Social Démocratique—PSD), led by Tsiranana—had nationwide support. The major political opposition was provided by the Party of the Congress for the Independence of Madagascar (Ankoton'ny Kongresi'ny Fahaleovantenan Madagaskara—AKFM). Its strength was limited to the largest and best educated ethnic group, the Merina, who were concentrated in the capital district. As a result, the PSD held the vast majority of governmental posts everywhere except in the capital, where most positions were consistently won by the AKFM.

Madagascar faced growing economic problems throughout its short span of sovereignty (see ch. 12). Factors contributing to a chronic condition of economic insufficiency included the country's distance from external markets, fluctuating world prices for its agricultural commodities, a shortage of investment funds for economic development plans, a scarcity of skilled technicians, and an inadequate transportation system to support its system of domestic trade. By the early 1970s the rapid growth of the population had brought new challenges to the national government in managing the economy; pressure on available resources increased, and strains on traditional economic and social institutions brought objections from political opposition groups.

The essentially agricultural economy, in which small farming predominated, concentrated primarily on cultivation except in a few districts of the south and the middle west where cattle were raised (see ch. 13). Although by the early 1970s the Malagasy had taken over most of the production of export crops that were introduced initially on French-owned plantations, roughly 80 percent of the farmers engaged primarily in the subsistence cultivation of rice. Most of them also managed to sell a portion of their limited crops, but such sales often barely sufficed for the payment of debts and taxes and the purchase of basic household necessities. The country was basically self-sufficient in staple foods, but at times the government had been obliged to import rice to keep up with demands of the rapidly increasing population.

The industrial sector was small but growing. Occupied chiefly with the processing of agricultural products grown domestically, local firms were beginning to manufacture some desired items that in former times had been imported. Privately owned French firms and some operated by resident Asians produced many of the locally manufactured items and provided a large share of the commercial services. Indians and Chinese assumed a dominant role as small retail merchants throughout rural areas.

Since independence the country's economic well-being had remained heavily dependent on France. The French continued to supply a large amount of the funds required for national development projects and a portion of the national government's current operating expenses. French technical assistance included personnel skilled in the technical knowledge that often was lacking among the Malagasy working force; management personnel also were supplied for much of Madagascar's industrial and commercial activities. A defense agreement with France aided the Malagasy military establishment and, in turn, provided the French with a strategic base in the southwestern Indian Ocean (see ch. 14).

The country's foreign trade remained oriented principally toward France and other members of the European Economic Community. Trade balances showed continuing deficits, which had to be covered by foreign assistance, largely from France.

Beginning in the late 1960s public criticism was leveled at the national government for its handling of the economic system. Discontent with foreign predominance in commerce and industry appeared to be gaining adherents of opposition demands for more state ownership in the area of industry and commerce. The rural population expressed dissatisfaction with the head tax and the tax on cattle, which substantially reduced their already meager income and which gave rise to abuses by collectors at the local level.

Tsiranana's efforts to broaden economic development were largely tied to programs outlined in three successive development plans. Most of the actions under these plans were carried forward with French and other European assistance. Economic improvement goals included an increase in the production of rice, beef, and export crops; the exploitation of mineral deposits; the development of local processing industries in order to reduce the growing level of consumer imports; and an increase of Malagasy participation in commerce, management, and jobs requiring skilled labor. Although some progress in this direction was made, the pace remained slow. As public demands for economic and governmental reform increased in early 1972, it was apparent that satisfactory solutions to the country's economic problems were yet to be found.

The governing political party lost much of its vitality during the late 1960s as it increasingly failed to serve as a spokeman for the people (see ch. 9). The earlier vigorous role played by the PSD and the national government gave way to bureaucratic stagnation, which was regarded as neo-colonialism by activist elements of the population. Moreover, a progressively disabling illness diminished Tsiranana's earlier ability to balance the various forces within the party and the society. Considerable unrest, stemming from local economic grievances and a growing public desire to end heavy French influence on the Malagasy society, resulted in an uprising in the south, a split in the PSD, the arrest and jailing of the vice president, and widespread unrest among students and other urban inhabitants. These actions led to riots in the capital in May 1972, and the government reacted by ordering units of the national security forces to suppress the rioters (see ch. 14). The intensity of the government's reaction shocked the traditionally peaceful Malagasy.

Fearing that the country was in danger of falling into a serious crisis that would develop into a confrontation between the Merina and the côtiers, Tsiranana's political advisers recommended an emergency solution. Acceding to many of the demonstrators' demands, the president dissolved his government and petitioned the nation's senior military officer to accept the position of prime minister and head of a new government.

General Ramanantsoa, a Merina, and his new cabinet of five

6

Merina military officers and five civilian technicians—all côtiers—
initially were expected to operate the governmental system, leaving
Tsiranana in the figurehead position of chief of state. In a national
referendum conducted on October 8, 1972, the new prime minister
received overwhelming support from the electorate, who gave him a
mandate to effect reforms within the society for the next five years.
Tsiranana resigned.

Although Ramanantsoa had not announced his definitive plans,
some general concepts had been indicated after his power takeover.
Chief among them was a public assurance that he would continue to
drive for national unity. In doing so, he indicated that his government would work to bring progress to the agricultural sector and to
improve the general condition of all Malagasy workers. He expressed concern for a restructuring of the educational system to
meet local needs and for a modernization of the tax system to relieve
the peasants' burden. Reform of the administrative structure of
government at all levels appeared to be targeted for early action,
and he called for austerity on the part of all Malagasy, including
those within government circles.

In the field of foreign relations he promised to review the
cooperation agreements signed with France in 1960 (see ch. 10).
Contrary to the unfavorable approach taken by his predecessor
toward communist nations, the new prime minister had agreed to
establish diplomatic relations with the Soviet Union. Expansion of
economic and cultural relations between the two countries was
anticipated. Ramanantsoa's reversal of Tsiranana's plans for
economic and political dialogue with the Republic of South Africa
was viewed as a major step in a rapprochement with the majority of
the African members of the Organization of African Unity, of which
Madagascar was a member.

CHAPTER 2
HISTORICAL SETTING

The people of Madagascar reflect a double line of origin—that is, races from both Africa and Indonesia. How the two groups came to the island and formed a population with a single, predominantly Indonesian language and culture remained unclear in 1972.

The divisions within the modern state are not those of race or of ancient history. Rather, the major division is between the peoples of the Central Highlands, primarily Merina, and the côtiers, or peoples of the coasts who surround them. The divisions follow the lines of economic diversity and political privilege created with the birth of organized states from the sixteenth through the nineteenth centuries and are reinforced by differing rates of assimilation of new, modernizing ideas introduced by contacts with Europe.

The major development in this precolonial period was the creation of a strong kingdom between the sixteenth and eighteenth centuries by the Merina people in a rich, remote, and well-protected portion of the Central Highlands. By the nineteenth century the Merina had defeated the other strong states on the island and exercised claims to suzerainty over nearly all of Madagascar. By the latter part of the nineteenth century they had accepted the military, material, organizational, and educational changes introduced from Europe and had made Protestant Christianity the state religion.

Colonial rule, when it came in the 1890s, was thus superimposed on an existing, semimodernized, independent state. The Merina, however, strengthened their initial educational and economic advantages under the French. Modern nationalism had its birth in Merina opposition to French rule; the Merina were joined later by those peoples of the eastern half of the island who had suffered losses and insults at the hands of French settlers. Throughout the colonial period, the primary interest of the majority of the côtiers remained a desire for equality with the Merina. The approach of independence in 1960 brought with it a change in relations as power fell into the hands of a political party led by representatives of the island's côtier majority.

EARLY HISTORY
Origins of the Population

The conflicting theories of the population's origins are debated in numerous works in French and English. All the theories are discussed in detail in an American work, *Early Kingdoms in Madagascar, 1500-1700*, by Raymond K. Kent. Particularly at issue are the timing and conditions of arrival of the African portion and its size, as well as the possible routes traveled by the Indonesian portion. Over and above the learned arguments, the modern Malagasy peoples feel that, although geography and the need for a wider association with countries having similar problems may tie them to the African continent, theirs is a culture distinct from all others—an Indian Ocean civilization. They prefer to stress their ancient ties to Indonesia while recognizing their secondary cultural ties with mainland Africa as a basis for more practical relations in the modern world.

As to the Malagasy peoples' origins, scholars disagree completely on the conclusions to be drawn from the limited indicators provided by geography, physical anthropology, linguistic analysis, and scattered obscure references in ancient writings. Despite Madagascar's close proximity to that portion of eastern Africa where early man is generally believed to have originated, there are no indications of a human population on the island earlier than 2,500 years ago.

The first arrivals were sailors whose route and motivation may never be known, although it is clear that a majority were not from neighboring Africa. Instead it is generally presumed that they were Indonesians who crossed the 6,000 miles of Indian Ocean, following the monsoon trade winds in outrigger canoes. These early sailors possibly crossed directly but more likely in stages, sailing first along well-established routes to India, thence to the Horn of Africa, and along the East African coast to Zanzibar, the Comoro Islands, and Madagascar. They may have included Africans or persons of mixed Indo-African descent who had been assimilated into their culture from earlier and as yet undiscovered settlements along the East African coast. One apparently common tie in modern times between all these areas is the use of outrigger canoes, otherwise a feature only of areas associated with East Asia and the Pacific.

Movement from the Far East is dated by the fact that the Malagasy language and culture appear to have made a complete break from the mainstream of Indonesian culture before about the twelfth century. According to most historians the migratory flow seems to have lasted for at least 1,000 years. Although some authorities attribute the undated African influx to the importation of slaves, others see a major African inflow. At the time of the arrival of the first Europeans at the end of the fifteenth century, the shores of the west coast were occupied by men who were apparently African immigrants speaking a mainland language, although Malagasy customs had already taken root among them. They may have come as a major migration from the former Monomatapa kingdom in the area of modern Rhodesia and may have brought with them more advanced political ideas than had the Indonesians.

Along the eastern and northwestern coasts of the great island, contact with the Arab traders who sailed the East African coast from the twelfth through the sixteenth centuries provided the Malagasy inhabitants a degree of contact with the African and Islamic worlds. Notable centers of contact were at Vohēmar in the northeast, on Ile Sainte-Marie, and far down the eastern coast between Mananjari and Fort Dauphin. These so-called Arabs may well have been African Muslims from Zanzibar or from the Muslim settlement of Sofala on the mainland coast of the Mozambique Channel.

These visitors may have been very limited in number, but they did introduce new ideas. They were the first to reduce the Malagasy language to writing, using Arabic script. The penetration of the Islamic faith was limited to small regions of the coast, but pseudo-Islamic religious and religico-magic practices found their way inland. Early European visitors to the kingdoms of the central plateau found that the rulers still depended upon nominally Arab officials to serve as their secretaries, since only they knew how to write. Several volumes of works on magic, including two never examined by historians, are intact; these works date from the pre-seventeenth century period and are still revered by some coastal peoples, particularly the group most influenced by Islam, the Antaimoro. Sporadic contact with the outside world was also provided by sailors whose ships were castaway on the long shoreline. Arabs, Indians, Indonesians, and Chinese have been included; after 1500 some Europeans were included.

Initial European Contacts

The first European visitors were Portuguese. In 1500 a Portuguese ship was blown off course after rounding the Cape of Good Hope en route to India, and the captain, Diogo Dias, sailed along the coast of the great island. By 1502 European cartographers had labeled the landmass *Madagascar,* a name taken from a comment on the existence of a great island in the Indian Ocean found in the writings of Marco Polo. Early Portuguese explorers, however, called the island Saint Lawrence. They quickly sought out and destroyed the few Arab settlements along the coast as part of their general campaign to control the trade routes in the western Indian Ocean. Whatever contacts the island's population may have continued to maintain with the Arab, Indian, or Indonesian worlds were thus brought to a definite end in the first part of the sixteenth century.

The earliest extended contacts between the Europeans and the Malagasy were made by Portuguese missionaries who, with short-lived success, attempted to establish missions along the coast between 1600 and 1619. The island was also of interest to the fleets of Portugal, Holland, France, and Great Britain.

At various times all four countries maintained reprovisioning stations, trading posts, and temporary settlements along the

11

Madagascar coast. Attemps at settlement included two by the English, in 1644 and 1650, to create colonies modeled on those of Virginia and New England. These efforts were inspired by a widespread belief that Madagascar was rich in minerals and other sources of wealth. Both colonies were crushed within a year, however, by the hostile Malagasy.

From 1642 to 1674 the French maintained a garrison colony at Fort Dauphin. Its governor, Etienne de Flacourt, wrote several detailed studies of the island's fauna, geography, and population. In 1674 the garrison incurred the wrath of the neighboring people, and all but a handful of the colonists were massacred. Although the French then withdrew from their possessions, the government of France continued vague claims to sovereignty over the entire island. Meaningful commercial contact was maintained by the French colonists on the small islands of Mauritius and Reunion, some 350 miles to the east, who bought cattle and slaves from the coastal peoples. The only foreign enclaves, however, were maintained by pirates from Europe and from the American colonies who used the island as a base for attacks on Indian Ocean commerce.

In the second half of the eighteenth century the French again undertook to create colonies on the island. Ile Sainte-Marie became a French colony in 1750 and remained a part of France for over two centuries. A fresh attempt to create a permanent base was made at Fort Dauphin. In addition, a Polish soldier of fortune, D'Aladar de Benyowski, was commissioned by the French king to take control of the island's interior; eventually, Benyowski proclaimed himself emperor of Madagascar, although his actual conquests were very limited.

THE MALAGASY KINGDOMS

Because the history of the island's inhabitants can only be adequately traced from the middle of the sixteenth century, just two historically important facts about earlier Malagasy society can be asserted. First, virtually all of the inhabitants originally lived in the coastal zones. Second, the people were divided into small units rarely larger than village chiefdoms, although they were linked by a common language and cultural characteristics. The two racial groups intermingled freely so that in general the people could not be traced by their racial lines (see ch. 4).

The concept of larger kingdoms (as replacements for small-scale chiefdoms) was introduced at the beginning of the sixteenth century through contacts with foreigners. The origin of this foreign influence is contested, some authorities believing it to be the result of a final wave from Asia, others attributing it to contacts with the Muslim world. The theory that the influence derived from the East African coastal Swahili or Bantu cultures has been given considerable weight. The first major Malagasy kingdom developed along the western coast—the most African-influenced portion of the island—at the end of the sixteenth century. The kingdom's original base was near the modern town of Tulear on the southwestern coast.

The kingdom was ruled from its beginning by the Maroserana dynasty, which adopted the term *Sakalava* to designate all its subjects regardless of their varied ethnic origins. The kingdom's power reached its greatest height in the mid-eighteenth century, when nearly half the island was either under direct Sakalava rule or organized into smaller states such as Imerina, which admitted vassalage to the Sakalava. The Sakalava lands were divided into two allied kingdoms under the sons of Andriandahifotsy (c.1610-1655). Despite diversity of ethnic origin, the Sakalava were united by geography and a common economy. All lived in the western grasslands and practiced the predominantly East African style of cattle herding. Tulear and later Majunga became major ports, where cattle and slaves were exchanged with European traders—primarily French colonists from Mauritius and Réunion—for guns and other manufactured goods.

The Sakalava state was weakened after the death of Andriandahifotsy's two sons, but its power was rejuvenated under Queen Ravahiny, who ruled the northern kingdom of Boina. The kingdom came to an end with her death in 1808, and the Merina were invited to step in to bring an end to the chaos that resulted from quarreling over the succession to the Sakalava throne.

The second major kingdom appeared in the seventeenth century among the people of the eastern coast, where each of the separate valleys was an independent chiefdom. One group, the Tsitambala confederation, conquered all the chiefdoms along a 100-mile stretch of the coast. The confederation was overthrown and replaced by a dynasty founded in the early eighteenth century by the mulatto son of an English pirate, Ratsimilaho, who had been educated in England. He united the people along a 400-mile stretch around Tamatave and gave the people a common name, the Betsimisaraka or "the many who do not separate." This kingdom fell apart upon the death of its third ruler in 1791.

South of the Betsimisaraka, the Antaimoro and the Antambahoaka—under Arab influence—had established small kingdoms at a much earlier but unidentified date. The new ideas introduced through these small states may have been a major influence on events elsewhere in the island.

Merina Hegemony

The last and most powerful of the Malagasy kingdoms was that of the Merina. The origins of the Merina have long intrigued historians and anthropologists because, as a group, they have a much more Asian appearance than the rest of the Malagasy peoples (see ch. 4). It has been suggested that they are the descendants of the last migratory wave from Indonesia or that they represent a group that had enforced strict rules against marriage between the races over many centuries; this and all other theories, however, are subject to well-based challenges. All that can be asserted with certainty is that this distinctive group had entered the almost unpopulated interior of the country by the fifteenth century and had settled along the forest edge south of the highlands around the present-day site of Tananarive.

This land to which they came had the advantages of isolation from other warlike people and of promising agricultural potential. They successfully imposed their power over the original inhabitants, the darker skinned Vazimba. At the beginning of the sixteenth century their first important ruler, Queen Rafohy, altered the traditional system of succession that most Malagasy peoples had followed by appointing her oldest son as chief and her successor instead of allowing her small domain to be divided among all her children. Her early successors introduced a number of other innovations, which may have been suggested to them by contacts with the outside world. Their changes included the construction of fortified towns, new weapons of iron, and eventually a few guns. They also diked the Ikapa River, which allowed the fertile Antanarivo marshes to be drained and East Asian-style rice paddies to be introduced.

These changes, generally in advance of events in the rest of the island, combined to influence the Merina kingdom's growth over the next three centuries. The growth, however, was not without challenge. Externally the Merina state was long threatened by the much larger Sakalava kingdoms to the west. Within the kingdom, a major and continuing problem was the conflict between the noble classes, called the Andriana, and the royalty.

In theory the king's power and rights were absolute. He held title to all property and was considered divinely appointed. In practice, however, the Andriana, then and later, sought to exert more power, particularly by supporting more amenable claimants to the throne. On a number of occasions they had kings assassinated in order that more pliant figures would be the successors.

The Merina society was rigidly stratified into the higher and lower nobles, the Hova or free citizens, and four levels of slaves. The structure of the state was organized around a dual system of appointive and popular control. Local villages had *fokon'olona*, or village councils, responsible for village administration, although supervision of such an area was also assigned to a male member of the noble or Hova classes. The king also appointed noblemen as

14

regional administrators. At the center of power was a council of nobles intended to serve the king as an advisory body; in times of weak rule this council became the king's rival rather than his adviser. Popular opinion of the Hova lower nobility could be expressed at the regional and even national levels through *kabary*, or great assemblies, called by the king or regional governor to announce major new government decisions to the people. The assembled people could express their opinion in support of, or in opposition to, the policy being considered. Popular opinion could be proclaimed and thus influence and even alter executive decisionmaking by popular demand.

In 1787 Andrianampoinimerina (literally, "the prince desired by the Merina") came to the throne. His first ten years of rule were spent in firmly uniting and reorganizing the divided Merina. By his death in 1810 he had extended his control to include much of the territory of the neighboring peoples of the Central Highlands and portions of the plains to the west.

Andrianampoinimerina chose as his successor his son and chief general, who assumed the throne as Radama I in 1810 with directions from his father to fulfill a task by extending his role over the entire island. Radama's army had already defeated portions of the Betsileo, Bezanozano, Sihanaka, and Sakalava peoples (see ch. 4).

Radama I and his wife and successor, Queen Ranavalona I, ruled for a total of fifty-one years and succeeded in extending Merina control to include the major portions of the island. During Radama's reign (1810-28) the country took its first steps toward the outside world in the form of contacts with the French and, more substantially, the British mission. The British efforts were directed by the governor of Mauritius, which had become a British possession after the Napoleonic wars. Although France still entertained vague claims to the great island, Great Britain in 1817 recognized Radama as king of Madagascar. Several foreign advisers assisted in the reorganization of the army along modern lines, creating a large professional force in place of the previous levies. The existing structure of government was formalized in a European-style cabinet.

Missionaries, particularly from the London Missionary Society, were given freedom to proselytize. They produced a Latin script for the Malagasy language and opened the first schools. By 1828 several thousand Malagasy were literate, and at least nine had been sent abroad to study. Along with new ideas came new bases for the economy with the introduction of manufactured goods and new crafts. Despite acceptance of these changes, Radama was sufficiently aware of the threat posed by the European powers to ban the construction of a road from the coast to Tananarive that could facilitate an invasion.

The reign of Queen Ranavalona I was dominated by a fear of foreign influences. The schools and churches were closed, Malagasy Christians were persecuted and killed, and nearly all Europeans were forced to flee. Among the handful to remain was French artisan Jean Laborde, protegé of the queen's influential prime minister, Rainiharo. Laborde, without outside assistance, created a manufacturing complex around an iron foundry that produced an incredible array of goods from cannons to soap. In addition, he strongly influenced the queen's heir, Rakoto, toward modernization and friendship with France. Rakoto became king as Radama II in 1861 but, because of his liberal and pro-French policies, was assassinated by the nobles in 1863. Nevertheless, the British and French embassies and missionaries were allowed to return, primarily because of the modernizing policies of Rainilaiarivony, prime minister from the 1850s until 1883 and the husband of three successive queens.

The prime minister introduced modernization of the administration, codified the laws, broke the threat often posed to the ruler by the strong nobles, and sought to play off the French against the British in order to maintain the island's independence. Nevertheless, British influences were much stronger at the royal court. In 1869 the newly ascended Queen Ranavalona II proclaimed the Protestant Christianity, which had been introduced and led by the London Missionary Society as the official religion of the Merina state. In addition, British instructors led the Merina army.

Establishment of the French Protectorate

As the British were associated with the church of the Merina upper classes, the French Roman Catholic missions concentrated on the Merina lower classes and the island's coastal people. The religious division thus developing was to have continuing political significance.

France had signed protectorate treaties with several Sakalava chiefs on the west coast and had occupied Nosy Be in addition to Ile Sainte-Marie. In the 1870s and 1880s England and France came to an understanding about the division of colonial spheres of influence. In return for allowing the British a free hand in Egypt and Zanzibar, French interests were given priority in Madagascar. France staged several attacks on the island between 1883 and 1885. In order to obtain peace the Merina were forced to recognize French control over Diégo-Suarez, to pay a large idemnity, and to allow a French resident at Tananarive to control the country's foreign relations.

As a result of the rise in influence of imperialist forces in France rather than any specific action in Madagascar, France declared the creation of a protectorate over the island in 1894. When Queen Ranavalona III refused to recognize this imposition, a French expeditionary force occupied Tananarive in September 1895 without encountering severe opposition from the Merina forces. The queen was required to sign the protectorate agreement. Peace, however, was temporary. A popular uprising broke out, led by conservative elements in Merina society who placed the blame for their defeat on the royal household's break with the traditional religion and practices. The missionaries and their converts and government officials were attacked. The first French reaction was to exile permanently the queen and the former prime minister to Algeria and to declare the island a French colony in 1896.

THE COLONIAL PERIOD

To the new French governor, General Joseph Gallieni, fell the task of ending the succession of revolts—first by the Merina, then by the Sakalava, and finally, in 1904, by the peoples of the southeast. Gallieni accomplished a number of major tasks in addition to his successful pacification efforts. He carried out the effective abolition of slavery, thus altering the status of roughly one-third of the island's inhabitants. He sought to carry out the official policy of lessening Merina hegemony over other groups by what was called *politique des races*, or tribal division. He granted an equal voice to all groups in government councils. He also began the economic development of the island through the construction of roads and began efforts to build a railroad. Gallieni spent nearly 30 percent of the government's tax income on these early efforts at building an infrastructure. Gallieni required his civil and military administrators to seek to understand the Malagasy people. He sought to ensure, whenever economically feasible, that priority would be given to the needs of the island's people rather than to those of France.

At the same time, the French governor broke the tie between the Merina and the British by bringing in French Protestant missionaries and by requiring that all instruction in the British missionary schools be given in French. As early as 1883 there were more than 150,000 students in these schools, and the instructors were provided by a teacher training school founded in 1862. Technical education programs were underway, and a secondary school at Faravohitra opened in 1881. The British Protestants opened an academy in 1886 to prepare medical personnel through a five-year program (see ch. 7).

Gallieni departed from Madagascar in 1905. The French governors who succeeded him were nearly all men of lesser stature and insight; they concentrated their efforts on formalizing the system of French control, on introducing foreign enterprise, and on increasing tax revenues to ensure a balanced budget. Several of them concentrated their efforts on the Central Highlands and reduced expenditures by closing the newly opened provincial schools, thus reversing the ethnic equality sought under Gallieni's administration.

The new colony served France well during World War I, providing agricultural and mineral supplies at low cost as well as 41,000 combat troops, most of whom served in France. Some 4,000 of them were killed in action, and several of their battalions were highly commended.

The impact of the war had effects that the French had not anticipated. New ideas were introduced to the island by those who had served in Europe. These included Western concepts of equality, socialism, and anticolonialism. A small number of Malagasy remained in France after the war as students.

The burdens imposed by the war increased tax levies, raised consumer prices, and caused market scarcities. These problems caused considerable bitterness, particularly among the Merina, adding material deprivation to the political humiliation they had encountered by their earlier loss of status. In addition, the war lessened the belief in the invincibility and superiority of the French, which had been created by the swiftness of their conquest and the material improvements that they had introduced.

Emergence of Nationalism

The earliest origins of nationalist movements are generally traced to a small group founded in Tananarive around 1909 by a Merina Protestant minister, Reverend Ravelojaona, who modeled it on principles followed by the Young Men's Christian Association. It was abolished by government order in 1910 on budgetary pretexts but in reality because the government had learned that its discussion groups talked about political affairs.

In 1912 the group's members formed an unregistered society that came to be known as the Vy Vato Sakelika (VVS), a Malagasy phrase meaning purity and discipline. The society's several hundred members, mostly Merina, were dedicated to the preservation of the Malagasy cultural heritage. Their imaginations had been stirred in particular by a speech Ravelojaona made in admiration of the Japanese, whose traditional society had successfully avoided colonial rule and had rejected European economic and political control while accepting Western technical advancement.

Two notable factors in the new movement were its Merina and Protestant orientations. It was the Merina upper classes who had lost the most through the imposition of colonial rule and the freeing of others (including the Merina lower strata) from their domination. This same group was closely associated with Protestantism because the Merina educated elite was almost entirely composed of adherents to the state church. Roman Catholic missionaries had largely restricted their efforts to the lower classes and the *côtiers*,

18

who had gained more than they lost with the arrival of French colonialism.

Among the VVS leadership were many students, several of whom were to become future nationalist leaders. Included among them were two medical students, Joseph Raseta and Joseph Ravoahangy.

In December 1915, at a low point in French fortunes in the war in Europe, the VVS made the withdrawal of colonial rule a part of its platform. The French treated the affair as a major plot against the government and announced that the VVS was planning to poison all the French residents. The entire VVS membership was arrested, and more than 200 of them—nearly all students—were jailed. Thirty-four were sentenced to major prison terms. The trials were strongly criticized by the French missionaries, and all those jailed were freed in 1921.

The end of World War I brought increased prosperity to the island and provided the basis for further economic development. The first steps were taken toward providing a representative voice in the government through the Consultation Committee for Native Affairs, composed of five Frenchmen and six Malagasy. This committee and its two 1924 successors, the Economic and Financial Delegations (Délégations Economiques et Financières—DEF) were given little, if any, meaningful weight in government decisionmaking, although the bodies did give the Malagasy some experience in parliamentary and executive affairs. One of the sections of the DEF was composed of French settlers; the other, of twenty-four Malagasy chosen by elections throughout the islands. The electorate was restricted to members of the Council of Notables in each of twenty-four districts, who in turn had been selected by all the Malagasy village chiefs.

Governor Marcel Olivier (1924-29) who created the DEF, also organized another body—the Public Works Labor Service (Service de la Main-D'Oeuvre des Travaux d'Intérêt Général—SMOTIG). Young men were drafted into SMOTIG as an alternative to military service and were required to work for two years on major public works projects. SMOTIG completed a number of important development projects. The workers received the same indemnity that they would have obtained in the army, but SMOTIG drew considerable external criticism because it was accused of violating international agreements against the use of forced labor. The Malagasy criticized SMOTIG on the grounds that its projects largely favored the interests of the French settlers and subjected the participants to degrading work. During this period Olivier also rearranged the colony's administrative structure into six provinces and forty-four districts.

The rapid change of governors brought a varied emphasis in educational efforts. Few of them matched Gallieni's initial efforts, and several were actually retrogressive because of short-sighted economy measures, a disagreement on the proper language and objective of instruction for the Malagasy, or conflicting ideologies, including an anticlericalism that deprived the mission schools of funds. A major problem was the continued concentration of educational efforts in Tananarive. This had the effect of further increasing the advantages of the Merina and the allied major highland groups—the Betsileo and the Sihanaka—over the côtiers.

In 1922 Jean Ralaimongo, one of the veterans who had remained in France after World War I, returned to Madagascar. He had experienced three years of association with radical French politicians, particularly a group called the French League for Madagascar, headed by Anatole France. The league's objective was the granting of French citizenship to all Malagasy as a reward for the island's contribution to French victory in the war. Upon his return, Ralaimongo had begun to apply the political techniques he had learned in France. His main objective at the time—far from being nationalistic—was to achieve for the island the status of an integral department of France.

In 1927 Ralaimongo and Joseph Varoatangy, assisted by French Communist Paul Dussac, began publication of a newspaper expressing these views. Shortly afterward Dussac moved to Tananarive; with two other French civil servants who were Communists, he started a second newspaper. The group encouraged demonstrations in the capital city in May 1929, beginning with an apolitical strike by the students of the medical school who demanded academic changes. The riot that followed was without bloodshed; thirty demonstrators were arrested, but the incident marked the first forceful political demands by Malagasy modernists.

In June 1930 a new governor, Leon Cayla, burdened by the impact of the worldwide depression on the island's fragile economy, took steps that effectively crushed any vocal opposition. The newspapers were closed, and the nationalists were restricted to remote areas.

During the long administration of Cayla (1930-39), considerable efforts were made to improve the local economy. Some 8,000 miles of roads were built, the southern railroad was completed, the port of Tamatave was rebuilt, and new cash crops were introduced. These efforts, however, did little to ameliorate the results of the economic depression, which had its most notable impact on the European sector of the economy.

Toward the end of the 1930s several steps were taken to liberalize Malagasy politics. The restriction of nationalists to remote areas was ended, their newspapers were allowed to reappear, and new civil rights were extended. The requirements under which individual Malagasy could obtain French citizenship were eased, although only

8,000 had taken advantage of these provisions by 1939. In 1939 Ravelojoana was elected to represent the Malagasy in Paris in a new Intercolonial body, the Superior Council for the Colonies (Conseil Supérieur des Colonies).

The World War II Era

Between September 1939 and the occupation of France by Nazi Germany in June 1940, some 15,000 Malagasy soldiers and construction troops were sent to France. The island's government wavered on the issue of joining the Free French of General Charles de Gaulle or supporting the Vichy government. By August 1940 the governor of Madagascar had been replaced by a Vichy appointee, who suspended the DEF, smothered all political expression, and gave the force of law to discrimination on purely racial grounds for the first time. Considerable support for the Free French was evident, however, among the informed Malagasy inhabitants.

In May 1942 British forces, fearful that the Vichy government might allow Japan to use the large naval base at Diégo-Suarez, staged a surprise attach and captured the base. In a largely bloodless campaign, but one hampered by French sabotage of the road system, the British captured the rest of the island by the end of September. Control was turned over to the Free French in January 1943.

The French military government that took over administration of Madagascar adopted several liberal measures. Notable among these were the creation of a replacement for the DEF in which an equal number of European and Malagasy were seated and the revitalization of the *fokon'olona*, or indigenous village councils, in order to allot some degree of power to people at the local level. In the main, however, the wartime government was so concerned with maximizing the island's contribution to the wider war effort that Franco-Malagasy relations deteriorated severely. Another 28,000 Malagasy were recruited into the French army, forced labor was instituted to repair the damage from the British military campaign, and a large war loan was raised.

Major antagonism, however, was created by French efforts to use the island as a granary for its forces elsewhere. Great animosity was the major product of the Rice Office, established in 1944 to control the rice crop—the staple of the Malagasy diet. All farmers were forced to sell their entire crop to this organization at artificially low prices and then to buy back what they needed for food. They were particularly incensed when they found that much of the crop taken from them found its way into the hands of black marketeers.

In March 1945 the mixed commissions and the DEF were replaced by the Representative Council, composed of sixty members. Thirty were popularly elected by the French residents; and thirty, by a much enlarged but still limited Malagasy electoral college of some

75,000 persons. In order to lessen Merina dominance, each Malagasy representative had to be a member of the ethnic group that was numerically predominant in his electoral district.

In the fall of 1945, the two electoral colleges also voted for the posts assigned to the island in the Constituent Assembly of the Fourth French Republic in Paris. The two delegates chosen by the Malagasy were Raseta and Ravoahangy, both of whom in their campaigns had demanded implementation of the ideals of self-government proffered by the Atlantic Charter of 1941 and by de Gaulle at the Brazzaville Conference of 1944.

Postwar Political Development

Under the impact of the French constitution of 1946, which granted to the Malagasy French citizenship and an extended right to vote, four political parties formed during that year. The first and most important of these was the Democratic Movement for Malagasy Restoration (Mouvement Démocratique de Rénovation Malgache—MDRM), organized by the two Malagasy representatives in Paris and a writer long resident in Paris, Jacques Rabemananjara. These men already had established a skeleton political organization throughout the island, formed to back their election bid. The party's growth was extremely rapid and stirred immediate opposition in the form of three much smaller rivals. The first of these was the Party of the Malagasy Disinherited (Parti des Déshérités Malgaches—PADESM). It purported to be a party of the coastal interests and the underprivileged but was open to accusations of being a government front, sponsored to weaken the nationalists by reinforcing the divisions between the Merina and other ethnic groups. Its main demand was the assignment of development priority to the country's poorer areas.

The Malagasy Democratic Party (Parti Démocratique Malgache—PDM) was an upper class Merina Protestant political grouping that favored independence. It opposed the MDRM because of personality clashes and dislike of the violence that some elements in the larger party had begun to foster. The PDM called for placing the island under a United Nations trusteeship while the educational and economic development needed for independence was completed. The third rival of the MDRM, the Malagasy Social Movement (Mouvement Social Malgache—MSM), was similar in approach to the PDM but was composed of the non-Merina Roman Catholic elite. For this reason it did not oppose the PADESM.

The MDRM proved itself to have an extremely large following, although its claims of 300,000 members were exaggerated. In the 1946 election to the five newly created provincial assemblies, the MDRM won all the seats in the provinces of Tananarive and Tamatave, won majorities in Tulear and Fianarantsoa provinces, and lost only in Majunga Province. The members of the new islandwide Representative Assembly should have reflected the composition of the provincial assemblies. The colonial government, however, changed the rules, giving the PADESM a majority of representation. The provincial assemblies were intended to exercise much of the supervision over local affairs. Nationalists, however, saw them as a further effort to divide the island's population.

The Anti-French Revolt of 1947

The growth of the MDRM and the violent anti-French revolt among the Malagasy that followed in 1947 have never been satisfactorily explained. The earlier nationalist aspirations had been concentrated among—if not limited to—the Merina. In what appeared to be a sudden switch, the demand for expulsion of the French from Madagascar extended throughout the central and eastern peoples and grew considerably in intensity.

The major causes of the unrest were the dislocations brought on or heightened by the events of World War II. Because of France's postwar economic problems, many of the French administration's wartime impositions in Madagascar had continued into 1947. Included were forced labor requirements, the rice scandals, deprivation caused by rationing, and the heightened racial tensions that derived from attitudes popular with the Vichy supporters.

Two other factors, however, further heightened the already increasing tensions between the Malagasy and the French administration. Promises of political improvements that began with the Brazzaville Doctrine had continued with improvements in the legal status of the Malagasy and the support in France for creation of a French commonwealth of autonomous states. These enticements led to increasing demands and more violent language in the many newspapers that appeared after government censorship was lifted. When a more conservative force gained control in France, considerable disappointment ensued.

Great weight also must be given to the return of 40,000 or more World War II veterans to Madagascar. In addition to the new ideas and attitudes they acquired in overseas service, their experiences had made these veterans politically volatile. Many thousands had been imprisoned by the Germans for as long as four years. Large numbers, including those surrendered to Germany in 1940, had been stranded in France long after the war because transportation to Madagascar was not available; most of them resented the more generous treatment accorded French soldiers. Many had either served in the French underground or had become familiar with its methods. The veterans—and other Malagasy as well—had seen France defeated by the Germans in 1940 and again on Madagascar by British forces in 1942. All of these events tended to bring an end to the mixture of fear, respect, and emulation on which Franco-Malagasy relations had been based.

With such factors at work only a little organization was needed to spark a revolt against French rule. This was provided by elements within the MDRM. Although the French blamed the party's leaders, their part has never been clarified. Those within the MDRM's ranks who were inclined toward violence were generally associated with two affiliated extremist groups, the Nationalist Youth (Jeunesse Nationaliste—JN) and the Malagasy Nationalist Party (Parti Nationaliste Malgache—PANAMA). A bloody uprising broke out simultaneously throughout much of the island on March 29, 1947. For a short time the French lost control of the eastern coast. Over 100 Europeans and several thousand pro-French and Christian Malagasy were killed. With reinforcements from abroad, the French army had broken the revolt by July 1947, although military operations continued in remote areas until the end of 1948.

An accurate estimate of the number of persons killed was never achieved, in part because most deaths occurred among Malagasy civilians who fled into the forest and swamps to avoid widespread reprisals. The official French government report in 1948 spoke of 60,000 to 80,000 victims, but this was later lowered to some 11,000. All but 180 were Malagasy.

The courts convicted between 5,000 and 6,000 for having taken an active part in the revolt. Several hundred were executed, some as late as 1951. Those jailed included the three leaders of the MDRM; two were sentenced to death but later were reprieved. Rabemananjara was sentenced to life imprisonment. Political activity in Madagascar virtually ceased until after 1955. The last of those sentenced were freed in 1957, but the key leaders remained in enforced exile in France until 1960.

The long-term reaction of the island's colonial adminstrators to the revolt was to suppress all political expression while attacking the root causes of the tensions. Martial law remained partially in effect until after 1950. Although the MDRM was suppressed, the other political parties continued in existence. They had little vitality, however, as they were under the weight of administrative pressure. Most of the population had become disillusioned with the political process and blamed the political campaigns of 1946 and 1947 for the bloody revolt and the 1947-49 repression. Those most strongly motivated toward nationalist political activity were left without a party.

At this juncture the Communist Party of France made a concerted effort to win Malagasy adherents—first in 1948 among the 200 Malagasy exiles and students in Paris. In 1945 and 1946 the MDRM leaders had established close relations with the Communists, not on ideological grounds, but because only the extreme left in French politics was willing to consider Malagasy demands for autonomy. The link was weakened, however, by the Communists' refusal to support complete independence for Madagascar. The Malagasy recognized that this reluctance was based on the anticipation of a colonial windfall should the Communists gain control of France.

A significant number of students with communist connections began returning to the island in 1950. With the help of several French Communists in the colonial administration, they served as the nucleus for the formation of communist cells in the new and infiltrated organizations. The party they later founded was known as the Party for the Union of the Malagasy People (Parti de l'Union du Peuple Malgache—PUPM).

The other center of opposition to the suppression of nationalist sentiments was composed of the liberal Frenchmen in the administration and the churches. The Roman Catholic and Protestant church leaders called for the restoration of civil rights, amnesty for the political prisoners, and recognition of the legitimacy of demands for independence. Espousal of these views by church leaders encouraged the island's Christians to take an active interest in political affairs. Most notably, the non-Merina of the west and the north who had been largely apolitical and among whom were many Roman Catholics were much influenced by the stand of the clergy.

The major impetus for Malagasy political advancement, however, arose from the changed attitudes toward colonialism fostered in France by governments of the 1950s. Instead of opposition, the Malagasy nationalists now met an important degree of encouragement on all sides.

During the early 1950s election to local office and to the provincial assemblies and the Representative Assembly, as well as to the intercolonial bodies in Paris, continued to be fought along party lines but with little vigor. The assemblies concerned themselves primarily with nonpolitical matters. With 5,000 Malagasy still in detention, few nationalist issues were raised, and provincial separatism became a major consideration. It was generally limited in form, however, to criticism by the majority of continued Merina dominance in educational and other opportunities.

In 1952 several new côtier political figures made their appearances. The most important among them was Philibert Tsiranana, a well-educated Tsimihety, who was elected to the Majunga provincial assembly and the Representative Assembly. At the instigation of a new socialist governor, André Soucadaux, Tsiranana was allowed to found a new political party, the Social Democratic Party of Madagascar (Parti Social Démocratique de Madagascar—PSD). Initially the party had its base of support in

Majunga Province. Another party with liberal Roman Catholic influence, the Union of Independents (Union des Independents—UI), was founded in 1953 by Stanislas Rakotonirina, who was elected mayor of Tananarive in 1956. The growth of these parties was spurred by a 1955 decision of the French National Assembly that abolished the dual electoral system under which French residents had voted in one constituency and indigenous peoples in another.

Real political development began with passage of the *loi cadre* (enabling act of June 23, 1956). This empire-wide law provided for universal suffrage and was the basis for parliamentary government in each colony. Its application to Madagascar was specifically designed by the French parliament to further weaken Merina dominance by granting each province an executive council having significant authority. The first election under the new law was held in May 1957. In the six provincial contests only sixty-five of the total of 240 seats were won by strong advocates of independence; radical majorities were elected only in the Tananarive and Diégo-Suarez provincial assemblies. The indirectly elected territorial assembly (elected by the members of the provincial bodies) had a moderate majority. The government council or cabinet that was chosen consisted of seven members, including Tsiranana. Elected to the highest post as vice president of the governing council, Tsiranana was second only to the appointed French governor.

THE MOVE TO INDEPENDENCE

The political parties that formed during the period included many that were only provincial interest groups. The broader based parties included the PSD and the closely associated Democratic and Social Union of Madagascar (Union Démocratique et Sociale de Madagascar—UDSM) in the south. Both parties found most of their strength among moderates who favored self-rule while advocating close ties to France. Placing greater emphasis on imminent independence, the doctrines of the National Malagasy Union (Union Nationale Malgache—UNAM) were based on French moderate but secular socialism. Further to the Left was the Roman Catholic socialist UI, which shared many attitudes with the UNAM and, like the UNAM, was opposed to any alliance with the Communists. The Union of Malagasy Intellectuals and Academicians (Union des Intellectuels et Universitaires Malgaches—UNIUM) had strong Marxist, but not orthodox, leanings. Although aligning itself with the UNAM and UI on most occasions, the UNIUM was willing to accept a tactical union with the communist elements.

The Far Left was represented by a group heavily influenced by communist members. Initially calling itself the Assemblage of Malagasy People (Rassemblement du Peuple Malgache), by 1959 it had become the Party of the Congress for the Independence of Madagascar (Ankoton'ny Kongresi'ny Fahaleovantenan Madagaskara—AKFM). The AKFM strongholds were Diégo-Suarez and Tananarive, having additional influence in Tamatave. Its leader was Richard Andriamanjato, a Merina and a Protestant minister who had Marxist leanings and who was elected mayor of the capital city in October 1959. The communist party, the PUPM, merged with the AKFM in late 1959 and at least for a time gained control of the larger party's leadership. The most notable Communist was a woman, Giselle Rabesahala.

The major policy of the AKFM was consistently to demand complete independence from France. Organized along communist party lines, it included many members who were interested in the party because of its attitudes toward independence rather than because of its ideology. The Communists, for their part, had accepted as their policy the need to concentrate on the nationalist issues and to adopt a common front stance. For this reason they occasionally had supported candidates who had rejected any communist association.

Whatever its policies and claims to national prominence, each of the parties found its key strength in a particular region, usually where a major party leader had a personal following. Thus the UNAM was centered on Tamatave; the UI, on Tananarive; and the PSD, on Majunga. Regionalism remained a major force in the territorial assembly, and the PSD supported a policy of dividing national powers equally between the central and regional governments.

The increasing opportunities to express themselves politically, the widening recognition that self-rule in one form or another might soon be a reality, and a taste of executive power caused a rapid evolution of these views within the PSD. By mid-1958 Tsiranana and his party were calling for a strong national government, an end to the limitations imposed by the *loi cadre*, and a raise in status of the Council of Ministers so that its leader would be recognized as the island's premier. These efforts coincided with the policies of all the other parties, even those whose demands did not stop there.

The PSD had rapidly expanded throughout the island and was the country's only well-organized political party. Its moderate approach appealed to most of the influential local leaders of the basically conservative rural society (see ch. 5). Most important to the growth of the PSD was the recognition by its leaders that its objectives should be aimed at gaining control of the government. The PSD leadership realized that success at the polls and in the assemblies would put the party in a position to determine policy; its opponents continued to voice demands without effectively organizing to gain power.

DeGaulle's return to power in France in 1958 brought new changes to the French colonial empire. As president, de Gaulle scheduled a referendum for September 1958 in which each colonial territory was to choose its own status. He assured all the territories that they could choose immediate independence if they wished but cautioned that all French assistance would be terminated immediately if they did so. The alternative was to accept an autonomous status within a French commonwealth of states, a step short of total independence but one that would grant far more self-government than the PSD had sought.

Tsiranana and the PSD campaigned effectively for autonomous status and were helped by de Gaulle's later statements that indicated that, after obtaining autonomy, independence might still be granted if requested by the newly sovereign state. The main PSD argument against independence was that it would leave Madagascar dependent on other great powers for aid, and the Communists could thus gain control of the island. Seventy-seven percent of the 1.3 million voters cast their ballots in favor of an autonomous status. On October 15, 1958. the French governor proclaimed an end to the annexation law of 1896. Amidst jubilation, Madagascar became the first self-governing republic of the French Commonwealth.

The new state continued to function under the existing laws while a new constitution was drawn up by a ninety-member constituent assembly, formed under PSD leadership from a congress of members of the provincial assemblies. The constituent assembly approved the new constitution on April 29, 1959. The new document created a mixed presidential-parliamentary form of government with a bicameral legislature. Two days later the constituent assembly, which had become the National Assembly, and its executive committee, which had become the Senate, chose Tsiranana as the country's first president.

By this time the unity and organizational ability of the PSD had assured it virtually all political power. Only the AKFM, which had limited appeal and few members, remained as an effective opponent—the others having been largely won over and absorbed by the PSD. Nevertheless, the government continued to listen to demands from outside the party.

Reflecting the attitudes adopted from political elements it had absorbed and taking its cue from events in other autonomous states of the commonwealth, the PSD requested total independence in February 1960. President Tsiranana led a delegation to Paris, and the French government agreed to its demands. On June 26, 1960, the autonomous status of the Malagasy Republic came to an end, and the country was recognized as a completely independent state.

Nevertheless, special economic, cultural, and military relationships still bound the country closely to France.

Most members of the country's political elite—even many of the AKFM opposition that demanded a break with France and close ties with member nations of the communist bloc—retained close personal cultural ties with France. These relationships were born of their education, personal associations or, in several cases, long residence as exiles in France. The policies of the ruling PSD, particularly the attitudes of its leader, President Tsiranana, favored close links to France. Particular warmth was widely felt for President de Gaulle, who was seen as responsible for France's granting of Malagasy independence.

At independence a defense and cooperation agreement with France was put into effect. French economic and military assistance, averaging the equivalent of US$40 million a year, was larger in the postindependence years than the combined foreign assistance received from all other countries. Primary dependence for external defense was placed on the large French force that remained on the island.

CHAPTER 3
GEOGRAPHY AND POPULATION

The Malagasy Republic consists of all of Madagascar—the fourth largest island in the world—and a number of small coastal reefs and islands, of which only about five have more than a handful of inhabitants (see fig. 1). Lying in the Indian Ocean astride the forty-seventh meridian some 250 miles east of southern Africa, the main island is about 1,000 miles long and averages 350 miles in width. Geographical isolation from major world industrial and trade centers is reinforced by a lack of natural harbors on the eastern coast, which is the logical area of access to shipping lanes for the nation's major areas of population density and agricultural production (see ch. 13).

A tropical marine climate is modified by complex factors associated with Madagascar's large landmass, particularly the elevated area known as the Central Highlands. This area, the site of Tananarive, the capital city, and of other population centers, is relatively comfortable for humans, as elevation moderates the tropical heat and humidity that prevail in the coastal lowlands. By partially blocking the trade winds that blow constantly from the Indian Ocean, the steep eastern slopes of the highlands become a major influence on rainfall patterns; they divide the nation into a humid windward (eastern) area, with rainfall during every month of the year, and a larger leeward (western) area, with a distinct four- to six-month dry season.

Natural vegetation in the east is humid, perennially green rain forest. The west has deciduous trees and various plant species that are adapted to an annual period of dormancy, during which the landscape is brown and dust blown.

Soils in most of the country consist of a shallow layer of laterite and clay, low in humus and plant nutrients. Over several centuries the original savanna and forests on most of the western half of the island have been stripped away or seriously degraded by shifting agriculture, by overgrazing, and by frequent burning by pastoralists. As these processes continue, the original forests and forage plants are replaced by fibrous grasses and scrub, and the weak soils are exposed to further leaching and erosion.

Most areas in the west and southwest support only a few people per square mile, although some areas of sedimentary soils offer development potential, especially in the heavier rainfall regions of the northwest. Somewhat better soils are found in the highlands, on the narrow eastern coastal plains, and in the far north; all of these areas have generated a moderately dense population, mostly on subsistence and commercial farms. In 1972 about 86 percent of the total population of 7.6 million people were essentially rural, making their living from agriculture or from closely related activities. The remainder were nominally urban, but there were few jobs, mostly in industries or commerce related to agriculture. A majority of the economically active population of 3.2 million were unskilled.

The transportation network is limited, especially in the sparsely settled west and southwest. Only a few thousand miles of roads, less than one-third of the system, can be kept in usable condition during the annual rainy season. Two relatively small areas in the highlands and the eastern plains are served by railroads. A comprehensive air transportation network compensates to some degree for the scarcity of railroads and all-season roads.

PHYSICAL SETTING

Boundaries and Political Subdivisions

The coastlines of Madgascar, plus those of the small offshore islands, are the nation's borders. Separated from other nations by the Mozambique Channel and the Indian Ocean, the republic has no border problems with other nations. Although the western ports are only a few hundred miles from the coast of Africa, the west was and is sparsely populated, and there has been neither active trade nor conflicts between the island people and those on the African continent (see ch. 10).

East-coast conditions have tended to increase the country's isolation. The eastern coastal plains face an empty ocean, and on most of the coastline there are few protected coves and no natural harbors. Offshore reefs, a high average wind velocity, and frequent hurricanes add to the hazards and expense of trading or traveling in this area.

Internal administrative divisions include six provinces, each bearing the same name as its provincial capital. Provincial borders were laid out by former French colonial administrators and retained by the Malagasy government after independence in 1960. They reflect attention to natural divisions as well as regional economic and ethnic differences (see ch. 4; ch. 12).

The provinces are divided into a total of eighteen prefectures, which are further divided into ninety-two subprefectures. The subprefecture system appears to be especially well adapted to local needs and customs. At the local level are rural or urban communes and cantons and various village administrative units (see ch. 8; ch. 5).

Landforms

Inside Madagascar's natural ocean boundaries, a broad, sparsely populated western coastal plain rises gradually to rolling foothills and low plateaus; the eastern plain is narrow and supports a comparatively dense population (see fig. 2). Between these dissimilar plains stands a complex of mountain ranges, rounded hills, and open valleys, extending from southwest to northeast throughout most of the length of the island. Most of the higher elevations are located east of the southwest-northeast central axis, but they are generally referred to as the Central Highlands or, less accurately, as the high plateaus.

The eastern slopes of these highlands rise abruptly above the narrow coastal plain—no more than ten miles wide in some areas—along the Indian Ocean. Mountain ranges above 4,000-foot elevation stand within sixty miles of this shore, rising from the coastal plains in a series of escarpments separated by narrow, hilly plateaus or benches.

Many of the agricultural regions and population centers in the Central Highlands are at elevations between 4,000 and 5,000 feet in a broad area of rolling grassy slopes, valleys, and numerous barren, rounded domes, overlooked by mountains rising in some cases above 8,000-foot altitude. Monotonous landscapes of rounded and sometimes baretopped hills of approximately equal height cover wide areas, but there is nevertheless considerable diversity in the landforms, elevations, and geologic origins of the highlands. Westward, this elevated central area descends gradually into rolling foothills and dissected plateaus, then into swamps and estuaries along the coast and the Mozambique Channel.

Much of the surface layer in the middle elevations and many prominent topographic features developed from the ancient granite structure underlying the island, which is similar to the substructure of the African continent. Most of the mountain ranges were apparently thrust upward by long-term lateral shifting in the foundation rock, but some of the highest mountains are of volcanic origin. Lava flows occurring in geologically recent times covered the older granite landforms in a few highland areas, providing the basis for some of the country's best soils. The Tsaratanana massif in northern Madagascar, surmounted at 9,450 feet by the highest mountain on the island, is primarily granite but is partially covered by lava from eruptions in the immediate area. Rock and soil from other volcanic activity are associated with the Ankaratra massif in the center of the country.

Another structure apparently created by ancient shifting of the granite substructure is a rift valley lying between mountain ranges northeast of the city of Tananarive. It is similar to the larger rift valleys of East Africa. Lake Alaotra, the largest of the lakes and swamps in this rift, lies below rock walls rising as much as 2,300 feet above the lake surface.

On the western slopes lateral shifting has also lifted, tilted, and

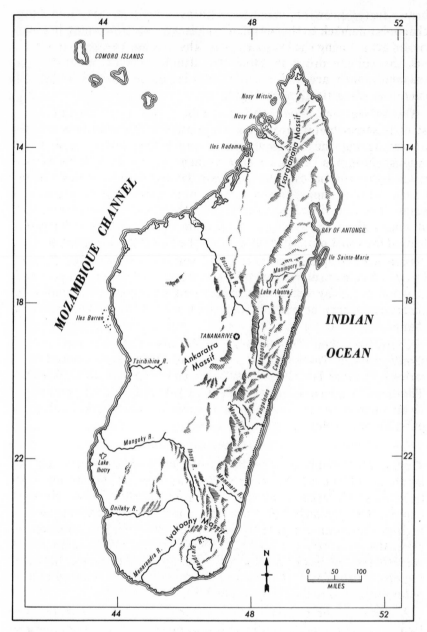

Figure 2. Physical Features of the Malagasy Republic, 1972

fractured old layers of sedimentary and alluvial rock and soil. Long-term erosion has worn down the resulting ridges, moving great quantities of decomposed rock and soil to the coastal plain.

Drainage

Rivers in the east are torrents rushing down steep slopes. Despite

34

heavy forest growths, rainwater drains quickly to the main river channels and back to the ocean. There is some flow of water in these rivers even during the least rainy months (September to November), but the volume drops to about one-fifth that of the summer wet season. In delta areas alluvial deposits have been shifted by littoral currents, distorting river mouths.

On the western slopes of the uplands, typical river gradients are steep in some stretches and shallow in others. Some sections may be empty during the height of the western dry season in July or August. Swamps in flood plains or near stagnant sections of the river are green oases in a red-brown landscape as the dry season advances; they support spots or strips of mosses, reeds, grasses, and trees. Western rivers are sluggish on the broad coastal plain, and alluvial soil material carried down from the highlands is deposited behind the coast or in the deltas along the Mozambique Channel.

Streams are ephemeral in the arid south and southwest, flowing briefly after sporadic rains. Problems of low rainfall are compounded in some areas by the porous nature of limestone soils and substructure, which allow the rainfall to seep away in underground channels.

There are about nineteen lakes, of which only a few are of significant size. The highland area west of Tamatave is marked by a series of former lake basins, of which the largest is Lake Alaotra. These various basins, which support a relatively dense population, were formed by lava flows that partially filled and divided an existing rift valley.

Climate

All of the republic has a basically tropical marine climate, but the landmass of the island, particularly the eastern mountains, contributes to the creation of important regional differences. No area experiences prolonged freezes, and snow is rare except on the highest mountains. Temperatures of 100° F or higher, common on several continents, are also rare here. The timing and amount of rainfall are the basic factors determining the differences between regions, particularly the important contrasts in vegetation and in potential for various agricultural uses.

A useful and simple description of climate divides the country into two areas: the humid, narrow belt east of the central mountains and the vast western slopes and plains, which have a distinct dry season (see fig. 3). A wet tropical climate with no entirely dry season prevails on the eastern coastal plain, the steep eastern faces of the mountains, and the peninsula in the extreme north. The northern peninsula's climate can be regarded as an extension of that along the eastern coast, although its rainfall pattern is somewhat different. The Central Highlands are a transition zone, influenced at different times by airmasses from both coasts. The western slope area, which includes much of the country, receives its rainfall from different storm patterns and has distinct wet (summer) and dry (winter) seasons. The four-to six-month dry season—longer in the southwest than in the northwest—is a major influence on natural vegetation and on agricultural use of the land, giving most of the west a landscape and character that are markedly different from that of the eastern slope or the northernmost peninsula area.

A more detailed analysis reflects five climatic regions (see fig. 4). Each of these areas also has distinct cultural and economic traits (see ch. 4; ch. 13). This breakdown includes the humid eastern belt; the wet extreme north, which is partially isolated from both east and west by mountains; the Central Highlands with a relatively pleasant tropical, high-altitude climate; the mid-level and lower western slopes shading into the broad west-coast plain, well-watered during the summer rainy season but dry for nearly half the year; and the south and southwest, a semidesert area.

Much of the rainfall in the east is carried from the Indian Ocean on the trade winds. These currents of warm wet air flow ceaselessly over the island from the east. Madagascar's steep mountain barrier—1,000 miles long—and the warmth of the island's landmass force the air currents upward, where they interact with cooler layers of air and develop great turbulence. Their moisture condenses into rain, often several inches per day, along the entire eastern slope area.

Precipitation in the east ranges from ten to eighteen inches per month during the southern hemisphere summer (from December to April). During the cool season, the trade winds blow persistently from a high-pressure area east-southeast of the island, striking the land at a direct right angle to the general orientation of the mountain ranges. These winds bring three to six inches of rain per month to the eastern region during its least rainy months (September, October, and November). Total annual rainfall in most of this relatively narrow belt is over eighty inches and in small areas near the Bay of Antongil, where landforms tend to trap the turbulent winds, exceeds 120 inches.

Some of the burden of moisture is carried over or between the eastern escarpments and inland as far as the general area of the capital city of Tananarive, but rainfall of any kind is minimal in the Central Highlands during the cool season between May and September. Having dropped their moisture over the eastern slopes and a small belt of the highlands, the east winds become drying winds, picking up moisture from the land as they move down the broad western slopes. This is a major factor in the creation of the annual western dry season, which lasts four to six months in most areas.

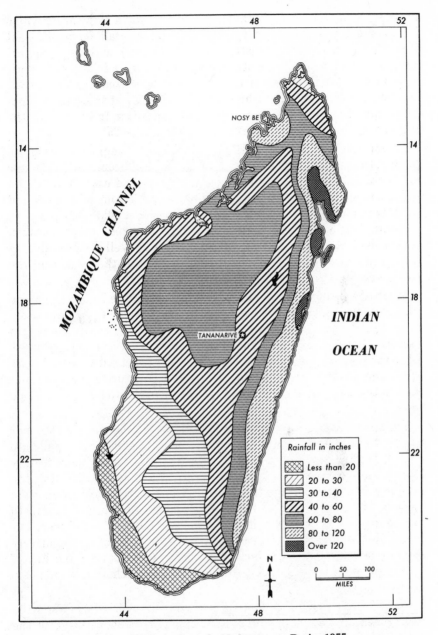

Source: Adapted from Hildebert Isnard, *Madagascar*, Paris, 1955.

Figure 3. Annual Rainfall in the Malagasy Republic

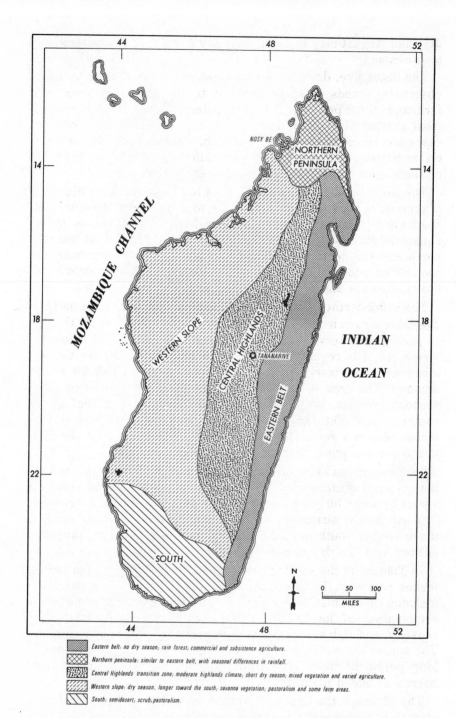

Eastern belt: no dry season; rain forest; commercial and subsistence agriculture.

Northern peninsula: similar to eastern belt, with seasonal differences in rainfall.

Central Highlands transition zone; moderate highlands climate; short dry season; mixed vegetation and varied agriculture.

Western slope: dry season, longer toward the south; savanna vegetation; pastoralism and some farm areas.

South: semidesert; scrub; pastoralism.

Figure 4. Geographical Regions of the Malagasy Republic

38

July and August may be completely dry in most of the western half of the island.

The desertlike, dry-season landscape, commented upon by many observers, stands in sharp contrast to the lush rain forest and farmland on the perennially humid eastern slopes. The difference is most sharply illustrated in the south, a few miles inland from the east-coast resort town of Fort Dauphin, where stands of rain forest on the eastern face of a narrow mountain range are within ten miles of semidesert vegetation on the western slopes.

The western slope dry season comes to an end with the approach of summer in the southern hemisphere, as the thermal equator shifts southward to latitudes near northern Madagascar. Warm, humid equatorial air moves in above the western half of the island from the north and the northwest. These wet airmasses interact with the cooler east winds over the island, producing prolonged drizzles or heavy showers and sometimes destructive tropical storms.

The small northern region, including the broad peninsula north of the Tsaratanana massif and the nearby island of Nosy Be, is the first to receive moisture from the southward shift of humid equatorial airmasses. The region continues to be affected even after the wet airmasses have retreated from most of the country at the end of summer. The area also gets rain clouds from the east during other seasons and has, in effect, a microclimate similar to that of the eastern coast. The Diégo-Suarez port area receives forty to fifty inches of rain a year; Nosy Be and the adjacent area on the main island receive more than eighty inches annually.

In Majunga on the northwestern coast and in most of the area between the western coast and the Central Highlands, precipitation varies between forty and eighty inches during the annual wet cycle. The equatorial airmasses become progressively weaker as they move farther south over the western half of the island; rainfall is lighter, and the dry season is longer.

In Tulear, on the southwestern coast, rainfall is less than twenty inches per year. In this southern and southwestern area, which includes approximately one-sixth of the island's total land surface, a combination of low rainfall, thin soil with little waterholding capacity, and high evaporation rates produces semidesert conditions. The sparse natural cover has been degraded by overgrazing over a long period of time, and large areas are becoming increasingly barren of useful plantlife.

The climate in the Central Highlands, which are above 4,000 feet in elevation, is generally regarded as relatively healthful and comfortable, as it is cooler and less humid than that of the coastal plains. During the dry months of the year mists form at night but are dissipated early. Usually, bright sunshine prevails for most of the day. Cool, dry trade winds, having been stripped of their moisture as they rise above the eastern slopes, tend to hold daytime temperatures and humidity near the ranges preferred by most residents, particularly by Europeans or by others unaccustomed to the extremes of tropical climates at lower altitudes.

Like upland areas almost everywhere, Tananarive and other highland areas show broader daily temperature ranges than areas nearer sea level. Even when days are hot, the nights are refreshingly cool. Above 5,000-foot elevation, frost or light snow occasionally appear.

Mean temperatures in the city of Tananarive (altitude, 4,500 feet) are about 70° F from December through March and about 60° F from June through September (see table 1). This contrasts with Tamatave, the port city only 150 miles to the northeast, where humidity is high and mean temperatures are usually about 10° F warmer (about 80° F during the warmest months and 70° F during the local winter). Majunga, a city on the northwest coast, has a quite different rainfall pattern but is nearly as warm and humid as Tamatave. Tulear, on the edge of the southern and southwestern semidesert region, records temperatures similar to those in other towns on both coasts but has, along with its lower annual rainfall, a lower average humidity.

Table 1. Mean Temperature and Rainfall at Selected
Stations, Malagasy Republic, 1967

	Tamatave		Tananarive		Tulear	
	Temperature (°F)	Rainfall (inches)	Temperature (°F)	Rainfall (inches)	Temperature (°F)	Rainfall (inches)
January	80	14.4	70	11.8	82	3.1
February	80	14.8	69	11.0	80	3.2
March	79	17.8	69	7.0	79	1.4
April	77	15.7	67	2.1	76	0.3
May	74	10.4	63	0.7	72	0.7
June	71	11.1	60	0.3	71	0.4
July	70	11.9	59	0.3	69	0.1
August	70	8.0	58	0.4	69	0.2
September	71	5.2	62	0.7	72	0.3
October	74	3.9	67	2.4	75	0.7
November	77	4.6	68	5.3	78	1.4
December	79	10.3	70	11.3	81	1.7
Annual	75	128.2	65	53.4	75	13.5
Altitude (in feet) .	20		4,500		20	

Source: Adapted from Alan B. Mountjoy and Clifford Embleton, *Africa: A New Geographical Survey*, New York, 1967.

The island's warmest temperatures occur in the inland areas of moderate altitude on the western slope. Northwestern coastal towns are cooled somewhat by daytime sea breezes, but a warm wind blows from the landward side of the coastal flatlands during the late night and early morning hours. Similarly, on the eastern coast a breeze from the foothills behind the coastline prevails at the surface during the early mornings. In late morning, the trade winds again begin to flow in from the Indian Ocean.

In the highlands, clouds accumulate in local valleys during the cool nights and dissipate over the mountains in the morning as the warmth of the sun creates updrafts. In some seasons, large thunderheads are visible over the eastern highlands by midday and rise to considerable heights. Winds push these turbulent rainbearing clouds westward over the Central Highlands; after a relatively pleasant day of tropical highland climate, rain often falls in the late afternoon or evening.

The continuing clashes of highly charged airmasses over Madagascar routinely produce impressive displays of thunder and lightning. Several dozen people are killed every year by lightning, and unprotected buildings are damaged; permanent homes and other larger buildings are usually provided with lightning arresters.

Violent tropical storms occur frequently enough—generally from one to five times a year—that they must be accepted as a regular part of island life. The annual storm season generally lasts from December to March. The towns, small farms, and commercial plantations from Mahanoro and Tamatave on the east-central coast to Diego-Suarez on the northern peninsula are struck by the full force of these storms as they sweep in from the Indian Ocean. West-coast and highlands residents also suffer. Storm tracks vary and may reach any part of the island except the extreme south. Entering the land area from the northeast or east, they curve southward over the west-coast area or the Mozambique Channel and then turn southeastward across the southern half of the country.

Even storms with wind velocities under seventy-three miles per hour (the technical minimum for storms to be labeled as hurricanes) may do considerable damage. During the worst storms, winds may exceed 100 or even 150 miles per hour, damaging or destroying buildings and uprooting trees that have stood for centuries. The lightly built huts of many rural inhabitants are especially vulnerable. Floods and high winds also erode away crops and farmland, the earthen dikes of rice paddies, or any other soil not protected by a well-established cover of vegetation.

Soils

Highly productive soils are found only on a small percentage of the total land surface (see fig. 5). Alluvial materials deposited in valley bottoms and in old lake beds in the highlands and on the eastern coastal plains make good farmland. Rich volcanic soils are found in a few areas of Tananarive Province and in the extreme north. Some of the lighter clays in extensive areas of Tananarive and Fianarantsoa provinces are not as seriously laterized or eroded as the soils on most of the lower slopes and are, therefore, relatively good soils. Erosional processes have resulted in mixtures of these and other soils, and many variations can be identified.

In broad areas of the highlands and the upper western and southwestern slopes, the surface layers are red, lateritic clay derived originally from the granite that forms the substructure of the island. Soils vary greatly, but they are generally low in plant nutrients and are only moderately productive. In some areas of the southwestern semidesert plateaus, the soil is no more than a skeletal crust of poorly developed clay or limestone, shading in the southwestern coastal area into a thin crust on a limestone base.

West of the highlands, the lower slopes include broad areas in which the underlying granite is exposed only here and there. The granite is covered elsewhere by varied mixtures of lateritic clay, limestone, gravels, and sediments from ancient and existing streams. Erosional debris, especially the finer sediments, has been carried down to the coastal plain by the rivers and deposited in flood plains and deltas.

Heavy runoff has carried much topsoil into the seas on both coasts and continues to do so wherever the soil is not held in place by vegetation. Erosion and leaching are not limited to heavy storm periods or to any single area. In the highlands and on the western slope in general, soils formerly protected by forests or by savanna mixtures of trees, shrubs, and grasses have been exposed by improper land use. Indiscriminate annual burning of brush and pastureland has been practiced for centuries. Repeated burning eventually kills most of the succulent plants and grasses, and the land is taken over by thorny scrub and less desirable varieties of grass.

During the dry season, soil exposed by the burning of vegetation or by shifting cultivation is damaged by the hot sun, which destroys humus in surface layers, and hot winds sweep away clouds of red dust. Heavy runoff continues the process of leaching and erosion of exposed soil during the rainy season, especially on the steeper slopes.

Minerals

Proven mineral deposits are meager, but about eight kinds of ores have been found in quantities that justified their development in the past or are regarded as possibilities for the future (see ch. 13). Graphite is shipped from a point near the eastern coast; and mica,

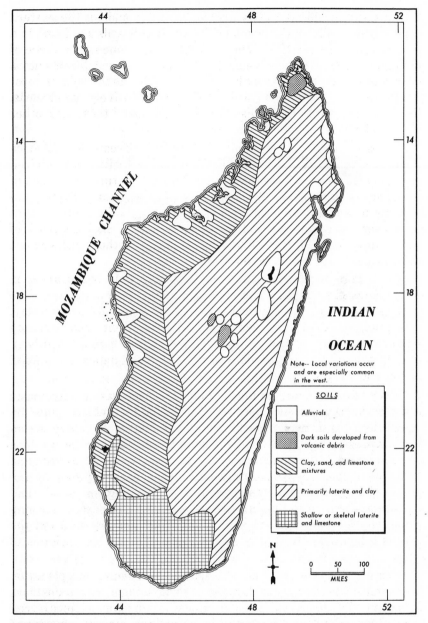

Source: Adapted from André Guilcher and René Battistini, *Madagascar: Géographie Régionale*, Paris, 1967.

Figure 5. Predominant Soil Varieties of the Malagasy Republic

from the southeast, inland from Fort Dauphin. Chromium ore is mined from sites west of Lake Alaotra in Tamatave Province, and a rail line was extended to the site to carry ore concentrate to the port at Tamatave.

43

Uranium and thorium compounds have been mined on a small scale near Behara in southern Tulear Province. A large deposit of coal at Sakoa, also in Tulear Province, is being studied. Minor deposits of quartz, garnets, monazite, beryllium, columbium, and tantalum have been identified. Small amounts of gold have been extracted at several sites in the highlands. A search for petroleum has been in progress since the early 1960s, including offshore exploration after 1967. Some references have been made to petroleum deposits under the southwestern plateaus inland from Tulear, but as of late 1972 no public announcements of major oil discoveries had been made.

Vegetation and Wildlife

In its profusion of plantlife, as in several other fields of study, Madagascar has its own unique character. Many species show close relationships to Asian or Indonesian plant families. Others appear to have descended, with little evolutionary change, from very ancient local species.

Natural vegetation in the perennially wet eastern (windward) face of the island is a complex mixture of tropical and subtropical species, dominated by trees and shrubs that retain their foliage all year. Extensive areas on the western (leeward) slopes and plains were originally covered by drought-resistant forest or by varying combinations of savanna plants, most of them well adapted to the rigors of an annual dry season. Some areas of the western savanna have few trees except those around villages. There are also several ecological subregions, including small areas of montane forest at the higher altitudes in the central mountains; mangrove swamps in the flat plains along the Mozambique Channel; and the cacti and other hardy species in the southern and southwestern semidesert.

The permanently green eastern slopes have conserved a number of ancient plants that are peculiar to Madagascar. Common native coastal species in this region include several kinds of pines and palms, which tower over marsh reeds and broad-leaved marsh plants. A few miles inland, in areas where the original forest still exists, the lower slopes of the mountains are covered by mixed trees that average eighty to 100 feet in height. Vines and parasitic flowering plants hang from the trees. Beneath them the forest floor is covered by short varieties of palm, bracken, and fern. The traveler's tree, which stores potable water in its fibers, is common.

In other eastern areas the native forests have been disrupted or destroyed by man. Even when left unused, such areas may produce scrub mixtures known as *savoka*, rather than revert to forest. Above an elevation of 2,500 feet, shorter trees and herbs with complicated root systems prevail. Bamboo thrives in the area, but it may be bent or distorted by the pounding winds.

The northern region of Madagascar, north of the Tsaratanana

massif, as well as the offshore island of Nosy Be, originally produced evergreen forests similar to those on the eastern coast. Small forested areas remain, but most of the trees have been removed and have been replaced by plantations or mixtures of grasses.

The western slopes, including parts of the Central Highlands, were probably covered originally by tropical mixed forests, primarily deciduous trees and shrubs adapted to an annual season of drought and dormancy. Most of the original forest has long since been removed by cutting or burning, leaving less than 10 percent of the original coverage, mostly on the taller peaks in the Central Highlands.

In some areas the high peaks are covered with thick stands of a kind of brush similar to heather. Other large areas in the highlands were originally covered with a mixture of savanna grasses and a few shrubs or trees that shaded into a mixture of shrubs, trees, and grasses farther west. Taller trees, including varieties that form gallery forests, thrived along watercourses, and stands of such trees still survive along some streams.

Many areas in the highlands are farmed, and in some areas the original succulent grasses have been destroyed by repeated annual burning. Broad areas, however, retain some of the original appearance of the open savanna. The landscape is bright green during the rainy months but turns brown and dormant during the dry season, except for strips of green along watercourses. The red earth shows through in partially barren areas, which expand as intensive grazing and annual burning continue. A few fire-resistant trees such as satrana (a type of palm) rise above the clutter of coarse grasses, thorny scrub, half-burned stumps, and fibers. At medium or low altitudes in the far west, the mixed plantlife includes baobab and raffia palm trees. Close to the coast, mangrove and palm trees stand above swamp grasses and reeds.

Toward the south and southwest, increasing numbers of mimosa trees and thorny drought-resistant bushes appear. The destruction of the original vegetative cover is more complete in southern and southwestern Tulear Province, where it regresses from the original semidesert, which had a rich and unique variety of dry-area plantlife, toward the barren sand and clay of true desert. Like the humid east, this isolated region has created and preserved unique and highly specialized botanic forms not found elsewhere. Some of them are in danger of extinction.

The moderate climate is favorable to many plants imported from foreign tropical and temperate climates; some have become standard subsistence or commercial crops. Trees that were introduced (in some cases these were foreign varieties of species already in the country) include eucalyptus, mimosa, oil palm, papaya, clove, and cocoa.

Eucalyptus trees are common in some towns. Their branches are used for fuel for cooking. Other common plantings in residential areas in the major towns include jacaranda, bougainvillea, lilac, poinsettia, and datura. A specie of cactus brought from Central America in the eighteenth century adapted so well that it crowded out several other kinds on some soils in the south.

Like its plantlife, the country's wildlife includes many types that are unknown elsewhere. There are about forty varieties of lemur, ranging in size from a few inches to the size of a large monkey. Small animals include hedgehogs, bats, civet cats, and various rodents. Altogether, about thirty types of insect-eating small mammals are known. When the island was first settled, there were no deer, monkeys, or any of the large carnivores among the native species.

Indigenous reptiles include various nonpoisonous snakes, crocodiles, tortoises, chameleons, geckoes, and large lizards. A great variety of insects includes silk-making moths and 800 butterfly species. Well-known birds include guinea fowl, francolin (a kind of partridge), various ducks, teal, snipe, heron, ibis, flamingo, egrets, owls, various birds of prey, and many small forest and savanna birds. A specie of dwarf hippopotamus formerly lived here, and in ancient times there were several large flightless birds. One specie probably survived until shortly before Europeans began to visit the island several centuries ago.

At least a dozen major species of native fish live in inland waters and are caught in all areas except the south. The tilapia (also found in Africa) lives in most areas of the island. Some introduced species have thrived, the best known being the rainbow trout and black bass. Offshore waters support nearly 100 kinds of ocean fish, including shellfish in the coastal waters. Two species, globefish and cofferfish, are known only in the Madagascar area. The coelacanth, a large fish formerly thought to have been extinct for millions of years, survives in offshore waters and is sometimes referred to as a living fossil.

Transportation Features

Despite improvements in transportation facilities since 1955, many local economic units and population centers in 1972 had little contact with distant towns or potential markets because of the country's limited transportation system.

Roads

In 1972 about 20,000 miles of roads and improved trails formed a sparse network, at least a few roads extending into most parts of the country (see fig. 6). As much as three-fourths of the system, however, was often unusable during the annual rainy season. Main routes extended throughout the north-south length of the island, and there were a few east-west connections to the seaports.

About 1,850 miles of the road network were hard surfaced, including the route through the highlands from Tananarive southward to Antsirabe and Fianarantsoa. Road connections between the Central Highlands and the eastern coast, as well as the 380-mile link between the capital and the northwestern port of Majunga, were considered primary routes and were either paved or scheduled for paving and other major improvements. In most areas of the country, however, only short segments in or near major towns were permanently surfaced. Major road improvement programs began during the late 1950s. Long-term financing of road construction was arranged during the early 1960s, and the improvement and maintenance programs continued in 1972.

Railroads

The only railroads in the Malagasy Republic in 1972 were two relatively small systems connecting two highland areas with the eastern coast. The first and largest of these, completed in 1913, covered a 229-mile route from Tananarive to the major east-coast port of Tamatave, serving thirty-six stations along the way. A branch line extended northward to the Lake Aloatra agricultural area and to a chromium ore mine west of the lake. Another branch extended southward to Antsirabe.

The second link, completed in 1936, had no branch lines and was not connected to the existing system. It served seventeen stations between Fianarantsoa and the minor eastern port of Manakara. Along the 110-mile route were nearly 100 tunnels, viaducts, and bridges. On both systems, original coasts and maintenance expenses have been high.

Some rolling stock was fairly modern, and more up-to-date equipment was being added. Thirty-two diesel-electric locomotives were in use during the late 1960s, and the purchase of three more was reportedly under consideration in 1970. Containerized freight units, including a few insulated containers for meat shipments, were being used. The two rail systems had about 850 freight cars and 100 passenger cars in use.

All trackage was meter gauge. Originally there were many tight curves, steep grades, and an insufficient number of crossing stations (sidetracks). The roadbed and rails were not adequate for the traffic demands made on them during the 1950s and early 1960s, and an extensive modernization and improvement program was initiated. It extended into every phase of operation: trackage, bridges, equipment, maintenance, communications, station improvements, and housing for railroad personnel. Major progress had been made by 1972, and the program was continuing.

Airports

Since the 1950s an expanding air network has improved contact

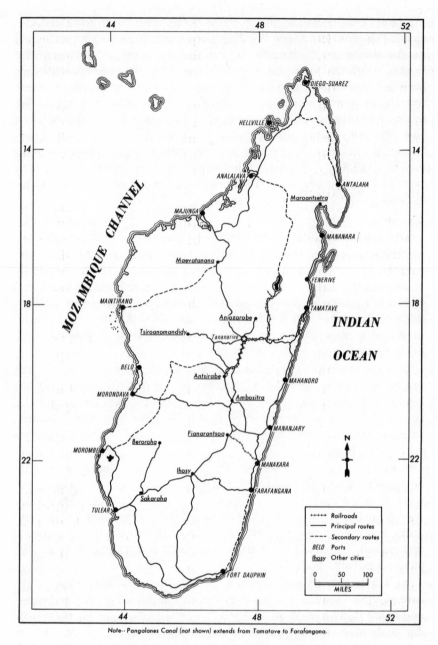

Note-- Pangalanes Canal (not shown) extends from Tamatave to Farafangana.

Source: Adapted from C. Robequain, *Madagascar et les Bases Dispersées de l'Union Francaise*, Paris, 1958; and Hubert Deschamps, *Madagascar*, Paris, 1968.

Figure 6. Transportation System of the Malagasy Republic, 1972

between regions. Air Madagascar (Société Nationale Malgache des Transports Aériens) was formed in 1962 to manage air transport services. By 1972 the civil air fleet included one Boeing 707 long-range heavy jet transport, one Boeing 737 medium jet, eleven piston-engine Douglas DC-4 and DC-3 transports, ten small Piper-built passenger carriers, and several other aircraft. Foreign airlines with connections to the Malagasy Republic were Air France, Alitalia, and South African Airways.

Of about 200 airfields and airstrips, about sixty-five were in regular use. Ivato airport was the hub of the internal air service and, since 1967, the primary port for international flights as well. Amborovy, on the eastern coast near Majunga, was also an entry and departure point for overseas air carriers (see fig. 7).

Ports and Inland Waterways

Twenty-three seaports served the country in 1972. Almost all were minor facilities that handled small amounts of freight with simple techniques and equipment. In the absence of natural harbors on the eastern coast, the trade winds have often posed a shipping problem. Nevertheless, Tamatave, with a manmade harbor, handled one-half of the nation's external trade, having been developed to serve the east-coast plantations and the agricultural areas in the highlands.

Majunga on the northwestern coast was the second largest port. It was naturally sheltered from rough water but had no deepwater quay. Tulear in the southwest had few facilities.

Diego-Suarez in the far north, one of the largest and best natural harbors in the world, was remote from the main areas of population and agricultural production in the highlands. The port served primarily as a naval base rather than as a facility for commercial shipping. The offshore island of Nosy Be was served by a small port at Hellville.

Lakes and short stretches of various rivers were used on a small scale as transportation routes but, in general, inland waterways were of minor significance, except for the moderate level of use and the local importance of the Pangalanes Canal paralleling the eastern coast. In this unique system, numerous manmade channels through natural rock sills (*pangalanes*) connected a series of shallow lagoons on the coastal plain, providing a quiet waterway for small boats. It served minor ports and agricultural communities along a 400-mile segment of the coastline from the city of Tamatave and the railhead east of Brickaville southward to Faranfangana.

Settlement Patterns

Soils and climate have been the primary determinants of the varying regional settlement patterns. Although the overall population density was about thirty-three persons per square mile in 1972, regions of alluvial or volcanic soils had produced considerably higher densities of population in a small percentage of the total land area. When combined with adequate rainfall, such soils had fostered

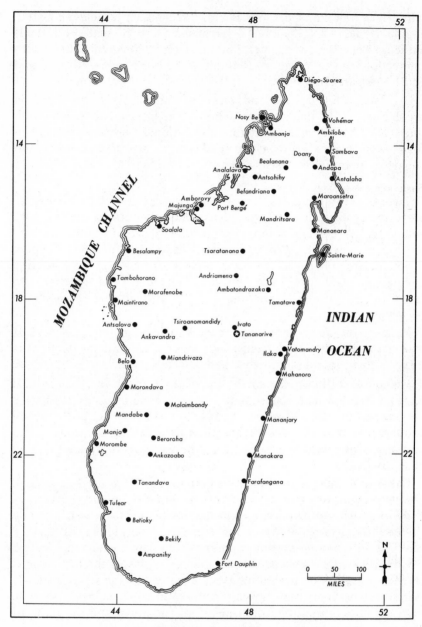

Figure 7. *Active Civil Airports, Malagasy Republic, 1972*

intensive agriculture and a limited amount of industry and trade
related to agriculture (see ch. 13).

More than one-fourth of the nation's population lived in the
eastern coastal plains and adjacent foothills—a belt 600 miles long

and averaging twenty-five miles in width. Settlement patterns in this area have grown out of a mixture of subsistence and commercial agriculture and the proximity of seaports that handled primarily agricultural products. In a number of districts scattered along the eastern coast, population densities were about 100 persons per square mile; much larger areas supported more than fifty persons per square mile.

Eastern settlements ranged from small farming communities and numerous large villages of more than 1,000 inhabitants to six coastal towns with populations of more than 5,000. Tamatave, by far the largest eastern town, was the most active seaport in the entire country. It served both the local agricultural hinterland and the population concentrations in the Central Highlands.

Most of the major concentrations of population in the highlands were in an area extending from Tananarive 200 miles southward to Fianarantsoa. In this area, varying in width from a few miles to about fifty miles, hundreds of open valleys contained better soils than the laterites that covered most of the western slopes. As the population increased in these upland areas, some villages grew until they coalesced with neighboring settlements. In areas where agricultural surpluses led to related commerce or industry, some of the multiple villages continued to grow. The Central Highlands thus had become a mixture of small villages, expanded villages of 1,000 to 2,000 people (about fifty in Tananarive Province, for example), and about six larger towns. Even the larger centers were unplanned agricultural settlements, farmland or grassland being interspersed with outlying residences. Population densities were similar to those of the eastern lowlands, varying from fifty to more than 150 persons per square mile.

Tananarive, the national capital, is an anomaly in this highland region, although it retains obvious ties to the surrounding agricultural economy. Its early origins as a group of large, neighboring Merina villages can still be detected. The site, on the slopes of a great rocky mound, appears to have been chosen for its advantages as a defensive position. Nearby productive soils, a moderate climate, and its central location contributed to its development during the eighteenth and nineteenth centuries as the seat of government of the Merina royal families as they extended their influence throughout the island (see ch. 2; ch. 4).

As France consolidated its control of the island after 1896, the capital city began to develop a new dimension as the primary focus of foreign technology and political philosophies and as the main center of government, education, industry, transportation, entertainment, and the arts. This trend has continued since independence. With an estimated 375,000 people in 1972, Tananarive was six times the size of any other city in the nation and continued to grow.

Despite its size and special characteristics, the capital city exhibits many of the traits of smaller towns. Large homes stand close to various smaller dwellings, and few areas are devoted to a single kind of structure or economic activity. Houses with small yards or gardens are close together. Rows of homes with stone steps up the steep slopes between them rise in terraces. Cultivated fields extend into some parts of the urban areas, and homes stand near fields of paddy rice, sugarcane, manioc, and fruits.

Additional small areas of relatively dense population were on the northern coast in Diégo-Suarez Province, on the offshore island of Nosy Be, and on a few small river deltas such as those in the Majunga area of the northwestern coast. This northwestern region and a few flood plains and delta areas along the central part of the western coastal plain were developing a heavier population and were believed to have the potential for considerable agricultural expansion (see ch. 13).

Few other areas offer any comparable potential that has not already been tested or exploited. Tens of thousands of square miles on the western plateaus and on the southern semidesert are covered with thin lateritic soils. Rainfall is variable and below the minimum needed for many food crops. A sparse population grows a few subsistence crops in small areas, but most of the land produces only scrub and forage for cattle. About 170,000 square miles, the majority of Madagascar's land area, thus supports an average of less than ten people per square mile.

POPULATION

The population in late 1972 was about 7.6 million, an estimate based upon data from an official population survey in 1966 and from additional analyses and projections published in 1971. The survey, an extensive official demographic study, covered about 10 percent of the population in seventy-seven selected areas. It provided the basis for an official estimate of about 6.2 million people on January 1, 1967, up from an estimated 4.1 million in 1948 and 5.3 million in 1960. Subsequent reviews of the 1966 data by survey officials and by other demographic specialists indicated that the survey and recent official estimates based in part on survey data have been reasonably accurate.

Population Dynamics

Population growth was probably limited to about 1 percent annually until the early 1950s, when programs of immunization, preventive medicine, and mosquito control were expanded. The growth rate for the 1960-72 period probably averaged about 2.1 percent. In the absence of a complete census, estimates of population growth ranged from 2 to 2.5 percent.

Data by province for the 1967-70 period showed growth in all areas. The highlands province of Tananarive and the northwestern province of Tamatave increased most rapidly (see table 2).

Table 2. Population Growth in the Malagasy Republic
from 1967 to 1970

Province	Population		Increase	
	1967	1970	Number	Percent
Tananarive	1,620,700	1,780,300	159,600	9.8
Fianarantsoa	1,701,500	1,805,300	103,800	6.1
Tamatave	1,057,550	1,174,900	117,350	11.0
Majunga	800,550	859,300	58,750	7.3
Tulear	1,046,800	1,117,700	70,900	6.8
Diégo-Suarez	549,900	583,900	34,000	6.2
TOTAL	6,777,000	7,321,400	544,400	....

Source: Adapted from Malagasy Republic, Institut National de la Statistique et de la Recherche Economique, *Population de Madagascar, Situation au 1er Janvier 1970*, Tananarive, Ministère des Finances et du Commerce, 1971.

Birth rates were estimated to be between forty-six and forty-nine per 1,000 a year during the early 1960s, and there was some evidence of a rate of about forty-five thereafter. Mortality rates were about twenty-five per 1,000 per year for the 1966-72 period, down from an estimated forty per 1,000 before improvements in preventive medicine and malaria control were instituted during the 1950s. Life expectancy at birth was estimated at about forty years (see ch. 6).

The government's demographic survey and projected estimates of 1970 revealed a relatively young population (see table 3). More than 57 percent of the people were under twenty-one years of age. The population was almost evenly divided between males and females, partly because male migration to foreign areas in search of work, which distrupts the balance in a number of countries, was not an important factor in the Malagasy Republic.

Rural-Urban Distribution

In 1972 more than 6 million people—about 86 percent of the population—lived in a rural setting, mostly as subsistence farmers or pastoralists. Most of them resided in villages that varied greatly in size and form according to ethnic group, terrain, type of agriculture practiced, and other factors (see ch. 6).

Above the village level, the typical population center (including many of the largest towns as well as the smaller towns and expanded villages) remained a part of the agricultural milieu, although the residents of some were nominally urban. Such centers have usually

Table 3. Age and Sex Distribution of the Population,
Malagasy Republic, 1970

Age Group	Male	Female	Total
Under 15 years	1,454,050	1,418,550	2,872,600
15 - 20 years	664,700	709,200	1,373,900
21 years or older	1,534,250	1,643,100	3,177,350
TOTAL	3,653,000	3,770,850	7,423,850

Source: Adapted from Malagasy Republic, Institut National de la Statistique
et de la Recherche Economique. *Population de Madagascar, Situation
au 1er Janvier 1970,* Tananarive, Ministère des Finances et du
Commerce, 1971.

grown into town status from a group of adjoining villages. In most
cases they have few centrally controlled services and limited interests outside the local farm area.

In 1972 the nominally urban population ranged from less than 5
percent in Tulear Province to a high of about 20 percent in
Tananarive Province, where most of the urbanites were in the
capital city and in the town of Antsirabe. The population of most
urban centers had grown at a rate of about 4 percent per year since
1950; more than half of this increase was attributed to internal
growth rather than to movement from rural areas, which was
reportedly slow.

For many decades villagers have traveled on foot or by bicycle or
cart to local market centers, and more recently there has been an
increase in travel by small buses and even by air. Most of those who
were forced to move because of drought or population pressures on
the land have apparently looked for other farm areas. There have
been few jobs in the towns, as industrialization is not far advanced
(see ch. 13). The smaller towns, and most of the larger ones as well,
provide few of the amenities, services, or entertainments that might
attract more migrants.

If residency in a town of at least 5,000 people is accepted as an
arbitrary standard, about 14 percent of the population, or about
1,050,000 people, were urban dwellers in late 1972 (see table 4). More
than half of this group lived in sixteen towns in the provinces of
Tananarive and Fianarantsoa, which are primarily highlands areas
but areas that also include a long segment of the eastern coastal
plains.

Tananarive is a mixture of cosmopolitan and agricultural interests.
All the other towns and cities show stronger agricultural ties,
although they may also be provincial capitals, ports, or both. The
next six cities in order of size in 1970 were Antsirabe (center of an
agricultural area in Tananarive Province with about 57,000 people)

Table 4. Estimated Urban Population of the Malagasy Republic, 1970

Province	Number of Towns [1]	Population
Tananarive	9	455,500
Fianarantsoa	3	137,250
Diégo-Suarez	9	138,900
Majunga	8	111,700
Tamatave	6	103,950
Tulear	5	82,000
TOTAL	40	1,029,300 [2]

[1] Over 5,000 population only.
[2] Increased to an estimated 1.05 million by late 1972.

Source: Adapted from Malagasy Republic, Institut National de la Statistique et de la Recherche Economique, *Population de Madagascar, Situation au 1er Janvier 1970*, Tananarive, Ministère des Finances et du Commerce, 1971.

and the capitals of the other five provinces. Each capital had local economic importance in addition to its function as an administrative center: Tamatave, the major east-coast port, had a population of 56,900; Majunga, the major northwestern port, 54,000; Fianarantsoa, center of a highlands agricultural area, 50,700; Diégo-Suarez, northern port and naval base near commercial agricultural lands, 46,900; and Tulear, southwestern coastal town, 35,950. All were relatively formless, having grown around their function as ports, agricultural centers, or both.

Forty-five additional towns each had more than 5,000 people. Towns of this size ranged from five in Tulear Province to nine in each of the provinces of Tananarive and Diégo-Suarez. The provinces of Tananarive and Diégo-Suarez had the smallest land area but the best soils. Another 340 towns or expanded villages each listed between 1,000 and 5,000 people. The plateaus and coastal plains of the large western provinces of Majunga and Tulear held about 105 of these smaller centers, as compared with 123 in the smaller area of Tananarive and Tamatave provinces—where climate and soil foster a richer agriculture and a heavier population.

Migration

About 35,000 people—perhaps 50,000 in years when subsistence farmers suffer from drought or other problems—work for part of the year outside their home areas. Some are seasonal workers who labor for several weeks or months on commercial rice farms in the highlands, on tobacco farms in the northwest, or with other crops in various areas. Most of these workers are young men, but some women also work away from home (see ch. 5).

In addition to seasonal agricultural workers, other temporary migrants go from home areas into the cities for varying periods of employment. Many are laborers; a few are artisans, such as masons or carpenters, who move from village to village offering their services. Those who travel only short distances usually go on foot, by bicycles, or in small buses. In the absence of an extensive system of all-weather roads and with the development of a relatively complete domestic air transportation system since the mid 1950s, more workers who must cover long distances have been traveling by air.

Most workers retain ties to their home area and return as the job or the work season comes to an end. A minority, estimated to be a few thousand each year, remain away indefinitely or settle permanently and become a part of the ethnic mixture in their new home area (see ch. 4; ch. 6).

Many of those who have resettled originated in the south and left their home area as temporary workers. Aridity, population pressure on the land in the south, and opportunities to work—at least seasonally—in the northwest or the extreme north have been important factors in a slow but continuing shift of population. The south-north drift of economically hard-pressed southerners, mostly young people, has been going on for several decades and continued in the early 1970s.

Although there were no active programs to help migrants resettle, Malagasy planning officials indicated in 1971 that such assistance should be a government concern. Some of the central areas of the western coastal plains appeared to offer good potential for agricultural development (see ch. 13).

The majority of migrants had no special skills and necessarily sought farmwork. The farms in the highlands of Tananarive and Fianarantsoa provinces were closer than those in the northwest, but the highlands were already relatively crowded. As a result few southerners have remained there permanently. Whereas the former ruling group in the highlands, the Merina, remained relatively unmixed, western and far northern coastal areas had developed a varied population that included many migrants from other provinces, especially from the south, as well as immigrants or descendants of immigrants from abroad.

In 1970 more than 90 percent of the population of Tananarive, Fianarantsoa, and Tamatave—the three eastern provinces—were locally born; in Tananarive the figure was nearly 99 percent. In the west, immigrants from other provinces or from areas outside the country ranged from 20 percent in Tulear to 40 percent in Majunga and more than 75 percent in Diégo-Suarez.

The Economically Active Population

About 90 percent of the males over fifteen years of age and 75 percent of the females were active in productive work in 1970, making a total of about 3.2 million in the country's work force (see ch. 12). Estimates indicated 238,000 employees in private enterprises and 49,000 in the public sector, leaving about 2.9 million categorized as self-employed, mostly family members sharing in the work on subsistence farms. About 56 percent of the labor force was considered unskilled. After the change of government leadership in May 1972, government spokesmen announced plans to train more people and create more jobs, acknowledging that the lack of adequate opportunities was considered to be one of the causes of the demonstrations in April and May (see ch. 9).

Skilled workers made up about 12 percent of the work force. The remaining 32 percent were foremen, managers, concessionaires, or others outside the primary categories of skilled and unskilled productive personnel.

CHAPTER 4
ETHNIC GROUPS AND LANGUAGES

The Malagasy people are usually divided into eighteen separate ethnic groups, each of which considers itself distinct, mainly because of different histories and isolation from each other—until the beginning of the twentieth century—in different parts of the island (see fig. 8). All speak the same Malagasy language and generally share the same culture; all have mixed African and Asian antecedents, although in varying proportions (see ch. 2).

The Malagasy language—polysyllabic and rich in metaphor and poetic imagery—belongs to the Malayo-Polynesian family. Added to a Malayo-Polynesian base are African, Sanskrit, Arabic, and European words. Different, mutually understandable dialects are spoken; of these, Merina, also called Hova and universally spoken in Tananarive Province, is considered standard Malagasy. In written form, Malagasy makes use of a Latin script, which was first produced by European missionaries in the early 1800s. The country's two official languages are Malagasy and French.

Certain cultural traits are derived from Indonesia, such as growing rice on irrigated, terraced land; the use of the long-handled spade; building steep-roofed, rectangular houses; and the custom of elaborate funeral rituals. African contributions include the culture of millet and the emotional attachment to cattle, which is characteristic of many Malagasy groups.

Among the country's ethnic groups, linguistic and cultural unity contrasts with physical diversity, and three major physical types can be distinguished. One of these is small boned, of short or medium height, and rather light skinned and has straight or slightly wavy hair. The second physical type has black skin, kinky hair, and thick lips and ranges in height from short to tall. The third and most common type is a mixture of the other two types: deep brown skin, tightly wavy or curly hair, and moderately thick lips. Physical appearance alone, however, is not an indication of ethnic affiliation. The variety rather testifies to the long and somewhat obscure history of the island's early migrations.

The immigrants who settled on Madagascar came in successive waves, by various routes, and at different times (see ch. 2). They settled in different parts of the country and then adapted to particular surroundings. This created the ethnic divisions that still survive. Significantly, most of the names that designate these groups describe the geographical areas of Madagascar in which each group originally settled.

Largest of the groups are the Merina, who in 1970 constituted

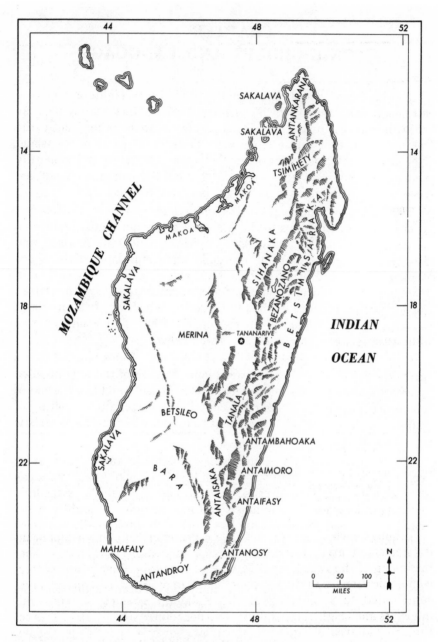

Source: Adapted from Conrad Phillip Kottak, "Cultural Adaptation, Kinship and Descent in Madagascar," *Southwestern Journal of Anthropology*, XXVII, 1971, pp. 194-247.

Figure 8. Ethnic Homelands of the Peoples of the Malagasy Republic

more than one-fourth of the island's total population (see table 5). Next in numerical size are the Betsimisaraka, followed by the Betsileo. The three groups together accountd for 53 percent of the population.

Table 5. *Ethnic Composition of the Population, Malagasy Republic, 1970*

Ethnic Group	Number of Persons	Percentage of Total Population
Merina	1,934,765	26.1
Betsimisaraka	1,106,991	14.9
Betsileo	892,352	12.0
Tsimihety	533,289	7.2
Sakalava	434,315	5.8
Antandroy	396,820	5.3
Antaisaka	377,110	5.0
Tanala	283,908	3.8
Antaimoro	255,161	3.4
Bara	250,261	3.3
Sihanaka	182,948	2.4
Antanosy	172,797	2.3
Mahafaly	120,620	1.6
Antaifasy	88,899	1.2
Makoa	80,069	1.1
Bezanozano	56,588	0.8
Antakarana	44,852	0.6
Antambahoaka	29,481	0.4
Other Malagasy	80,245	1.1
Total in entire country	7,321,471	....
Foreigners	102,393	1.4
GRAND TOTAL	7,423,864	99.7*

* Figures do not reflect 100 percent because of rounding.

Source: Adapted from Malagasy Republic, Institut National de la Statistique et de la Recherche Economique, *Population de Madagascar, Situation au 1er Janvier 1970*, Tananarive, Ministère des Finances et du Commerce, 1971.

Although each of the various groups is numerically predominant in its homeland area, intensive internal migrations (started at the beginning of the twentieth century and encouraged by peace, better communications, and the introduction of an exchange economy) have contributed to a blending of the Malagasy peoples. Usually immigrants and original inhabitants live peacefully side by side. Ties to the original area of settlement persist, however, and most people who have migrated, or who are descendants of migrants, are aware of their historical origins. Thus the people of Madagascar can be divided by their areas of origin into peoples of the Central Highlands, the north, the east, the south, and the west. A little more than one-third of the Malagasy people belong to Christian churches. The others consider themselves primarily adherents to the traditional religious system. A very small minority are Muslims (see ch. 5).

The memory of former Merina conquests still accounts for the major division between the peoples of the Central Highlands and the others who are lumped together under the term *côtiers* (coastal peoples) even if they live inland. It is a division that has mainly political implications (see ch. 9).

PEOPLES OF THE CENTRAL HIGHLANDS

The Merina

Largest of all the ethnic groups of Madagascar are the Merina, who live in the northern section of the Central Highlands. Their name means "those from the country where one can see far." Although culturally not very distinct from their neighbors, they are prominent because of their association with the former Merina kingdom (see ch. 2). Their growth rate—the highest in Madagascar—reached 4 percent after special eradication programs wiped out malaria after World War II. Their home region is called Imerina, a name which may refer either to the area of the Merina kingdom as it was at the end of the eighteenth century or to the much larger province of Tananarive.

Variously said to have come from the east by the valley of the Mangoro or from the northeast by the valley of the Razafintsalana, the Merina pushed back, intermarried with, and finally absorbed the original inhabitants (Vazimba), whose origin is clouded in controversy. They divide themselves into two kinds of people: the *fotsy* (whites), who are descendants of free Merina; and the *mainty* (blacks), descendants of slaves. The division is mainly a social one, but often physical criteria provide a clue.

Merina society is hierarachical and highly structured (see ch. 5). Within the segment regarded as white a class of nobles, called Andriana, is distinguished from commoners or freemen, who are called Hova, a name that is sometimes applied to all the Merina. The Andevo are the descendants of former slaves—usually taken in wars—who were employed as domestic help or as agricultural laborers. The Andevo adopted the traditions and customs of their masters and in time identified with them. By 1895 when the French assumed control of Madagascar, it was estimated that about half the Merina were slaves. Some of the liberated slaves went back to the coast to their place of origin or to other parts of the island where they established Merina villages and started irrigated ricefields.

Usually well educated, the Merina are heavily represented in the modern middle class and in the intellectual elite. Except for Tsimihety country in the north, the extreme south, and portions of the west coast, Merina are found everywhere as businessmen who compete successfully with Chinese and Indians; they also serve as doctors, ministers, managers of plantations, technicians, and government officials. Fifty-nine percent of the government officials were Merina at independence in 1960. Their rate of urbanization in the 1960s was 19 percent, as compared with 6.8 percent for the entire population (see ch. 5).

Nevertheless, the Merina have remained clannish and conservative in their habits. They live, if possible, near the tombs of their ancestors. When they migrate to other places outside Imerina, they do so for very precise reasons. They either return eventually or call for relatives to come and live nearby, forming exclusive Merina colonies whose members refuse to mix with others and in turn are resented. Many Merina settle elsewhere because there are not enough jobs for them in their homeland and because other regions of Madagascar are in need of their professional skills. In 1970 about 13 percent were living outside Tananarive Province (see table 6).

The Betsileo

The Betsileo are believed to have come to their present region in the fifteenth century from the eastern coast and to be related to the Antaimoro. Similar to the Merina, they pushed back and mixed with the original inhabitants, the Vazimba. Resembling the Merina in customs, beliefs, and historical traditions but less warlike and less well organized, the Betsileo were easily conquered. The Merina, however, treated them favorably, employed them in their armies, and encouraged their expansion, as the French were to do later.

The Betsileo are model cultivators and are noted for their mastery of growing irrigated rice on terraced fields (see ch. 13). They make use of even the steepest terrain and manage to grow cassava on the poorest soil. They are also expert raisers of household cattle and pigs, although their region does not permit the development of large herds. The limited resources of their homeland have forced many to settle in other parts of the island, so that about one-fourth live outside their homeland. Wherever they have lived, they have increased the productivity of the land.

Many Betsileo participate in short-term seasonal migrations to do agricultural work, some as often as two or three times a year. The men are sometimes accompanied by unattached sisters or other female relatives who are responsible for the transplanting of the rice shoots. Wives, however, stay behind in the villages, where they and their children do all the work during the absence of their husbands.

The men, too, work hard and live frugally during their migratory ventures. They bring back their earnings either in the form of cattle or in money that they save in order to go into commerce, build a house, or buy a ricefield. Their social structure has not been significantly affected by these short absences (see ch. 5).

Many Betsileo, including some who have settled permanently on the eastern coast, are skilled craftsmen. Some go from village to

Ethnic Group	Province					
	Tananarive	Fianarantsoa	Tamatave	Majunga	Tulear	Diègo-Suarez
Merina	87.1	3.1	4.0	3.7	0.5	1.0
Betsimisaraka	0.5	11.9	73.2	2.1	0.1	11.9
Betsileo	6.0	76.9	1.0	8.2	6.1	1.5
Tsimihety	0.2	0	3.7	64.7	0.1	33.1
Sakalava	0.8	0.1	0.2	33.1	47.0	18.0
Antandroy	2.5	1.8	2.1	4.0	84.3	5.2
Antaisaka	0.7	64.4	2.2	10.5	14.4	7.6
Tanala	0.4	89.7	0.1	3.5	4.5	1.6
Antaimoro	0.7	76.0	4.3	7.5	0.2	9.7
Bara	2.3	32.6	0.4	5.5	57.4	1.5
Sihanaka	1.1	0.1	79.4	18.0	0.4	1.2
Antanosy	0.4	1.6	1.4	2.2	91.4	2.8
Mahafaly	0.4	0.2	1.0	2.9	92.5	2.8
Antaifasy	0.9	78.3	4.2	4.8	6.1	5.6
Makoa	0.2	0	2.4	64.2	6.3	26.7
Bezanozano	2.3	0	90.8	4.9	0.6	1.2
Antakarana	0.5	0.2	1.1	1.4	0.5	96.1
Antambahoaka	1.2	73.1	18.9	1.3	1.3	4.0

*Figures do not reflect 100 percent because of rounding.

Source: Adapted from Malagasy Republic, Institut National de la Statistique
et de la Recherche Economique, *Population de Madagascar, Situation
au 1er Janvier 1970*, Tananarive, Ministère des Finances et du
Commerce, 1971.

village offering their services. Groups of carpenters or bricklayers,
often related to each other, wander with their tools through the
countryside during the dry season, usually in Betsileo or Merina
country. Betsileo women are noted for the multicolored silk cloth,
which they weave in small bands.

The Betsileo often settle permanently in other parts of the island
as merchants, buyers of produce, or traders of cattle. Like the
Merina, they are often found in government service; in the mid-1960s
they constituted 13 percent of the government's working force. Also
like the Merina, they live together in separate sections of the towns
or villages to which they have migrated. The Betsileo, however, have
closer relationships with their new neighbors than the more aloof
Merina.

The Sihanaka

About 80 percent of the Sihanaka live in Tamatave Province as
rice farmers, cattle herders, and fishermen in the basin of Lake
Alaotra (where they went in the eighteenth century to escape ab-
sorption by the Betsimisaraka and conquest by the Merina in the
nineteenth century). Their name means "those who wandered in the

marshes."

They resemble the Merina and live next to them but refuse to mix. In the early 1970s massive government investment, originally for the benefit of French settlers, was turning Alaotra into one of the most productive areas of the island (see ch. 13).

PEOPLES OF THE NORTH

The Antakarana

The Antakarana, whose name means "people of the rocks, " occupy the extreme northern tip of Madagascar from Cap d'Ambre to the Sambirano River. They are a heterogeneous group of mixed Sakalava, Betsimisaraka, and Arab ancestry. During the Merina conquests, part of the group settled on the northwestern coast where they managed to preserve considerable independence. This group became Muslim, although they retained their traditional customs regarding family relations and burial ceremonies.

The Antakarana are mainly cattle raisers, but they also grow maize (corn), rice, cassava, and other crops. Since the mid-1940s many of them have gone to work in the factories and meat canneries of Ambilobe, Diégo-Suarez, and Vohémar or on the plantations of the eastern coast.

The Tsimihety

According to their own traditions, the Tsimihety are descendants of Sihanaka who sought refuge in the high valleys of the eastern coast. There they were joined by groups from the Bay of Antongil, including perhaps some European sailors.

Numbering about 35,000 at the beginning of the twentieth century, the Tsimihety in 1970 constituted the fourth largest group on the island. Robust, prolific, and having a reputation as hard workers, they have spread over much of Majunga and Diégo-Suarez provinces. Their expansion has resulted not from conquest or massive emigration but rather from slow, peaceful, and progressive penetration. They have infiltrated and intermarried with other people, without forgetting their genealogical ties to those they left generations ago. Although separated by great distances, they continue to send presents and contributions towards funerals and the upkeep of family tombs. In contrast to other Malagasy, the Tsimihety never migrate to parts of the islands where they will be cut off from their own people. Few are found outside the north.

Eager for education, they are considered one of Madagascar's most dynamic peoples. Philibert Tsiranana—the island republic's president from 1958 to 1972—is a Tsimihety. The Tsimihety have never been politically unified but are fragmented into about forty localized kinship groups, of which the largest are the Antandrona, the Maronmena, and the Maromainty. They have the reputation of disliking political restraints and of moving to a new area whenever a settled group numbers more than fifty people. Their name, which signifies "those who do not cut their hair," (as is commonly done as a sign of sorrow at the death of a ruler), is indicative of their spirit of independence. They managed to remain independent of the former Sakalava and the Betsimisaraka kingdoms and submitted to rule by the Merina in 1823 and later to the French in 1895, only after their subgroups were assured local autonomy.

The Tsimihety are the most mobile of Malagasy peoples, largely because of a high growth rate of above 3 percent; strict rules of exogamy that forbid marriage of two persons with a common ancestor as far back as eight generations; inheritance laws favoring the first born; and tight social constraints. Some apparently find the constraints difficult to take and leave their home communities.

The Tsimihety are farmers and cattle herders. Rice is their staple crop and basic food, but cattle are of enormous social importance. Cultivable areas belong to kinship units but are used and inherited by individuals. The oldest son inherits the main house and the best terrain close to the villages, but the younger ones often lack enough land to support a family. Work is done collectively, the lands of father and older brothers being worked first. All land not under cultivation can be used for pasture by all; in this case also the older people have priority, and the younger men must move away if they want to enlarge their herds. The search for new pastures is another incentive to migrate.

The usual pattern is for a man to set out in search of free land, to clear it, and to establish a home. His sons will probably remain, but one or more of his younger grandsons is likely to move on to new land. Other young men tend to take salaried employment in the coffee plantations on the eastern coast or on the tobacco plantations near Port Bergé. Many of these migrants go away for specified periods, returning in November and December to help with the ricefields. They usually borrow a little money from the head of the family on their departure and reimburse him when they return. During their absence they save for taxes, clothes, and presents. Although they become accustomed to new foods and distractions, their seasonal migrations do not modify conservative, patriarchal Tsimihety society.

Those who have gone westward to settle permanently on empty land have gradually supplanted their western neighbors, the Sakalava, in the northern part of that group's territory. This is the main area of Tsimihety expansion.

They also move north to settle among the Antakarana, who allow them to cultivate their lands and with whom they intermarry. In the east they move into the high valleys of Betsimisaraka territory.

EASTERN PEOPLES

The Betsimisaraka

The country's second largest group is the Betsimisaraka who live in a long coastal belt in the east, reaching 400 miles from the Bay of Antongil south to the Manajary River and varying in width from twenty to fifty miles. The group's name means "the many who do not separate" and refers to the time in the eighteenth century when their numerous kinship groups united in a mighty confederation.

Predominantly cultivators, they have been influenced by early European traders who came to their shores; long ago they turned to cash crops such as coffee. The men migrate within Betsimisaraka country, going to work in the coffee plantations, in the graphite mines near Vatomandry and Brickaville, in the docks and sugar-processing plants of Tamatave, and in the three vanilla-producing northern districts of Antalaha, Andapa, and Sambaba. The women work as domestic servants in the towns or help with the coffee crop during harvest. They are the main inhabitants of Ile Sainte-Marie, located off the eastern coast, where they cultivate cloves. Betsimisaraka society is rapidly changing under the impact of an export-oriented economy.

The Bezanozano

The Bezanozano live in the upper and middle valley of the Mangoro River between the Merina and the Betsimisaraka peoples. In former times their chiefs were elected only for brief periods and lacked genuine authority. The Bezanozano were easily conquered in the eighteenth century by the Merina, who found them as hard to control as did the French during their later period of administration.

In many ways the Bezanozano resemble the Betsimisaraka with whom they live intermingled in the subprefecture of Moramanga. They are predominantly herders and woodsmen, but they also cultivate some rice. Their name means "many little braids," a reference to their traditional hair style.

The Tanala

The Tanala, "people of the forest," occupy roughly the southern third of the eastern mountain massif. They are divided into two subgroups, the northern Tanala Menabe and the southern Tanala Ikongo. The region where the Menabe live (not to be confused with the Menabe of the Sakalava area on the western coast) is less favored by nature. Its high mountains, covered with impenetrable vegetation and receiving heavy rainfall, provided a refuge for groups fleeing after defeat in war; the region of the Ikongo has often been penetrated by the Bara from the west and the Antaimoro from the east, however.

The Tanala traditionally have lacked strong political organization.

Thus in the eighteenth century the northern part or their homeland was easily conquered by the Merina, and later all of their region was overtaken by the French; however, the Tanala were frequently rebellious against both.

They are skilled hunters, food gatherers, and woodsmen. Their traditional slash-and-burn method of agriculture has proved most destructive to their area and has been banned by the government (see ch. 13). In recent times they have been learning more modern methods of agriculture—especially the cultivation of coffee and the irrigation of rice—which were introduced by the Bara, Antaimoro, and Betsileo who migrated to the Tanala homeland.

The Antambahoaka

The Antambahoaka live mostly in the lower Mananjary Valley, and there are a few isolated clusters of them further north. The only ethnic group having a single common genealogy, they are believed to have descended from a common ancestor, King Raminia, who came from Mecca in the fourteenth century. They no longer have any contact with the Islam world but retain some fairly strong Muslim influences. They are divided into eight kin groups and resemble the Betsimisaraka whose homeland surrounds them.

Rice is their main crop and their main food along with cassava. They also fish and have a reputation of being good boatsmen. They are found fairly frequently in towns as government employees or on the staffs of private enterprises.

The Antaimoro

The Antaimoro, "people of the coast," live south of the Betsimisaraka on the eastern coast in a narrow band about 100 miles long and twenty-five miles wide. Their region comprises a series of valleys divided by low barren hills. They are the only ones who knew writing before the arrival of the London Missionary Society in 1830. Their unique contribution to Malagasy culture consists of a number of manuscripts dealing with historical and religious matters written in Malagasy but in Arabic script and ink made from local materials.

The Antaimoro claim that they are descended from Arabs who arrived in two boats from Mecca in the thirteenth century, married local women, and founded a kingdom. Their society is still divided into castes, of which the upper level claims direct descent from the early Arab settlers. In addition to this vertical division of society, there exists a horizontal division that groups people according to age and assigns each group specific functions and a particular status for a given number of years.

An important position is held in Antaimoro society by the *ombiasi* (diviner-healers), who settle disputes and interpret Islamic laws using Arab procedures, although they have long lost contact with the Muslim world. The *ombiasi* were the first of the southeastern peoples to travel outside their region. They practiced *sidiki* (divination) and sold amulets to earn their living and to bring back cattle and money. Some *ombiasi* became diviners at the courts of the Sakalava, Betsileo, and Merina rulers. After the Antaimoro submitted to Merina domination in the nineteenth century, the *ombiasi* were free to circulate throughout the entire island. In modern times, therefore, the name Antaimoro is often applied by northerners to all the peoples of the southeastern coast. Some Antaimoro have become wealthy coffee growers; others leave their home region to work seasonally or permanently in the north.

The Antaifasy

Members of the small Antaifasy group live mostly in the vicinity of the coastal town of Farafangana, in Fianarantsoa Province, but many migrate as laborers to the north and the northeast of the island. According to some oral traditions the Antaifasy, "people of the sands," originally came from the African continent by way of the western coast of Madagascar. They were never conquered by the Merina.

Antaifasy society is divided into strata of nobles, commoners, and descendants of slaves. Members of each stratum marry solely within their own group.

The Antaisaka

The Antaisaka, largest of the southeastern ethnic groups, live generally in the area centered on the coastal town of Farafangana. The noble element, consisting of the Rabehava, Zarafaniliha, and Zaramanampi kinship groups, came originally from the area of the Mangoky River in the western coastal plain during the seventeenth century. They settled in the Mananara River valley of the eastern coast. Kinship groups comprising the commoner class of Antaisaka society are of mixed Bara, Sakalava, or other origin and include assimilated kinship groups of various antecedents, such as the Antemanambondre of Tanala descent. Despite this variety of origins Antaisaka society is cohesive, and their customs are uniform.

The Antaisaka constitute the main reservoir of migrant workers in Madagascar. The poverty of their region and a high growth rate have long led the young Antaisaka men to migrate either to work as seasonal laborers in the plantations of the north and west or to remain permanently outside their homeland area. In certain western areas they are simply known as *korao* (young men). Of the 5,000 or 6,000 *korao* who leave the southeast every year, three-quarters are members of the Antaisaka group. Moreover, in 1970 nearly 40 percent of the Antaisaka lived permanently outside their home region.

The head of the family designates which young men must migrate to earn money for taxes, cattle, cloth, imported goods, and—most of all—contributions toward family tombs and funerals (see ch.5). He consults the *ombiasi* for a propitious day of departure and arranges a small ceremony to reconcile the dead ancestors. Upon the return of the migrants, the head of the family oversees the purification ritual that they must undergo. He will take all their wage earnings, spend them in the best interests of the community, and perhaps send some young men away again the following year. Even those who settle permanently outside Antaisaka territory continue to send contributions to kinship groups in the homelands.

The Antaisaka represent a pioneering element in the western area of Madagascar where they introduce their more advanced agricultural techniques, especially the inundating and transplanting of rice. Their joking relationship with the Makoa makes it easy for them to obtain land in that part of the west, just as the Sakalava origin of some Antaisaka kinship groups has accommodated their settling in Sakalava country (see Interethnic Relations, this ch.)

SOUTHERN PEOPLES

The Antanosy

The region around Fort Dauphin is the homeland of the Antanosy. According to their traditions, they were conquered some time before the sixteenth century by Arabized invaders who were related to the Antambahoaka. Later they mixed with Indians and Europeans, especially the French, whose ships were wrecked on the southern shores.

The group was subdued by the Merina in 1830 but rebelled ten years later. A number of Antanosy then emigrated westward and settled in the valleys of the Onilahy River tributaries, transforming the land in the valleys into ricefields and using the hillsides for pasture. They adapted to their new surroundings, dressed like the neighboring Bara and Mahafaly, and began building round houses made of wattle over wooden frames instead of their former retangular houses raised on stilts. They also introduced their more advanced agricultural techniques. In modern times they still represent a progressive element in the west, where they continue to expand. A number of Antanosy have also emigrated northward to Manja, Miandrivazo, Majunga, and the small offshore island of Nosy Be.

The Antanosy are divided into a number of small chiefdoms; the chiefs belong to the noble class, consisting of descendants of the conquerors. Although the traditional social structures are disintegrating in the Fort Dauphin area, they still exist among the more conservative western Antanosy.

The Antandroy

The Antandroy, "people of the thornbush," inhabit the southernmost tip of the island between the Mandrare and Menarandra rivers. Many are of Sakalava origin; others are related to the Antanosy, and some, to the Bara. Various kinship groups of different descent have in the past formed powerful confederations, but the majority have remained autonomous groups. During the nineteenth century the Merina tried unsuccessfully to conquer the Antandroy, and the French later subdued them only after promising that no Merina officials would be sent to the Antandroy homeland and that no schools would be built.

Frequent droughts and locust invasions make life difficult for these people. Primarily pastoral, they take cattle every year to northern pastures and bring them back a few months later to the home villages. They also grow some crops, such as sweet potatoes, maize, cassava, millet, and some rice (see ch. 13). They are isolated from the rest of Madagascar, their harsh arid country constituting a sort of island within an island. Unlike other Malagasy peoples, the Antandroy did not know how to grow rice and learned reluctantly only in recent times. Intergroup warfare and cattle raiding were formerly common. A 1958 law that imposed severe penalties for cattle stealing had to be moderated in recognition of the fact that it applied to an accepted custom and not to an ordinary crime.

The Antandroy began emigrating in 1922 when settlers on the island of Réunion asked for workers and the French administration sent them there by force. The migratory pattern became firmly entrenched among the Antandroy, although in modern times some local employment is available in sisal plantations and in mica and uranothorianite mines. Many seek employment in the urban centers of Tulear, Diégo-Suarez, Majunga, and Tamatave and, to a lesser degree, in Fianarantsoa and Tananarive. They are highly regarded as diligent workers.

The migrant Antandroy live frugally in order to save as much money as possible, anticipating the day when they can return home with clothes, presents, and especially with money to buy cattle. Their foremost ambition is to own a herd and enlarge it. Most Antandroy remain passionately attached to their homeland. It has been estimated that 80 percent of those who migrate only for short distances return within a year and that 15 percent of the migrants return within two years. Wives stay behind with the parents; those who return are quickly reabsorbed into the social body. Of those who go far away, however, a third does not come back at all.

The migratory pattern brings about subtle changes. The returnees dress differently, substituting shirt and shorts for the traditional breechclout. They build houses that are higher than the low ones in the homeland; in the case of illness returned migrants go to a medical center rather than to the local healer. The authority of the elders has also begun to weaken.

The Mahafaly

West of the Antandroy, in an arid stretch of land between the Menarandra and Onilahy rivers, live the Mahafaly. Until they were conquered by the French in the late nineteenth century, they had kings who were related to the kings of the Sakalava. Primarily pastoralists who herd goats and cattle, the Mahafaly also grow some crops and do considerable fishing on the southern coast. They usually live in small huts in isolated villages.

The Mahafaly move their livestock seasonally from one region to another, and some of the men go to work in the urban centers of Majunga and Diégo-Suarez. They engage less in the practice of migratory labor, however, then the Antandroy, with whom they are often confused. They are renowned as gifted artists who carve long, elegant wooden staffs with which they adorn their family tombs. New economic opportunities, such as work at local sisal plantations and in the fairly remunerative mohair rug-weaving and rug-dyeing industry, have somewhat lessened the traditional authority of the group's political and religious chiefs.

The Bara

Seminomadic herders, the Bara live on the low, south-central plateaus. According to their traditional belief—and as indicated by the name of the noble element of their society—they formerly had "white" kings, related perhaps to those of the Sakalava of the western coast. In the past, two Bara kingdoms existed, one of which was subdued by the Merina; the other remained independent until the French arrived in the late nineteenth century.

The Bara are divided into five great localized kinship groups: Bara-Bés in the valley of the Ihosy River; the Bara-Imamono near Andazoabo; the Bara-Iantsantsa near Ivohibé; the Bara-Vinda near the Onilahy River; and the Bara-Antaivondro on the upper Intomampapy River. Beginning early in the twentieth century the Antaisaka, the Antanosy, the Betsileo, and other groups began settling among them. The immigrants, especially the Betsileo, occasionally intermarried with the Bara, and the newcomers adopted their social customs. The Bara also kept expanding in their sparsely populated area, the sons of chiefs often gathering a group of followers to go off in search of new pastures where cattle raising seemed more profitable.

The Bara used to regard agriculture as a lowly occupation, but they learned the cultivation of rice from the Betsileo. They do this unwillingly, however, and often allow the land to be farmed by immigrants. Some Bara work as sharecroppers on the tobacco plantations of Miandrivazo and Malaimbandy (see ch. 13).

WESTERN PEOPLES

The Sakalava

The Sakalava, whose name means "people who inhabit the long valleys," occupy a large area on the west coast stretching from Nosy Be to Tulear. In the seventeenth century two Sakalava kingdoms, Menabe and Boina, were founded and absorbed many local people (see ch. 2). The Merina conquered Boina and part of Menabe in the beginning of the nineteenth century, but Sakalava chiefs have continued to exercise considerable authority. Some Sakalava in the center of their territory have been Islamized through long contact with the people who have migrated to Madgascar from the nearby Comoro Islands.

Warriors in the past, most Sakalava are seminomadic pastoralists who practice only a rudimentary form of agriculture. They grow rice by broadcasting it in riverbeds. Until recently the Sakalava had a high disease rate and a very low birthrate and were considered a doomed race, but the trend has been reversed, partly because of the influence of the more progressive immigrants who have settled among them.

The vast grassy plains of their thinly populated area, representing one-fifth of the island's total surface, are intersected at intervals by sedimentary river basins that have long attracted many enterprising people from other parts of the island, particularly Merina, Betsileo, and (in the far north) Tsimihety, who have put the land to productive use. In 1970 the Sakalava constituted only a minority in their own region, and only 6.6 percent of the population of Majunga were Sakalava. Immigrants and Sakalava usually live in separate villages.

Independent, but grouped customarily with the Sakalava, are some 60,000 Masikoro in the Mangoky delta and about 45,000 Vezo fishermen near Tulear. Intermixed with the Vezo and maintaining an exchange relationship are several thousand Tanalana (not to be confused with the Tanala in the east) who are cultivators.

The Makoa

In Malagasy, Makoa refers to small compact groups living dispersed in northern Sakalava country. In Africa it designates a large ethnic group living in northeastern Mozambique. Makoa and 'Masombiki' were also the names given by the Merina to all slaves when they were freed by Ranavalona II after her conversion to Christianity (see ch. 2). Very likely the Makoa living in the northwest are descendants of slaves brought across the Mozambique Channel by Arab slavers from Zanzibar, although some may have crossed earlier of their own volition. The Makoa are the most African of all Malagasy people.

Most Makoa keep aloof from other Malgasy peoples. A few have intermarried with Tsimihety who have wandered away from their homeland in the north. Some small clusters of Makoa live in far northern Sakalava country where they are known as hard workers. The descendants of these immigrants regard themselves as Sakalava.

MAJOR FOREIGN GROUPS

Fairly large foreign minorities live on the island. Ethnically and socially closest to the Malagasy peoples are the Comorians. Since 1947 they have been leaving their overpopulated islands to work in northern and western Madagascar as laborers, domestic help, and shopkeepers, but rarely as farmers. In 1970 there were 39, 184 Comorians living on the island, and half the population of Majunga were Comorians. Because they are Muslims and because their language differs from that of the Malagasy, they tend to live apart. Many return to the Comoro Islands after a few years. In the early 1960s, however, 16 percent of Comorians living in Madagascar had been born there.

Immigration by Comorians and all other outsiders had almost stopped by about 1970, and permanent departures of Malagasy citizens to other countries were also relatively rare. In the early 1970s the net annual change in total population through immigration or emigration was negligible.

The French, who numbered 31, 071 in 1970, are by far the most numerous of the Europeans living in the country, although the size of this group has decreased from a maximum of about 70,000 before independence. Approximately one-fourth were born in the Malagasy Republic or came from Réunion. They are concentrated in the cities, particularly in the capital city of Tananarive. Also counted as French are the Creoles from Réunion and Ile Sainte-Marie who came to Madagascar after 1900 when the French government encouraged French settlers by giving them land. Creoles began farming in the coffee lands of the eastern coast and the hinterland of Diégo-Suarez, but few of them have been successful. They tend to look down on the Malagasy peoples and are disliked in turn.

There are about 500 Greeks among the foreign population, distributed throughout the island except for the eastern coast. They are planters, merchants, and hotel owners.

Both Chinese and Indians—numbering 9,017 and 17,299, respectively, in 1970—have their own schools and associations. The Indians live mainly in cities on the western coast, such as Diégo-Suarez, Majunga, and Tulear, and on the great plains of the west and south. They started coming to Madagascar via East Africa and the Comoro Islands centuries ago and still keep in touch with their home areas in northwestern India and Pakistan. Many more arrived in 1901 to work on the railroad linking the eastern coast with Tananarive. They are merchants, small enterpreneurs, and bankers, and they monopolize the wholesale and retail trade in textiles. In the villages they own small general stores and buy the agricultural produce directly from the farmers (see ch. 13). They are divided into a great number of religious groups, of which the largest are Ismalians (Shiite Muslims).

Most of the Chinese came from South China in the early 1930s and settled on the eastern coast and its hinterland. In the 1970s there were fairly large Chinese minorities in Tamatave and Tananarive provinces. They are mainly small merchants and are found even in the smallest villages where they live isolated from the Malagasy, buying agricultural produce for import-export companies. Occasionally they own small plantations or are involved in transport activities.

INTERETHNIC RELATIONS

The essential unity of Malagasy ethnic groups, as expressed in a common language and similar customs, was largely veiled because they lived apart from each other. Internal migrations during the twentieth century, however, have brought a number of the various groups into contact with each other, thus attenuating the differences that had derived mainly from separate histories.

The main impetus for these migrations was the beginning of a money economy. Salaried work, however, was a strange, unpleasant, and even dishonorable notion for people who voluntarily helped their neighbors to whom they were, moreover, tied by bonds of kinship. They could not do such work for a relative. In order to earn money, they had to emigrate.

The migrations were undertaken at first and for a long time predominantly by people from the southeast. Forced to pay taxes and obliged to find cattle for sacrifices in a region not suitable for livestock raising, the Antaisaka and other southeasterners set out toward the north, where public works, plantations, and mines provided economic opportunities. In 1972 they remained the people who traveled the longest distances in order to find salaried work.

Somewhat later the Antandroy were forced to migrate in great numbers because of repeated famines in their home region. In most instances emigration has been strongest among these highly conservative societies. Usually the young men were told to go and bring back money and cattle, but the rapid distribution of their earnings would soon force them to go away again. Thirty-five percent of the

Antaisaka and 16 percent of the Antandroy eventually stayed away permanently.

On the other hand, such highly mobile people as the Sakalava and other western pastoralists have migrated least, and the wide open spaces of their region have instead been penetrated by others. For example, the Menabe region of Sakalava country has attracted Antaisaka and Betsileo.

The effect of emigration has been to bring money into the region of origin, along with new skills and new needs, but without destroying the prevailing social fabric. In the regions of immigration, economic development became possible because of the influx of much needed labor. There is rarely conflict between people of differing origin. Usually they live side by side and maintain ties to their home region even after several generations. Nevertheless, in some cases people have fused by intermarrying, as the Bara and Betsileo have done in Ihosy Subprefecture, or as the Sakalava, Makoa, and Tsimihety have done in Analalava Subprefecture. In other cases cultural traits have been blended, as with the Tsimihety, who have adopted Sakalava customs, and the Betsileo, who have adopted certain Bara values.

Internal migrations that have helped to break down barriers between ethnic groups have been facilitated by an institution called *ziva* (joking relationship). It creates an unbreakable tie by establishing a fictive kinship between groups. It confers an obligation to behave with familiarity in a relaxed, informal, burlesque fashion, including even the right to insult with impunity. *Ziva* might originate in an alliance concluded after a long forgotten war or after one group immigrates into the territory of another.

According to local belief the newcomers had to be made acceptable to the land's tutelary spirits—that is, to the souls of the original inhabitant's dead ancestors who were traditionally believed to own the land. *Ziva* thus served the function of turning the newcomers into quasi-relatives and integrating them into the community. The Merina are said to have had *ziva* with the legendary Vazimba for the same reason. Even in modern times they look after Vazimba tombs found here and there in Imerina. *Ziva* has linked the Antandroy and the Antanosy since the nineteenth century, when some Antanosy migrated westward into Antandroy country. It very often links a group from the interior to one living on the coast, such as the Betsileo and the Betsimisaraka. It sometimes allies such distant groups as the Sakalava and the Antaimoro or the Antaimoro and the Makoa. In such cases the existence of the tie is remembered and acted upon, although its origin may be obscure. Sometimes *ziva* exists when the relationship was one of historical dominance and dependence, as between Sihanaka masters and Makoa slaves. The existence of *ziva* between two groups still facilitates immigration, although in modern times it has become less important.

In any case, quarrels do erupt occasionally between inhabitants. The Betsimisaraka, for example, often claim ownership to land after it has been made productive by immigrant *tatsimo* (people of the south), the name given indiscriminately to Antaisaka, Antaimoro, Antaifasy, Antanosy, Tanala, and Antandroy. In the same fashion the Tsimihety in the northern part of their region sometimes do not renounce customary rights to their land after it has been bought and registered by Merina.

In regions of immigration, members of different ethnic groups usually continue to live side by side in homogeneous sections of the towns and villages. Segregation is enforced by the widespread custom of endogamy, which forces a man to look for a wife within his own ethnic group and even within his own social stratum. A Tanala would rather not marry a Betsileo or a Merina, although they are neighbors.

People living in close proximity, however, cannot help influencing each other. When rice growers settle in the region of pastoralists, they bring along not only new agricultural techniques but also social rules that meticulously regulate the communal work connected with terracing, flooding, and transplanting as well as individual rights to water and crops. New rules and new institutions evolve for matters concerning an entire community composed of different ethnic groups, although their members continue to follow different pursuits.

Sometimes aloofness or even animosity between groups goes back to memories of wars and old controversies. The Sakalava, for example, recall that the Merina were their vassals in the eighteenth century and that they were conquered by them in turn in the nineteenth century. This historical awareness still affects the relationship between the two peoples.

The Merina proudly remember their past and tend to look down upon the people their ancestors conquered, an attitude that others deeply resent. Not all of the formerly conquered people, however, react this way. To the Betsileo and to many Tsimihety, the educated Merina rather than the European represents the model of modern man. Both groups have tried to imitate the Merina. The Tsirnihety give Merina names to their children, and Tsimihety women braid their hair in Merina style. Both groups eagerly send their children to school to receive a modern education. The Merina and the Betsileo easily cooperate whenever the occasion arises.

The coastal people of the south and the west, who are mostly pastoralists in contrast to the cultivators of the highlands, long remained impervious to alien influences and, until fairly recently, objected to modern education. The coastal people of the east were more receptive to progressive ideas, but the Betsimisaraka did not wish to emulate the Merina and scornfully labelled them *vazaha*

(Europeans). The tensions between highland peoples and *côtiers* still are manifested in subtle and sometimes violent ways, such as political affiliations before and after independence (see ch. 2; ch. 9).

CHAPTER 5
THE SOCIAL SYSTEM

Despite political upheaval and economic changes Malagasy society was basically stable in 1972. An often-quoted proverb that "the people are one mat" still expressed the popular thought that individuals need each other and that everyone has his secure place in the social structure—in family, larger kin group, ethnic group, or rank. For the vast majority of the people this well-ordered, tradition-bound world included the dead, to whom the living were linked by insoluble ties. They saw their ancestors as invisible roots of the family tree of which the living represented only temporary shoots. The dead were the guardians of moral codes whose prescriptions must be followed. Whoever acted against their wishes, whoever disturbed the social order would suffer mystical sanctions.

Innumerable taboos trace the limitations imposed on each individual and provide precise rules for behavior. They also tend to foster conformity, lack of initiative, and fear of taking risks. Change is occurring, but by an almost imperceptible degree. Wherever the traditional concepts were no longer acted upon, they were still shared as ideals that linked people otherwise diverse in attitude and lifestyle.

Change was more marked in the cities, where a modern economy forced increased social interaction between people who were unrelated and where new classes, based on wealth and individual achievement, had emerged. In the countryside people usually still lived in fairly homogeneous groups, but there, too, modern economic development had encouraged internal migrations, escape from parental controls, and a weakening of traditional patterns.

In both town and country, solidarity, especially among kin, remained the foremost social value. Family reunions, religious feasts (whether Christian or traditional), attending visiting chiefs or government officials, even going to the market without trading were highly prized occasions because of the social and emotional rewards.

KIN GROUPS AND KINSHIP

Everywhere in Madagascar groups defined by common descent and residence have served traditionally as the local basis of social structure. Outside observes commonly refer to them as clans, but they are not organized as corporate groups that trace their descent exclusively through either males or females from a common ancestor. Except for royal families, Malagasy genealogies are very shallow, tracing ancestry back no farther than the grandfather of the oldest living member of the group. Ancestors beyond that point are undifferentiated, even if the group carries a founder's name.

Most Malagasy use the term *karazana*, meaning "species" or "of the same root," when they speak of the extended family (see Glossary) and the term *foko* when they refer to larger kinship groups. These notions are almost interchangeable however, and the lines between them are not sharply drawn because the larger unit is also considered a family. Members of a *foko* share veneration of common ancestors, follow the same taboos, and engage in collective ceremonies, particularly burial in the same tomb.

Political and economic cohesion originally did not extend beyond the *foko*. In time, several of these groups often combined to form chiefdoms or confederations. In the late eighteenth and nineteenth centuries most were incorporated into the Merina kingdom (see ch. 2). After the establishment of peace people began to move out of their homeland areas, sometimes settling permanently elsewhere. Kinship ties were rarely broken, however, largely because of the continuing custom of burial in common tombs.

Within the *foko* patrilineal descent is stressed in theory, but in practice individuals generally have a choice and for one reason or another may claim affiliation with their mother's group. The degree to which this is done varies from one ethnic group to another. Generally, people do not relinquish one affiliation unequivocally but retain the option of exploiting multiple ancestral ties.

Different ecological conditions may well account for variations in reckoning descent. Where people are cultivators and densely settled, as on the southeastern coast, they stress patrilineal affiliation to claim scarce land through inheritance from their father. On the other hand, cattle pastoralists, such as the Bara, who live in a thinly settled region, calculate kinship bilaterally through affiliation with their mother's family in order to take advantage of better pastures.

The Tsimihety emphasize patrilineal descent, perhaps for reasons of social identity to counterbalance the unsettling effects of constant migrations; however, they do not record the patriline beyond three generations. Children may claim their mother's ancestral land and through residence may acquire membership in their kinship group. Thus a Tsimihety can activate descent lines to each of his maternal and paternal grandparents.

The Masikoro, who are usually grouped with the Sakalava, emphasize the father's line against the others. A man generally settles in his father's village after marriage. Yet a Masikoro reserves the right to withdraw his married daughters and their offspring should their husbands behave badly. Nowhere in Madagascar does marriage give the bridegroom and his family exclusive rights to the children.

The Betsileo settle in the village of their father, and farmland is inherited from him, but they also reckon kinship bilaterally and can act upon this at any time. Sometimes they cultivate ricefields inherited from both sides. Since population density in Betsileo country varies from one area to another, bilateral kinship calculations make it possible for an individual to move from his father's high-density area to his mother's less densely settled region if necessary. Moreover, people may activate bilateral affiliation for limited periods of time; thus they identify with their father's group while living in his village but with their mother's group while visiting hers.

Of all ethnic groups, the Merina are most ambilineally inclined in their descent reckoning. Terms for maternal and paternal relatives are given complete equivalence in all generations. Members of a Merina *foko* consider themselves as being descended from one or several common founding ancestors, but they do not trace the intervening steps through the father's or the mother's line because they assume that both the parents are members of the same *foko*. A Merina *foko* is thus a descent group because it has a descent ideology, but in practice it is the custom of in-marriage that establishes it as a corporate group. A Merina will trace his relationship to another *foko* member laterally rather than through a common ancestor.

The easiest way of finding out to what *foko* someone belongs is to ask for the name of his *tanindrazana* (ancestral village or land). In former times people lived there, and they often still do; today many live elsewhere, but they continue to be buried in their ancestral homeland. Territories of a *foko* are thus defined primarily in terms of tombs, and the ultimate criterion of membership in a *foko* is burial in a common tomb. The essential social unit is often that of people who are to be buried in the same tomb and not of those who live together.

In conformity with the customary patrilineal bias in descent reckoning, a person is often buried in the tomb of his father, but he usually has a number of choices, including the tomb of his mother's group. A woman may choose burial in her father's, mother's, or husband's tomb (if she has borne him children). Thus, there are people with clear claims to burial and others who have potential claims connected with each tomb.

The decision regarding the choice of tomb must be made fairly early because of the considerable expense connected with building and upkeep. People who are denied burial in the tomb because they failed to contribute or because of some grave infraction are buried near the entrance to what is called "graves of *vahiny*" (stranger).

The oldest or perhaps the most notable member of the group, such as a government employee or a wealthy man, is in charge of all activities connected with the tomb. His power includes the right to deny burial. Usually the very threat of such action proves sufficient to enforce behavior that conforms to traditional standards. It is the cult of the tomb that provides social cohesion even in modern times when internal migrations and political, social, and economic changes are weakening the social fabric. Kinship ties weaken, however, whenever migrants stay away permanently and build a tomb in the new location.

Marriage

In many ethnic groups the tendency is to marry within the kinship group. The Merina have the highest degree of in-marriage, followed closely by the Betsileo. In both groups, the descendants of nobles are somewhat more insistent on this point than the descendants of commoners. Descendants of slaves prefer to marry someone with whom they cannot trace kinship up to the third cousin.

The Merina call marriage between close kinsmen *lova tsy mifindra* ("the inheritance which does not go away"). Land in Imerina is inherited by both sons and daughters and is thus endlessly fragmented. The rules of in-marriage kept scarce riceland in the *tanindrazana* within a small local group; the same is still true, but rights to such land become tenuous when owners move away and leave the land in trust with local relatives, sometimes for generations. The best way of reaffirming these rights is by in-marriage.

At the same time people feel that there is something incestuous about marriage with close kin and therefore perform certain ceremonies of purification, especially when the marriage is between children of two brothers or two sisters. Marriage between the children of two sisters is considered most incestuous of all because it is the mother, not the father, who gives *ra* (blood) to the child, according to Malagasy beliefs.

Some groups, such as the Tsimihety and the southeastern groups, insist on marrying with nonkin. The Bara prefer such marriage but, according to a study undertaken in the mid-1950s, more than one-fifth actually married within the kinship group after sacrificing some cattle in a purification ritual.

In-marriage reaffirms existing kinship links, but marriage with nonkin neighbors strengthens links within a village. If they occur fairly frequently, they will eventually lead to the establishment of villages where everyone is related. The general trend is increasingly toward mixed marriages as people migrate, intermingle, and cooperate more and more with people to whom they are not related. For example, a 1964 demographic survey showed that in the Andapa River basin, which attracts many immigrants, one woman out of five married a man not only of a different *foko* but also of a different ethnic group.

In general, people still follow the traditional rule that decrees marriage within one's social rank. Marriages between descendants of freemen and slaves take place only when the higher ranking family is highly sophisticated, or when a small rural family of freemen lives surrounded by a community of slave descendants.

Most people still marry within their ethnic group. This habit is the basis for the occasional custom of temporary marriage among the Betsimisaraka, the Tsimihety, and the Sakalava who wish to migrate. A migrant chooses a woman who wants to go away with him. They are married before the *fokon'olona* (village council) for the length of the migration. Their bond is dissolved upon their return, and all earnings are divided.

Polygamy, which formerly was frequent, has almost disappeared except for the Muslim Comorians and some people in the south and southwest, such as the Antandroy, Antanosy, Mahafaly, and Antaisaka. According to a study published in 1962, in the extreme south 19 percent of family heads had more than one wife, compared with only 2 percent in Sakalava country, less than 1 percent among the Betsimisaraka, and none in the Central Highlands.

Marriages are preceded by lengthy discussions between representatives of the two families. Bride price is usually very low, not more than a few thousand Malagasy francs (for value of the Malagasy franc—see Glossary) or perhaps one head of cattle. Sometimes the family of the bride will be reimbursed for the expenses incurred in giving her an education. Women are expected to obey their husbands, but in practice they have a lot of independence and influence. They manage, inherit, and bequeath property and often hold the family purse strings.

The Family

Most social life revolves within the family, which quite often includes three generations. Members may live in one household or in a number of households. In the countryside the family coincides with the nucleus of the cooperative agricultural team; in the city it tends to be smaller. A survey taken in Tamatave in the mid-1960s showed that about one-third of the households consisted of nuclear families— husband, wife, and unmarried children.

Within the family, terms refer not to a particular relative but to the member of a particular generation. Someone called father, for example, might be the real father but can also be an uncle; brothers and sisters may be what in the West would be called cousins. Children list all the houses of their local family without singling out that of their parents. They have the right to enter any one of these houses where they expect to be fed and looked after and, on occasion, reprimanded.

The head of the local family is usually the oldest male and is sometimes the oldest female. Sometimes the head is the richest and strongest, especially in the case of a man who started a new village and was followed by others later on. He makes the major decisions that affect the family interests, represents it in dealings with the outside, and punishes those who act counter to the welfare and reputation of the family. He has his own honored place in the house, either in the eastern or northern corner, and he eats before the rest of the family. When he is also head of a *foko*, he lives in a house larger than those of the other villagers, and sometimes he has special ricefields at his disposal, whose crops are used for entertaining.

His power is shrinking in the cities where he can no longer protect family members as in the past and where the young can escape his control. Even there, however, although parental power is diminished, it remains far stronger than in Western countries. The most significant social values in Malagasy society can still be summed up in the word *fihavanana*, which means at once kinship and solidarity. The Malagasy radio, typically, addresses its listeners as *havana* (kinsmen). Family loyalties override all others, and help with expense occasioned by marriages, funerals, and sickness continues to be a moral imperative.

Fictive Kinship

Before the establishment of better communications and the beginning of internal migrations, people living in one village were usually related to one another and to the *fokon'olona* (see ch. 8). The idiom of kinship is still used, although at present the people living in one village and meeting in council are very often not related. *Fokon'olona* members still help each other, however, such as at the time of death, when the real blood relatives have not yet been summoned. In conformity with Malagasy kinship ideology, such mutual help is not thought of as an exchange of economic services but as the demonstration of a moral link between kin. The Merina call *fokon'olona* members *mpifakatiavana* ("people who love each other"). They are considered to be quasi-kinsmen because they are loved.

For the same reason blood brotherhood is established between strangers who must deal with each other for one reason or another. Merchants, migrants, chiefs who travel outside their homeland, or even two wives of the same man might take the blood oath (*fatidra*). It requires a number of symbolic actions, but it centers on drinking mingled drops of blood from the two persons concerned and swearing an oath before a witness. Misfortune is said to befall whoever breaks this oath.

Another example of fictive kinship is *ziva*, or joking relationship, which is concluded between groups and confers the right to familiarity and even the right to inflict damage without provoking revenge. *Ziva* sometimes ties groups of people who live far apart and thus has facilitated peaceful circulation and expansion (see ch. 4).

STRATIFICATION

Traditional Ranking

Almost everywhere in Malagasy society, the *foko* are ranked according to social importance, in categories commonly referred to by outside observers as "castes." Traditionally the major categories were nobles, commoners, and slaves. This hierarchical ordering usually originated when conquering strangers created chiefdoms or kingdoms. Nobles had certain privileges. In some cases they had the exclusive right to sacrifice cattle. Among the Antaimoro, only the noble *foko* of the Antenoni could elect the king. They were, however, more tightly constrained by taboos than were commoners. The Merina call their nobles Andriana, but the Betsileo and the Bara call them Hova—the name the Merina use to designate their commoners.

Sometimes each of these social strata was further subdivided. In Merina society seven different ranks of nobles existed, their prestige increasing the closer their relationship was to the then-current royal family. This meticulously ranked hierarchy was established in the eighteenth century by King Andrianampoinimerina to avoid power struggles between competing groups of nobles. Commoner kinship groups also often differed in prestige. Certain Hova groups in Merina society still consider themselves superior not only to other Hova groups but also to certain Andriana.

In the beginning of the nineteenth century these Hova groups had slowly become more influential. The murder of Radama II in 1863 and the investiture of Queen Ranavalona II confirmed the power of these groups, especially of the Andafy-Avafatra family, who from then on furnished the country's prime ministers. The last of these was Rainilaiarivony, who chose and married in succession three Merina queens. It was the Hova, less constrained by rigid taboos than the Andriana, who first embraced Christianity (see ch. 2).

At the bottom of the social ladder were the slaves, usually either prisoners of war or freemen who had committed a crime. After the establishment of the Sakalava kingdoms on the western coast in the eighteenth century, they were also imported from Africa. The Betsileo called the slaves "lost people" because they had been forcibly separated from their kin. Slaves were not considered part of the social system but only an extension of their masters. They were buried outside the villages in earthen tombs. They, too, were ranked, the highest being owned by royalty. Radama I forbade the taking of slaves within the country in 1865. In 1874 Ranavalona II freed all the slaves who had been imported from Mozambique since 1865. In 1896, after the French had annexed the island, all slaves were legally freed.

New Developments

These historical divisions have been perpetuated partly because of strict rules requiring marriage within one's social stratum. Children of mésalliances automatically belong to the lower ranking group, and the higher ranking parent is forbidden burial in his family tomb. The higher the status of a kinship group, the stronger is the insistence on marrying within it. When immigrants settle in new surroundings, they are still ranked according to the status their kinship group had in their region of origin.

Social distinctions between nobles and commoners are nevertheless becoming blurred. What has remained is the right of nobles to speak first at public meetings and of being greeted in a deferential manner. In Imerina, Andriana tombs are still inside the villages, and often Hova tombs are still outside. Sometimes pride in noble ancestry leads a family to conspicuous consumption, such as building a church with the highest steeple, killing the greatest number of cattle for a ceremony, or spending the most during a funeral. Among the Bara a modern profession still counts less than high rank, although nobles no longer demonstrate their descent by wearing the traditional red-brown toga.

The great distinction at present remains that between descendants of freemen and slaves. Although not visible among rural people who tend to live alike regardless of status, the descent ideology of Malagasy society has social and economic effects that perpetuate stratification. Descendants of freemen maintain a tomb in their ancestral land and—because of this—close ties with a now often-dispersed kinship group. They can, for example, easily board their children with relatives in town to let them attend better schools and later on get better jobs in government and private enterprises. Through the kinship grapevine they hear of better opportunities elsewhere.

Descendants of slaves have no ancestral land and no ancestral tombs. They establish tombs and are buried in the village in which they live. Usually they marry someone who lives nearby, and their lives focus on the local community. This makes it easy for them to cooperate with neighbors, but they lack the advantages of a widespread net of relatives. When a slave descendant moves to town, he marries someone there and soon severs ties with his old village. People who remain in the village thus do not profit from an urban contact. Those who have gone to live in the cities often hesitate to take advantage of opportunities in the modern sector of the economy and the professions because of ingrained feelings of inferiority. Descendants of former slaves in eminent positions remain the exception, despite government intentions to eliminate advantages due to birth.

Nevertheless, new social classes based on wealth are emerging. Besides propertyless wage earners, a middle class has developed that is educated, more individualistically minded, and largely urban. This class is composed of public administrators, merchants, entrepreneurs, clerics, doctors, and other representatives of modern professions. In some contexts, individual achievement has become more important that inherited rank.

Age Groups

Some ethnic groups, such as the Bara and Antaimoro, divide into age groups that cut across hierarchical strata. This institution assigns specific roles to men and women during certain years of their lives.

Among the southeastern people, the age group of the *zazalahi* (unmarried young men) has the right to carry the dead to the tomb. Young men thus have some leverage with the older generation. They make the litter on which the dead are carried and enlarge the tomb whenever necessary. They also kill and cut up the cattle for the funeral ceremony and are called upon to do tasks requested by the government, such as cleaning the village streets or repairing roads and bridges. Later they pass on to other grades, each having their duties and prerogatives, until they join the old men who no longer pay taxes and who have a right to leisure and respect.

Old age confers prestige everywhere in Malagasy society and, in theory, the right to command. The elders are called *raiamandreny*, a term that means literally "father and mother," although it refers usually to men. Boys are introduced into the world of men through circumcision. It is a group ceremony that unites the heads of families and that remains an element of social cohesion. The act itself is performed in the house of the chief. Today circumcision rites often no longer unite all of the dispersed kin, but only neighbors.

RELIGION

The Traditional Religious System

Traditional Malagasy religion has no dogma and no clergy. Its most important element is the cult of the dead. Men who die "leave to become God," having powers commensurate with the rank they held in life. Prayers always ask for a blessing of both Zanahary (God) and the ancestors. Zanahary, however, the creator of the universe, is distant and unrepresentable, whereas ancestors are believed to be intensely concerned with the fate of their living descendants.

Death is thus no absolute end to life and can be met calmly and serenely. A man knows that after his death he will continue to interest himself in the affairs of his family, influence their decisions, and be honored, even though his originality and particularity will soon be forgotten and he will merge with the anonymous group of ancestors. Even his name will not be remembered long and will be supplanted by those of "younger" dead. The relation between him and the living will be permanent, however. That is why tombs are usually far more luxurious and far more solidly built than the houses of the living. Erected on unalienable land, they are partly underground and have a burial chamber reached by a subterranean staircase and closed off by a massive stone slab. The portion protruding above the ground, usually no more than four or five feet high, is often decorated, brightly painted, or topped with elaborate stone arcades.

In addition to the numerous tombs that dot the Malagasy landscape, there are everywhere, especially on the highlands and in the south, tall narrow monoliths up to twelve or fifteen feet high on top of mountains or by the side of the street, near villages or inside courtyards, and made either of stone or of wood. Some are erected to commemorate an important event such as a military victory, but often they are funeral monuments to remind the living of those who could not be buried in the land of their ancestors and to give the soul of the dead a place to rest. Otherwise, it is feared, the errant soul will grieve and be driven to revenge.

Unusual funeral rites, too, testify to the intense and enduring relationship between the living and dead. For a variety of reasons, people are often buried in a temporary grave. Either the family tomb is too far away and relatives cannot be gathered quickly; or a child under four or five years of age has died and must wait for an adult to die to be buried with him; or the family tomb that can only be opened once within a year has already had a burial within that time. All neighbors, including those not related to the dead person, will help with this funeral and contribute time, money, rice, or other necessities. The permanent burial is in the family tomb and is the concern of the *foko*. Here the dead will join his ancestors forever and watch with them over the living kin.

The Merina and the Betsileo have another customary funeral rite called *famadihana* (turning over the dead). During this ceremony the remains of a number of bodies who have long been dead are rewrapped in new, very fine and colorful silk, then placed inside a mat and carried through the streets. During this happy and almost riotous reunion with beloved ancestors, men drink and women dance, touching their long dead kinsmen and tossing them playfully up into the air. Eventually the bodies are returned to the tomb, the most prominent place given to those who died most recently, unless a skeleton is believed to be that of the original founder. Some dead are only wrapped in a new silk shroud and not taken out in order to avoid the taxes that the government levies on each exhumed body. Afterwards the mats in which the dead were carried around are thrown away, and the women fight for them because they believe that sleeping on them ensures fertility.

In each house a hallowed place—either in the northeastern corner or near the door on the east side—is reserved for the ancestors. Here the head of the family prays, asking for a healing or the prevention of a misfortune, and offers rice, honey, alcohol, a chicken, or another animal.

Besides the belief in one God and in the immortality of the soul, many Malagasy believe in secondary spirits living in notable natural features, such as trees, mountain tops, caves, or running streams. There is also a widespread fear of the spirits of unknown dead who frighten people by strange noises. Such spirits can take possession of the living, put them into a trance, and make them dance. This phenomenon is called *tromba* and is said to occur particularly in the northeast of the island. The Sakalava, among whom traditional chiefs are still powerful, are convinced that the soul of a dead prince can get possession of a person, a belief that buttresses the old social structure. In another type of *tromba* a malevolent spirit takes possession of a person, who must be delivered through a ritual.

Certain concepts and practices, prevalent throughout the island, can be traced to Islamic beliefs, which originated in Antaimoro country on the southeastern coast (see ch. 4). They have been accepted by Malagasy holding traditional beliefs as well as by those professing Christianity.

They were disseminated by the *ombiasi* (diviner-healers), who are reputed to have knowledge of supernatural forces and especially of the heavenly constellations. Among the Antandroy it is the *ombiasi* who are often asked to eradicate a mistake made by neglecting a taboo. The Bara consult the *ombiasi* to look after the sick and dying. Family heads ask them about the proper date to begin certain agricultural tasks or when to marry or to circumcise. Merina families have their personal diviners who consult the stars; their advice is requested on all enterprises that are thought to involve dangers; and they are paid a regular salary as well as additional fees for extra services. They set the auspicious day for a *famadihana*. Even a highly educated Merina would not think of building a house without consulting the *ombiasi* for the favorable day to begin work. When a marriage is contemplated, both sets of parents will ask the *ombiasi* whether the partners will be compatible.

The science of the *ombiasi* is tied to the concept of *vintana*, which means fate ordained by the position of moon, sun, and stars. Accordingly, different values and different forces, either active or passive, are attributed to each fraction of time. Space, too, is thought to be affected by these forces, east being superior to west, and north to south. Northeast is believed to be the most favorable direction. People build their houses on the north-south axis and reserve the northeastern corner for prayers. Guests are seated on the northern side, and chickens are kept in the southwestern corner.

Fate is impersonal and cannot be changed, but certain aspects can be foretold and avoided. For divination the *ombiasi* use the system of *sikidi* (method of divination of Arabic origin) in which fruit seeds or grains of maize are put into rows of eight each. Various figure combinations indicate the future and what to do regarding sickness, love, business, and other enterprises. The *ombiasi* also sell *ody* (talisman) made of such objects as dried or powdered vegetables, glass beads, or animal teeth.

As to Islam proper, apart from the Comorians there are only about 70,000 nominal Muslims in Madagascar, mostly in the northwest among the Sakalava and the Antakarana. In some cases believers practice a modified form of Islam called the Kharidjite heresy. This was once an important Islam sect, elements of which survive in Algeria, Zanzibar, and Oman.

Christianity

Christian missions have been in Madagascar since the early nineteenth century (see ch. 2). Today they claim more than one-third of the population as converts. In August 1968, on the 150th anniversary of the arrival of the London Missionary Society, three Protestant churches united. They were the Church of Christ in Madagascar, the Malagasy Friends Church, and the Evangelical Church of Madagascar. This new united church, having a Presbyterian synodal constitution, claims over 800,000 members and forms with the 300,000 members of the Malagasy Lutheran Church the Protestant Federation of Madagascar.

The Protestant churches have long had Malagasy pastors. They became independent from their mother organizations in 1958, and lay Christians and pastors were integrated with the Malagasy church at all levels. As of the early 1970s five missionary societies, having a total of 167 missionaries, were still represented in the country. They were the American Lutheran, the Franco-Swiss Mission de Paris, the Norwegian Lutheran, and two English societies.

The Roman Catholic Church claims 1.5 million members. Three archdioceses are based in Diégo-Suarez, Tananarive, and Fianarantsoa. In the early 1970s about a third of the priests were Malagasy, including the archbishop of Tananarive. About a dozen Roman Catholic missionary societies were active, including the Jesuits, the Fathers of the Holy Ghost, and the Lazarists.

Because it was first espoused by Merina freemen, Protestantism has been historically the denomination of the upper classes; Catholicism, that of slaves and the *côtiers* (see Glossary). These divisions, however, are no longer clear cut as Roman Catholics have made more converts in the highlands and among the descendants of nobles and freemen.

Traditional religion was tied to the concept of a narrow world limited by kin group, village, and ancestral tomb. Christianity, by stressing the individual relationship between the believer and God, had the effect of encouraging personal development and achievement while opening the vista of belonging to a worldwide congregation. Most Christians however, have not been able to free themselves from traditional notions of the supernatural. They still believe in witchcraft, ghosts, and astrology.

After the Merina espoused Christianity, they began building churches in their *tanindrazana* so that today almost all small villages in the ancestral homelands in Imerina have at least one but sometimes two churches—one Roman Catholic and one Protestant. This means that the Merina who migrated elsewhere belong to two congregations, that of the village or town in which they live and that near their family tomb. The church in the *tanindrazana* is frequently far more impressive because it is maintained by those who have moved away and are often in remunerative professions. Members of a *foko* thus meet not only for family ceremonies but also on Christian feast days.

Malagasy Christians have found the cult of the dead compatible with their religious beliefs. They have their dead blessed at the church before burying them according to traditional rites. They invite the pastor to attend a *famadahina,* and they may well put a cross on the ancestral tomb. They will even say that the dead ancestors have become Christians and thus continue to be the arbiters of what is morally good.

TRADITION IN THE SOCIAL ORDER

Taboos

Ancestors are considered to be the originators and guardians of customs (*fombe*). Far more than mere habits these customs provide a framework for everyday behavior. Specifically, innumerable taboos (*fady*) are considered commands of the ancestors that must be avoided under peril of incurring their wrath and inviting calamities, such as sickness, infertility, and even death. In fact, they are often called *fady mody* (taboos that take vengeance). They are precise proscriptions telling which foods not to eat, which features not to include in a house or tombs, and which words and actions to avoid.

Taboos are imprinted on the minds of children and form an important part of their education. Elders tell their grandchildren about past events that explain their historical origin, such as the rescue of a prince by an animal that must, therefore, never be killed; the plant that made some ancestor sick and must never be eaten; or the specific disaster that renders certain days evil so that special rites must be performed for children born on them. Such tales always emphasize the evil that will befall the breaker of a taboo. There are taboos applying to individuals, to families, to kinship groups, and to ethnic groups. In fact, the different taboos followed by different people in villages whose inhabitants are of mixed origins make it at times impossible to unite them all for a common task, such as repairing an irrigation canal. An individual is hedged in by so many taboos that it is almost impossible for him to do something without making a false move. The ever-present possibility of transgression for the least bold action or untoward word, the constant fear of incurring blame (*tsiny*) and punishment, leads to circumspection, moderation, and even a certain fatalism.

This explains the extreme prudence concerning new enterprises and the mistrust and fear of originality and innovation. Whenever the exigencies of modern living demand a departure from ancestral values, a rite is required. Whatever is new is charged with danger. A Bara who builds a nontraditional type of house, one of earth instead of straw, will place a ritual object into a prominent spot to reconcile the ancestors.

There is great reverence for what is old and proven. Old age overrides social rank, and in former times even a prince would listen to the advice of an old slave. Enough of this attitude survives today to make it difficult for young men in responsible government positions to enforce their decisions with the older generation.

For the Merina and Betsileo, the holding of *famadihana* is one way of lightening the ever-present burden of guilt occasioned by the breaking of a taboo. Being financially able to have a *famadihana*, but failing to do so, increases *tsiny*.

Fear of *tsiny* also explains the extreme politeness that Malagasy exhibit toward each other and their reluctance to contradict. At a *fokon'olona* meeting, for example, a speaker will always begin with a lengthy introduction called *miala tsiny* (removing of faults) in which he apologizes at length for his unworthiness. "Excuse me for speaking," he will say, "I am not a father, but a son, not an elder, but a young man." This is not dictated by excessive humility but by the conviction that every statement is bound to hurt someone's expectations. Then the speaker will launch into a general moral statement expressing love of kin, family, and nation, and respect for elders; all of it will be embellished with copious proverbs and perhaps a quote or two from the Bible. Only after a very long time will he discuss the matter at hand and state his opinion.

The people will listen silently from beginning to end. Those who disagree will not express their opinion but will counter with a speech that at first seems to support the first speaker but that actually contains a hidden counterproposal. They might express their views by telling jokes. If people laugh or if they simply act according to the second speaker's proposal, the first has lost. There will never be an open confrontation, however.

Social Change

Attachment to a fixed social order has not prevented change. It began earlier and touched more people in the Central Highlands than anywhere else on the island. When the Merina established their rule, the influence of kinship groups, of local chiefs, and of ethnic loyalties was undermined. Instead, fear and a certain respect developed for the Merina king, provincial governors, and other officials. Even the *fokon'olona* was often summoned from then on to discuss the latest regulations from Tananarive rather than local initiative.

Under French colonial rule, the development of a money economy, the introduction of cash crops and wage labor, the growth of urban centers, and internal migrations created a world in which the old beliefs and the wisdom of the ancestors seemed no longer quite adequate for practical guidance. Old age itself no longer commands the influence it once wielded. The advice of the Protestant minister or a government official might be taken rather than that of the elder. Traditionally the heads of kinship groups are also ritual chiefs who give the signal to begin the harvest after having eaten the "first fruits." When people move to a region where the climate is different and crops ripen earlier, they can no longer wait for the message of a faraway chief.

Everywhere it is the older generation that is more attached to traditions. Among the cattle pastoralists of the south and west, the older people still consider raising cattle a far more noble pastime than cultivation. South of the Mangoky River, Bara cattle raisers plant living thorn hedges to isolate themselves from immigrant Betsileo cultivators, who are Christians, grow rice, and raise pigs, all of which is taboo for the Bara. Young Bara cattlemen who have gone to settle north of the Mangoky River among farmers, however, no longer balk at living in close proximity with people holding different beliefs and following different life-styles. Occasionally, they begin cultivating the land themselves.

New ideas are spread in the countryside by traders, itinerant craftsmen, musicians, magicians, and government officials. When new techniques are proposed, villagers will not accept them until after thorough discussion and perhaps the performance of a ritual to avoid the dire consequences of breaking a taboo. Hardy individuals who embark on a new course before it has been accepted by the elders of the *fokon'olona* are eagerly watched in expectation of disaster that is bound to overtake them.

Sometimes new plants and agricultural methods are accepted because the ancestors could not possibly have established rules about something that was unknown to them. For example, traditionally it is taboo to cultivate a wild plant. To this day, raffia palms are exploited and destroyed for their fibers, and new ones are never planted. The cactus and various new plants from Africa were introduced and cultivated in the seventeenth and eighteenth centuries, however.

For the older generation, the deepest and most unavoidable conflict remains that between what is *razana* ("of the ancestor") and that which is *vazaha* ("of the stranger"), which means anything even remotely associated with Europe. One is considered good and trustworthy; the other, disturbing and doubtful, even by those who have studied abroad. One way of reconciling claims by two incompatible sets of values is by continuing the custom of burial in the family tomb. Another is to cooperate with *foko* members for important events, such as circumcision and marriage, and to give hospitality and financial help. Modern politicians have used appeals to such ancestral values to curry votes. The young intellectual elite that has not been traumatized by the *razana-vazaha* dichotomy has been able to accept Western values—sometimes even Marxism—without inhibition and to integrate them with traditional Malagasy values.

CHAPTER 6
LIVING CONDITIONS

In the early 1970s living conditions in the urban centers differed sharply from those prevailing in the countryside. A southern herder inhabiting a hut constructed by his own hands, clothed in garments woven and dyed at home, and eating the products of his cattle and garden contrasted markedly with the wealthy trader or high-ranking government official who lived in Tananarive in a two-storied house maintained by servants and who wore Western-style clothing and bought imported goods.

Income levels differed broadly not only between inhabitants of rural and urban areas but also between those of the various geographic regions (see ch. 3). Richest was Tananarive Province, where for centuries farmers had painstakingly coaxed the highest yields on the island from land not particularly rich in natural resources and where the cash economy had penetrated the local society more thoroughly than elsewhere. In Tananarive Province the greatest number of children went to school. More than two-thirds of the people knew how to read and write, and at least half of them spoke French as well as Malagasy. Housing was adequate, and diets were more substantial; health facilities were available to most of the people. Conditions were similar but not quite as favorable in Fianarantsoa Province, home of the Betsileo, who were capable farmers but who lacked a city the size of Tananarive as a market for their surplus produce.

Living standards were lower in the provinces of Tamatave and Diégo-Suarez, although much of this region was favored by nature and was capable of producing export crops. Large plantations were usually owned by foreigners, whereas those belonging to the Betsimisaraka, Tsimihety, and Antakarana were usually small, amounting to no more than two or four acres. The owners of these small properties sold their coffee, vanilla, cloves, and other crops to Chinese or Indian middlemen and often had to borrow money from them at high interest rates during hard times. Their housing and diet patterns had generally not been affected by the introduction of cash crops, and educational and health standards were lower than in the Central Highlands. Still lower were the living standards in Majunga Province, where most land, except for small oases of cultivable ground in the river valleys, was arid and fit only for cattle raising.

Poorest of the country's six provinces was Tulear in the south, where most people subsisted with difficulty in an inhospitable setting. Cash needed for taxes and cattle purchases was earned by selling products that grew wild and were painfully collected in the bush, by working at sisal plantations, or often by migrating to other parts of the island.

In the early 1960s the average annual per capita income had been estimated roughly at the equivalent of US$92. By the early 1970s the population had increased at a faster pace than the national product, and prices had risen. Accurate estimates were difficult to obtain as almost half the personal incomes were considered to be non-monetary, consisting mainly of goods and foods produced and consumed at home or bartered. They also included services and gifts that played a large social role as mutual obligations.

PATTERNS OF LIVING

The 85 percent of the Malagasy people who live in the countryside follow the natural pattern of the days and the seasons. They rise at sunup and work in the fields and pastures in the morning and the early afternoon. A Malagasy term for a cattle herder, for example, is *mpanarak'andro*, which means "those who follow the day." Villages are often nearly deserted during the day. Only a few women go back and forth carrying water, while children play in the dust and old people doze in the shadow of a tree. In the late afternoon people come home from their work to eat and then to chat, usually discussing local affairs. When it is cool, they sit on the western side of their house in the rays of the setting sun; in hot weather they sit on the southern or the eastern side. Moonlit evenings are occasions for staying up late.

Rural people spend a great deal of their working time satisfying immediate household needs. Because of the lack of a division of labor beyond the domestic level, each household is obliged to perform a great number of tasks—from the raising of food to the building of houses. Within the household, however, the division of labor is strict. Men prepare the ricefields, raise cattle, construct houses, hunt, and catch fish with a line. Women transplant the rice shoots, cultivate the gardens, net fish with wicker baskets, and gather wild crops. They weave mats, sweep out their houses at least once a day, and collect firewood. Meals are simple, and cooking takes little of their time, in contrast to the task of keeping a supply of water, which in most cases is a time-consuming job. Where water is scarce, as in the south, clothes are seldom washed, and people clean themselves by rubbing their skin with crushed leaves. In some places enterprising individuals haul water by wagon, selling it by the bucketful from door to door.

Seasonal changes affect not only the people's work schedules but also their nourishment. Times of plenty after the harvest are followed by difficult periods—even famines—when supplies are exhausted and people are forced to look for roots and wild fruits in the bush.

Rural people who manage to have a cash surplus put metal roofs on their houses and buy Western-style clothing, a bicycle, a phonograph, or a sewing machine. In the early 1970s, however, few rural Malagasy had such luxuries. They spent an estimated 4 percent of their monetary income (2 percent of their total income) on tombs and funerals. This estimate did not include the number of cattle bought, raised, and slaughtered for funeral ceremonies. Economists have contended that money thus spent could be put to better use, but many Malagasy farmers and herders considered these expenditures part of a minimum living standard. Funeral ceremonies provided spiritual communion with the ancestors, an intangible requisite for all social and economic activities.

The much higher living standard of some urban people is most strikingly demonstrated in Tananarive Province, where people in the capital earn on the average three times as much as those in the countryside. Moreover, this gap is increasing because the rural population grows at a higher rate.

Within the city, living conditions vary greatly. A tiny minority, composed of high-ranking government employees, wealthy merchants, and top officials of private enterprise, lives at a high level of affluence. Their houses are equipped with most modern amenities; they own at least one means of private transport; and they are able to save. They invest these savings profitably in apartment houses, for example, or they contribute to various community projects in their *tanindrazana* (ancestral village).

A rather large middle class lives on a decent but far more modest scale. Included in this group are the lower echelons of the administration and private enterprise—the small and medium-scale merchants and the owners of ricefields that are leased to tenants. Basically, their life-style is traditional, although they have adopted some Western habits regarding food, clothing, lodging, and leisure activities.

The majority of the capital's inhabitants are poor. Unskilled laborers, messengers, and domestic servants, they are almost exclusively Merina *mainty* (blacks) and descendants of former slaves. They cling to their traditional way of life, living in overcrowded sections of the city without the simplest comforts. When their money is gone, they are often forced to borrow. They have no savings, and sickness and unemployment represent genuine catastrophes. Below this group of poor people exists a still poorer one, composed of recently uprooted farmers. They live from day to day in sordid lodgings at the periphery of the city, perpetually looking for work and seldom finding it. A thorough study of 1,951 Tananarive families undertaken in the 1960s revealed that 13.3 percent earned less than the equivalent of US$30 per month; more than half earned less than

US$60; and only 16 percent had incomes of more than US$100. These figures usually represented the combined monthly incomes of several family members.

The same study indicated that on the average these people spent 37 percent of their income on food, 9.3 percent on clothing, and 6.6 percent on rent. An important 3.3 percent was spent for intercity transport.

Despite generally low incomes, 80 percent of these households had transitor radios, and 55 percent had sewing machines. Four percent of all households owned bicycles, and 3.8 percent had autombiles, usually secondhand models that required costly upkeep. To have such modern conveniences people took on high-interest debts so that, on an average, 4.3 percent of their incomes were spent on loan repayments. Few people spent money on books, newspapers, or motion pictures. Walking in the parks or journeying into the nearby countryside were favorite family pastimes.

HOUSING

Houses vary from small mud or bamboo thatch-covered huts to elaborate two-storied brick structures. Regardless of individual or regional variations, all share certain customary features linked to astrological beliefs. Usually rectangular, they are almost always built along a north-south axis, anything else being considered unhealthy. Most houses have steeply pitched two-sided roofs because strict taboos forbid having a roof with only one slope. The building of a house begins on a day determined by the *ombiasi* (diviner-healer), who also sets the date for occupancy.

Because of their orientation Malagasy houses also serve as sundials. Madagascar is in the southern hemisphere, and the sun's path is north of the zenith for most of the year. Local inhabitants consider that it is 8:00 A.M. when the sun is above the roof, 11:00 A.M. when it crosses the threshold, and 2:00 P.M. when it lights up the southwestern corner of the house.

The building material and the size of the houses depend mainly on regional location. In Imerina and in Betsileo areas, houses often have two stories and are made of sun-dried mud bricks of the same red color as the surrounding earth. They have small square windows and no chimneys so that the smoke blackens the inside with soot and escapes as best it can through the thatch or tile of the roof. The outside and inside walls are plastered with a mixture of earth and cow dung. Floors are usually of compacted soil covered with mats. The more affluent Merina add a balcony, supported by four brick columns and shaded by a projecting roof, at the second-floor level.

The usual house in Tananarive has a second story reached by an interior staircase and has two or three rooms on each floor, including a separate kitchen and a balcony. They resemble Victorian cottages, the edges of their roofs often being decorated with wooden fretwork. The same kind of house is found in the less prestigious sections of the city, but there the ground floor is occupied by vendors of fruit or charcoal or by hairdressers, tailors, and carpenters. Children play, and women wash clothes on second-floor balconies that face the street. In the outlying districts a great many people are crowded into traditional one-room houses of mud bricks and thatched roofs, a phenomenon made bearable because so many activities are pursued out-of-doors.

Typical of the houses in the Ankaratra region southwest of Tananarive are roofs extending all the way to the ground. The entrance door is cut into one of the two roof slopes above a raised threshold; the inside room is below ground. Protection from winds and preservation of heat are the reason for this unusual style of building.

Interior migrations have introduced into other regions certain kinds of houses that may or may not be suited to local conditions. Brick houses, for example, built by Merina living outside Imerina, are often copied by local people for reasons of prestige.

In the northeast, where vanilla is grown, the Chinese shop made of stone, brick, or corrugated iron is often the most solid structure in the village. It also serves as a social meetingplace because even the smallest purchase by a customer becomes a lengthy transaction.

In the south and the east, houses are often built entirely of vegetable matter. Large panels made of rushes or the midribs of traveler's palms are fitted into a framework, made either of wood or of palm stalks, that supports a steep, two-sided roof of palm leaves. The panels are attached to the inside wall so that the framework is visible from the outside. When such houses are built in higher and cooler regions, the stalks in the paneling are more closely tied and sometimes are interlaced with mud to keep out the draft. These structures are not very high and usually consist of a single room. They are quickly built by teams of men, who afterwards are given a feast by the owner. In Antandroy country, a number of houses belonging to the same family are surrounded by thorn or aloe hedges, which also enclose the cattle pen and the small gardens.

The Tsimihety in the north build thatch-roofed houses of sun-dried mud brick caked over a framework of raffia palm ribs. Such houses can last up to twenty years, but villages in this region often include homes that have fallen into disrepair because their owners have migrated.

In the forest regions, such as the eastern escarpment, and in some parts of the extreme south, houses, including their roofs, are made entirely of wood. Vertical timbers, peeled but not dressed, are usually planted directly into the ground. Floors are made of planks or from split and flattened bamboo mats, which are woven in a checkerboard design.

Where rainfall is heavy, houses are raised on posts; the floors are often up to two feet above the ground. Where there is less rain, only the threshold is above ground level. Near Lake Alaotra, where flooding is likely, the houses are put on large footings of earth and stones. When the waters rise higher than expected, bundles of interlaced rushes are piled on the floor to raise the family above the water level. More layers are added if necessary.

Houses in rural areas are thus extremely simple, except perhaps for the number of openings. Usually there is at least a second door or a window even in one-room houses, and some have three doors. In such an arrangement the door on the east is reserved for the carrying out of the dead; the one on the west is used by the descendants of slaves.

Traditional beliefs also govern the arrangement of furnishings inside the house. The northesastern corner is considered the domain of dead ancestors. It is devoid of furnishings except for the family *ody* (talisman) and a mat on which the head of the house says his prayers; he also sleeps near that corner along the eastern wall. This is the part of the house where honored guests are received, people of inferior position sitting on the western side.

Inside a one-room house, as in about half of all Malagasy houses, the hearth is usually situated in the southeastern triangle; in the southern part of the island, it is constructed in the middle of the room. The hearth consists of three stones or three iron legs supporting the cooking pot. Underneath a fire is lighted, using wood, straw, or occasionally charcoal. The water reservoir is often a large piece of bamboo. In houses raised on posts, another bamboo section might be fastened vertically, its top flush with the floor, to serve as a drain. Some women cook outside in the courtyard or under a separate small shelter.

Belongings, such as bowls, plates, small calabashes, and cooking pots, are arranged on shelves along the walls. Chests or sometimes a cupboard contain clothing and other belongings. Rooms are lighted either by the cooking fire or sometimes by a burning raffia cord submerged in a mixture of kerosine and water.

There is usually little furniture. Many people eat their meals while sitting on the floor in a circle around a plate or large palm leaf piled high with rice. They sleep on mats, which are rolled up during the day. Returning veterans of military service and more prosperous farmers, especially in the Central Highlands, have beds, simple tables, chairs, and perhaps a mirror or a framed military citation on the wall.

A great many granaries, looking like miniature houses and raised on four posts six feet or more above the ground, are characteristic of villages in the southwest. They are found in smaller numbers elsewhere except in the Central Highlands.

Urban people similarly have very little furniture. Usually they own a few chairs and tables in addition to mats or beds that often accommodate several people. Fifty-four percent of the 1,951 families interviewed in Tananarive in the mid-1960s, however, had a room reserved for visitors and for special occasions. This room contained upholstered furniture and was not used regularly despite crowded conditions in other parts of the house. More than half these families also owned a house in the country, situated in the *tanindrazana* of the head of the household in 71 percent of the cases. This second house was not rented out, and the family used it from time to time for vacations, weddings, funerals, and other family ceremonies. These houses, although empty most of the year, were often far better than the surrounding houses of permanent village inhabitants.

The outstanding edifices almost everywhere on the island are the family tombs. Solidly built, they contrast with the houses of the living, which in comparison seem flimsy and impermanent.

CLOTHING

The most common item of Malagasy clothing is the *lamba*, a cloth shawl worn over the shoulder by men and women. Even wealthy women who want to demonstrate their attachment to the Malagasy cultural tradition wear it over their Western-style dresses. Usually white and of rough cloth, the *lamba* that is worn on Sunday is often of attractive silk and is frequently woven by Betsileo women. A woman carries her baby in her *lamba*, and the dead are wrapped in a *lamba* before they are placed inside the tomb. Some people wear a cotton blanket, which they drape in such a manner that a triangle hangs down in front and another in back. In cold weather they let it hang down like a toga.

The typical Malagasy suit worn by men in the Central Highlands is of light flannel and consists of a long shirt called *malabar*, which reaches down to the knees over long, loose trousers. In more remote areas of the highlands the *malabar* is worn without the pants.

In parts of the southeast, people still wear a traditional one-piece sleeveless garment woven of raffia. Elsewhere in many remote rural areas men still wear the *salaka*, a band of soft cloth, six to ten inches wide and six to eight feet long, which is passed through the legs and then wound three times around the hips with the ends hanging down in the front and the back. These traditional clothes are increasingly being replaced everywhere by shirts worn with shorts or trousers.

Some Sakalava and Antakarana chiefs, who have adopted Islam, wear the white ample robe of the Arabs.

In the cities the majority of people wear Western-style clothing. Women's dresses are usually of colorful cotton imported from Japan or from France. Secondhand clothing, imported frequently from the United States, is sold in the markets. There is a great variety in hat styles. They are made from different vegetable materials and in many colors. The most popular style in the Central Highlands has a wide rim. In the southwest and in the south, hats are square and rimless, resembling baskets turned upside down. In Tananarive many Western styles of hats are worn, including homburgs and Tyrolean models.

Women wear their hair long and plaited in many different ways. They often use cacao oil to give it a glossy sheen. Merina women wear gold jewelry on Sunday when they go to church. It is made by craftsmen who have learned their skill from Indian immigrants. Many rural people, especially women and children, go barefoot, as shoes and sandals are still a luxury.

DIET AND NUTRITION

The diet of the average Malagasy is monotonous, based almost entirely on rice. Originally a prestige food, its use has spread throughout the island, replacing in most areas the former traditional diet of cassava and other tubers. In modern times these foods are eaten as snacks between meals and during the meager months before the new rice harvest. Only the Antanosy, the Antandroy, and other southern peoples still eat them as a main food. Even among these peoples, however, rice is becoming increasingly popular.

A Malagasy eats on the average 297 pounds of rice per year, which ranks him as the world's fifth largest consumer of this staple. The national average caloric intake is 2,290 per day, but this figure hides wide variations, depending on geographic location and the time of the year. Large numbers of Malagasy do not get enough nutritious food either in quantity or in quality. In regions that are favorable for farming, cash crops have often replaced food crops, and the money earned is not spent on adequate diets (see ch. 13). In poorer regions migrations provide temporary solutions to undernourishment and often prevent starvation.

The national dish is *romazava*, which is eaten in the middle of the day. It consists of boiled rice with or without greens and sometimes with a little meat or fish. No sauces and very little fat are used, in contrast to the typical African diet. Often Malagasy food is cooked without salt, but occasionally it is spiced with chili. The national beverage (*ranopango*) is always drunk after the meal. It is water boiled with the rice that has become stuck to the side of the cooking pot. Coffee is popular between meals among those who can afford it.

Women buy it green and roast it at home. A strong alcoholic beverage is made by distilling a mixture of sugarcane and tree bark.

Regional dietary differences are great. The Antaimoro subsist almost entirely on rice, supplemented by a little fish. The Betsileo, who are skilled farmers living on fairly fertile land, consume on the average over 3,000 calories daily. The Betsimisaraka who live near the coast have a more varied diet by adding fish and vegetables to their rice, but they use the polished, less nutritious variety. The inland Betsimisaraka hull the rice by crude methods and thus retain more of its nutrients. The Sakalava in the west eat very little rice, subsisting on a meager diet of maize (corn) and taro, supplemented on rare occasions by meat.

Consumption of meat is generally limited to occasions of sacrifices at traditional ceremonies, especially funerals. Otherwise animals are killed occasionally in honor of a guest or if they are injured, sick, or old. Meat must be consumed at once because surpluses cannot be stored or sold. Occasionally excess meat is buried and is eaten after it has rotted. The Sakalava often smoke their meat and then cut it up in small strips.

A variety of fruit grows wild on the island, and children pick it usually as snacks between meals. There is little systematic growing of vegetables. Few eggs are eaten, partly because they are not fresh when found. Because frequent epidemics have reduced the number of fowl, eggs are often kept for hatching. Poultry also is used in religious sacrifices or as gifts.

Rural people buy few food items at the shop or market. They walk great distances, however, to purchase minute quantities of coffee, salt, or sugar, sometimes in the form of sugarcane, which they crush in a rice mortar.

Few Malagasy farmers and herders have a balanced diet. Because they produce, on the average, four-fifths of what they consume, they are dependent on the weather and natural resources. The difference between the lean and plentiful months is usually enormous. Caloric intake may drop from an average of 2,587 during the summer months to 1,430 during the winter months, when people subsist mainly on tubers and maize supplemented by wild grains and fruits. The season of hunger touches the lives of 39 percent of all households. This is the period when rice reserves have been exhausted—either because the harvest was too small or too much was sold—and the new crop has not yet been harvested. For 13 percent of the people, this period lasts five months. The worst time is from October through December. Two bad harvests in succession will produce serious famines.

Generally, people accept such calamities fatalistically and do little to prepare for them. Hospitable by nature, they eat surreptitiously during lean times, hiding with shame the fact that they are without proper food. Should they receive a sudden windfall, however, they quickly invite all their neighbors and save nothing for the next day.

People in the cities, especially in Tananarive, have more varied diets. They complement the traditional rice dish with bread, fresh vegetables, meat, a little fresh or condensed milk, and fruit. Bananas are often boiled, or they are dried, pounded with a pestle, mixed with rice, and fried in peanut oil.

Children are usually breast fed for nine to eighteen months after birth. A mother with insufficient milk supplements the baby's diet with rice water or sweetened herb tea. Milk is seldom available and is a luxury for most people.

Sociocultural factors influence the Malagasy diet, especially dietary taboos, of which no fewer than 275 have been listed. Many people believe, for example, that children who eat eggs before they have learned to speak will become mute or that eating fish will cause syphilis. The consumption of green bananas is said to produce dental cavities. The Tsimihety have the greatest number of food taboos—a total of 144—followed by the Betsimisaraka, who have 133. The great majority of these refer, however, to marginal items, and they seem to be forgotten under certain conditions. When Lake Matsaborimena near Bealanana was stocked with rapidly multiplying fish in 1957, the Tsimihety eagerly took to eating them despite a traditional taboo against fish, just as only one-tenth of the Antandroy continue to observe their taboo against ocean fish. Migrants in a strange environment tend to cling to their food taboos for a while as a way of ethnic identification but forget them eventually.

HEALTH

A low life expectancy, which was estimated to be about forty years at birth in the early 1970s, was a reflection of inadequate sanitation, medical care, and diet. Adults and especially children suffered from a variety of nutritional insufficiencies and consequently had poor resistance against illness. Lack of animal protein in diets was widespread. Vitamin A was totally lacking for many months of the year for some people and during the entire year for others. Frequent dental caries, bleeding gums, and rickets resulted from a lack of vitamin C. Investigations revealed that 40.74 percent of the children showed signs of malnutrition during the first year of life.

On the other hand, the island did not have sleeping sickness, cholera, brucellosis, and yellow fever, which are prevalent in many other tropical countries. Not a single case of smallpox had been recorded for more than forty years, and heart attacks were almost unknown.

Prevalent Diseases

In 1972 malaria remained the most serious tropical disease, although eradication campaigns waged since 1948 had resulted in spectacular declines in its incidence and a dramatic decrease in the island's mortality rate. In some regions, especially the Central Highlands, these campaigns have been almost completely successful, but malaria continued to be prevalent in the coastal regions, especially the east.

Schistosomiasis, a parasitic ailment that spreads primarily through the passing of human wastes into ponds, irrigation canals, and slow-moving streams, threatens to exceed malaria in extent. The disease-producing organism, picked up through the skin of the foot, develops in the human liver, reproduces, is passed through the urine into the water, goes through a stage of development in snails, and lives in stagnant water until it finds another human host. Typical symptoms are lassitude, low vitality, and blood in the urine. All of the island, except the far north, is affected. Eradication campaigns are still in the stage of research and preliminary planning.

Tuberculosis, which is spread by close contact with infected patients, was gaining ground and claimed some 10,000 victims in the early 1970s. The government conducts vaccination campaigns on a mass scale. Since 1962 the antitubercular vaccine has been produced at the Tananarive-based Pasteur Institute.

Leprosy is endemic on the island. In 1881, long before the French arrived, the Merina queen, Ranavalona I, issued a royal decree for an antileprosy drive. In the early 1970s it was estimated that there were between 50,000 and 60,000 infected persons, most of them in the coastal regions. Many were treated at home and depended on yearly or twice-yearly visits from itinerant physicians or made trips to treatment centers headed by male nurses. Some 35,000 were treated in thirteen leprosariums as of 1972. Cured lepers were not readmitted to their villages but lived in nine special settlements.

Bubonic plague, spread by rats and formerly endemic, reappears sporadically, although on a tiny scale. Many other diseases—some serious—are widespread and include diphtheria, typhoid and paratyphoid fever, veneral diseases, tetanus, hepatitis, and gastroenteric parasites.

Modern Medical Services

Health services were capable of handling major outbreaks of contagious diseases, but preventive and curative medical facilities were still modest. In the early 1970s two large hospitals in Tananarive and five smaller hospitals in other provincial capitals served predominantly urban people. In addition a sanatorium was situated in Fenoarivo, a psychiatric hospital in Ambohidratrimo, a physical therapy center for polio victims in Antsirabe, and a children's hospital in Tananarive. A network of 610 medical centers and dispensaries provided modern medical care for rural people. Patients frequently arrived with their families, consisting often of up to five or more people who brought sleeping mats, cooking utensils, and other necessities. Most of them stayed with the patient around the clock, sleeping next to his bed or camping in the courtyard.

The first five-year plan after independence had called for more than doubling the existing number of 14,140 hospital beds. By the end of the 1960s this objective had been achieved in urban areas and to the extent of 95 percent in rural districts. At that time the great majority of the country's 657 doctors and eighty-nine dentists were Malagasy who had been trained in foreign, mainly French, universities or locally at the Befelatanana School of Medicine at Tananarive. They were assisted by almost 2,000 professional nurses and 677 midwives.

A government-sponsored program called Mother and Child Care (Protection Maternelle et Infantile—PMI), which had been started by the French, provided mothers with information based on modern health principles. PMI centers were mostly located in villages and market towns. In the cities women were given information on how to take better care of their children when they went to the hospital to give birth. Such programs were supplemented by public lectures, newspaper articles, and radio publicity. Special teams of women, trained in nutrition at Tananarive, spread health education in rural districts, usually stressing better use of available foods.

A great number of Malagasy women belong to the Red Cross. In Tananarive Province membership is almost compulsory. Members in the villages take care of the weekly distribution of antimalaria drugs and, when available, parcel out clothes and powdered milk to needy children.

Folk Medicine

Most Malagasy go to hospitals and medical centers, sometimes walking great distances to reach these facilities, but traditional methods of diagnosis and treatment are still widely practiced. Vendors at the market sell concoctions and ointments for a variety of ills. The *ombiasi* is still often asked for advice and will consult the *sikidi* (diviner) for the cause of the disease and its proper remedy. He prescribes powerful *ody* as preventive measure and infusions from roots and leaves for treatment.

Some Sakalava still believe that certain diseases are caused by possession of malicious spirits and try to effect cures by means of animal sacrifices or by *bilo*, a chanting prayer followed by paroxysms of shouting and dancing.

Sanitation

Many common ailments were attributable to unsanitary conditions. Rivers, canals, stagnant pools, and wells that served for laundering, bathing, and washing of food as well as for drinking water were polluted with human and animal waste. Flies bred in open latrines and waste disposal sites. Disease also resulted from improper handling of perishable foods and from congested housing in towns.

In June 1971 the Governing Council of the United Nations Development Program approved a project for a survey of the water supply and sewage systems of Tananarive to be carried out by the World Health Organization. Slightly more than four-fifths of the cost of this project was covered by a United Nations grant of US$842,000, and the remainder, by a contribution from the Malagasy government.

Even in the capital the great majority of houses had no running water, and people had to fetch their drinking water at fountains in the streets. Most houses were without modern sewage disposal. A concerned but vastly understaffed Municipal Health Office tried to cope with these conditions. It led a persistent fight against sickness vectors, such as fleas, lice, mosquitoes, and flies, from outhouses and open-pit latrines. Houses were annually treated with insecticides. Brush was eliminated from roads and empty lots. Drainage canals from swamps and open sewers were treated with chemicals, especially in the half-urban, half-rural zone between the city proper and the swampy areas in the west and north. Flies had consequently almost totally disappeared from Tananarive. Garbage was collected regularly. Intensive measures were also taken against rats and the dogs that swarmed through the cities at night. Such does were impounded or killed because of the danger of rabies.

Visiting nurses regularly checked different city districts whenever there seemed to be a danger of contagious disease. The sick were taken to the hospital, and inhabitants who had come in contact with them were thoroughly examined. Regular vaccinations were given against smallpox, cholera, diphtheria, and typhoid fever. A central milk bureau collected, pasteurized, and bottled milk.

WELFARE

Government welfare programs were concerned with health and sanitation services, municipal and rural development, education, and a social security system for wage earners under the general supervision of the Ministry of Labor and Social Affairs. Implementation of such programs, however, was often difficult because of insufficient funds.

Wage earners in the private sector were insured for old age, disability, and death by paying 1 percent of their earnings into the National Social Insurance Fund, as against 3.5 percent contributed to the fund by employers. Another 1.25 percent was paid by employers to insure wage earners for benefit s during temporary disability after work injury. An additional 8.25 percent paid by employers and supplemented by government subsidies paid family allowances for children under fourteen years of age (up to twenty-one if they were students) and 50 percent of the salaries of employed pregnant women for up to eight weeks before and six weeks after confinement. A separate social security system insured government employees.

Alongside these programs that benefited the comparatively low number of wage earners, older methods of ensuring individuals and of providing group welfare continued to operate in both town and rural areas, sometimes equaling and often surpassing government programs in scope and effectiveness. In the traditional system, the welfare agent was the family or larger kinship group to which the individual was bound by mutual obligation, to which he could turn for protection or aid, and on which he could rely in old age.

The traditional welfare system became less adequate when the family was no longer a self-sufficient economic unit, as in the city of the market economy. Even in the large towns, however, it continued to function in providing protection for relatives who had come to seek employment, in furnishing them housing, and generally in cushioning them against the effects of rapid change.

CHAPTER 7
EDUCATION AND THE ARTS AND SCIENCES

The country possesses a rich tradition of cultural expression, part of which parallels the cultural traditions of Asian peoples, from whom some of the Malagasy peoples have descended (see ch. 2; ch. 4). The Malagasy have not, however, been confined by these traditions and have created their own original forms of artistic and intellectual expression. Elements of Arabic and African cultures also have been assimilated, and during the past century the island has been heavily exposed to French cultural influences.

In 1972 various cultural organizations in the republic ranged from foreign-oriented groups, such as the French Alliance (Alliance Française) and the Goethe Institute, to affiliates of the Malagasy Academy (Académie Malgache). There were numerous smaller associations whose stated purpose was the encouragement of the cultural and educational advancement of their members. In addition to their stated cultural goals, these organizations provided occasions for informal social interaction and organized recreational activities (see ch. 11).

These groups differed regarding the direction the national culture should take, but many increasingly emphasized traditional, indigenous artistic and intellectual forms. Forms of government support included: the sponsoring of exhibitions and cultural fairs; the maintenance of academic facilities and museums; financial aid for persons studying at Malagasy schools and aid for those studying abroad; purchase guarantees to selected artists; and legislation protecting the island's historic sites and monuments. Concern in the 1960s shifted from the earlier stress on the equal worth of local and foreign traditions of cultural expression to a search for forms serving the evolving society.

Among the more pressing realities faced by the government were the economic and social disparities existing between peoples of the Central Highlands—primarily the Merina—and the côtiers (coastal peoples) (see ch. 4; ch. 6). Government efforts to eliminate these inequalities had placed heavy emphasis on education. The major aims of the educational system included furnishing the country with the skilled manpower and intellectuals needed to further economic and cultural development. A basic feature of this approach has been an attempt to provide all children with equal educational opportunities. In accordance with these goals, the government had assumed responsibility for national education, ranging from primary to advanced levels. Limited success was evidenced in the attempts to increase the pace of national development through the classroom, but by 1972 the expanded horizons acquired through education had produced a more politically influential student element among the country's academic institutions (see ch. 9).

EDUCATION

With the support of the Merina monarchy, English Protestant missionaries introduced formal education to the island at the beginning of the nineteenth century. The success of the mission schools was immediate. By 1836—sixty years before the assumption of political administration by the French—there were more than 3,000 students, including several hundred girls, in attendance at some forty schools. At the time it was estimated that nearly 10,000 Malagasy could read and write their own language, and a Malagasy-English and English-Malagasy dictionary had been published. The Merina quickly accepted literacy as a means of both personal advancement and administrative control. By 1896 there were 164,000 Malagasy children attending primary mission schools; three generations of Malagasy intellectuals had contributed to Malagasy language publications; and sophisticated Malagasy diplomats discussed regional and international issues in the capitals of Europe.

The achievements of the educational system that developed under the Merina state, however, were limited in several respects. Although secondary schools existed, most institutions of learning offered only a primary education. The quality of instruction was in many cases rudimentary, and in all cases it was affected by the religious views of the denomination operating each school. Although the Merina government in 1880 had made primary education compulsory for all children between the ages of eight and sixteen, the majority of mission schools were located within a 100-square-mile area around Tananarive. The educational system thus favored the Merina and, to a lesser extent, the Betsileo. The end result was the creation of a small, well-educated Merina elite and a widening of the cultural gap between the peoples of the Central Highlands and the côtiers.

Public education was established in 1899 under the adminstration of French Governor Joseph Gallieni. Its basic structure and operation remained unchanged until after World War II. Public schools were separated into two groups. Those for French children were modeled on metropolitan educational facilities. The Malagasy schools offered practical and utilitarian education. Contrary to the overall French policy of assimilation, local administrators after World War I favored the use of Malagasy as the language of instruction for indigenous primary schools. New curriculum proposals in the early 1930s offered increased instruction in French for Malagasy students, but inauguration of these proposals and educational development as a whole were halted by the fiscal economies of the depression years and by manpower shortages during World War II (see ch. 2).

The French stress on secular education reduced but did not eliminate the role of mission education. The policy of subsidies for private schools varied widely during the colonial period. In general the requirement that schools having academic curricula offer French culture and language instruction favored the Roman Catholic mission schools. All schools receiving state aid were required to conform to fixed requirements, giving the administration considerable leverage over private facilities. During those periods when all subsidy programs were suspended, the greatest hardship was experienced by private secondary facilities.

Educational policy adopted after World War II reflected the recommendations of the 1944 Brazzaville Conference. The heavily utilitarian education offered to Malagasy children was rejected for more technical and academic curriculum. During the 1950s the issue of linguistic policy remained unsettled, but increased emphasis was given French language instruction. School facilities remained concentrated in the Central Highlands, but decentralization of the system was being implemented. As independence approached, the issue of education assumed increasing importance. New côtier political leaders looked for the advancement of their peoples, who had been disfavored by the previous educational system.

Under the education decree of January 6, 1959, provision was made for free, compulsory, nondenominational education for both sexes between the ages of six and fifteen. In late 1972, however, compulsory attendance for children had not become a reality even in urban centers, and the rate of population growth made the achievement of this goal within the near future seem unlikely. At times after independence, school fees were required at some institutions, and government grants and scholarships have been a political issue.

Estimates of the number of people able to read and write in any language varied between 30 and 40 percent of the total population. Literacy rates for different portions of the country were quite disparate; the rate for Tananarive was more than double the national average, and for some rural areas—particularly in the south—it was less than half the national average.

Adult literacy programs were usually associated with functional literacy projects that attempted not only to teach the Malagasy to read and write but also how to achieve better standard of living and to utilize local resources more effectively. Such programs were first implemented in 1950, were temporarily abandoned in the mid-1950s, and were resumed shortly before independence. Functional literacy was closely linked to overall national development in the guidelines established by economic planners in the late 1960s. In 1969 a major

111

functional literacy program, with a budget equivalent to US$2.1 million, was approved in cooperation with the United Nations Development Program (UNDP); about 60 percent of the program budget was provided by the Malagasy government. Because the program focused on agriculture, the Food and Agriculture Organization (FAO), a specialized agency of the United Nations, served as executive agent for the project.

Administration and Financing

With the exception of agricultural training, which was coordinated and supervised by the Ministry of Agriculture, public and private education at all levels in 1972 was the responsibility of the Ministry of Cultural Affairs; decentralization of certain aspects of primary education had been affected. The administrative structure included the national government's inspector general and the ministry directorates of academic services, secondary education, and higher education. The director of higher education was also rector of the University of Madagascar in Tananarive. General policy for higher education was placed in the special charge of the National Foundation of Higher Education (Fondation Nationale de l'Enseignement Supérieur), over which the president of the republic directly presided. Ministerial reorganization in 1968 resulted in the establishment of an educational unit to analyze educational operations at all levels. An interministerial committee also was created that, along with such bodies as the Employment-Training Committee, sought to closely coordinate the educational activities of all ministries and departments. The multiplicity of government programs and agencies engaged in educational activities seemed overly complex, and the effectiveness of the system and its coordination could not be readily determined.

Because budgetary expenditures were split among separate ministries and local funds were channeled into primary education, the precise amount allocated to education was difficult to determine. In 1971 the total public expenditure for education was estimated at about the equivalent of US$31.3 million. This represented roughly 18.2 percent of the total estimated budget, as compared to an average of about 16.5 percent during the late 1960s. Comparative figures for the percentage of gross domestic product (GDP) devoted to education were not available, but provisional estimates for 1970 would indicate that it represented about 3.1 percent, as compared to 4.2 percent in 1967.

Budgetary considerations had limited the development of public preschool education, which in 1972 was offered only by private institutions. The most recent statistics available indicated that in the mid-1960s about 8,400 children between the ages of three and six were enrolled in preschool programs at fifty-two private institutions.

The education decree of September 25, 1964, outlined the provisions under which preschool programs were to be regulated. Supervision was carried out by provincial educational services under the directives of the Ministry of Cultural Affairs, which was concerned mainly with the qualification of professional staff members, with hygiene, and with the age of children in attendance.

The government actively sought aid for its educational program from a variety of international organizations. School lunch programs had been aided by the United Nations Children's Fund (UNICEF) and several projects operated in cooperation with the United Nations Educational, Scientific and Cultural Organization (UNESCO). Technical literary projects were supported by the UNDP. A major channel of aid was provided by the French through the Aid and Cooperation Fund (Fonds d'Aide et Coopération).

The national government was an active member of the University Association for the Development of Teaching and Culture in Africa and Madagascar (Association Universitaire pour le Développement de l'Enseignement et de la Culture en Afrique et a Madagascar). which since 1960 had sponsored a biannual conference of national education ministers of French-speaking African countries. The first meeting each year has been in Africa and the second in France. In February 1972 the conference was held in Tananarive.

Primary Education

In 1972 primary education lasted for six years and was divided into three ascending levels, each of which lasted two years: a preparatory course (cours préparatoire); an elementary course (cours élémentaire); and a middle class (cours moyen). Most children entered primary school at the age of six. Despite variations among public and private schools and among schools in different regions, the major emphasis in all curricula was on reading, writing, mathematics, history, and geography. Technical and applied instruction was increasing. Upon completion of primary education, students were awarded an elementary school certificate (certificat d'études primaires élementaires).

In 1970 about 882,000 students were enrolled in primary schools, and projections indicated that by 1972 enrollment may have exceeded 1 million children. About 50 percent of all children between the ages of six and twelve were attending school, but figures for urban and rural areas were quite disparate. The enrollment percentage had remained relatively constant since the mid-1960s, the effects of the expansion of educational facilities having been offset by population increases (see ch. 3).

Among the many factors affecting the inability of the system to increase the percentage of enrollment of eligible school-age children, was the fact that the costs of educational expansion on the primary level, including building costs and teachers' salaries, was supported largely by local budgets. In most cases, the budgets were smallest where the need for expansion was greatest. The quality of primary education, moreover, varied widely. Most classrooms had more than eighty students, and some were as large as 150. Half-time classes were common in remote rural schools.

Secondary Education

Students who successfully passed the primary grade-six entrance examination could directly enter a secondary school to pursue academic, technical, or teacher training programs. Most of them entered at the age of twelve. Most secondary schools offered two academic programs. The *enseignement court* (short cycle) consisted of a four-year program, progressing from class six to class three. The longer academic program, *enseignement long* (long cycle), required an additional three years and included class two, class one, and a terminal year. Different branches of classic and modern coursework were structured according to difficulty. Each offered various curricula, in which were included foreign languages, philosophy, literature, history, geography, mathematics, the arts, physical sciences, physical education, and technical subjects. Upon completion of the four-year *enseignement court*, a student received a *brevet élementaire* (elementary certificate). Those enrolled in the *enseignement long* program received a *brevet d'études de premier cycle* (first cycle certificate) before continuing to the secondary cycle. Both certificates gave the holder access to lower level civil service positions. Upon completion of the first two years of the second cycle a student took a qualifying examination and, upon completion of the terminal class, a *baccalauréat* (diploma) was awarded.

Estimates of the number of students enrolled in secondary schools in 1970 varied between 55,000 and 67,000. About 35 percent of all secondary students attended public schools, and roughly 40 percent of the total were girls. Enrollment was largest at the lower level of class six, and only a third of those students presenting themselves for the 1970 *brevet d'études de premier cycle* examination were successful. Curriculum evaluation to match both the preparation and examination processes to the needs of Malagasy society was underway, and programs offering increased training to teachers were being stressed.

Higher Education

Although the University of Madagascar in Tananarive represented the major facility offering advanced education in 1972, programs of higher learning were also provided by other facilities, such as the Institute of Judicial Studies, the National Institute of Telecommunications and Postal Services, the Radioisotope

Laboratory, and the National Institute of Advanced Research and Teacher Training. Administrative responsibility for all advanced programs was the responsibility of the Charles de Gaulle National Foundation of Higher Education.

Although various institutes originating in the late nineteenth century offered specialized training, the first coordination of higher education programs was initiated in 1955. Certification was extended through the University of Aix-Marseille. Under the terms of the Franco-Malagasy Cooperation Agreement on Higher Education of June 27, 1960, the University of Madagascar was established, and its degrees and diplomas were given equivalence in France to similar French certification. A building program costing an amount equivalent to about US$12 million was begun in 1963 in the suburbs of Tananarive and had been completed by 1970, with the exception of some faculty housing, science facilities, and services.

The university was divided into three faculties: law and economic studies; the sciences; and letters and human sciences. All three offered four-year undergraduate programs leading to a bachelor's degree and graduate programs leading to a doctorate. The National Medical School offered a doctor of medicine degree to graduates, and a variety of certificates were provided by the nine other institutes and schools associated with the university. In addition to on-campus study, some institutes offered programs of study through correspondence.

A total of about 5,650 students were enrolled in university programs in the 1971 / 72 school year; an estimated 25 percent of those enrolled were female. The largest enrollments were, respectively, in the Faculty of Law and Economic Studies; the Faculty of Sciences; the Institute of Applied Linguistics; and the Faculty of Letters and Human Sciences. The remaining institutes provided about 22 percent of the total enrollment; the National Higher School of Agronomy, for example, had fourteen students. The major increase in university enrollment occurred between school years 1969 / 70 and 1970 / 71, when figures rose from about 3,880 to 5,290—an increase of about 40 percent.

Vocational Training

In 1972 vocational training programs in more than forty specializations were available to Malagasy who had a primary school education. The most popular course provided training in housecrafts or for employment as general mechanics, automobile mechanics, electricians, carpenters, and printers. Basic courses of three or four years' duration led to the award of professional certificates. Four-year programs in technical colleges brought graduates the equivalent of a secondary school diploma. Five institutes offered seven-year technical training courses. There were about 2,600 students enrolled in technical colleges in 1970, and the total number of students in all technical programs may have numbered 8,000.

Technical education faced numerous problems. Privately operated training programs existed outside the structure of the public institutes, and the programs offered by the two sources were not always coordinated. In the early 1970s at least half of the sixteen technical educational colleges were housed in facilities dating from before World War II. Although the number of technical-school teachers had increased, almost 50 percent of the tools and machinery used in the training was more than forty years old.

Teacher Training

There were numerous teacher training programs; many were experimental or were undergoing modification. Some students passed from primary education directly into teacher training programs; others continued into secondary schools before specializing in education. By attending a teacher training school for one year, students who had completed four years of secondary school were able to obtain a certificate entitling them to teach in primary schools. Students entering teacher training programs directly from primary school were also able to obtain a teaching certificate after completing a five-year residence program.

Various factors, including low salaries after graduation, made it difficult to encourage students to enter teacher training programs. Teacher shortages consequently existed on almost every level of the school system. In view of the major shortage of primary teachers, secondary students had been encouraged for some time to transfer to teacher training schools before completing the work required for a *brevet élémentaire*. By 1971, however, this policy had been discontinued.

Holders of certificates from secondary or technical schools were able to obtain specialized certificate as teachers after completing a year of training at special institutes. Preparation for teaching at secondary and higher levels was provided by the National Institute of Advanced Research and Teacher Training. The various teaching certificates available to graduates recognized such practical factors as inservice training and professional experience as well as the scope of the individual's classroom study and his institutional certification.

Recent Educational Innovations

Curriculum and syllabus modification began shortly after independence in a progressive effort to end the rigid separation between technical and academic preparation instituted under the French. Malagsy was adopted as the language of instruction in all primary schools, and in 1967 it became a compulsory examination subject for all Malagasy students. In the same year new history and geography syllabuses were introduced on the secondary level.

During the late 1960s various experimental programs were initiated; many of these were implemented only on a regional basis. Information was generally lacking in late 1972 regarding the success of most of these experiments or their likely adoption on a national basis.

The most publicized proposals for curriculum modification for primary and secondary education emphasized technology. Based on preliminary experiments, the new proposals were designed to open the minds of Malagasy youth to the reality of the modern world by introducing technology, not as an additional discipline but in terms of its relationship to the student and his environment. Specific modifications outlined the introduction of new technology training programs on the secondary level and increased emphasis on practical living at the primary level.

Especially in primary education, the method of classroom instruction adopted during the 1960s placed greatest emphasis on firm relations between the subject matter and the students' environment. The use of school gardens, for example, provided students with practical knowledge about their environment and served as a means of teaching related subjects, such as nutrition and mathematics. Modern mathematical instruction techniques, as opposed to former rote memorization of mathematical tables, were being introduced but were limited by the necessity of teacher retraining. The direct method of language instruction, essentially avoiding intermediate translations by the instructor, had been adopted on the primary level for teaching French. The use of audiovisual aids was on the increase. Because of budgetary considerations, the flannelgraph was the most widely used teaching aid on the primary level—especially in rural areas—but slides and films were being used increasingly. By the end of the 1960s textbook revisions had been initiated, and an educational equipment center had been established to supply teaching equipment for science classes.

In addition to standard classroom instruction, various auxiliary educational programs were in operation. The Malagasy Union, an organization interested in promoting artistic and cultural expression in a secular context, offered a cultural training program for schoolteachers. Physical, moral, and social retraining of juvenile delinquents was offered by the Malagasy Education League under the auspices of the Ministry of Cultural Affairs. The Malagasy National Broadcasting Company (Radiodiffusion Nationale Malgache—RNM) offered periodic broadcasts in civic education and promoted parental understanding of educational development.

A special educational series was begun in 1961 by RNM in cooperation with the National Foundation of Higher Education. Expanded during the 1960s, this series has become known as Radio Université. In 1972 mediumwave and shortwave broadcasts of one and four kilowatts, respectively, were operated by univeristy personnel for nearly four hours on weekdays and for seven hours on Sundays throughout the school year, excluding holidays. Instruction was offered for various levels, but major emphasis was given to higher education and to the training of schoolteachers.

Students as a Political Force

The educational systems that were established under the Merina monarchy and continued under the French rule were regarded as means to administrative jobs for Malagasy graduates. Because an education was available mainly to the Merina, it served to widen social disparities between them and the côtiers. As dissatisfaction with social and political inequalities increased, educational policy assumed political significance, and organized student movements became increasingly important.

The first lasting student organization was the Association of Students of Malagasy Origin (Association des Etudiants d'Origine Malgache—AEOM). Composed largely of young people from affluent Merina families, it was organized in Paris in 1934. Until after World War II its major concern, with the exception of a limited interest in educational reform, was cultural. After the anti-French revolt of 1947, AEOM was transformed into a political organization and assumed the position of overseas spokesman for Malagasy nationalism (see ch. 2).

The affluent Merina membership of AEOM was altered after the war as a result of the increased numbers of middle class Malagasy studying abroad. In 1949, however, only nine of its members— including Philibert Tsiranana, who was to become president—were non-Merina côtiers. The interest of these nine in the advancement of their own peoples more than in the issue of independence led them to form the Association of Coastal Malagasy Students (Amicale des Etudiants Malgaches Côtiers), which later broke completely from AEOM and formed the Malagasy Student Union (Union des Etudiants Malgaches—UEM). Increasingly, UEM interests identified with the policy of the Social Democratic Party (Parti Social Démocratique—PSD), founded in the early 1950s by Philibert Tsiranana (see ch. 9).

After the mid-1950s AEOM membership increased rapidly, and its political orientation became increasingly leftist. It had developed close relations with the French Communist Party and the International Students' Union, both of which aided Malagasy student travel and study in the Soviet Union and countries of Eastern Europe. AEOM continued to press for Malagasy independence and amnesty for political prisoners while it denounced capitalist and colonialist exploitation. PSD concern about the influence that these leftist students had after their return to Madagascar continued after independence; it led to the support of advanced educational facilities at home and to a decrease in financial support for study abroad.

With the coming of independence, the location of organized student protests became domestic. A variety of student associations were established during the 1960s under the coordination of the Federation of Malagasy Student Associations (Fédération des Associations d'Etudiants de Madagascar—FAEM). During the late 1960s student dissatisfaction increased. Protests attacked curriculum structure, examination phasing, lack of employment opportunities, insufficient student participation in educational planning, scholarships, and admission policies. Despite reform attempts dissatisfaction increased, and communications between the government and student organizations became increasingly ineffective.

Student and faculty dissatisfaction with university education increased markedly during 1972. In January 1972 students at the Befelatanana School of Medicine went on strike and called for a reform of the medical school curriculum and admissions policy. Negotiations between the government and the Association of Medical and Pharmaceutical Students (Association d'Etudiants de Médecine et Pharmacie—AEMP) broke down in late April, and the cabinet called for the dissolution of the AEMP. The AEMP was joined in protest by student organizations throughout the country, the Union of Malagasy Public School Teachers, and organized labor.

In February the University Teachers and Researchers Union (Syndicat des Enseignants et Chercheurs de l'Enseignement Supérieur—SECES) had sponsored a week-long seminar that included students and university personnel as well as faculty members. The session focused on adapting the university programs to the needs of the country and called for increased democratization and wider use of Malagasy faculty and staff personnel. Specific recommendations included: the use of Malagasy as the language of instruction in all disciplines; increased participation by students and assistants in university planning; more professional and technical training institutes; and administration reorganization that would reduce the size of the individual colleges of the university.

Although the government received these recommendations, concern about the likelihood of their implementation was one of the factors contributing to civic unrest, to the declaration of a state of national emergency, and to the transfer of executive powers to the army chief of staff in May 1972 (see ch. 9; ch. 14). The new prime minister, General Gabriel Ramanantsoa, announced in July 1972 his government's intention to revolutionize the educational system, which he termed responsible for longstanding economic and social imbalances within Malagasy society. Immediate attention was given to plans for reducing the number of university dropouts and increasing employment opportunities for graduates.

ARTISTIC EXPRESSION AND SOCIETY

Traditionally, artistic expression has been judged by the Malagasy both in terms of the fulfillment of tasks regarded as essential to the survival of particular social groups and on the basis of each form's aesthetic merits. Thus, although recitations of oral literature provide a measure of entertainment—particularly in coastal areas—their more fundamental purpose often is to establish guidelines for social action for both children and adults and to facilitate the transmission of myths and sacred beliefs. Some plastic and graphic art forms, the value of which may be defined mainly in aesthetic terms, have evolved. Utilitarian items, however, such as food and water containers or ritual objects to which decoration has been added, are seen more often. In the performing arts, group participation rather than individual performance is the pattern.

Except for songs and chants related to work and the celebration of certain holidays, group gatherings for song and dance occur mainly in the evening after the completion of daily tasks. Songs and dances are frequently related to religious occasions or to seasonal events, such as crop planting and harvesting. Some are associated with events in the life cycle of group members: birth, puberty, marriage, and death. Similar celebrations are often used to repay social debts or to demonstrate social position or wealth (see ch. 5).

The social status of those engaged in cultural expression varies in several ways. Specialists in oral recitation and those who are literate are generally held in high esteem. Among the educated urban portion of the population, the composition of literary works is a symbol of prestige. On the other hand, traditional musicians can seldom support themselves solely by their performances, and they must supplement their income through such work as carpentry or by begging. Although the popularity of entertainers in urban areas has modified the status of the performer, musicians traditionally have held low status; and in many cases they are subjected to socioreligious restrictions, including dress and housing. Strict rules exist for the performance of various ceremonies, but the special role played by musicians, especially popular entertainers, allows them some flexibility in adherence to social standards.

Although the majority of residents outside the Central Highlands participate in traditional culture, since the end of the nineteenth century a small, highly educated urban elite has enjoyed and participated in forms of Western cultural expression. Literary expression is particularly popular among this group, and a diverse body of literary forms in both Malagasy and French has evolved. Although at times urban elite cultural expression seemed to be cut off from the traditional indigenous culture, it was demonstrating an increasing interest in the heritage of traditional forms.

Observable changes in Malagasy artistic forms and themes, providing a useful index of social change, can be observed most readily in literary movements within the country. One of the first reflections of growing national identity among the educated elite during the late nineteenth century and of the call for self-government in the twentieth century were poems, essays, and short stories. Dramatic productions have also served this function. Since World War II the lyrics of popular songs have become a major form of popular culture and a means of social and political protest among both literate and illiterate; one of the more current social themes of popular music has been the advancement of Malagasy rather than French as the national language. The search for a new sense of nationality has also become evident in the graphic arts.

LITERARY TRADITIONS

Although written texts existed in the south, until the nineteenth century oral literary traditions were the most pervasive. Oral forms of legendary histories, sacred myths, rituals, folktales, scenes from family life, riddles, and children's stories vary in length and seriousness. Some have a moral message; others are comic. Proverbs passed in conversation were a common literary tradition, and appropriate sayings existed for almost every phase of life. Oral forms often were sung or recited with rhythmic accompaniment.

Oral literary forms were not always rigidly memorized, and there has been considerable flexibility and variation in their development. The same tale may be told differently from village to village, but common themes often cross ethnic boundaries. Some variations were developed to serve particular social needs and were later incorporated into the larger literary tradition of specific peoples. Several ethnic groups possess legendary serials or cycles detailing the exploits of one individual or a common problem.

Many of the traditional tales and legends resemble portions of the legendary cycles of Arab, Indian, Indonesian, and Chinese mythology. The lengendary cycle of Tandrokomana of the Sakalava, each episode of which teaches a basic moral, unmistakably resembles the Malaysian Bangswan Legend, itself adapted from Hindu mythology. Authorities disagree on the extent to which some of these themes were developed independently by the Malagasy after their arrival on the island and on the extent of literary transfer and cultural assimilation that resulted from early migrations and trade.

Early contact with Arab traders did expose the Malagasy to Arabic script, which they modified and adapted to their own language. How far this form of written Malagasy spread is uncertain, but by the sixteenth century a scribe aristocracy was well established among the Antaimoro and some of their neighbors, and both ink and paper were being manufactured locally. Sacred manuscripts called *sorabe* (great writings) included myths explaining the origins of several southeastern ethnic groups and works on medicine, divination, and astrology. These works are not believed to be original but rather translations of earlier Arabic treatises. Antaimoro scribes traveled to the courts of other ethnic groups and provided such services as land and genealogical registration.

By 1800 *sorabe* were in use at the Merina court, there is evidence that a small class or school may have been in operation under the direction of Antaimoro scribes. In 1820, however, two British missionaries aided by a Frenchman produced a version of Roman script for Malagasy that rapidly replaced *sorabe*. By 1866 literacy in Malagasy was reflected in the codification of Merina social legislation and the existence of Malagasy language periodicals. The most extensive history of the Merina—*Tantaran'ny Adriana eto Imerina*, written by Father Callet— and the first indigenous scholarship on Malagasy history and culture—*Tantara sy fombandrazana*, written by a minister of the Merina government, Rainandriandriamampandry—appeared shortly afterward.

Although Malagasy authors were quick to show an interest in a variety of written literary forms, the most striking developments were in the field of poetry. Until the early twentieth century most poets wrote in Malagasy, but by World War I French was becoming increasingly popular. The mission education of these poets was apparent in their frequent use of Biblical references. Their works possessed an exciting, lyrical quality, and their search for an expanded, precise vocabulary served to enrich the Malagasy language as a whole.

The first Malagasy poet to publish in French was Jean-Joseph Ravearivelo. The thirteen prolific years following his first publication in 1924 became increasingly melancholy, and in 1937 he committed suicide. *La coupe de cendres* (Cup of Ashes), *Chants pour Abéone* (Songs for Abéone), and *Traduit de la nuit* (Night Translation) are some of the works that place him at the forefront of all Malagasy poets. The foremost contemporary poet in the early 1970s was Jacques Rabemananjara, who had served as foreign minister and vice president under the Tsiranana administration. He was also known for his plays, essays, and other works. Other French-language poets included Regis Raolison Rajenmisa, Elie-Charles Abraham, and Richard Raherivelo. Representing an increasing interest in traditional roots were the Malagasy-language poems of Dox Razakandraina.

Although adaptations of Western plays have been performed on occasion and numerous Malagasy authors have written plays—most of which have never been published—theater in the Western tradition has not been an established Malagasy art form. The closest traditional approximation was the group chant. During the first half of the twentieth century folk theater evolved from the chant form and from a blending of legends, songs, and dances. Most folk theater has little unity of plot. Idealistic and romantic themes set in an historical context were most common. In the late 1960s folk theater was being performed by about twenty theatrical troupes who were either resident in the Tananarive area or touring nearby communities. Reformist efforts were underway to remove chants and long poetic narrations, to create plot unity, and to introduce realism and relevance into theatrical productions. The development of a modern dramatic form, however, continued to be restricted by the limited physical facilities available.

MUSIC AND DANCE

Music plays an integral part in all Malagasy entertainment and ceremony. The popularity of music as a medium of cultural expression is increasingly displacing the preeminent position held formerly by literary art forms. Instrumental music has served traditionally as an accompaniment to songs, hymns, recitations, or dances; the introduction of radio broadcasting, however, has increased the independent performance of instrumental music (see ch. 11). Traditional Malagasy music has origins that many authorities attribute to Asia, but indigenous and highly original local developments have been added.

Common musical instruments include a variety of drums and stringed instruments such as the *valiha*, a harp-like instrument formed by stretching strings across a curved piece of bamboo. Although these instruments have oriental prototypes, they have been modified considerably, and the degree of foreign contribution to their development is open to debate. Other traditional instruments include flutes, believed to have been introduced by Arab traders, and several kinds of xylophones that seem to have African origins. Since the early nineteenth century Western instruments, such as trumpets, clarinets, accordions, and harmoniums, have been introduced.

Malagasy songs vary in form and mood. Most traditional ceremonial songs incorporate a scale of only five notes and are melancholic. Sentimental love songs that have beautiful melodies are also popular. Many songs have incorporated the melodies and harmonies of Protestant hymns, Creole dances introduced from Réunion, and—most recently—twentieth-century Western dance music. Comic songs having complex plays on words and mocking songs exchanged between two groups are also common in traditional music.

Music is sometimes performed by community groups, but most frequently small professional and semiprofessional groups are engaged. A typical group consists of six to fifteen players of either sex. Some of the men play instruments to accompany the singing and dancing of the others. A leader begins with a lively oratory, the mood of which is designed to fit the occasion. After a musical introduction, the singers join in, frequently dancing at the same time. The dances have measured steps similar to forms popular in eighteenth-century Europe. Harmonic developments are complex and often incorporate descants and minor thirds. Skillful adaptations of traditional forms and themes, performed by professional groups such as the Ny Antasly Trio, were well received abroad in the 1950s and 1960s.

Traditional dances vary considerably in form and purpose. Solo dances are seldom performed, even by the very young, and most dances involve a group of several people. Men and women usually do not dance together as couples but are divided into separate, well-defined groups. Dances are characterized by precise hand and leg movements and graceful patterns of motion. They are almost always performed out-of-doors, frequently as part of an evening of competitive events sponsored by neighboring villages.

THE VISUAL ARTS

The visual arts include both graphic and plastic forms, most of which have ritual or practical functions. Two general decorative approaches have evolved. In the Central Highlands geometric motifs are popular, whereas three-dimensional human and animal forms are more common in coastal art. Internal migrations, however, have eroded this basic distinction to some degree, and interesting combinations of the two approaches are often seen.

Painting as an art form was first introduced in the early 1800s during the reign of Radama I, when Malagasy artisans were trained to execute frescoes for the Silver Palace in Tananarive. The paintings depicted military scenes and parades and were executed in primitive style. Indigenous experimentation followed. Oil paint was used on wood, matting, and ticking. Varying intensities of gray, green, and ochre were the hues mainly used in these works. Three-dimensional effects were sometimes achieved by attaching wood and vegetable fibers to the surface of the painting. Landscapes were popular subjects. Bright watercolors depicting scenes from everyday life were also executed. Few of these works reflected international trends and developments.

During the 1920s painters became much more aware of artistic developments abroad. The color range for oil painting expanded, and compositions became more dynamic. Some artists attempted to abandon local traditions and imitate French styles, but as a result much of their work was without merit. Since World War II styles have become more flexible, experimental, and abstract, and artists have tended to return to traditional subjects as a source of inspiration. Increasingly refined techniques have brought international recognition. Etchings and woodcuts have also increased in popularity.

Although diverse traditions of sculpture exist, the most pervasive and fully developed forms are seen in Malagasy woodcarvings. The rigors of a tropical climate, however, have left few examples that date before the nineteenth century. Major examples of prehistoric stone sculpture include a near half-scale sized elephant found at the mouth of the Mananjary River and a ritual guardian figure presently placed in the cemetery of the royal family in Tananarive. Although small stone fertility charms and human figures have been found, molded artifacts of terra cotta are far more common. The only major tradition of stone carving comparable to the scale of the Mananjary elephant were stelae carved in the nineteenth century. They were engraved with representations of human beings or carved to achieve varying degrees of three-dimensionalism. The majority are representations of a Vikinankarata chief and are located in the Central Highlands to the southwest of Tananarive.

The major traditions of wood sculpture include elaborately carved tomb stelae, small ritual figures, children's toys (also modeled in terra cotta), and relief carving on wood panels or on craft items. Pyroengraving on gourds and charred-wood-chiseling are used by certain groups to obtain interesting two-color designs. Straight- and broken-line patterns are more common than those with curved lines, and open spaces are often filled with stippling. Small, highly realistic human figures are carved by the Mahafaly. Some express emotion, which is usually lacking in traditional carving; more recently executed examples are dressed with cloth garments. Realistic animal figures, including spiders and insects and painted in natural colors, were carved as a hobby during the first half of the twentieth century. Various wood figures are still being produced for sale to tourists.

The most advanced sculptural form in terms of size and complexity is the tomb stela, which ranges from six to fifteen feet in height. The more complex of these stake-like monuments have elaborately carved middle sections of several feet in length surmounted by a realistic human figure; more recently, representations of some important event in the life of the deceased person or some quality for which he is remembered have substituted as terminations. The erection of these stelae is still common, and their survival marks them as the most enduring traditional visual art form.

CRAFTS

Archaeological excavations have revealed a long-established tradition of pottery manufacture, using techniques believed to have been introduced from India several hundred years ago. Among people living near Lake Alaotra and some other groups the application of graphite to wet clay before it was baked by the sun created a shiny, black pseudoglaze. Some groups decorated their work with simple geometric designs or topped them with finials shaped like animals. Pots were sometimes mounted on legs and fitted with covers.

Although decorated pottery was still being produced by some Tsimihety, Vezo, Merina, and Betsileo potters, most ceramic work was utilitarian and did not display traditional refinements. A few potters had been trained professionally at educational facilities, and their work had been well received at international exhibitions as early as the 1930s. The manufacture of ceramic tiles depicting traditional scenes, many of which were used for the tops of wrought iron tables, and smll pottery figurines represented a healthy local craft industry in 1972.

Throughout the country baskets are manufactured and used as food containers, cradles, sun shades, and animal cages. Woven mats are used as building material and as sleeping mats. Loom weaving is widespread, but weavers in the Betsileo region—especially women— have the highest reputation for their finely woven silks. Brightly colored cloth is used as a draped garment called *lamba* or as a burial shroud (see ch. 6). Originally, vegetable dyes were used to yield solid colors and patterns, but in modern times most weavers use analine dyes. Imported fabrics are becoming increasingly competitive.

Metal working, believed to have been introduced originally by Asian migrants, includes utilitarian objects, such as wrought iron lamps, as well as delicate filigree. Pendants, clasps, knife handles, combs, and small animals are popular items. The most common metals are silver and copper, obtained by melting down old coins, gun cartridges, or telegraph wire. Gold is a highly popular material for filigree jewelry, but until recently its use had been forbidden by the government.

Rapidly disappearing, even among the coastal peoples, was *tombokalana* or tattooing, which was still popular among some highland peoples during the 1930s. Introduced from Africa as early as the tenth century, the most highly developed use of the tattoo was among the Makoa and among some Antanosy women. Patterns with artistic qualities as well as ritual symbolism sometimes covered major portions of an individual's body.

Several crafts represent adaptations of European techniques introduced during the nineteenth century. Embroidery and lacemaking, first introduced by missionaries, are still popular among older women. Both feature unique indigenous designs based on local flora and fauna; dragonflies and butterflies are especially popular and are intricately executed. Fine cabinetry, veneering, and inlay work has also developed. Nineteenth-century craftsmen produced interesting pieces of furniture, especially beds, chairs, and sofas, which combined French, English, and indigenous styles.

By 1972 the manufacture of traditional handicraft items had been disrupted by changes in the country's economic and social structure. Certain objects had lost their former sacred meanings, and there was less time to produce time-consuming secular handicrafts. Many traditional items had thus been displaced by the introduction of new methods and products. Pottery and baskets had been replaced by tin and plastic items. Handmade clothing and shoes were being replaced by readymade items that were manufactured locally or were imported. Some crafts, however, had been improved by the introduction of new techniques. Mohair rugs and decorative paper sheets into which dried flowers had been pressed had become popular export items. Other craft industries, such as woodcarving, were also aiming at commercial outlets.

ARCHITECTURE

Diverse architectural styles reflect varying environmental needs, ethnic backgrounds, and historical traditions. Stone ruins that are believed to have been built by Arab or Portuguese traders are seen in coastal areas, and stone sepulchers built by indigenous people are found throughout the island. Although thorough excavations have been undertaken at several locations, precise conclusions based on the diggings are complicated by repeated reconstruction of these tombs and their continued reuse for burials (see ch. 5).

Except among some southern and southeastern peoples, tombs either are enclosed by a low wall or set into low stone platforms. The placement of the casket holding the body, as well as its size and construction, varies; exhumation of the body and its subsequent reburial are common. The tomb is sometimes embellished with decorations to which color or whitewash is applied; those of the Mahafaly in the southern region are covered with syncretic religious symbols. Some tombs cover large areas. The nineteeth-century tombs of one Tananarive family have arched galleries and arcades supported by granite column; those of the royal family in Tananarive are surmounted by wooden structures several stories high. Most tombs are flat platforms into which intricately carved stakes, zebu horns, or small stone monoliths have been embedded. Many ancient tombs are still used, and newly constructed burial sites frequently follow traditional forms. Concrete, however, is replacing stone as a building material.

Traditional dwelling structures are usually rectangular and are built of wood and woven vegetable fibers. Many are placed on wooden pillars or posts, and roofs are characteristically two-sided, with high-pitched gables. Roofing material is usually thatch, but during the nineteenth century wooden shingles were introduced. Walls are frequently made of woven matting, but the Bara use a board and batten technique. The same construction is also used in a few homes belonging to the elite of other ethnic groups (see ch. 6). Some groups terminate eaves posts with zebu horns or finials shaped like animals.

During the eighteenth and early nineteenth centuries Merina nobles built fortifications and homes of laterite blocks cut from deposits of earth having a hard, brick-like consistency. Ruins of many of these structures remain, and some are intact or provide the foundations and main walls of more recently built structures. The original roofs were of thatch, but wooden shingles or tin sheets top many of those examples still in use. The buildings were often narrow and had several stories, which gave them a tower-like appearance. They were often connected to outbuildings by walls made of the same cut blocks; gardens and small fields were sometimes similarly protected.

During the last half of the nineteenth century the introduction of European architectural forms modified traditional techniques and styles of construction. Hip roofs, glass windows, louvred shutters, and wooden and wrought iron balconies gave urban centers the atmosphere of a small town in the south of France. The importation of European styles was not wholesale, however, and in many cases interesting combinations resulted. Victorian gingerbread tracery and traditional decorative designs were interchanged and used to ornament doors, window headings, eaves, and railings. Most construction was in wood and was limited to a few stories. One of the finest examples of the period, however, was the stone facade built around an earlier wooden structure for the Merina queen in Tananarive. The style mixed classical Italian and Second Empire French periods. At the corner were offset square towers, one of which housed a clock, connected by arched galleries. The structure was topped by a mansard roof and was surrounded by formal, landscaped gardens and a reflecting pool. The palace was maintained by the state and remained a major tourist attraction in 1972.

Architectural styles during the twentieth century followed developments in metropolitan France. The greatest advances came after World War II and especially after independence, when major building booms occurred. Reinforced concrete, glass, modular panel construction, and sculpturally designed facades had been introduced. The best examples were public buildings, including communication and education facilities, office buildings and, to a lesser degree, some hotels and private homes.

SCIENTIFIC RESEARCH

An indigenous tradition of scientific research concerning Madagascar was stimulated initially by scholarly European studies dating back to the first Western contacts with the island (see ch. 2). It has continued into modern times. Until well into the twentieth century European scientists dominated research efforts in the natural and social sciences, and the educated Malagasy concentrated in the fields of literature and history. The emergence after World War II of two generations of diversely specialized Malagasy scholars had considerably increased Malagasy participation in research activity, especially in education and in the social sciences as a whole.

During the last half of the nineteenth century British and French scholars competed for leadership in the scientific study of the area. In 1864 Alfred Grandidier initiated an important study of the island's geography and a compilation of bibliographic information that, later carried on by his son, was to represent almost a century of research regarding Madagascar. About the same time French Jesuits established an observatory near Tananarive, where astronomical and meteorological research continues. English efforts were led by the missionary and naturalist James Sibree, who in 1875 founded the *Antananarivo Annual.* This periodical, published until 1900, was the first to be devoted to the scientific study of the island and contained numerous scholarly articles that are still highly valued.

Although the Merina monarchy had encouraged various research projects in the nineteenth century, the assumption of administrative authority by the French in 1896 under General Joseph Gallieni brought not only increased government support for research but also organizations and institutionalized methods for its collection and publication. Three organizations provided the major support for government-supported research. The Committee of Madagascar (Comité de Madagascar), established in the mid-1890s, published a journal known as the *Revue de Madagascar* between 1899 and 1911 and another, the *Bulletin Economique de Madagascar,* from 1901 to 1939. The Malagasy Academy (Académie Malgache), founded in 1902, had published over 160 articles on the natural and social sciences and continued to play a major role in scholarly research in the country in 1972. The Pasteur Institute (Institut Pasteur), also founded in the early 1900s, remained the major medical research facility in the country in 1972. In 1935 two French scientists at this institute developed a vaccine that is still used throughout the world to control bubonic plague.

Interest in the geographical survey of the island after World War I led to the establishment in 1926 of the Geological Service (Service

Géologique). The service has published a variety of reports and periodicals, which include *Travaux du Bureau Géologique, Annales Géologiques*, and *Documentation du Service Géologique*. The world has been aided since 1945 by research and educational opportunities provided by the National Geographical Institute of Madagascar (Institut Géographique National de Madagascar).

In the interest of coordinating research operations, the Scientific and Economic Studies Committee (Comité d'Etudes Scientifiques et Economiques) was founded in 1937 under the direction of the Museum of Natural History in Paris. It was replaced by the Scientific Research Service (Service de Recherche Scientifique), whose functions were in turn assumed in 1946 by the Institute of Scientific Research in Madagascar (Institut de Recherches Scientifiques au Madagascar—IRSM). For about ten years IRSM devoted its efforts to pure and applied research, emphasizing studies of Malagasy soils, flora, and fauna. Numerous monographs and two major demographic studies were produced during its ten-year existence. In 1957 IRSM was incorporated as a territorial committee of the French Office of Scientific and Technical Research Overseas (Office de la Recherche Scientifique et Technique Outre-Mer—ORSTOM). In 1972 two ORSTOM centers were maintained in the republic. The Nosy Be center specialized in oceanography, geology, and nutrition. Research at the Tananarive center included study in the fields of geology, hydrology, botany, agronomy, economics, sociology, and ethnology.

Coordinating responsbility for research activity was redirected in 1961 by the creation of the Interministerial Committee of Scientific and Technical Research (Comité Interministeriel de la Recherche Scientifique et Technique—CIRST). The interministerial membership of CIRST proved to be an encumbrance, however, and in 1963 it was reorganized as the Committee of Scientific and Technical Research (Comité de la Recherche Scientifique et Technique—CRST). Administrative authority for CRST was placed directly under the office of the vice president, aided by a special staff. In addition to budgetary and program planning, special interests of the committee included communication links between Malagasy research institutes and the exchange of information and technicians with foreign research organizations, particularly those of other African states. The committee directed Malagasy participation in various international programs operated by the specialized agencies of the United Nations, the Organization of African Unity, and the Common Organization of African and Malagasy States and Mauritius (Organisation Commune Africaine, Malgache, et Mauritien—OCAMM).

During the 1960s several new Malagasy research institutes were established, a number of which maintained affiliations with research institutes abroad. The Technical Tropical Forestry Center (Centre

Technique Forestier Tropical), created in 1961, functioned as a branch of the central organization of the same name in France. The same was true for the French Overseas Fruitgrowing Research Institute (Institut Français de Recherches Frutières d'Outre-Mer) and the District of Veterinary and Zootechnical Research of Madagascar (Région de Recherches Veterinaires et Zootechniques de Madagascar), which was directed by the French Institute of Tropical Countries Stockraising and Veterinary Medicine (Institut d'Elevage et de Médecine Veterinaire des Pays Tropicaux). Other research institutes in 1972 included the Office of Geological and Mineral Research (Bureau de Recherche Géologique et Minières), the Agronomy Research Institue (Institut de Recherches Agronomiques), and the Social Hygiene Institue (Institut d'Hygiène Sociale).

Research efforts since Madagascar's independence have been greatly aided by French subsidies. In addition to funds channeled through ORSTOM and grants for medical research to the Pasteur Institute, the seven major national research institutes have received aid under the Aid and Cooperation Fund (Fonds d'Aide et de Coopération—FAC). FAC had required equal matching of French funds by the Malagasy government, and program continuance had been subject to annual riders attached to the original agreement of August 5, 1960. Joint contributions during the 1960s reached about FMG6.2 billion (for value of the Malagasy franc—see Glossary). It was expected that similar cooperation would continue throught the 1970s.

LIBRARIES AND MUSEUMS

Although at independence the country possessed an established tradition of scholarly research, most public library facilities did not predate the late 1950s. In 1972 there were ten major libraries in the country. Most were administered by government ministries or agencies, and all but two were located in Tananarive. The 123,000-volume collection of the National Library (Bibliotheque Nationale) was the largest in the country. Although it was formally established in 1961, the main core of the original collection was provided by the library of the government-general, which was started in 1920. The library housed specialized collections in history, literature, the arts, the applied sciences, and information files on Madagascar. The Library of the University of Madagascar (Bibliothèque Universitaire), the second largest in the country, contained a collection of 85,000 volumes. The Archives and Document Service of the National Government (Service des Archives et de la Documentation) in Tananarive maintained about 2,500 volumes as well as an extensive collection of government documents dating to 1820.

Although preceded by government collections and small religious library holdings, the 42,900-volume collection of the Geological Service, founded in 1926, represented the oldest continuous public facility in the country. ORSTOM also maintained libraries at its centers in Nosy Be and Tananarive. A 13,630-volume collection with strong stress on belles lettres was maintained by the Albert Camus Cultural Center (Centre Culturel Albert Camus), founded in 1962. Tananarive also had a public library with 4,350 volumes and a library of about equal size operated by the United States Information Agency.

Antsirabe had a small municipal library, but facilities for other areas outside Tananarive were mostly limited to twenty-one small collections associated with various schools. The combined total number of books in these libraries was fewer than 30,000 volumes. Reading materials were available at local Malagasy information and cultural centers, but their limited collections were used mainly for entertainment. Teachers were able to borrow materials from various research and library facilities, but information detailing the operation and effectiveness of such loans was not readily available.

Both of the two major museums in 1972 were located in Tananarive. The Museum of Art and Archaeology (Musée d'Art et d'Archéologie) was affiliated with the University of Madagascar. It specialized in traditional and contemporary arts and crafts and in prehistoric artifacts. The History Museum (Musée Historique), located adjacent to the Queen's Palace, specialized in the history of the former Merina state. It also included other items relevant to the development of the Malagasy state during the nineteenth and twentieth centuries.

SECTION II. POLITICAL
CHAPTER 8
THE GOVERNMENTAL SYSTEM

Until mid-1972 the country had been governed according to a constitution that had been in effect with little change since 1958, when France granted the country self-governing status. The changes made at independence in 1960 were limited, if vital, serving only to place the last vestige of executive and legislative power in Malagasy hands (see ch. 2). A major political upheaval occurred in May and June 1972, but the effects this would have on the governmental system had not become clear by early fall (see ch. 9).

Until this time, the basic political structure had been formed in practice as outlined in the constitution. This provided for a parliamentary form of government in which the executive was responsible to Parliament while retaining the power to dissolve the legislature's more powerful lower house, the National Assembly. It also provided for judicial review of all legislation in order to ensure that all laws and all applications of law were in compliance with the constitution and with the basic civil rights guaranteed in its preamble. The governmental organization—like the constitution—reflected strong French influence, although in general it was well adapted to Malagasy sentiments regarding leadership, justice, and the relations between national and local interests.

During the first ten years of independence the extensive bill of rights provided by the preamble to the constitution had been consistently honored by the national government. By 1970, however, the guarantees of freedom of the press and of personal freedoms were frequently violated. There were increasing numbers of arbitrary arrests, detentions without trial, and harassments of the press. Yet even in these acts, the preeminence of the law was acknowledged, the government pleading that special circumstances existed to require action against its opponents.

The main criticism directed against the operations of the government resulted from a weakness apparently unforeseen by the constitution's drafters. Although ample protection was granted for minority political parties to operate, the electoral method had the effect of creating a winner-take-all system that effectively denied the opposition a voice (see ch. 9).

The first changes following the May 1972 riots were the steps taken by the president to create the new post of prime minister, who was to serve as head of government. The state of national emergency that was proclaimed on May 13, 1972, the suspension of Parliament, and the dismissal of governmental ministers were all in line with provisions of the constitution. All real power, however, now lay in the hands of the army general who had been appointed as prime minister. He subsequently convened a new cabinet and, with its concurrence, issued laws by decree. For the first few months no changes were made in the structure of government. In early September, however, the prime minister announced that he intended to hold a national referendum, the result of which would be to allow the government to make any changes to the governmental and political order that it deemed necessary.

CONSTITUTIONAL STRUCTURE OF GOVERNMENT

The constitution still in effect in mid-1972 had been drafted by the Representative Assembly and approved by the French parliament on April 29, 1959. The country's change of status from an autonomous unit of the French Community to a totally independent state had been effected by an amendment of June 28, 1960, which simply deleted all references in the document to ties with France and the French Community (see ch. 2). Further short amendments in 1962 had made the choice of the president dependent upon popular election and had lessened the powers of the upper house of Parliament and those of the provincial governments.

Responsibility for ensuring that laws and ordinances conform to the constitution rests with the High Council of Institutions (Conseil Supérieur des Institutions). The council is a special body that exists independently of the executive, legislative, and judicial branches of the national governmental structure.

The Executive

According to the constitution, the president serves as head of state and head of government. Until the introduction of a prime minister as head of government in May 1972, President Philibert Tsiranana had exercised authority in both roles since national independence.

The president is elected by direct universal suffrage for a seven-year term and may seek reelection. In these contests he must obtain an absolute majority of the votes cast; failing this, a second balloting must be held in which the winner need only obtain the largest number of votes. Although directly elected by the people, the president is responsible to Parliament for his actions throughout his elected term. In case the president is unable to perform his duties because of absence from the country, illness, resignation, impeachment, or death, the vice president shall succeed him temporarily. If the president's removal is permanent, the High Council of Institutions must declare the position vacant and call for new presidential elections.

Under the constitution, the duties assigned to the president are diverse and extensive, reflecting his dual role. He nominates certain members of the Senate (the upper house of Parliament) and the High Council of Institutions and the incumbents of high-ranking civil and military posts. He opens and closes parliamentary sessions and proclaims laws to the people. He may call for referendums, confer distinctions of state, appoint and receive ambassadors, and negotiate and sign treaties. Parliament, however, must approve treaties of alliance, of commerce, and of peace and treaties that modify existing legislation or alter national territory.

As chairman of the Council of Ministers, the president must approve and sign decrees and ordinances. He supervises the preparation of draft legislation to be presented to Parliament and calls for votes of confidence. He chooses the vice president and other members of the Council of Ministers, although they must be confirmed by Parliament. He also assigns their duties and removes them at will.

The president is responsible for national defense and is the commander in chief of both the armed forces and the National Gendarmerie. He has the power to declare a state of national emergency, after consulting the Council of Ministers and obtaining the agreement of the presidents of both the National Assembly and the Senate. Under this constitutional provision he may then conditionally suspend the functioning of the constitution and take any measures he deems necessary for the defense of the state against internal or external threats.

The Council of Ministers is composed of the president, the vice president, the senior ministers (ministers of state), the various other ministers, and the secretaries of state, who are subordinate to the ministers. The number of members was not fixed by law. When the council convenes without the president, it is referred to officially as the Cabinet of Ministers.

In the early 1970s the vice president filled a dual function, heading the Ministry of Labor and Social Affairs. Two ministers of state headed the ministries of interior and of foreign affairs, and the third served as the president's personal assistant or handled special problem areas in the government. For a short time all four of these officials were called vice presidents and, in a novel effort to lighten the presidential burden, the four chief assistants were given executive authority over large ministerial areas. There were usually about eight other ministers and up to eleven secretaries of state. In June 1972 one of the first acts of the newly appointed prime minister was to reduce the number of members of the cabinet to ten.

The organization of the government and of the cabinet has been altered a number of times; however, a typical structure would consist of about ten ministries plus several bodies attached to the presidency or office of the president. One common feature of all governments has been the lack of any element serving as a defense ministry. Defense matters have always been handled by small military and gendarmerie staffs in the presidency (see ch. 14).

Within this governmental structure, several bodies have a primarily political function; under the presidency there are a number of such offices. The General Secretariat of the Government serves as the staff of the Council of Ministers. This unit publishes the *Journal Officiel de la République Malgache*, the journal in which new laws and decrees are officially promulgated, and serves as the office of the government's general counsel or chief administrative legal officer. The adjacent offices of the inspector general of the state and the controller provide the government with fiscal and administrative auditing services, covering all national and local government units and the semigovernmental bodies. It also serves as a management analysis center.

The minister of state delegated to the presidency serves as the president's personal deputy. His duties have varied considerably; sometimes he has been given responsibility for the management of problem ministries.

The secretary of state for the civil service is responsible for directing the activities of all permanent or temporary employees of national and regional governmental organizations. His office establishes civil service policy, sets pay scales, and handles matters involving disciplinary procedure. In making decisions involving substantive policy he is required to consult with the Higher Council for the Civil Service, composed of appointed officials and civil servants. Lesser councils function at the provincial level and are concerned with specific groups of employees; all are under centralized control.

Regarding the ministries, the minister of state for the interior has two major areas of responsibility: the civil police and regional and local administration, each organized under separate ministerial directorates. Ministerial responsibility for the police is exercised through the National Security Directorate and extends to the control of the Republican Security Force but not to the National Gendarmerie, which is directed from a headquarters within the presidency (see ch. 14). Within the Directorate of the Interior, which is charged with regional and local administrative matters, the Political Affairs Service is responsible for collecting political information from regional officials. It registers political parties or associations and trade unions and conducts the arrangements for elections. With help from the Ministry of Information, Tourism, and Traditional Arts, the Political Affairs Service also handles matters relating to press control and censorship.

The minister of state is the head of a hierarchical structure beginning at the local level with the canton and rising through the administrative district (*arrondissement administratif*), sub-prefecture, prefecture, and province. Administrative officials at each level are representatives of the Ministry of Interior, but they also function as local representatives of various other ministries. At the national level of government, the Ministry of Interior provides administrative representation of the organs of local government; the rural and urban communes and the local self-help organizations, notably the *fokon'olona* (traditional village council). Within the ministry this mission is the responsibility of a designated secretary of state.

The Ministry of Justice is responsible for providing administrative support needed by the judiciary; it also operates the country's prisons. The operation of the courts is overseen by the president of the Court of Appeals, as a result of the separation of the executive and judicial branches of government. The Ministry of Justice also handles population registration and records such events as births, deaths, marriages, and divorces.

Within the ministry is the government's criminal prosecution organ, called the *ministère publique*. This body is headed nationally by a procurator general, and in each region, by the procurator of each of the major courts.

Parliament

The legislature consists of two houses, the National Assembly and the Senate. Membership of the National Assembly, the more powerful lower house, is composed of one deputy for every 50,000 Malagasy inhabitants. In the 1969 elections 107 members were chosen. According to the constitution, the Senate is designed to function as the representative body for regional, economic, and cultural interests. It consists of fifty-four members.

Method of Election

The members of the National Assembly are chosen by direct universal suffrage. With exceptions, all adult Malagasy citizens are eligible to serve in the lower legislative body. High-ranking civil servants and judges, however, are barred by the constitution from running for any elective office for three years after the end of their official duties. Most other government officials cannot stand for election until one year after serving in their particular districts.

Each province and the capital district (prefecture) of Tananarive form an electoral district. In each one the various political parties present a single list of candidates to fill all the seats sought in the National Assembly. The voters cast their ballots for the list they prefer. If any party's list receives 55 percent or more of the total votes cast, all the seats in the electoral district are awarded to the winning party. If no party's list receives such a majority of the total votes cast, the assembly seats are divided among the competing parties in proportion to the percentage of the vote each one receives. No seats are given to parties receiving less than 5 percent of the votes cast. Seats are assigned to candidates in the order in which their names appear on the list. Since independence this single-list system has had the effect of limiting the chance that any opposition party would obtain a significant voice in Parliament. In each election the Social Democratic Party (Parti Social Démocratique—PSD) of President Philibert Tsiranana had easily captured more than 55 percent of the votes in six of the seven electoral districts.

Thirty-six of the members of the Senate are elected by a single-list system—six from each province. They are not popularly elected but rather are chosen by a special electoral college composed of the members of the province's general council and all the members of the province's various municipal and rural councils. The eighteen other senators are named by the government. Four are chosen from nominees of the chambers of commerce; four, from nominees of labor unions; and four, from suggestions by cultural bodies and private educational groups. An additional six senators are selected by the government on the basis of their particular ability to contribute to the nation's legislative process. All senators serve six-year terms. Elections of senators are staggered so that they are held every three years in half of the provinces. The Senate is not subject to dissolution by the government.

Legislation

Proposed legislation is considered by commissions of deputies, each of which deals with a particular field of legislation, such as foreign affairs, education, or national security. Special commissions, called commissions of inquiry, may be appointed to conduct special investigations of complex affairs. The Senate, like the National Assembly, organizes itself into permanent commissions.

New legislation may be introduced either by the government or by the members of Parliament. In the latter case a draft must first be sent to the ministry concerned before being considered on the floor of the legislature. The deputies may amend measures presented by the government, although they may not propose amendments that would have the effect of unbalancing the government's proposed budget. Ordinarily, Parliament may also pass portions of a government bill while defeating others. When introducing legislation, however, the government may attach a demand that a particular measure be considered by block vote—that is, in its entirety. In such a case the measure must be passed or defeated as a whole. Such measures must be submitted eight days in advance of the opening of a parliamentary session.

All legislation passed by the lower house goes to the Senate for

138

confirmation. If the Senate defeats the bill, it is returned to the National Assembly for a second consideration. If the bill again passes in the lower chamber, the measure becomes law without Senate approval. In any case, the Senate has only twenty days to act on a measure forwarded to it after passage by the National Assembly. If the Senate has not acted by this time, the measure is considered as having been automatically approved, and it becomes law.

The constitution provides that certain types of legislation require an act of Parliament. In other matters Parliament provides the basic, or enabling, legislation, leaving actual control to be exercised through regulations decided upon by the Council of Ministers. It can also give the government the right to make laws by decree on specific subjects for a limited period of time.

Amendments to the constitution must be introduced on a motion supported by a fourth of the members of either house. Such legislation must receive the support of the Council of Ministers and must then win a two-thirds majority in the National Assembly and a three-fifths vote in the Senate.

Particularly important pieces of basic legislation are called organic laws. Although no special methods of passing such legislation are provided, they are recognized as being supplements to the constitution. The passage of such organic laws as those creating the High Court of Justice and the High Council of Institutions was specifically provided for in the constitution. Other laws and acts that do not conform to organic laws may be declared unconstitutional, just as if they were in conflict with the constitution itself.

There are two legislative sessions each year, beginning in May and again in October. The October session is charged primarily with examining the national budget and must be complete within sixty-five days of the opening; otherwise, the budget becomes law without parliamentary approval. Special sessions of Parliament can be convened by the president or by a request of the majority of the members of the National Assembly.

When Parliament is not in session, a major responsibility rests with its bureau or permanent commission. The bureau is composed of the president of the National Assembly and other officers elected by the deputies. Each of these officers serves for a term of one year.

Presidential and Parliamentary Relations

The dual responsibility and power of the National Assembly and the president make it imperative that both are in agreement on the basic policies the country is to follow. If not, the National Assembly may force the fall of the Council of Ministers, the president may dissolve the assembly, and finally a new assembly may require the resignation of the president.

The first challenge in such a series may come from the National

Assembly's refusal, via a motion of censure or a vote of no-confidence, to support a particular portion of the government's program. The introduction of a motion of censure requires the support of one-fifth of the members of the assembly. To pass, it requires the votes of an absolute majority of all deputies. Within ten days after the dissolution of government (which must follow a motion of censure or the loss of a vote of confidence) the president must present to the Senate the names of a new cabinet and the general outline of the proposed new government's political program.

After consulting the Senate the president presents his nominees and their programs to the National Assembly, which votes whether to accept or reject them. If the assembly again refuses to agree to the president's platform or to his cabinet nominees, the assembly is automatically dissolved, and new national elections are held within forty days. If the new assembly again refuses to accept the president's program, the president must immediately resign. The election of a new president must take place within thirty days. His functions are taken over during this interregnum by the president of the National Assembly. The direction of the ministries becomes the responsibility of the presidents of the two houses of Parliament and their vice presidents. From 1960 until 1972, however, the president's party was both numerically dominant in the assembly and well disciplined. As a result there was no occasion to dissolve either the government or the assembly. The many changes in government that took place were all carried out on presidential initiative.

The president may choose to dissolve the assembly without a defeat of the government. In such a case, however, his motion requires support of two-thirds of the Senate.

The president must promulgate all new legislation within fifteen days after its enactment by Parliament. He may, however, return such newly passed legislation to the legislature for reconsideration within this period. He may demand that the members reconsider either all or a part of such a bill, giving his reasons for opposing the measure. To pass over this effort, which amounts to a presidential veto power, the offending articles must receive a majority vote in both the National Assembly and the Senate. The president and the leaders of either house have the right to request the High Council of Institutions to examine proposed or newly passed legislation to see if it is in conformity with the constitution or with the organic laws.

The High Council of Institutions

The High Council of Institutions is responsible for ensuring that laws and ordinances are in conformity with the constitution. The council is composed of five members, three of them chosen for their judicial experience. Two are named by the president; two, by the leader of the assembly; and one, by the president of the Senate. Each serves for a seven-year term. New legislation referred to them is suspended during their consideration. If the council decides that a law is unconstitutional, it must be returned to Parliament for correction.

As the arbiter of constitutionality the council may be called upon to interpret the laws. The body also serves to judge the regularity of national and provincial electoral procedures and supervises the conducting of referenda.

REGIONAL ADMINISTRATION AND LOCAL GOVERNMENT

In mid-1972 the country had six provinces, eighteen prefectures, and ninety-two subprefectures. Ideally, each subprefecture was intended to have about 60,000 inhabitants. The larger sub-prefectures were partially split, and the administrative district (*arrondissement administratif*) was formed in order to lessen the workload of the subprefect; there were forty-three of these units. At the lowest level of the central government's regional administration were the 705 cantons. The local heads of regional divisions, such as the province chiefs, prefects, subprefects, and cantonal chiefs, are the coordinating heads of their regions. They are responsible for directing all government activities except those of the National Gendarmerie, the Ministry of Justice, the courts, and the Treasury.

Representative institutions are found only at the highest level in the form of provincial assemblies called general councils and at the lowest level in the 734 local communes, headed by communal councils, which are popularly elected organs of local government; more than 90 percent of the communes are coterminus with the cantons. Most of the exceptions are in Majunva Province. There are also forty-four urban communes, some including entire towns, whereas others are subdivisions of the few large cities. Provincial and lesser boundaries may be altered or abolished by decision of the central government's Council of Ministers.

The provinces are intended to give regional interests a focal point through which they can influence affairs below the national level and a collective voice in national affairs through provincial represen-tation in the Senate. Unlike the provinces, the prefectures—without a popular voice and headed by a prefect—are supposed to be geographically and economically natural units. The city of Tananarive constitutes a prefecture by itself. This prefecture is subdivided only into urban communes. The Tananarive prefect, like his fellow prefects a central government appointee, has many of the powers assigned elsewhere to mayors, but the capital city also has a popularly elected mayor.

The prefect is responsible for keeping the population informed of government decisions, of publicizing and explaining new laws, of ensuring the enforcement of laws and regulations, and of keeping the government informed about popular opinion within his area of responsibility. He is held responsible for public order in the prefecture and is in command of the civil police. He oversees the operations of the officials heading the smaller administrative units within his area and oversees the operations of the popularly elected communes.

The size of the area of responsibility for subprefects and chiefs of administrative districts are nearly the same. These officers have primary responsibility for advising the rural communes and their mayors on administrative matters and guiding their relations with higher government units. Subprefects and administrative district chiefs are expected to establish direct and personal contact with the local people. They organize municipal and communal elections, set up price controls, prepare the local portions of development plans, and preside over the local draft board for the Civic Service (Service Civique) and for the military (see ch. 14).

The lowest official in the regional administrative hierarchy is the chief of the canton, an officer chosen by the subprefect. He serves as the collector of both national and local taxes, controls the movement of cattle, supervises the local population registration, serves as the immediate counselor to the local mayor and the communal council, and often serves as the postmaster. He is assisted by chiefs of villages or wards (*quartiers*), who are selected by the communal councils.

The Provincial General Council

The provincial general council serves as the regional administrative assembly. Each is composed of the province's parliamentary deputies and senators and the general councillors, who are elected by direct popular vote for five-year terms on the basis of one seat for each subprefecture. The prefecture of Tananarive, which is not divided into subprefectures, is arbitrarily assigned four seats. Each province is divided into three election districts, having an average of five seats. As in parliamentary elections, each party presents a ticket listing all of its candidates for seats within the election district. The voters indicate their support for a full ticket rather than for individual candidates. The general council may be dissolved by decree of the national Council of Ministers, and new elections must be held within two months.

The council holds two sessions annually, but extraordinary sessions may be called by the province chief to consider specific matters. The council's own officers compose a bureau or permanent commission similar to that of the National Assembly. The bureau functions throughout the year, exercising the powers of the council when it is not in session. The council establishes the provincial budget and sets taxation, controls primary education, contributes to cultural and sports programs, and decides upon provincial public works. It must be consulted by the national government on matters pertaining to provincial contributions to the national development program. The general council, however, is specifically forbidden by the constitution to voice its opinion on national political matters.

The Communes

The only organs of elected local government are at the level of the rural and urban communes. The rural communes—each with an average population of about 8,000—group several small villages or hamlets under a communal council, generally called the *conseil municipal.* Each rural council has ten members, if the commune's population is under 4,000, or sixteen if it is greater. The actual powers of these units vary considerably, depending on the size of the population and its wealth; significant differences also exist in the rules governing the forty-four urban communal councils.

The urban communes are headed by councils composed of twenty-three to thirty-five members. Included in the list of urban communes are those of Ile Sainte-Marie and Nosy Be, which govern the entire area of the two offshore islands. They were granted special communal status under French rule before the twentieth century. In all other cases, an urban council represents a single major town.

Each commune has limited local taxing authority and receives a portion of the national taxes collected within its domain. All the councillors are elected for six-year terms, although for convenience the government is authorized to shorten or extend the term by one year in order to avoid conflicts with a national election. Communal council elections are held under a party-list system similar to the national and provincial examples.

Any communal council may be dissolved by decree of the national Council of Ministers and replaced by an appointed special delegation composed of at least three members. This occurs if the communal council is torn by dissension or displays a poor management record. New communal elections must be held within six months.

The officials of the regional administration maintain considerable power over the actions of the communal councils both directly and through their advisory role. The prefect and, in some cases, lower officials have the right to nullify council decisions on many matters.

Each rural or urban commune is headed by a mayor, chosen by the councillors from among their own ranks for the full term of the council. The duties of the mayor and the council include: directing the work of council employees; preparing the communal budget; operating a bureau of social assistance; organizing such additional primary schools as their budget may allow; installation and maintenance of local and town roads, street lighting, public water, and electric service (except where these are handled by private or state companies); control of markets; regulation of local traffic; granting of building permits; and levying local taxes on property, vehicles, and animals.

The Village Organization

The *fokon'olona* is the Merina name for a village or hamlet organization traditionally composed of the heads of all the village households. Historically all would have been members of the same kinship group. In modern times this is often no longer true, but people still act as if they were related (see ch. 5). The *fokon'olona* was the basic unit of local government under the Merina kings. After being alternately suppressed and encouraged by the former colonial government, they were given reinforced status in 1962 by the new Malagasy government, which sought to encourage the *fokon'olona* in its traditional role of responsibility for order in the village and the provision for social and economic assistance to the members. The organization is charged with ensuring the apprehension of criminals among its members and with major responsibility for the suppression of cattle stealing, which is traditional and endemic in much of the country's south and west.

The government's major aim in strengthening the *fokon'olona*, however, was to gain its assistance in plans for rural economic and social development, particularly through self-help programs. Its major power stems from traditional social sanctions supplemented by the legal provisions that allow the *fokon'olona* to expel anyone from the village for consistently refusing to cooperate in projects under its leadership.

THE COURT SYSTEM

The separation of powers between the executive and judicial branches is a prime objective of the Malagasy constitution. Only at the lowest level of the judicial structure is there any overlap between the two: subprefecture tribunals are presided over by the subprefect or his deputy. All actions, however, are open to review by the higher courts of the judicial system.

With the subprefectural exception, all judges are completely independent of the executive and have an extensive legal background. Nearly all are graduates of the University of Madagascar's law school or have studied law in Paris. They may be called to the bench only if they have completed the course of the Institute of Judicial Studies or hold a master's degree in law. The only exception is that notaries and court clerks with ten years of experience in their field may also be designated as magistrates. Initial appointment to a specific post is made by the president on the recommendation of the minister of justice, but the executive branch of government has no control over the judge's career.

There are six ranks of magistrate. Transfers must be agreed to by the individual magistrate, and promotions are controlled by a commission headed by the ranking member of the judiciary, who is the president of the Court of Appeals. The commission's other members include the procurator general and the presidents of the various chambers of the Court of Appeals. The judicial disciplinary body is the general assembly of the magistrates of the Court of Appeals. The prosecutor's staff is also composed of a number of magistrates, but they spend their careers as prosecutors rather than as judges.

As in France, the Malagasy courts apply law according to fixed codes, designed to cover all applications and to leave little room for interpretation by the individual courts. In practice, the codes do not begin to cover the variety of material presented before the courts for decision, and the courts are obliged to expand the laws. It is up to the higher courts to ensure uniformity in application, particularly as no requirements exist for following legal precedent set by other courts.

An entire series of codes, which attempted to include indigenous elements, were introduced in the early 1960s. These included penal, penal procedure, civil, civil procedure, military, maritime, labor, and personal law codes. The acceptance of such codes was effected by the existence of extensive codification in Merina traditional law before the arrival of the colonial era. The customary law systems of the island's other peoples were often unrecorded, however. A major distinction between the traditional and modern systems that effected popular attitudes toward the courts was the fact that in criminal prosecutions the modern code placed emphasis on inflicting punishment, whereas the Malagasy system emphasized the seeking of compensation for the injured parties. As a result, many crimes were not brought to the courts but were settled by the *fokon'olona*, without the sanction of law.

Lower Courts

The court involved in most cases is one of the tribunals of first instance or one of the sections of such a tribunal. A tribunal of first instance is located in each provincial capital; its sections are found at other major locations within the province. The court has complete jurisdiction over civil matters and limited jurisdiction over criminal cases. It has five chambers. Single chambers deal with matters of civil, commercial, and labor law. The fourth chamber, at the level of the police court (*simple police*) or the court of petty sessions (*correctionnelle*), deals with criminal charges. Jurisdiction of police courts is limited to crimes punishable by less than thirty days in jail; the court of petty sessions may try cases involving crimes punishable by less than ten years imprisonment or a fine of more than FMG25,000 (for value of the Malagasy franc—see Glossary). The fifth chamber—chambre d'immatriculation—deals with such matters as land registration. In some areas there is also a chamber for juvenile offenders.

The size of the judicial staff varies with the number of cases handled in the province. All cases tried by a tribunal of first instance are heard by at least two judges. At this and all higher levels, another judge must be assigned as investigating magistrate (juge d'instruction), a post peculiar to the French judicial system on which the Malagasy system has been modeled. This magistrate examines the charge laid by the prosecutor's office, questions the accused and the witnesses, directs the police investigators, and decides whether the case should go to trial. He then prepares a report for the court with the results of his examination in which he states his conclusions about the case. His report is available to the presecution and defense staffs. The tribunal's conclusions may not be appealed unless they involve a prison sentence or a civil case concerning a loss of more than FMG50,000.

The tribunal's sections are located in the twenty-five largest population centers. At section level, cases are heard by a single magistrate. Except in the busiest section courts, he acts as investigating magistrate, judge, and prosecutor. He does not hear serious or complex cases but refers all such matters directly to the tribunal of first instance.

Below the tribunals of first instance are those of the subprefecture and the parallel administrative district headed by the subprefect or district chief. These tribunals, which numbered 105 in 1970, do not have jurisdiction over commercial or labor matters or land registration cases. They hear only limited civil and police court cases. An appeal on the facts may be made from any of these lower level courts in all but petty cases. On appeal, the entire case is retried in the next highest court.

Criminal Courts

All cases classified as criminel—those involving crimes punishable by a sentence of at least ten years in prison—are tried by the criminal courts. Ten such courts, all without a permanent location, are assigned to areas of the country as they are needed. The bench in a criminal court consists of a magistrate, who sits as president or chief judge, and four assessors. The assessors, who are laymen rather than trained magistrates, are picked from a list of eighteen men designated at the beginning of each court term for a period of one year. Two substitute assessors also are chosen from the list by the magistrate for each case. The verdict in all cases is reached by a majority vote of all five members of the bench.

Cases heard by a criminal court are investigated by the investigating magistrate and are presented before the court on his recommendation. In serious cases, his report is first reviewed by the Chamber of Accusations of the Court of Appeals.

In contrast with appeals from decisions of the tribunals, appeals of the decisions of the criminal courts are permissible only on the grounds of an error in law. Such appeals are carried to the Chamber of Cassation, a division of the Supreme Court. Six special criminal courts devote their activities to cases involving juveniles. Criminal cases involving the armed forces are heard by the military tribunal, which ordinarily functions in the capital city of Tananarive.

The High Court of Justice

The High Court of Justice is composed of the first president of the Court of Appeals, the two presidents of the chambers of the Court of Appeals, five other judges of the court drawn by lots, and eight members of Parliament—five from the National Assembly and three from the Senate. These eight legislators are elected at the beginning of each term of the National Assembly. The court's Chamber of Accusations functions as the examining magistrate.

The High Court of Justice was created by the constitution and is intended solely to hear cases in which the president or members of the Council of Ministers are accused of crimes committed in the exercise of their duties. An accusation can only be presented to the court on a parliamentary motion, which must pass by a majority vote in both houses of the legislature. As of mid-1972 the court had not been used.

The Court of Appeals

The Court of Appeals is the highest court with appellate jurisdiction over matters of both law and fact; its president is the country's ranking jurist. Appeals of verdicts handed down by criminal courts may be brought before the Court of Appeals either by the prosecution or by the defense. Cases are always presented before a bench composed of three judges. The court has six chambers, five corresponding to those of the tribunals of first instance from which appeals ordinarily come: the civil chamber, the commercial chamber, the land registration chamber, the labor law chamber, and the minor criminal chamber. The sixth chamber—the Chamber of Accusations—reviews the decisions of the investigating magistrates for matters pertaining to evidence, decision to prosecute, and the granting of bail.

The Court of Appeals, whose judges all sit on the bench, is the court to which cases are returned for retrial after a successful appeal to the Supreme Court. This full bench also hears disciplinary cases against magistrates and advocates.

The Supreme Court

At the apex of the court structure is the Supreme Court; it is composed of three chambers, each having very distinct duties. The

Chamber of Cassation hears the final appeals brought on grounds that a lower court made an error in interpreting the law or in following legal procedure. The Chamber of Cassation's major function thus is to ensure that the law is uniformly and correctly applied by the courts throughout the republic. Fully constituted, the Chamber of Cassation consists of five magistrates.

The Chamber of Administrative Law, composed of three judges, hears charges against the state concerning illegal, improper, or unfair acts by organs of the government in suits brought by individuals or lower levels of government. The Chamber of Accounts acts in a similar fashion to oversee proper control of government expenditures. It functions as a general accounting office and reports to Parliament and the president concerning the execution of the annual budget.

THE CIVIL SERVICE

All national and regional government employees are members of the civil service. They are divided broadly into three classes: functionaries, or those with full tenure; auxiliaries, or persons hired without permanent tenure, who may, nevertheless, participate in retirement programs and other long-term benefits; and contractual employees, generally hired for a limited period of time. The last class includes highly skilled professionals, who are hired usually for two years. All three classes are divided further into categories according to educational qualifications. Five categories, Class A being the highest, are designated for functionaries. Parallel groupings exist for employees without tenure.

Entry into the civil service is achieved by competitive examination and, as required by the constitution, is open to all Malagasy without regard to ethnic origin, sex, religion, or political philosophy. In 1971 a large percentage of the technical posts and even many politically sensitive positions continued to be occupied by the 2,000 French technical assistance personnel in the republic.

CHAPTER 9
POLITICAL DYNAMICS AND ATTITUDES

Two themes can be distinguished in the country's political dynamics since independence. The first of these, salient during the early 1960s, was the consolidation of power in the hands of President Philibert Tsiranana and his Social Democratic Party (Parti Social Democratique—PSD). This position of political dominance was acquired without violating the constitution's democratic precepts; it was accomplished as a result of organizational ability and popular support at the polls.

The second theme—the reverse of the first—was the growth of opposition to the party and to the president in the late 1960s and early 1970s. This growing opposition was brought about in good part by the Tsiranana government's failure to offer solutions to the country's problems. It was also attributable to the stagnation that set in as the governing party assumed a bureaucratic role rather than serving as a spokesman for popular sentiments. A major but unmeasurable factor in this degeneration was the gradually intensifying cerebral disease, hemiplegia, which first struck the president in 1966 and reduced the vigor and ability with which he had earlier been able to balance the various forces at work in party and nation.

A major cause of political problems was the failure of the economy to improve the position of the peasant majority. The peasants' resentment was compounded by rising taxes, a burdensome bureaucracy, and a domestic trade system that incurred high prices that weighed heavily on the individual consumer (see ch. 12). As events developed, however, an educational crisis resulting from a large increase in the number of secondary school graduates and university students had greater immediate impact on the political situation. These young people had depended on the elite status acquired through education to provide them with opportunities after graduation. Instead, the sluggish economy resulted in a general lack of job prospects. The students blamed their difficulties on the educational system itself, which they felt lacked relevance to their own and their country's needs because it was a system designed for the needs of France (see ch. 7). The government's failure to ease the problem of the peasants and also the resentment caused by continued French economic and military dominance were of major significance.

The crisis that built up to a collapse of the Tsiranana government in mid-1972 occurred in four stages over a period of a little more than a year. First came a revolt against the government in April 1971 by farmers in the country's poorest province, Tulear. Second, President

Tsiranana in June suddenly arrested a man who had always appeared to be his closest supporter; André Resampa, minister of interior and secretary general of the PSD. Resampa was accused of plotting against the government and of accepting covert assistance from the United States. Resampa was the leader of the PSD wing that had the most support among the country's students. No evidence was offered to support the charges.

The third stage occurred in October 1971 when the president announced another purported antigovernment plot; again he offered no evidence. Fifteen intellectuals and scientists were arrested as alleged ringleaders and charged with having both French and Maoist connections. In February 1972 considerable protest was raised over the way in which the uncontested presidential election had been conducted.

Finally, student protests, which began in early March 1972, brought down the government in mid-May. President Tsiranana retained his post as head of state, but all power was placed in the hands of the ranking army officer, General Gabriel Ramanantsoa, who was named as prime minister and who chose a cabinet composed of technicians and military officers.

CONCENTRATION OF POLITICAL POWER, 1960-65

At independence on June 26, 1960, Malagasy political parties found themselves in a radically changed situation. The sole objective of many supporters of the Party of the Congress for the Independence of Madagascar (Ankoton'ny Kongresi'ny Fahaleovantenan Madagaskara—AKFM), for example, had been the achievement of independence and the return to the island of the exiled political heroes of the 1947 rebellion: Joseph Raseta; Joseph Ravoahangy; and Jacques Rabemanenjara (see ch. 2). When these objectives were achieved—and particularly because they were achieved by a coalition of parties under Tsiranana's chairmanship having the backing of the exiled heroes—the radicals were left without a popular cause.

The PSD leadership, on the other hand, was sufficiently skilled to take full advantage of its position. It captured the support of those nationalists whose objectives had been obtained, held onto its traditionalist rural constituents, and was successful in efforts to incorporate into its ranks the leaders of the smaller parties by offering them important posts in the government. Most notably, Rabemananjara, the only one of the three exiles young enough to be politically active, was given a high-ranking cabinet post.

The first elections after independence were held in September and October 1960. President Tsiranana led his party's efforts to form a common front that would include all other parties except the AKFM. This appeal met with limited success. Many of the small parties accepted ties with the PSD in order to reinforce their leaders' hopes of gaining office. The most important opposition parties, notably the Democratic and Social Union of Madagascar (Union Démocratique et Sociale de Madagascar—UDSM) and the National Movement for the Independence of Madagascar (Mouvement National pour l'Independence de Madagascar—MONIMA), presented candidates of their own, as did the AKFM. As a result, there was an average of four candidates for each post.

Nevertheless the PSD won eighty-one of 107 parliamentary seats. Another sixteen went to a slate of Roman Catholic candidates centered in Tamatave and led by Rabemananjara, who had already pledged his support to the president. The PSD's only clear losses were in Tananarive, where a temporary coalition of moderates won seven seats and the AKFM won three. PSD dominance in the Senate election and in the provincial General Council elections assumed a similar pattern. Overall, the president and his allies captured 104 of the 107 National Assembly seats, 231 of 236 provincial General Council seats, and all thirty-six elected posts in the Senate.

In the government formed after the elections were completed, four cabinet posts went to leaders of the other parties, despite the objections of the left wing of the PSD. This faction, led by Resampa, sought to have the posts go as rewards to loyal PSD members. Resampa also sought constitutional changes to centralize all power in the president's hands and to achieve support for a more socialist economic policy. Despite these differences with the president, Resampa was named to the important post of minister of interior. Calvin Tsiebo, a personal friend of Tsiranana, was elevated from the presidency of the National Assembly to the position of national vice president. Rabemananjara, Ravoahangy, leaders of two other moderate parties, and two Frenchmen were included among the ten government ministers.

Major differences arose in 1960 and 1961 between the executive branch and Parliament as each sought to increase its share of power. In part the differences resulted from clashes over policy. A majority of the members of both houses, including the members of the president's own party, were in favor of loosening the close ties that the country had with France and increasing the role of the Malagasy language and customs. A reduction of the number of French in the civil service was advocated. As a cultural protest, the Senate insisted on conducting all of its business in the Malagasy language. The executive branch was the ultimate victor in each challenge, however, because the president's leadership within the ruling party enabled him to mobilize the votes he needed on key issues. On several occasions he even obtained parliamentary approval of legislation that weakened the power of Parliament—notably acts that lessened the Senate's right to delay measures approved by the lower house and that permitted the executive branch to make laws in certain broad areas by decree (see ch. 8).

Despite the preeminence of the PSD, the country in late 1961 still had about thirty-three political parties, although many of these were little more than small clubs. Most of the parties were associated with a specific leader, but those of importance generally represented either an ethnic or an ideological interest group.

The majority of the medium-sized parties were regional, and differences among them could not be clearly distinguished. The PSD remained a party dominated by the côtiers (see Glossary) but was one that sought increasingly to be truly national. As a step in this direction—and in the hope of reducing the number of opposition parties—President Tsiranana instigated a series of meetings in late 1961 and 1962 among the leaders of all the parties, including his only ideological opponent, the AKFM. These led to a major coup for the PSD because most members of the small Malagasy National Renewal Party (Renouveau National Malgache—RNM) and several important opposition members—including Rabemananjara and Ravoahangy—joined the PSD. Several other groups formed a united front. Although they did not actually join the PSD, these groups announced their support for the president. A few small groups remained in existence, notably MONIMA and a wing of the RNM under Alexis Bezaka, but from this point onward only the PSD and the AKFM had a significant voice in the political arena.

The achievement of self-rule, the return from exile of the popular leaders of the 1947 revolt, and the attainment of national independence diminished much of the AKFM's strength, as these demands had been the source of its attraction to many of its members. The party, however, was not destroyed. The basis of its remaining strength was threefold. First, it was the party to which educated persons who favored radical social reform continued to adhere. At the same time, it was the party that served as the country's main communist front organization. Although a Malagasy communist party did exist, most individual Communists found a more effective voice through a wing of the AKFM whose leaders were pro-Communist and had close ties with the Soviet Union.

Second, the party drew much of its noncommunist strength from an entirely different source: the basic ethnopolitical split between the highland Merina and the côtiers and the reinforcing division between Protestants and Roman Catholics. The Protestants had historically been concentrated among the Merina upper classes; in most areas the majority of educated côtiers were Roman Catholics. The PSD represented the triumph of the "disinherited," as the original côtier party had been called. Many of the Merina elite, as the island's historical rulers, were embittered by their own loss of status. For that reason, they were willing to give their allegiance at election time to the AKFM—regardless of its political philosophy—because it was a party dominated outwardly by their fellow Merina.

Third, the AKFM as part of both its radical and Merina orientation, assumed an anti-French position that attracted many Malagasy. The PSD and particularly President Tsiranana favored the retention of close ties with France—in effect continuing many of the relationships created in the colonial period. He and many other Malagasy of his generation were genuine francophiles and preferred to recognize openly the positive contributions of the colonial era. They cherished the internationally recognized French cultural standards to which their education had made them adherents. In the area of foreign affairs, they welcomed the security and the more extensive contacts that were provided for the island by a continous association with France and its other former colonies.

For several reasons they were not opposed to a continuation of the strong French presence on the island. They approved the retention of French military forces, which reduced the need to create a strong army and also lessened the chance that the army might later copy the examples occuring in many African states and seize the power from the civilian government. They also approved the retention of French teachers and technicans who filled posts that otherwise would have been left vacant because of lack of qualified personnel, thus impeding national development. In addition, the PSD leaders accepted the continuance of marked French influence on the island's economy (see ch. 12).

The major factor that militated against the AKFM's obtaining more than limited political success was the strength of the PSD's influence within the government, which made membership in the sole active opposition party an unlikely route to personal success. The AKFM thus failed to attract into its ranks the new men who displayed the dynamism the party needed, particularly as its preindependence leaders grew older and drew further away from the country's students and urban youth, who had originally been a major source of its political support.

Tsiranana's efforts to unify the parties had failed to separate Richard Andriamanjato, a Merina Protestant clergyman, and his nationalist wing of the AKFM from the extremists. He had greatly strengthened his own party, however, by gaining the support of major portions of the small political groups known collectively as the Third Force and had left the AKFM further isolated. By the end of 1960 the PSD had 500,000 members organized into 900 sections. To this was added the strength of the parties that amalgamated during 1961.

THE SOCIAL DEMOCRATIC PARTY

Political Philosophy and Attitudes

The victories of the Social Democratic Party (Parti Social Démocratique—PSD) were most remarkable for having been won in a democratic system functioning under rules composed for a European society and followed only with great difficulty in a developing society. It was President Tsiranana who insisted on adhering to those rules and who refused to adopt a single-party system, seeing in an open political system a means to provide an outlet for expression of opposition and to assure all observers of his government's legitimacy.

The sources of Tsiranana's political ability and the control he successfully exercised over party and country have been discribed as being most nearly that of a popular paternal monarch. He was regarded as the inheritor of the traditions of the island's former dynasties, ruling neither by force nor by personal charisma but rather as the properly chosen and the ordained holder of the post of leadership.

Others have said that the people viewed him as the chief who guides his people or as the father of a national family. This last concept is particularly important in a society where the concept of family has such great significance for the individual. In the Malagasy pattern of thought the legitimate holder of power and authority is for his subordinates *ray amen'dreny* (both father and mother). Moreover, the ideas of a government composed of two branches and based on representative leadership were entirely unfamiliar to the Malagasy, who at best saw the members of the legislature as their spokesmen to the national executive. Such traditional concepts, never interfered with by the former colonial administration, were further reinforced for the educated Malagasy by conditions in France, which was then adapting to a strong presidential regime under Charles de Gaulle.

More than most Malagasy leaders, Tsiranana was a pragmatist, interested neither in philosophies nor in appearances but seeking instead the reality of political power through successful organization. His apparent humility, his ability to work with his most bitter opponents without projecting bitterness himself, and his great energy enabled him to maintain close contact with all elements and thus to become and remain aware of the forces building within the society.

President Tsiranana was most interested in using Israel as an example because he felt the Israeli people had developed their country by innovation and hard work. He also favored the gradual establishment of a socialist economy through the extension of cooperative agricultural and industrial movements, again showing an inclination toward the Israeli example.

Malagasy students and high-ranking servants alike were sent to Israel for training. The Civic Service was also copied from Israeli movements. Israelis were brought to Madagascar to help draft the first national development plan and to reorganize the PSD's labor unions. The Social Democratic Party of the Federal Republic of Germany (West Germany) replaced the French Socialist Party (Section Francaise de l'Internationale Ouvrière) as the PSD's chief foreign supporter, contributing the funds and staff for a training center for PSD leaders and a center that served as a hostel for PSD students at the university.

Tsiranana's major objective was to achieve a national unity that crossed ethnic and regional as well as political lines. He made use of Rabemanajara in foreign political and economic relations because he recognized that his stature in Europe as an internationally recognized author and poet as well as a politician would be an asset to the country's diplomatic prestige. He diverted Resampa's energy, organizational genius, and desire for social change into useful channels within the party in order to maintain ties with those most eager for change.

The PSD's directors labeled the party the instrument for social and economic renovation of their country. Its motto became "Better to Work than to Palaver." Although accepting a socialist economy as its goal, the PSD rejected all attempts to define its form of socialism; it declared that, given the peculiar requirement of the country, Malagasy socialism could be defined as whatever would do the most to provide its people with benefits. Party leaders saw the country's primary problem as the people's unwillingness to work toward national development. This unwillingness was blamed on their refusal to accept new methods and on their preference for leisure. Other observers, however, emphasized that an understanding of Malagasy passivity and insularity is essential to an understanding of Malagasy political values and attitudes.

The progressive or socialist wing of the PSD advocated policies strikingly similar to those of the AKFM. These included cutting or at least loosening the ties to France, avoiding close association with the European Economic Community (EEC, known as the Common Market) and with the Common Organization of African and Malagasy States and Mauritius (Organization Commune Africaine, Malgache, et Mauritien—OCAMM), replacing foreign technicians and all foreigners in politically sensitive posts with Malagasy officials, and nationalizing much of the economy. Most importantly, the socialist contingent advocated a major agrarian reform, which would begin with the nationalization of all foreign-owned estates, which were the main producers of certain export crops. Their view of socialism rejected the Marxist theory of class struggle in favor of a belief in the fundamental unity of Malagasy society.

The government adopted a liberal attitude toward the entrance of foreign capital in order to encourage projects that would aid national development because the country itself was not able to mobilize the human and financial investment required. The very large French investment on the island was viewed as irreplaceable and as an assurance of continuing large-scale French aid.

More out of a desire to stimulate industrialization than as a response to demands for a policy of state control, the government took several steps to establish state farms and enterprises. Among these was the National Investment Corporation (Société Nationale d'Investissement—SNI), created in 1964 and given a monopoly over transportation, electricity, and fuel production. The legislation allowed the private sector to operate these industries under the SNI's general direction. The SNI was also authorized to finance the creation of Malagasy-owned private industry or the purchase of foreign enterprises by Malagasy capitalists. In addition, it was to provide financial assistance to industrial cooperatives.

The government's most socialistic step was to alter the constitution to allow the expropriation of neglected properties without payment of compensation. These modest actions were condemned as inadequate by much of the PSD membership. Some of the left wing wished to see a complete collectivization of agriculture; many more favored an agrarian reform that would take over all foreign-held agricultural estates. The government consistently refused on the grounds that these estates provided the country with most of its export crops.

Internal Divisions

The major political division having any potential for conflict during much of the 1960s appeared to be that among the adherents of the three different philosophies within the PSD: Christian socialism, socialism, and conservatism. These three major divisions were supplemented or paralleled by divisions between the Merina and the côtiers and among other ethnic groups as well as by personal and clan rivalries.

The liberal or Christian socialist wing of the party aligned behind Jacques Rabemananjara contained most of those who had previously belonged to the Roman Catholic and Protestant parties of the Third Force (see Opposition Parties, this ch.). Its other leaders included Jules Razafimbahiny, former secretary of state for foreign affairs, as well as Jean-François Jarison and Jean Jacques Natai—both of whom were long-time cabinet ministers.

This group was accused by the rest of the party of being composed of opportunists who had joined the PSD only when they saw that it was a means to power. The left wing accused them of being covert sympathizers of capitalism because Rabemananjara, as the minister responsible for encouraging foreign investment, had taken a very conciliatory attitude toward foreign business. Much of the hostility between these two wings was a manifestation of parallel personal and regional conflicts, for both were led by rivals for the position of heir-apparent to President Tsiranana. Rabemananjara was the sole politician of importance to have inherited the mantle of the 1947 revolution's leadership. He was also generally considered the undisputed leader of the people of Tamatave.

The largest portion of the party's strength was in the hands of conservative interests. Included were many local and ethnic groups whose allegiance was often to their own leaders. This portion of the party in particular had strong links to President Tsiranana. Their numbers were greatest among the traditionalist côtiers but included many of the party's minor bureaucrats and French as well as Malagasy business interests.

The strongest wing in strength of organization appeared to be the progressive or socialist wing, led by Resampa. It had the support of the party's younger educated members and many students. Its followers sought to have the government take strong measures to achieve a reformation of the social and economic system. It favored an agrarian socialism on the model of Israel or the African socialist states, particularly Tanzania. It demanded the progressive nationalization of the vital sectors of the economy (although leaving other sectors open to capitalism) and the revision of the 1960 agreement with France. At the same time, it was strongly anti-AKFM and anticommunist and rejected relations with nations of the communist bloc; it even rejected the neutralism of the Afro-Asian countries, preferring to continue ties with the West.

Until 1971 the personal position of Resampa appeared very strong, despite protests that he was putting party above national interests. In the late 1960s, particularly after President Tsiranana began to suffer from a continuing serious illness that clearly impaired his abilities, Resampa urged him to create a post of prime minister to which many of his heavy duties as head of government and head of state could be transferred. Naturally Resampa would have been the chief candidate for this post.

Party Organization

The lowest level of organization within the PSD was the local section at the commune level, composed of dues-paying party members. At the level of the country's subprefectures, which numbered more than ninety in 1972, these local sections were grouped into a federation (see ch. 8). The secretaries of the federations were represented on the national Executive Committee (Comité Directeur). The highest body was the National Congress of the PSD, which met annually and elected the national Executive

Committee. This large committee in turn appointed from its members the party's Political Bureau and the secretary general. The secretary-generalship, the most powerful post in the party, was held from 1959 until 1971 by André Resampa. Urgent decisions were made by the National Council, a body which sat in place of the annual congress. The National Council was composed of the national Executive Committee, the Political Bureau, and PSD members of Parliament.

At the higher levels the party's old guard provided an effective working force, many of its members being employed as government officials; at the local levels there was always a shortage of volunteers willing and able to carry a work load. Most party members were content to limit their duty to paying their dues. This lack of local interest deprived the PSD and ultimately the government of the contact they both needed to carry policies and reforms down to the people. The weakness was due in part to the people's general lack of interest in things that are not part of their traditions and in part to their memories of what happened to active party members in the 1947 revolt. It was also caused, however, by major political weaknesses, notably a predilection within the party and the civil service for bureaucratic decisionmaking, which had been inherited from both the Merina and colonial eras. In violation of party rules and national laws, these men preferred to dictate to the peasants rather than to seek their active democratic participation.

Affiliated Groups

The groups associated with the PSD included professional organizations and the 40,000-member Confederation of Malagasy Workers (Fivondronan'ny Mpiasa Malagasy—FMM). The FMM, originally completely separate from the party, became very closely associated with it during the 1960s and came to include most of the members of the previously rival Christian Confederation of Malagasy Labor Unions (Confédération Chrétienne des Syndicats Malgaches—CCSM). The AKFM also had a closely aligned labor organization, the Federation of Malagasy Labor Unions (Firaisana Sendikaly Malagasy—FISEMA). FISEMA was associated with the All African Trade Union Federation, which had headquarters in Ghana during the era of Kwame Nkrumah, and the World Federation of Trade Unions, based in Prague. FISEMA's membership, however, was very small.

In 1960 the PSD founded a youth wing, the Young Social Democrats (Jeunesse Sociale-Démocrate—JSD). The JSD's leader was a nephew of Resampa. It became a powerful force within the left wing of the party. In 1962 a second youth body specifically aimed at the students, the Union of Malagasy Socialist Students (Union des Etudiantes Socialists Malgaches—UESM) was founded, with a staff trained by the French Socialist Party. Its major purpose was to counteract the strength of the AKFM's attraction to students at the university in Tananarive. Instead, however, the UESM established good working relations with the AKFM's associated student group, placing the UESM well to the left of the PSD. It voiced demands for renegotiating the agreements with France, a stronger voice in government for the peasants, and an end to the political interference in the cooperative movement.

The PSD women's organization, which exercised considerable power in the party hierarchy—not surprising in a country where women have traditionally filled powerful positions—was the National Council of the Association of Women of Madagascar (Conseil National des Associations de Femmes de Madagascar).

The party also published several daily and weekly newspapers. Its preeminence in the communications media, however, resulted from its ability to control the government press, radio, and television through its hold over the cabinet post directing the Ministry of Information. Despite the large number of opposition newspapers, the governing party was able to exercise considerable influence over public opinion through its control of radio broadcasting (see ch. 11). Until about 1967 a considerable degree of freedom was left to the station's personnel, in accordance with the government's liberal policies toward the opposition. After 1968, however, increasingly strict control was exercised, first by blocking information favorable to the opposition and later by structuring the news in the governing party's favor. Still later, control was so strict that the radio did not report the events of April and May 1972, leaving many Malagasy unaware of the events that led to General Ramanantsoa's takeover.

The party made effective use in rural areas and villages of the administrative structure through which its appointees served as prefects and subprefects. The prefect had the power to bring considerable pressure to bear on opponents of the party. He could also use the *fokon'olona* (see Glossary) to accomplish political aims, particularly in enlisting support for government programs. Despite Tsiranana's continued support for allowing the opposition a voice and a function in the democratic forum, the majority of the people in the civil service as well as among the peasantry regarded the party, the government, and the state as a single entity. Thus the administration became, in effect, synonymous with the party because the people could not distinguish between the two. This lack of comprehension was a result not only of traditional concepts but also of the heritage of colonial rule. In neither case had any distinction existed between the political leadership and the civil administration.

OPPOSITION PARTIES
The AKFM

In early 1972 the Party of the Congress for the Independence of Madagascar (Ankoton'ny Kongresi'ny Fahaleovantenan Madagaskara—AKFM) had 300 sections and about 30,000 members but could count on the occasional support of up to 250,000 voters. The majority of its support came from Tananarive, drawn from the Protestant Merina intellectuals, from the university students who were members of the Federation of Malagasy Student Associations (Fédération des Associations d'Etudiants de Madagascar—FAEM), and from the ranks of FISEMA, its labor union.

The most debated question about the AKFM was its communist connection. It had undeniable links with the Soviet variety of communism, presenting the Soviet Union as a model for Malagasy and advocating scientific socialism as the only way to a happy future for the world. The leaders, including Richard Andriamanjato, had frequent contacts with European communist leaders and had made many trips to Moscow. Various European communist parties had been regularly invited to attend AKFM meetings, as had the leading Communists from Mauritius, Réunion, and the Comoro Islands. Despite its anticolonial origins, the party even refused to speak out against the Soviet invasion of Czechoslovakia in 1968, a refusal that appeared to put the AKFM more in the Soviet camp than many explicitly communist parties of Western Europe.

Nevertheless, the AKFM claimed that it was not a communist party. Andriamanjato, AKFM leader and a Protestant minister, was particularly eager to deny that he was a Communist. He was, however, eager to prove that Christianity and communism not only can coexist but also can be reconciled, and he asserted that Christians in the Soviet Union are well treated. Although he was apparently not a Communist, many of the party's other leaders were.

During most periods the PSD refrained from direct attacks on the AKFM, continuing the efforts begun at independence to attract the noncommunist elements in the party to join or form a coalition with the PSD. By 1964 even Resampa was publicly considering the possibility of what he called a socialist front composed of the AKFM and the PSD in order to gain support for social reforms favored by both parties. Portions of the AKFM, particularly Andriamanjato and his followers, were eager to form such a coalition because it was the party's only hope of gaining a voice in the government. In the AKFM stronghold of Tananarive, the PSD—aware that it could not defeat Andriamanjato—declined to attempt to weaken his popularity, notably in the 1968 municipal elections. In the mid-1960s even the communist wing of his party followed Andriamanjato's leadership in seeking a rapprochement with the PSD.

The Malagasy Communist Party

The Malagasy Communist Party (Antoko Kaominista Malagasy—AKM) was formed in 1956 but never became active. Its sympathies appeared generally to be with the variety of communism followed by the People's Republic of China (PRC). Its existence was helpful to the AKFM leaders because they could use it to justify claims that theirs was not a communist party. At the same time, despite the AKM's apparent lack of power, the PSD used the party's existence and its favorable attitude toward the PRC to justify fears that subversives from the extreme Left, with support from the PRC were planning to overthrow the Malagasy government. By the late 1960s the AKM all but disappeared as the Soviet Union expressed growing interest in the AKFM.

The Third Force

The other political parties were often lumped together and labeled the Third Force because they tried to form a bloc between the PSD and the extreme Left. The Third Force, although generally composed of several parties, could be divided into two sets: one of left-wing nationalists, opposed to all foreign influences; the other of Christians, including Roman Catholics and Protestants, who were generally advocates of moderate socialism (see The Social Democratic Party, this ch.). Both of these groupings were weakened politically by the existence within the two major parties of wings that attracted their own political supporters. Nationalists were attracted to the noncommunist nationalist wing of the AKFM, and the liberals to the Rabemenanjara or Resampa wings of the PSD.

The only enduring ultranationalist party was the National Movement for the Independence of Madagascar (Mouvement National pour l'Indépendance de Madagascar—MONIMA). Founded before independence, its strength was concentrated among the personal followers and ethnic associates of a man sometimes described as a political mystic, Monja Jaona, an Antandroy and a former mayor of Tulear (see ch. 4). At times Jaona cooperated with the AKFM, thus enabling his party to win a seat on the Tananarive municipal council in 1964. He preferred to seek ties with the other small parties, however. In these efforts, and particularly in his relations with the government, he was plagued by the propensity of extremists among his followers to resort to violence. As a result the party was continually viewed with great suspicion by the government and the PSD leaders—particularly by Resampa, who first saw it as an anarchist force and then as a Maoist movement capable of armed insurrection. In his roles of minister of interior and secretary general of the PSD, Resampa encouraged or allowed his subordinates to persecute MONIMA members.

In 1965 Jaona aligned his party with the small splinter group of the far Left led by the old exiled nationalist leader, Raseta. This union between ultranationalists broke apart later in the same year, however, in a conflict over who should run for the presidency. Raseta died in 1968, and his party disbanded.

In October 1967 MONIMA was reorganized after new goals were announced at a national congress. These new aims included making MONIMA the party of the disenchanted peasants throughout the island; abolishing the Civic Service, state farms, and cooperative societies; supressing the Senate; and disbanding the Ministry of Interior's paramilitary force, the Republican Security Force (Force Républicaine de Sécurité—FRS). MONIMA also demanded the expulsion of all French military personnel from the island, supported a total nationalization of all government posts, and sought ties with the communist countries. Two other small parties, the New Malagasy National Renewal Party (Neo-Renouveau National Malgache—Neo-RNM) and the Manjakavahoaka, aligned themselves with MONIMA at that time.

The party condemned both the scientific socialism of the AKFM and the Malagasy socialist doctrine of the PSD. It declared itself a "national socialist" party, causing opponents to promptly label it a resurgence of the Nazi Fascists. Its major practical objective appeared to be to attempt to strengthen local interests at the expense of the national government; all decisions on regional and local affairs were to be made by popularly elected local officials.

Christian Churches in Politics

The PSD went out of its way to maintain good relations with the Protestant and Roman Catholic clergy. The Roman Catholic hierarchy respected the party for its anticommunist stance and because of the preponderance of Christians in its leadership. There was a degree of hostility, however, among some PSD members toward the Merina Anglican Episcopal Church. This was caused by the hostility of many Merina to the PSD and because several AKFM leaders and other radical elements were Merina Protestant clergyman.

Certain Roman Catholic clergyman, particularly Jesuits in the Fianarantsoa diocese, continued to be hostile to the PSD because of its early origins as the offspring of an anticlerical Marxist French party. Also, they resented the PSD's defeat between 1956 and 1962 of the Christian parties, some of which the clergy had controlled or inspired. They preferred to continue their efforts to see those parties reborn. Party names frequently changed, but these Christian parties were generally the most important portion of the Third Force. The most outspoken publicist for the movement, a French Jesuit critic of the government, had been expelled in early 1962, but Catholic criticism of the government was never silenced. Its primary vehicle was a pair of weekly journals published in Fianarantsoa diocese, one of which—*Lumière*—was published in French. Both journals remained highly critical of what they regarded as the government's failure to root out corruption, ensure civil rights, affirm Malagasy nationalism, or improve the life of the peasant majority.

These parties' strongest showing was in the 1960 parliamentary elections, when they won 30 percent of the vote in Fianarantsoa Province. At that time their hope was in Rabemananjara, who had been the Third Force's most outstanding Roman Catholic leader. Rabemananjara supporters won 63 percent of the vote in Tamatave and a portion of the vote in Tananarive, but he and his associates had already begun the moves that led to their joining the PSD.

ELECTIONS OF 1964-65

The dominance of Tsiranana's Social Democratic Party through the mid-1960s was demonstrated in the elections of 1964-65. In the local council elections of December 1964, the PSD candidates won 598 seats, and the AKFM captured 132. The RNM won eight seats, MONIMA candidates received two, and two Tananarive splinter parties won a total of four. An additional forty-four seats were divided among independent candidates.

On March 30, 1965, the country held its first popular presidential election, in accordance with the earlier constitutional changes. President Tsiranana commanded an impressive array of support. His only opponents were the elderly left-wing nationalist Raseta, who was not supported by the AKFM, and a local businessman in Antsirabe. The president received a considerable boost to his prestige when he won the support of 97 percent of the voters. Finally, to complete this period of nearly continuous electoral activity, legislative elections were held in August 1965. The PSD candidates polled as high a number of votes as the president. The AKFM was again successful in the capital city, winning three out of the five seats. The impressive 43,377 votes the AKFM won in the capital, however, was not matched by its showing in the other three provinces it contested; its national total was only 82,936 votes as compared to the PSD's 2,304,304. The two parties of the Third Force contested the elections in the capital and two provinces but won a total of only 57,451 votes (see Opposition Parties, this ch.). Finally, MONIMA presented candidates in Tulear Province. The officially reported results gave that party only a tenth of the province's ballots. Thus again, the PSD controlled 104 of the National Assembly's 107 seats and all the seats in the Senate except for two apolitical presidential appointees.

THE CRISIS YEARS, 1970-72

New local government elections were held in December 1969.

Again the PSD scored a resounding overall victory. Nevertheless, the support for the party had noticeably weakened in some crucial areas. The PSD vote in Tananarive remained constant, while support for the AKFM doubled, leaving the PSD with seven fewer seats. In Tamatave the PSD won only 49 percent of the vote, the AKFM won 31 percent, and a newly formed Third Force coalition received 20 percent; thus the opposition held one more seat than the PSD in the city council. These relative setbacks should have served as an indicator to the PSD's leaders of discontent, at least among the urban electorate.

Because of Tsiranana's progressive illness, by 1970 or earlier it was widely believed that he would not run for a third term in 1972 at the end of his fourteenth year as president. Therefore, the question of succession became of vital importance.

In October 1970 the ailing president took a major step to lessen his workload by appointing four vice presidents, each being responsible for a major area of governmental effort. The restructuring of the government was not viewed favorably by the Merina because all four vice presidents were côtiers. Only two relatively unimportant ministries went to Merina. Their most important spokesman in the government and the PSD executive element, Joseph Ravoahangy, had died a short time before. On the other hand, the middle and upper ranks of the civil service, including a majority of subcabinet posts, were filled by Merina, as were the institutions of higher education. These holdings gave the Merina considerable political power, compensating to some extent for their lack of power at the top of the political hierarchy.

The government and party bureaucrats were not at all pleased when Resampa, the cabinet member most associated with socialism and least associated with either the Merina or French culture, was given the post of first vice president—apparently making him Tsiranana's heir apparent. Unlike nearly all the other ranking political figures, Resampa had no personal ties to French culture, was largely self-educated, reportedly was incorruptible, and was uninterested in Tananarive's affluent society.

During 1970 Resampa had received presidential support for policies that would restore the party's dynamism. Particularly after his promotion, Resampa pushed for the replacement of the older party functionaries by younger men. Many of the changes—even the relatively minor ones—were regarded as challenges by conservative members of the PSD. He also immediately announced his intention of assuring the nationalization of all unproductive foreign-owned lands; this was interpreted as another reflection of his opposition to French interests.

Four months after creating the system of four vice presidents,

President Tsiranana dramatically demoted Resampa from first vice president and minister of interior to second vice president and minister of agriculture. The president personally took over the Ministry of Interior. He also took steps to strengthen his own hold over the PSD organization, which had long been Resampa's responsibility. Rumors spread that Resampa had begun to plot against the president after learning that despite his illness Tsiranana planned to run for a third seven-year term in 1972. Tsiranana's change of mind was influenced by the fact that the threat of Resampa succeeding to the presidency had alarmed many vested interests among the PSD's traditionalists and among the economically powerful French community.

Revolt in the Southwest

The people of the southwest—particularly the Antandroy, a group never effectively governed by the French except with the aid of military forces—were stirred to rebellion in April 1971 (see ch. 14). Although traditional ethnic alignments were the major basis of their organization, complaints rooted in modern conditions drove them to violent protest. The southwest is the poorest portion of the country and is always threatened by droughts (see ch. 3; ch. 13). The people are forced to seek work as laborers throughout the island in order to survive, but they tend to return to their home villages (see ch. 4). Their meager earnings and long absences from their home territory had caused them problems with the tax collectors. Further, they were little understood by the more educated highland peoples, who were sent among them as local administrators. Maladministration in the region was increased rather than relieved by a government decision in 1967 to localize administration. This brought the withdrawal of many Merina who, if unfriendly to the Antandroy, were at least technically qualified to govern them. They were replaced by local people without qualifications, who only increased the gap between the government and the governed.

Modern and traditional values were mixed closely in the motivation and objectives of the restive people; local mystical groups also played a part. Despite the proclaimed national objectives of its leaders, MONIMA, the regional political party, was closely tied to the traditional social organizations at the local level. Although ideas introduced by the party played a major role in instigating the unrest, the revolt was apparently planned and carried out by traditional forces.

By its drastic action to suppress the revolt, the government magnified the scale of an affair that otherwise might have been dismissed as a curious incident. Moreover, government leaders rejected the need for administrative and political reform underlined by the protest action in the southwest. The outbreak of violence—the first on the island in the twenty-four years since the 1947 rebellion against the French—weakened popular confidence in the government, particularly as many equated its action with the repression carried out by the French in 1947.

The Resampa Affair

The facade of PSD unity had already been shaken by Resampa's reduction in rank. In June 1971 he and thirteen supporters were arrested and charged with plotting to overthrow the government. Despite his record as a longtime enemy of MONIMA, he was accused of complicity in the southwestern rebellion and of setting up committees throughout the PSD to facilitate his seizure of power. He also was accused of having received support from a foreign power, in this case not the PRC but the United States. This accusation by the president caused a major strain on diplomatic relations between the two countries (see ch. 10). President Tsiranana later withdrew this charge. No evidence against Resampa was ever made public, and he was not brought to trial. Instead he and his associates were placed in exile and kept under strict supervision on Ile Sainte-Marie.

In October 1971 Tsiranana announced the discovery of a second plot, purportedly led by two known Maoist employees of the French Office of Scientific and Technical Research Overseas (Office de la Recherche Scientifique et Technique Outre-Mer—ORSTOM). Again virtually no proof was offered by the president to support his contention that a plot existed.

New presidential elections were scheduled for early 1972. No opposition candidates had any hope of obtaining a respectable showing against the PSD, and Tsiranana ran unopposed. The announced results gave him the support of 99.72 percent of the electorate.

Collapse of the Government

The increasing hostility between the government and the people began to come to a head in March 1972. The key event was a seemingly unimportant strike by students at the medical school associated with the University of Madagascar (see ch. 7). Gradually the unrest and a strike spread to other students, both out of sympathy for the medical students and in support of additional demands for educational reform.

Civil strife spread in April and May. Student strikes that began over minor educational issues were broadened to include problems that troubled the rest of the population as well. The university students, joined after mid-April by Tananarive's secondary school students, demanded sweeping educational, economic, and political reforms. The major theme was adoption of a Malagasy framework for national life and the elimination of much of the dominant French influence, especially in higher education. Specifically, the demonstrators sought the abrogation of the 1960 agreements with France, which had been the basis of cooperation in Malagasy military and educational programs. Strikes had become a serious problem by April 21, and the dissidents expressed opposition to the forthcoming May inauguration of aging President Tsiranana for a third seven-year term.

Even as they opposed the conservatism of the government, the strikers favored a takeover by Malagasy military officers—apparently because they felt that the nation had been drifting and the economy deteriorating for lack of strong centralized leadership. Before and after the May 1 presidential inauguration, unrest and demonstrations in the urban centers increased (see ch. 14). Up to that time the government appeared to have ignored much of the unrest or to have acted only to maintain its conservative policies. On May 15 rioting students directed their attack against both the ruling PSD and the opposition AKFM, which had lost its student supporters because of its ineffectiveness and its association with the established order. President Tsiranana and his advisers, apparently shocked by the resulting violence and unwilling or unable to use the security forces for further suppression, moved to accept most of the strikers' demands and announced that far-reaching reforms would be initiated.

The army began to be drawn into the government on May 16, 1972. Amid demands for the president's resignation, a general officer was appointed as governor of Tananarive. The president attempted to hold the government together by calling for a special session of Parliament in order to make radical changes to appease the strikers. Before this action could be taken, however, Tsiranana dissolved his cabinet and appointed General Ramanantsoa to the newly created post of prime minister. As demands continued for the president's removal, all powers were transferred to the prime minister, who dismissed Parliament and created a ten-member cabinet composed of five military and gendarmerie officers and five civilians. All five civilians were chosen for their technical abilities; politicians from both the PSD and the opposition parties were banned.

On June 7, 1972, the new prime minister announced that his government would function under state of emergency legislation, exercising all executive and legislative power. The structure and functions of the judiciary were undisturbed.

Former Vice President Resampa was still popular with the younger elements of the population and—despite his long association with the now-unpopular police, regional administration, and the PSD—was something of a hero. He was released on June 8, 1972, and all charges against him were dropped. All other political prisoners, including Jaona, were gradually released. Resampa resigned from the PSD, announcing that his disaffection was a result of the party's failure to denounce repeated violations of human rights and its failure to confront the problems of the nation or to advance its proclaimed socialist principles. He gave his support to the prime minister. His example was soon followed by all of the opposition parties—apparently including the Communists—as well as the newly formed Joint Struggle Committee (Komity Iombonan'ny Mpitolona—KIM), which was composed of the leaders of the radical students and workers (see ch. 14).

Ramanantsoa announced plans to hold a national plebiscite to win popular support for an interim constitutional measure that would grant him five years in office and give him the power to make laws without legislative approval in order to reform the entire state. Despite his earlier reputation as a pro-French conservative, Ramanantsoa's actions gained the support of those elements within the society that demanded major changes and a complete break with France. In mid-1972 it was too early to judge whether this support would continue. Moreover, the specific objectives that the new government would set for itself had not been clearly defined.

CHAPTER 10
FOREIGN RELATIONS

At independence in 1960 pragmatic and ideological considerations led Malagasy government leaders who formulated foreign policy to choose alignment with the West. The rejection of nonalignment—the more popular stance of most newly independent states in the early 1960s—reflected President Philibert Tsiranana's fear of communist infiltration and subversion and reflected the decision to maintain close cooperation with France in both economic and security affairs during the first decade of Malagasy sovereignty. Diplomatic relations were quickly established with the United States, which was regarded as the defender of the Western bloc, and with major West European states; overtures by the Soviet Union and East European states initially were rejected.

Although France and her partners in the European Economic Community (EEC, known as the Common Market) were the primary centers of attention in Malagasy foreign policy during the 1960s, diversification of political and economic relations was initiated. Relations with countries on the African continent mainly involved former French African colonies and were developed largely through regional cooperation. Contacts with Asian countries also were initiated. Foreign policy generally advanced pragmatic rather than idealistic solutions. Although the Tsiranana government's refusal to recognize the People's Republic of China (PRC) might be seen as an idealistic stance, the government in fact regarded the PRC as the major threat to the security of Madagascar. When France began its initiatives toward the PRC in the 1960s, the Malagasy representatives joined the United States in attempting to prevent votes in favor of seating the PRC in the United Nations.

The assumption of executive power by the military in May 1972 did not result in any immediate realignment of foreign policy. A shift, however, occurred in September of that year when the former government's policy toward the Republic of South Africa was revised. Since the mid-1960s the Tsiranana government had gradually increased its contacts with that country. This policy had become an issue of domestic as well as international controversy. The limitations of national sovereignty, implied by the international agreements specifying close cooperation with France, provided one of the major issues leading to the fall of the Tsiranana government (see ch. 9). When it was formed in May 1972, the new government of General Gabriel Ramanantsoa stated its intention to adjust the terms of some of these agreements, but as of late 1972 definitive steps in this direction had not been outlined.

THE FOREIGN MINISTRY AND DIPLOMATIC TIES

Under the provisions of the 1960 Constitution the president, serving as both head of state and head of government, was entrusted with major responsibility for the conduct of foreign relations. He was granted authority to negotiate and ratify treaties, to accredit ambassadors and envoys to foreign states, and to accept the credentials of foreign ambassadors and envoys. Policy formation by the president was constitutionally limited by the requirement that he conduct state policy in conformity with general directives adopted by the Council of Ministers. The authority of the president was further restricted by the necessity for parliamentary approval of treaties of alliance, commerce, or peace, treaties of membership in international organizations, and treaties modifying existing legislation or altering national territory.

The president was assisted in the execution of foreign policy by the minister of foreign affairs. Generally the post was given to one of the three senior ministers of state (see ch. 8). The minister was aided by a ministerial staff in the development of political, economic, and cultural relations as well as in the coordination of foreign assistance programs. The specific organization of the ministry, which was revised several times during the 1960s, provided both geographic and functional specialization. The ministry also contained a research staff engaged in studies and surveys—particularly in the area of economic cooperation—designed to evaluate its effectiveness and aid in the formulation of national policy. The ministries handling educational affairs and economic cooperation also played roles in foreign relations.

When General Ramanantsoa assumed executive power from President Tsiranana in May 1972, the executive branch was restructured. The majority, if not all, of the powers formerly held by the president were transferred to the newly created office of the prime minister. The cabinet under Ramanantsoa in late 1972 was meeting twice a week to discuss all matters of importance. Although additional information about the structure and dimensions of foreign policy formulation under the new cabinet was not available, it was clear that all foreign affairs decisions rested in the hands of the prime minister and his cabinet.

In 1972 financial considerations limited the number of countries in which Malagasy maintained resident ambassadors to fewer than ten. Most Malagasy ambassadors held multiple accreditation, expanding the total number of countries with which regularized diplomatic relations were maintained to about thirty. The ambassador to the United States, for example, was also accredited to Canada, the Republic of Korea (South Korea), and the United Nations. The ambassador to Belgium was accredited to the Netherlands, Switzerland, Luxembourg, and the Common Market. The ambassador to

France was also accredited to Sierra Leone, and the ambassador to the United Kingdom also served Italy, Israel, and Greece. Budget reductions under consideration by the new Ramanantsoa government included both the reduction of foreign service personnel abroad and the downgrading of certain diplomatic missions, including those in Algeria, the Republic of China (Nationalist China), Mauritius, and France.

In mid-1972 eleven countries maintained diplomatic missions in the Malagasy Republic at ambassadorial level. Of these, five were those of West European countries: Austria, France, the Federal Republic of Germany (West Germany), Italy, and the United Kingdom. No African countries had diplomatic representatives in Madagascar. The three Asian states maintaining embassies in the national capital were the Republic of China, India, and Japan; South Korea had announced its intention to establish a permanent diplomatic representative in Tananarive. Embassies were maintained by Greece, Israel, and the United States; the United Nations and the Vatican also had diplomatic representatives in Tananarive.

THE MAJOR ELEMENTS OF FOREIGN POLICY

Malagasy foreign policy has been structured to achieve a variety of explicitly stated objectives. The most dominant of these ranged from the theoretical application of general principles inherent in the Malagasy concept of foreign relations to the practical considerations related to the search for external sources of aid to support the domestic struggle for economic development. The policies designed to fulfill these objectives have been relatively consistent with one another; they have generally taken into account the realities of the international political system and have considered the strength of the Malagasy state vis-à-vis other states.

The first and foremost principle enunciated by the government has been respect for the sovereignty of all foreign countries and, correspondingly, nonintervention in the domestic affairs of any state. The government has been sensitive to the possibility of subversion encouraged from abroad, particularly from communist countries. The government's view of nonintervention extended beyond simple noninterference in a country's domestic political affairs and included an awareness that economic aid, trade, or other assistance could serve as a pretext for interference. Close ties with France, however, have been accepted by the government as compatible with national sovereignty.

Despite the fact that the Tsiranana government had opened economic relations with South Africa, it voiced strong support for the right of all people to self-determination. This second principle of Malagasy foreign policy, clearly advanced by the Ramanantsoa government in 1972, was particularly concerned with African

171

peoples still under colonial domination in the Portuguese colonies of Mozambique and Angola and those under the domination of a racial minority in Rhodesia and South Africa. In this as in all other affairs, however, the Malagasy emphasize a reliance on negotiations—the third major principle of foreign policy—as the sole solution for international conflict. The republic has systematically urged the adoption of negotiated settlements in the context of international and regional organizations, such as the United Nations and the Organization of African Unity (OAU), and it has offered its offices as a mediator and its territory as a site for negotiation between disputing parties. The principle is based on the rejection of violence and the belief that dialogue leads to understanding and is, therefore, the best route to the resolution of tension. Its stand in the OAU has been notable because it put the country in the ranks of the moderate minority on questions concerning South Africa.

Malagasy foreign policy was based on a perception of the world as being divided into two antagonistic blocs. The president's view of international relations allowed no room for a position of nonalignment between the free world and totalitarian communism. He regarded a nonaligned position as economic blackmail by opportunistic states attempting to play both sides for the maximization of parochial interests at the expense of larger free-world interests.

RELATIONS WITH FRANCE AND WESTERN EUROPE

Of the seventeen former French African colonies, the Malagasy government has appeared to be one of the three or four that seem least troubled over French neocolonialism, and firm relations have been maintained with France. Although Tsiranana did not support French policy toward the PRC, he firmly backed French policy in Algeria and defended nuclear testing in the Sahara. Mutual consultation between the two governments, particularly during the first half of the 1960s, occurred frequently in order to inform the other of positions and proposed actions each intended to take.

No single factor accounts for the general cordiality of relations between the two countries. Although there had been considerable cultural transfer from France, including the educational system, the replacement of foreign personnel with Malagasy nationals was an increasingly important issue during the 1960s. The transfer from French control during the 1950s was relatively smooth when compared to some other colonies, but resentment of the repressions of the 1947 revolt had not died at the time of independence (see ch. 2). One of the major explanations for the development of increased cordiality was the rapport between French President Charles de Gaulle and President Tsiranana; Tsiranana vistied de Gaulle in Paris several times during the early 1960s.

Government concern over communist subversion had led at

various times to the control of printed material imported into the country and to the close observation of groups suspected of communist activity. The country had relied on defense arrangements with the French and on its pro-Western orientation as a deterrent to communist incursions. Concern had been expressed over the increased Soviet presence in the Indian Ocean area, and by the early 1970s the Tsiranana government's earlier fears of communist subversion had been only slightly moderated, despite the general East-West detente.

In 1969 Foreign Minister Jacques Rabemananjara was quoted as saying that underdevelopment was the only enemy of the Malagasy state. Thus a major objective of diplomacy has been to work for the achievement of national development goals. After independence this task became a prime determinant of policy, but it received increasing emphasis during the late 1960s. The country has entered into various bilateral commercial, technical, and economic cooperation, and investment protection agreements. It has encouraged all sources and forms of development assistance, including many that—according to opposition critics—were infringing on the country's sovereignty and harming its best economic interests. Participation in multilateral activities included meetings and programs under the auspices of such groups as the United Nations and the Common Market. In 1972 concern continued to be expressed, however, that the search for economic development aid should not sacrifice political independence.

The fact that the government and ruling party felt the necessity of close cooperation with France was as influential as the intangible factors. The Malagasy, as a result, were dependent upon the French for administrative and technical assistance, and the Malagasy currency was tied to the stability of the French franc (see ch. 12). Not only was France the first trading partner of Madagascar, but also French-oriented business interests monopolized various sectors of the Malagasy economy. This general dependence was further institutionalized after independence by a multiplicity of agreements concerning defense, raw materials and strategic products, civil aviation, the merchant marine, justice, higher education, and postal and telecommunications matters.

French personnel have played a dominant role in technical and administrative assistance programs in Madagascar. In the early 1970s about 90 percent of the approximately 2,000 foreign technical assistance personnel in the country were French. About 70 percent of these were teachers, and about 14 percent were assigned to security operations. French citizens also played a direct role in government administration; numerous political posts, including roughly one-fifth of the presidential staff, were held by Frenchmen. About two-thirds of the higher civil service ranks and a weighted percentage of managerial posts in the private sector were held by French citizens.

Official government policy has not gone without protest from various opposition groups within the country. The Party of the Congress for the Independence of Madagascar (Ankoton'ny Kongresi'ny Fahaleovantenan Madagaskara—AKFM) and the nationalist press have been the most vocal. Although the French military presence often has been the target of protest, the number and cost of French technical assistants and the continuing treaty obligations with France have been more common issues. Extreme nationalists and procommunist elements of the population have expressed the greatest desire to disassociate from France, and even a probable majority of Social Democratic Party (Parti Social Démocratique—PSD) members support calls for reduced dependence on the French (see ch. 9).

During the early 1970s protest increased over these and other issues. The practical realities of the country's economy gave the Tsiranana government little room in which to maneuver and finally forced it to relinquish executive power to the military. In the fall of 1972 radical groups continued to press the new government for the expulsion of French military personnel, for the abolition of dual citizenship, and for moves to loosen ties with France. The ability of the government to satisfy domestic demands vis-à-vis its foreign policy position would be a contributing factor in maintaining continued popular support.

Under the terms of the Treaty of Rome that established the Common Market, associate status was granted to all of the French colonial territories. Under the Yaoundé Convention of 1960 this status was extended to these territories after they became independent states. The Malagasy were quick to establish diplomatic relations with all six Common Market members and used their status not only to diversify their economic relations but also to increase investment and aid its flow into the Malagasy economy. During the 1960s the country was the largest recipient of development funds granted by the European Development Fund, the development agency of the Common Market.

After France, the Common Market country with which Madagascar has developed the closest relations has been West Germany, which in the early 1970s was also a valued trade partner (see ch. 12). Strong support had been given West Germany in its defense of West Berlin, and the Malagasy had strongly condemned the erection of the Berlin wall in 1961. In return for its support Madagascar received various benefits, including educational assistance to Malagasy students and the establishment of a local chapter of the Goethe Institute in Tananarive (see ch. 7). The cadre training center of the PSD was also indirectly supported by the West

German Social Democratic Party through the Friedrich Ebert Foundation.

A variety of intergovernmental relations was maintained with other Common Market member states. The Ifagraria state enterprise of Italy, for example, supported agricultural development projects in Madagascar, but the terms of Italian cooperation agreements were regarded as overly severe. Economic relations had also been established with the Scandinavian countries.

Relations with the Netherlands had been marred in early 1972 by the disclosure of an information bulletin by the World Radio Broadcasting Company of the Netherlands for its personnel stationed in Madagascar; in it, relations with domestic servants and Malagasy social manners were discussed in what was considered a prejudiced and condescending manner. Domestic protest over this issue led to demands by protest groups for the expulsion of Radio Netherlands from Madagascar. The issure had become less important by mid-1972 but reappeared among the demands of more radical groups after the assumption of power by the military.

Although relations with Great Britain date from the early nineteenth century, British influence was largely displaced by the French presence during the colonial period. The British presence during World War II temporarily reopened relations with London. After independence cordial relations developed between the two countries, and in the mid-1960s the Malagasy consented to a British request that a squadron of the Royal Air Force be permitted to use the Majunga airfield in order to aid in the British blockade of Rhodesia. Consent was withdrawn in 1971, and by March 1972 the British had begun the withdrawal of their planes.

RELATIONS WITH THE UNITED STATES

Diplomatic relations with the United States were initiated by the Merina monarchy in the nineteenth century; a United States consul was installed in Tananarive in 1866. The consulate was maintained after the assumption of control by the French, but it closed temporarily at various times for lack of business or because of periods of international crisis. Upon Malagasy independence United States diplomatic representation was upgraded to the ambassadorial level.

At the outset the Malagasy were anxious to develop good relations with the United States, whose government was an obvious source of development aid and whose industrial corporations were potential investors in the private sector of the Malagasy economy. Other factors encouraging close relations with the United States included its influence on international financial institutions and the security role it played as a defender against potential communist intrusions.

After Malagasy independence the United States sent trade and

175

scientific missions to Tananarive and offered grants in American commodities. By 1963, in addition to standard aid programs, the United States had agreed to guarantee private investment in the island's economy and had made available a number of educational fellowships to Malagasy students. In return the Malagasy government consented in October 1963 to the construction of a National Aeronautics and Space Administration (NASA) tracking station. The NASA facility was established at Imerintsiatosika, southwest of Tananarive near the old Arivoniamamo airport. The tracking station was still in operation in late 1972.

At various times the United States has come under attack by the AKFM and other small left-wing groups. Conservative French residents spread rumors that the United States was supporting the rebels during the 1947 revolt (see ch. 2). Protests by the AKFM somewhat complicated negotiations and parliamentary debates over the acceptance of aid under the United States Point Four Program before independence and commodity grants after independence.

Relations between the two countries during the 1960s were cordial. The only Malagasy government complaint concerned what it considered to be the small amount of United States aid and investments. President Tsiranana made a trip to Washington in 1964 in the hope of obtaining a greater United States aid commitment. Such a commitment never reached the level Tsiranana had hoped it would because the United States continued to prefer minimal involvement in the Indian Ocean area.

In mid-1971, however, relations were disrupted between the two countries when the Malagasy government implied that the United States had participated in a plan by Vice President André Resampa to overthrow the Tsiranana government (see ch. 9). The United States ambassador and several other members of his staff were recalled to Washington. Diplomatic relations in Tananarive continued on a reduced level, and the United States refused to appoint a new ambassador until the Malagasy government offered an apology.

Nevertheless, in March 1972 the United States authorized emergency aid equivalent to FMG1.5 million (for value of the Malagasy franc—see Glossary) for the victims of a cyclonic wind disaster, and relations gradually improved. In May, shortly before the riots that forced him to cede executive power to General Ramanantsoa, President Tsiranana offered his government's official apology regarding the Resampa affair. The appointment by the United States government of a new ambassador, scheduled to assume his position in Tananarive during the fall of 1972, returned relations between the two governments to their pre-1971 level.

RELATIONS WITH THE SOVIET UNION AND EASTERN EUROPE

Relations between Soviet-bloc countries and the Malagasy Republic were slow in developing during the strongly anticommunist Tsiranana administration. In 1960 the Soviet Union expressed interest in an exchange of diplomatic representatives and sent a commercial mission to Tananarive in 1961 to establish economic relations, but the Soviet Union was unable to obtain a definitive response from the Malagasy government. Although the Malagasy indicated some interest in selling goods to the Soviet Union, they were unwilling to make commitments regarding the purchase of Soviet goods.

Contacts between the two countries had increased slightly by early 1964. Scientists and a group of tourists from the Soviet Union visited Tananarive, and a delegation of Malagasy students attended a youth festival in Moscow. These events were followed by the signing of commercial agreements with the Soviet Union, Poland, and Hungary. Implementation of the agreements was delayed by the Malagasy government until 1966 as a result of apprehension of communist subversive efforts, particularly as PRC interest in black Africa increased and procommunist groups overthrew the government in nearby Zanzibar. Decreasing Malagasy interest in the goods the East European states were offering also played a part.

In 1967 the country agreed for the first time to consider the exchange of commercial representatives with the Soviet Union. In 1968 diplomatic relations were established with Romania. Representatives of the Soviet Committee of Afro-Asian Solidarity were invited to the eighth anniversary of Malagasy independence. Malagasy representatives attended a film festival in Moscow; and new commercial agreements granting permission for the temporary establishment of a Soviet commercial mission in Tananarive were signed. This position was reversed, however, after the Soviet interference in Czechoslovakia in 1968 and after the Malagasy learned that the proposed mission was to be staffed by about 100 Russians. With the exception of the establishment of relations with Yugoslavia in 1969, relations with the countries of Eastern Europe remained static.

Faced with domestic unrest, President Tsiranana had increased his attacks against the dangers of communist subversion and directly blamed foreign Communists for supporting student strikes as a maneuver designed to widen local political divisions. In mid-1972 the AKFM and the more extreme political factions pressured the Ramanantsoa government to expand relations with communist states. The Malagasy foreign minister stopped in Moscow in September on his way to the United Nations in New York. This sign of improving relations between the Malagasy Republic and the Soviet Union was culminated in October by the announcement of an agreement between the two states to establish diplomatic relations. The two countries also announced their intentions to renegotiate the 1967 commercial agreements.

RELATIONS WITH AFRICA AND THE MIDDLE EAST

Geographical separation, budgetary limitations, the Malagasy concept of diplomacy, and diverse cultural traditions had limited the development of relations with continental Africa. The Malagasy have taken greater pride in the Asian aspect of their origins and have not identified closely with the pan-African movements of black Africa. Thus, although they have been active in regional organizations, their participation has been out of an interest in the promotion of regional peace and cooperation rather than in the creation of supranational unification. Contacts with members of these organizations were particularly important as a result of the lack of resident Malagasy diplomatic representation in many African capitals. Relations were largely oriented toward French-speaking African states.

The move toward relations with South Africa by the Tsiranana government during the late 1960s was the subject of considerable controversy. Motivated by a variety of factors, including economic benefits and possible cooperation between French and South African security forces in the southwestern Indian Ocean, the Malagasy government agreed to an exchange of visits of high-level officials in the late 1960s. Malawi was quick to applaud such action, but most African states and various Malagasy groups opposed such action. President Tsiranana was firm in stating his opposition to apartheid, but he was equally firm in his belief that the most effective policy was dialogue and not the economic and military strategies proposed by other states.

By 1971 negotiations between Madagascar and South Africa had expanded to include tourism, and agreements had been signed providing for South African investment in Malagasy tourist facilities, infrastructure, and docking and naval repair services (see ch. 12). A joint technical committee was established to promote trade, and other agreements had been signed, including the granting of mining concessions to South African companies. The possibility of diplomatic exchanges between the two countries was reported, and domestic protest over contacts with South Africa increased in the weeks leading to the May 1972 riots (see ch. 9).

In early June, after the assumption of control by the new government, the Malagasy foreign minister announced that relations with South Africa were under review. On June 23 the government announced that it had decided to break all official ties with South Africa and was cancelling the various conventions that previously had been negotiated. As the summer ended, there was some indication that his policy would not be applied uniformly to all investment agreements with South Africa, and the dimensions of future developments between the two states were unclear.

Officially, the Malagasy have maintained a position of neutrality regarding the situation in the Middle East and have called upon all parties concerned to enter into serious negotiation, which it considers the only solution to the issue. Governmental attitudes, however, have clearly favored Israel, which, along with Algeria and Tunisia, was one of the three Middle Eastern countries with whom the Malagasy maintained diplomatic relations. Although the government was reported to have been concerned in the early 1960s over the possibility of Arab penetration via the Comoro Islands and the Comorian minority living near Majunga, the pro-Israeli position appeared to have been motivated by the basic pro-Western stance of Malagasy foreign policy and the multiple economic benefits of cooperation with Israel.

Israel was regarded by the Tsiranana government as a model developing state, and exchanges of government officials in the early 1960s led to a variety of technical assistance programs, which provided training, on a limited scale, for civil servants, security forces, and urban police units. Malagasy communal associations were also modeled on Israeli cooperatives. Although scholarships had been offered by several North African countries, student exchanges had not been effected, and as late as 1972 the Malagasy government was reportedly unwilling to accept Arab Muslim technicians in programs sponsored by international organizations.

RELATIONS WITH ASIA

The anticommunist thrust of Malagasy foreign policy clearly has been aimed principally at the PRC, which in the opinion of the Malagasy government has intended to establish an Asian hegemony extending all the way to the African continent. In addition to maintaining relations with Nationalist China, the Tsiranana government had actively sought to prevent the seating of the PRC in the United Nations. Political factions within the country pressed for the opening of relations with the PRC after its admission to the United Nations and after the visit of President Richard Nixon of the United States to Peking in 1972. The government expressed satisfaction that the United States and the PRC were engaging in negotiations and voiced the belief that the opening of Sino-American relations would fundamentally affect all aspects of international relations. Indicating that every nation would have to decide for itself how its national interests were affected by this turn of events, the Malagasy government maintained that it would coninue its friendship with Nationalist China.

Relations with Nationalist China were strengthened in April 1962 when President Tsiranana vistied Taiwan. In early 1964 the two countries decided to establish diplomatic relations and subsequently exchanged ambassadors. Relations between the two countries included Nationalist Chinese aid and technical assistance to the Malagasy, especially in the areas of rice cultivation and bamboo handcrafts. These agreements were renewed in early 1972.

In the early 1970s there was a resident Chinese community of about 9,000 in Madagascar. The community had strong commercial interests, especially in grocery sales and moneylending. Although most members had retained Nationalist Chinese citizenship and allegiance, the Malagasy government had expressed concern that the PRC might attempt to use the ethnic identity of the Chinese community to its advantage. Careful distinction was maintained by the government, however, between the Chinese people—whom they regarded as friends—and groups that advocated Maoist revolutionary tactics.

As a counter to PRC influence the Malagasy government had sought firm relations with other noncommunist Asian states in addition to Nationalist China. Relations with India were cordial, but they were complicated by the presence in Madagascar of an Indian community estimated at roughly 17,000 in 1970. Only about 3,000 of these Indians were registered as aliens with the Indian embassy in Tananarive. Some of the more prosperous members of this community had obtained French citizenship during the colonial period, and hundreds more were without citizenship in any country. The Indian community also played a role in commerce disproportionate to its size; Indian capitalists had figured significantly in moves toward industrial development, particularly in the textile and food industries. The community was not well integrated into Malagasy society, however, and resentment of Indian economic success was openly expressed. Both the PSD and opposition groups had been united in their desire to maintain restrictions on Indian immigration that had been instituted under the French.

Trade agreements were initiated with Japan in 1963. Although the entrance of Japanese goods into the Malagasy market was limited by preferential agreements between the Malagasy Republic and the Common Market, Japanese manufactured goods were becoming increasingly competitive. The Japanese had expressed increasing interest in offshore fishing and in the construction of fishing industry facilities on the island.

Contacts had also been established during the 1960s with the Philippines and Singapore as well as with Indonesia after the fall of President Sukarno. Sentiment was strongly favorable toward Indonesia, which educated Malagasy regarded as the remote source of their ethnic and cultural origins (see ch. 2). The Tsiranana government had received the official representatives of the South Vietnamese government on several occasions but had officially expressed in various international bodies its opposition to the Vietnamese war and had urged its resolution by negotiation.

INTERNATIONAL ORGANIZATIONS

Upon receiving independence the Malagasy Republic applied immediately for membership in the United Nations. The application was approved promptly by the Security Council, and on September 20, 1960, the republic and ten African states were elected to membership during the first meeting of the fifteenth session of the General Assembly. In the following month the country became the first developing state to become a member of the executive council of the United Nations Educational, Scientific and Cultural Organization (UNESCO). Since then the country has become affiliated with all thirteen of the specialized agencies of the United Nations, including groups such as the World Health Organization (WHO), the Food and Agriculture Organization (FAO), and the International Bank for Reconstruction and Development (IBRD, commonly known as the World Bank). The Malagasy representatives have played an active role in the General Assembly and its various committee sessions. In February 1972 the republic cited its pressing obligations as a member of three other committees and one council as overriding reasons for its resignation from the United Nations Council on Decolonialisation.

Membership was also maintained in 1972 in such United Nations bodies as the General Agreement on Tariffs and Trade (GATT) and the International Atomic Energy Agency (IAEA). The country had served as a member of the executive council of the Office of the United Nations High Commissioner for Refugees and, in addition to receiving aid under various programs associated with the United Nations, was a contributor to the United Nations Development Program (UNDP).

Although initially concerned that membership in regional African organizations might adversely affect relations with France, President Tsiranana became one of the major supporters of such groups. In September 1961 the Charter of the African and Malagasy Union (Union Africaine et Malgache—UAM), which linked former French territories in a loose political and economic association, was signed in Tananarive. The government was active in plans leading to the establishment of the Organization of African Unity (OAU) and in the gradual reorganization of UAM into the Common Organization of African and Malagasy States and Mauritius (Organisation Commune Africaine, Malgache, et Mauritien—OCAMM). The widened membership of OCAMM included black African states that were former French and Belgian territories, but OCAMM cooperative efforts were largely limited to the economic sphere. In 1972 the republic remained an active member in both OCAMM and the OAU.

Participation in OCAMM included membership in a variety of associated cooperative organizations. Included were the African and Malagasy Council on Higher Education (Conseil Africain et Malgache de l'Enseignement Supérieur—CAMES), the African and Malagasy Postal and Telecommunication Union (Union Africaine et Malgache des postes et Télécommunication—UAMPT), and the African and Malagasy Union of Development Banks (Union Africaine et Malgache des Banques pour le Développement—UAMBD). The Malagasy government had also entered into agreements with Indian Ocean neighbors, including the Tourist Alliance of the Indian Ocean and the Vanilla Alliance of the Indian Ocean.

Although the government has sought for leadership in these organizations, the moderate and realistic positions advanced by its representatives have not always been popular with other African states. At the OAU conference of 1964, Tsiranana was the only head of state who supported the admission of Moise Tshombe of the Republic of the Congo to the conference; the Malagasy position was based on the premise that, regardless of internal developments, Tshombe was the legal representative of the Congolese government.

The Tsiranana government long opposed the use of insurgent groups against African states controlled by a racial minority and refused to pay assessments for the support of such organizations. The position on assessments was reversed in June 1972 by the Ramanantsoa government's agreement to pay both the current and outstanding assessments. The Malagasy membership in regional bodies has clearly indicated support for African unity, but the Malagasy have opposed the concept of supranational organizations such as that advocated by Kwame Nkrumah, former president of Ghana. The recognition of regional differences has remained inherent in Malagasy foreign policy.

CHAPTER 11
MASS COMMUNICATIONS

In 1972, despite an active and proliferous press and the existence of radio and television broadcasting facilities, traditional modes of communication remained the most widely used means of spreading information among the mass of the Malagasy people. A variety of interpersonal situations arising from the living habits of a predominantly agricultural population offered ample opportunity for face-to-face dialogue (see ch. 4). As a source of information for topics extending beyond local affairs, however, traditional channels were often unreliable mixtures of fact and rumor.

Efforts had been made to increase the spread of information to rural areas—particularly through the use of radio—but modern methods of mass communication had served the goals of national development only minimally. The sources of news and information about the national society were often limited to urban centers in the highlands, and the impact of information disseminated through modern channels was strongest among the more educated urban population. The printed word did not easily penetrate rural regions in which literacy and personal income levels were low.

Althought the number of persons reached by the modern media represented a small portion of the total population, those who relied on its elements for information tended to be the most politically active. The press has played a major role in expressing opposition opinion but has been restricted in its freedom both during the country's colonial period and since national independence in 1960. From its inception, radio broadcasting has been owned and administered by the central government. Its use as a means of political control often had been protested by opposition groups, including a segment of the partisan press.

TRADITIONAL COMMUNICATION CHANNELS

News and other information traditionally have been communicated by word of mouth within small groups meeting for social purposes or to perform work. The most common examples are gatherings of families and larger kinship groups, religious associations, and groups engaged in cultivation and herding. Although the Malagasy peoples do not regard participation in these groups primarily as a means of gathering information, such encounters provide a primary channel for exchanges regarding local affairs.

The number of such associations in which an individual participates varies within different ethnic groups, depending on their location and individual interests. Even when an individual participates in several groups, one is usually accepted as the principal and most reliable source of information. Local assemblages are also linked together as communication media by less formally structured exchanges that occur at marketplaces, coffeehouses, cultural clubs, wells, and other sources of water that are vital features of pastoral life.

The structure and regularity of group contact vary widely. Some nomadic or semisedentary groups—the Antandroy, for example—tend to use the same water sources without major variance. Other peoples may be more mobile and play a greater role in the dissemination of information between various groups. Migratory herders and semisedentary peoples often pick up news from village radio sets or in conversations with the residents of villages with whom they trade. These reports, as well as the listener's interpretations of them, are later passed on in the course of pastoral activities or during religious or social occasions.

The exchange of information between ethnic groups is often related to occupational considerations and thus may be seasonal in frequency. Among the Betsileo short-term seasonal migrations for agricultural employment occur sometimes two or three times a year. Groups of Betsileo carpenters or bricklayers wander throughout the countryside during the dry season; others serve as merchants and itinerant traders. In each case the transmission of news and other information occurs concurrently with the performance of the particular task at hand (see ch. 4).

Many groups possess formal decisionmaking bodies, such as the *kabary* of Merina society, which serve not only to settle issues at debate but also as information channels (see ch. 2). News and information received from a source outside the group are often treated with suspicion, but information attributed to a prestigious source, such as a visiting religious leader, is more often believed. In some cases group acceptance is virtually assured if the information conforms to existent ethnic beliefs and if it is presented in the group's conventional literary style. Introductory pleasantries and the exchange of traditional proverbs are often essential steps that must precede the discussion of any substantive issue or problem.

Although adequate for the dissemination of local information, the reliance on face-to-face communication often increases the incidence of misinformation and rumor. The system of informal communication tends to reinforce traditional local beliefs and often impedes acceptance of new concepts of national development that the government attempts to communicate to the people through modern channels. Links between traditional channels and the modern media thus are insufficient for the flow of news and information to all segments of the population. Similarly, the government often encounters difficulty in assessing the effect of its formal communication efforts.

THE MODERN MEDIA

The Role of the Government

The modern mass media of the republic have served throughout their history as channels for the dissemination of information supporting various political parties or official views of the government. The press in particular has played an active role in the political affairs of the country. Government regulation of the press by the government of Philibert Tsiranana has included measures designed to stimulate and improve publishing in the country, but it has also included acts of censorship and confiscation, such as the seizure of particular issues, the suspension of opposition newspapers, and the arrests of journalists. The government attitude toward free expression since independence, however, is one of the most liberal in the world.

After the establishment of the French Protectorate in 1894, the Malagasy press became subject to the French Metropolitan Act of July 19, 1881. The first strict application of censorship occurred during the World War I administration of Governor Hubert Garbit, who ironically favored a more liberal attitude toward the press than dictated by metropolitan policy directives. Major press restrictions in the years between the two world wars included the decree of December 15, 1929, requiring that the managing editor of a local newspaper be a Frenchman, and the decree of December 4, 1930, under which the government assumed powers to suppress and suspend local publications. Although more liberal policies were followed in the immediate years before World War II, the colonial government used the 1930 decree as the basis for similar suspension of the press following the 1947 revolt (see ch. 2).

A major shift in policy occurred during the 1950-54 administration of French Governor Robert Bargues, who supported a free press on the grounds that responsible and professional newspapers would aid French administrative efforts. He initiated the holding of regularly scheduled press conferences and supplied newspapers with accurate information designed to reduce the frequency of rumor. Other contributions included the establishment of an official information service, expansion of official publications, and related media developments, including the introduction of documentary films.

Freedom of the press became an important issue in the promulgation of the Malagasy constitution in 1959. Freedom of the press was specified as one of the fundamental forms of the right of free expression as long as it did not violate the interests of public order and security. As detailed in the Act of February 1959, the press was granted complete freedom to write and publish without any form of censorship; government action could be taken only after publication had occurred. Material designed to incite disruption of public order or which was false or slanderous was subject to confiscation by the Ministry of Interior. Heavy fines were specified as punishment for violators.

The terms of the 1959 act benefited larger publications, which either paid their fines or initiated countersuits, placing a heavy burden on an already overloaded court system. Small newspapers were often unable to satisfy the judgments of the courts and were forced out of business. Moreover, there were sufficient loopholes to allow a convicted newspaper to resume publication after a few days under a new name. Several ordinances were passed in an effort to remedy these deficiencies, but the reforms were generally marginal.

Government activities relating to the press and other elements of the mass media were placed under the jurisdiction of the Ministry of Information, Tourism, and Traditional Arts, whose organizational structure was provided under the decrees of August 24 and December 12, 1967. Among its various roles, the ministry was designated as a spokesman for the national government's Council of Ministers, and it disseminated government directives and information to the press. Under its direction were several divisions that also provided separate services for radio, television, and films. The ministry also operated a technical service and related administrative services, such as the sale of radio and television commercials. The government news service, the Madagascar Press Agency (L'Agence Madagascar Presse—MADPRESS), was also directed by the ministry. It was responsible for the gathering and dissemination of news to regional, national, and international subscribers, and it published a daily bulletin.

Throughout his administration as the republic's first head of state, President Tsiranana was proud of the existence of an opposition press. The sincerity of his pride was demonstrated by his initiatives designed to preserve an independent French-language press, which led to the creation of the influential daily newspaper *Le Courrier de Madagascar*. Domestic and international developments, however, led Tsiranana's government on several occasions to suspend unsympathetic publications or to confiscate particular issues. The government claimed such action was necessitated by irresponsible elements of the press, and the newspapers replied with objections to the limitations imposed on constitutionally guaranteed freedoms.

The politics of the early 1970s brought increased newspaper seizures. In late January and early February 1972 editions containing articles on the validity of the elections of January 30, 1970, were seized by order of the Ministry of Interior (see ch. 9). Included among the publications seized were issues of the daily newspapers

Maresaka, *Imongo Vaovao*, and *Basy Vava* and the thrice-weekly *Hehy*. By March 1972 additional seizures had been made of other periodicals, including issues of *Lumière* and *Réalités Malgaches*. The Press Association of Madagascar made an official appeal to the president, calling for an end to government seizures and requesting a joint discussion of new press laws.

Mounting political unrest led to the May 1972 assumption of executive power by General Gabriel Ramanantsoa (see ch. 9). At the start of the crisis the government suspended publication of the daily *Le Courrier de Madagascar*. The newspaper remained closed for sixteen days and then began publishing under the new name of *Madagascar Matin*. Government action at that time also included confiscation of issues of a number of foreign publications carrying articles about Malagasy domestic unrest. Included were the British periodical the *Economist* and French publications *Valeurs Actuelles*, *Paris Match*, *L'Express*, *Jeune Afrique*, and the weekly issue of *Le Monde*.

Radio and Television

In 1972 radio was the most effective modern medium of mass communication, especially among the rural areas where a low literacy rate and distribution problem greatly limited the effectiveness of the printed word. The value of radio was reinforced by the use in broadcasting of the standard Merina dialect, which was universally understood (see ch. 4). Separate programming in French was aimed at the more educated segments of the population. English was used to supplement French and Malagasy in programs designed for audiences outside the republic.

Public radio broadcasting was initiated in 1931 by the French administration of Governor Leon Cayla. Reception of the signal emitted by the 500-watt transmitter serving Radio Tananarive, as the station identified itself, was limited to a fifty-mile radius of the capital. Early programming provided a two-hour daily schedule. A more powerful transmitter was built in 1938 at Alarobia. On the eve of World War II there were about 2,000 receiving sets on the island; about half were battery powered. During the war the government made much use of the station to broadcast its orders and news, and a musical request program was introduced. By the end of the war, however, Radio Tananarive had lost its early broadcasting lead over the stations of other African colonies.

Although broadcasting facilities were expanded in the immediate postwar years, dissatisfaction with local program offerings significantly decreased the popularity of radio. During the 1950-54 administration of Governor Bargues, substantial improvements in radio broadcasting occurred, including refinements in the quality and duration of broadcasting, the initiation of islandwide listener reaction surveys, and the inclusion of Malagasy-language programs. Vernacular broadcasting had not been encouraged in French colonies, and its initiation in Madagascar represented one of the first revisions of this policy.

Technical difficulties, however, continued to limit the development of radio broadcasting. In 1957, in an effort to obtain increased financial and technical aid from France, Radio Tananarive was placed under the direct administration of the French Overseas Radio Broadcasting Company (Société de Radiodiffusion de la France d'Outre-Mer—SORAFOM) and was renamed Radiodiffusion de Madagascar. Administrative responsibility continued under SORAFOM until after independence in 1960, and major technical assistance was provided by the French company. By 1961 the broadcast schedule provided 145 hours of weekly programming.

In January 1962 control of all broadcasting was transferred to the Malagasy state company, the Malagasy National Radio Broadcasting Company (Société Nationale Malgache de Radiodiffusion). Although the broadcasting service maintained its own staff, it operated in compliance with the directives of the Ministry of Information, Tourism, and Traditional Arts. The broadcast service in 1972 was known as the Malagasy National Broadcasting Company (Radiodiffusion Nationale Malgache—RNM).

The facilities of the government's Broadcasting House in Tananarive were modern and could transmit three programs simultaneously. Transmission equipment included two mediumwave band transmitters, each with peak powers of four kilowatts, and eight shortwave band transmitters, with peak powers ranging from ten to 100 kilowatts. The major transmitter site was located southwest of Tananarive at Antanetibe. Booster facilities to increase the strength of the broadcast signals were reportedly planned.

In the late 1960s three separate networks were maintained by RNM. The first of these—Chaine Une—provided domestic service broadcasts in Malagasy, and the second network—Chaine Deux—broadcast a domestic service in French. The third network—Chaine Trois—provided a noncontinuous daily schedule with a total air time of about seven hours. Broadcasts in French, supplemented by Malagasy and English, were designed for overseas audiences. Experimentation with commercial use of this network had been implemented. Staffing and fiscal problems led the government to merge the first and third networks in September 1970.

In 1972 the broadcast schedules for the two remaining networks remained unchanged from previous years. Although schedules varied for each transmitter, a basic daily service of sixteen hours was transmitted by both networks. Daily broadcasting began at 3:00 A.M. and 3:30 A.M., respectively, and continued until 7:30 P.M.; the weekend schedules were shorter. Information about overseas programming was not readily available. The government, in cooperation with the University of Madagascar, also operated additional broadcasting facilities known as Radio Université (see ch. 7). There were no frequency modulation (FM) facilities.

Both RNM networks emphasized information services, focusing heavily on news and musical programs. Varied programming, however, was designed for separate audiences. Both networks devoted about 24 percent of their broadcasting time to information programs. Chaine Une, whose listeners tended to belong to the rural, less educated sector of the population, devoted another 25 percent of its broadcasting time to educational and instructional programs; the remainder featured music, major emphasis being put on traditional Malagasy folk music. The programs of Chaine Deux were designed for the better educated French speakers. This network devoted about 20 percent of its broadcasting time to educational and instructional programs and 42 percent to music, most of which was non-Malagasy in origin. The remaining programming consisted mainly of cultural programs, including dramatic and literary features, some of which were imported from France.

Surveys in the late 1960s indicated that the majority of people who listened to the Malagasy-language programs paid greater attention to program content than did the French-speaking listeners. Those who listened to Malagasy broadcasts also regarded radio listening as a serious activity. They tended to gather in groups for selected programs and gave their entire attention to its content. The audiences of French-language programs were less serious about radio listening and regarded radio as a means of entertainment. Many of them frequently used it as a diversion while performing some other task. As a whole, French speakers tended to be more critical of program content, particularly material they considered repetitious and biased. They were more likely to listen individually than as a group.

Conservative estimates for the early 1970s indicated that there were over 300,000 radio receiving sets providing service for over 2 million listeners, or about 28 percent of the population. This compared with roughly 70,000 receiving sets and an audience of about 500,000 in the early 1960s. The substantial increase in the role of radio broadcasting indicated by these figures was largely the result of two government programs. The first of these, calling for the establishment of information centers equipped with radio receivers in rural areas, was actually begun in the 1950s. The program had never been popular, and much of the equipment had fallen into disuse and disrepair by 1960. The government, however, reequipped ninety-six of the 160 centers with new receivers. At the same time a program known as Operation Transistor was launched to provide easy payment loans for the purchase of transistor radios. Rural groups were encouraged to buy a radio as a communal activity, and in the early 1970s this practice continued. Receivers and loudspeakers were also installed in public buildings, marketplaces, and coffeehouses, and the discussion of radio news programs had become an integral part of social life in many urban centers.

An agreement signed in 1967 granted Radio Netherlands permission to construct facilities extending the range of the Dutch Hilvers International Service. It also provided for the construction of transmitter boosters in each province for use by RNM and gave RNM the right to use the new Dutch international broadcast facilities. Installation of two shortwave band transmitters of 300 kilowatts, designed to beam Dutch programs to Africa, Australia, India, Indonesia, and various other Southeast Asian countries, was begun in 1970 and completed in late 1971. Information was not available in mid-1972 concerning the status of the facilities to be constructed for RNM or the use of its international broadcasting rights. Local opposition to the Dutch presence had developed in early 1972 as a result of an information bulletin—considered by the Malagasy as patronizing—that Radio Netherlands had published for its personnel. As of mid-1972 the issue appeared to have subsided.

Television service was inititated by the government in 1967 in cooperation with RNM studio facilities in Tananarive, providing a transmission schedule in mid-1972 of fifteen to eighteen hours each week. Although variations in programming occurred, a fairly regular schedule was published daily in the local press. Programs in both French and Malagasy gave emphasis to news and cultural features. Serialized dramas and general entertainment programs were also included. Audience size was limited by the high cost of receiving sets and the limited power of transmission equipment. The number of television receivers in operation in 1970 was estimated at just under 2,000.

The Press

Printing facilities were first established on the island by Protestant missionaries in the 1860s. Roman Catholic printers arrived soon afterward and contributed to the publication of widely divergent sacred and secular works. For a time the press of the London Missionary Society held the title of Official Printer to the Queen, but in the 1880s, in a move to avoid reliance on mission facilities, the Merina government established its own press. In addition to official documents, such as a new legal code, the new government press joined the Christian missions in publishing works of varying lengths by both European and Malagasy authors. The existence of these facilities served as one of the stimuli to the early and original literary achievements of the Malagasy (see ch. 7).

The first newspaper, *Gazety Malagasy*, appeared in the 1870s. It was followed in the next decade by the *Madagascar Times* and *Le Progrès de l'Imerina*. The press passed through various stages in its development but, from the beginning, was marked by political overtones. Initial growth occurred under the influence of Protestant missionaries between 1870 and 1895 when British religious influence played an important role among the ruling class of the powerful Merina kingdom (see ch. 2). During this period the English-language press—including the *Madagascar Times*, the *Madagascar News*, and the *Madagascar World*—flourished in Tananarive. All were anti-French. The French press was limited to provincial centers, such as Tamatave and Diégo-Suarez, and was largely a reflection of the views of French planters and traders.

The establishment of the French Protectorate in 1894 brought an end to the lead held by the English-language press in the capital. In 1900 the official Malagasy-language newspaper *Vaovao* was established, and by the eve of World War I privately owned French-language newspapers, such as *L'Echo de Tananarive*, *L'Echo du Sud*, *Madecasse*, and *Le Colon*, dominated the newspaper trade.

During the interwar period newspapers took on an increased literary tone. This was also reflected in the brief success of some French-language literary monthlies. Nationalist sentiment began to develop in such publications as *L'Aurore* and *L'Opinion*. In the decade before World War II the Malagasy-language press expanded, and several newspapers, including *Takariva*, *Firenena Malagasy*, *Ny Pariny*, and *Ny Gazetinsika*, survived through the war.

The improved colonial government attitude toward the press during the late 1950s, after rigid governmental control exercised as a result of the 1947 revolt, encouraged expansion of the publishing trade. By the early 1960s there were eighteen dailies, forty-eight weeklies, and almost ninety other periodicals competing for the potential readership of only 5.5 million literate persons. Survival was to be reserved for only the larger newspapers or those financially supported by political factions, religious groups, or income from related publishing enterprises and was particularly difficult for the small French-language publications.

The most recent figures available in 1972 indicated that seven major daily newspapers were being published (see table 7). All were located in Tananarive, and total circulation was estimated at about 60,000. Those dailies that had the largest circulation were *Madagascar Matin* and *Vaovao*. All dailies were published in Malagasy; *Madagascar Matin* was bilingual in Malagasy and French. Each issue of most of the dailies was limited in size to about eight pages. Editorials and lead articles of international significance and important domestic items usually appeared on the front page. Inside pages included social news, sports, entertainment, letters to the

Table 7. Principal Newspapers and Periodicals in the Malagasy Republic, 1972

Publication	Language	Place of Publication	Circulation	Comments
DAILY:				
Basy Vava	Malagasy	Tananarive	2,500	Daily organ of the Social Democratic Party.
Imongo Vaovao	-do-	-do-	3,000	Opposition newspaper; mouthpiece of AKFM; pro-left wing.
Madagascar Matin	French and Malagasy	-do-	16,200	Formerly *Le Courier de Madagascar;* official government newspaper.
Madagasikara Mahaleotena	-do-	-do-	15,000	Organ of Social Democratic Party.
Marêsaka	-do-	-do-	5,000	Independent.
Ny Gazetinsika	-do-	-do-	n.a.	Independent.
Vaovao	-do-	-do-	17,000	Official government newspaper.
WEEKLY:				
Ady Gasy [1]	French and Malagasy	-do-	n.a.	Nonpartisan.
L'Aurore	French	Majunga	5,000	Independent; apolitical; mainly local news.
Fanasina	Malagasy	Tananarive	10,000	Independent with occasional AKFM leanings.
Fanilo	-do-	Fianarantsoa	4,500	Roman Catholic oriented.
Info-Madagascar	French	Tananarive	1,000	Government press service publication.
Journal Officiel de la République Malgache	-do-	-do-	n.a.	Government publication.
Hehy [2]	Malagasy	-do-	15,000	Politically moderate.

Table 7. Principal Newspapers and Periodicals in the Malagasy Republic, 1972 — Continued

Publication	Language	Place of Publication	Circulation	Comments
Lakroan'i Madagasikara	-do-	Fianarantsoa	8,000	Roman Catholic.
Lumière	French	-do-	n.a.	Roman Catholic; socialist orientation.
La République	French and Malagasy	Tananarive	8,000	Reflects government policy.
MONTHLY:				
Bulletin de la Société de Corps Medical Malgache	French	-do-	n.a.	---
Bulletin de Madagascar	-do-	-do-	1,800	---
L'Ecole Publique de Madagascar	-do-	-do-	n.a.	---
L'Information Economique Juridique de Madagascar[3]	-do-	-do-	n.a.	---
Revue Medicale de Madagascar	-do-	-do-	n.a.	---
TWICE YEARLY:				
Revue de Madagascar	-do-	-do-	1,600	Government press service.

n.a. — not available.
[1] Published two times a week.
[2] Published three times a week.
[3] Published every two months.

Source: Adapted from Virginia Thompson and Richard Adloff, *The Malagasy Republic: Madagascar Today,* Stanford, 1965, pp. 228-242; Virginia Thompson, "Madagascar," page 460 in *Africa South of the Sahara, 1972,* London, 1972, and "Tananarive," *Notes et Documentaires* [Paris], October 28, 1969, pp. 63-64.

editor, and advertisements. Some newspapers had daily columns or featured editorials by foreign correspondents. Subscription rates were high, and distribution systems were limited.

In addition to the dailies there were sixteen major periodicals; about two-thirds were French-language newspapers, and about half were printed weekly. All but four weeklies were published in Tananarive. Periodicals that had limited circulations serviced some smaller urban centers. A variety of government reports and research publications were not included in this category. Several of the periodicals began publication in the early 1950s, and the *Journal Officiel de la République Malgache* dates from 1883.

The press in 1972 continued its political role and could be divided into various factions, reflecting the political divisions in the country (see ch. 9). The progovernment press was led by the official government dailies, *Vaovao* and *Madagascar Matin*. The major newspaper supporting the ruling Social Democratic Party (Parti Social Démocratique—PSD) was the daily *Madagasikara Mahaleotena*. *Revue de Madagascar* was the major progovernment periodical.

Among the opposition press, *Imongo Vaovao* supported policy positions of the leftist Party of the Congress for the Independence of Madagascar (Ankoton'ny Kongresi'ny Fahaleovantenan Madagaskara—AKFM). The thrice-weekly *Hehy* was moderately in support of AKFM positions, and on occasion the independent weekly *Fanasina* also supported the leftist political group. Roman Catholic socialist positions critical of the Tsiranana government were supported by the weekly *Lumière*. Basically independent positions were maintained by the daily *Ny Gazetinsika* and the weekly *L'Aurore*.

The larger dailies contained news provided by their own foreign correspondents or by the Madagascar Press Agency. Founded in Tananarive in 1962, the news agency published a daily information sheet called *Bulletin Quotidien d'Information*. Most newspapers did not have correspondents throughout the island but maintained local post office boxes for reader contributions. Lack of trained personnel affected the professional standards of some newspapers, and the political interests of most of them were reflected in their coverage of news events. Most reflective of Western journalistic standards was *Madagascar Matin*, founded in 1961 upon the request of President Tsiranana. In a move designed to stimulate the lagging French-language press and to improve journalistic standards, two French press services and four regional French dailies cooperated in establishing this publication, which has become the second most widely read newspaper in the country.

Publishing

In addition to the National Printing Company (Imprimerie Nationale), which published all official government publications, there were six private publishing houses in 1972. With the exception of the Catholic Industrial Printing Company (Imprimerie Industrielle Catholique), located in Fianarantsoa, all publishing houses were located in Tananarive. The two oldest firms, the Protestant Bookstore and Publishing House (Librarie-Imprimerie Protestant) and the Lutheran Publishing House (Trano Printy Loterana— formerly Imprimerie Lútherienne), were founded in 1865 and 1877, respectively. Both specialized in religious, educational, and fictional publications. Other publishing houses included the Malagasy Publishing Society (Sociēté Malgache d'Edition), founded in 1943; the Central Printing House (Imprimerie Centrale), which specialized in university and other school texts; and Fanontam-Boky Malagasy.

The country was listed among the top ten in the African area in terms of the number of books published annually. In 1969, of a total of 156 different titles, about 76 percent were first editions. About 66 percent were in Malagasy, and all but one of the remainder were in French. Topically, 29 percent were on religious subjects, 29 percent were of a literary nature, and 22 percent pertained to the social sciences. No works on the pure sciences or children's books were published, but publications included books in such fields as philosophy, linguistics, the fine arts, history, and the applied sciences.

Films

Motion pictures were growing in popularity but fell far below sports and radio listening as a preferred form of diversion. The majority of the population as a whole, including 25 percent of urban dwellers, had never seen a motion picture. Film attendance had made its greatest advance among students, professional people, and workers possessing Western-oriented skills. Members of traditional Malagasy communities found little in film viewing that was relevant to their daily needs, and various groups in urban communities protested the degree of violence presented in the films most commonly shown.

There were forty-five film theaters in the country in 1969. Facilities were about equally divided between those equipped with sixteen-millimeter and thirty-five-millimeter projectors. Almost all public theaters were located in major urban centers, and most were privately owned and operated. Private clubs offering film showings to their members existed in a few of the larger cities. The Cinema and Photo Section of the Ministry of Information, Tourism, and Traditional Arts operated mobile vans having sixteen-millimeter projection equipment, which provided educational films for schools and villages. The service was limited, however, by the physical condition of the country's road network (see ch. 3).

. Feature-length films were not produced in the country. In the late 1960s about half of all the films shown were imported from the United States, and a third came from France. Other sources included the United Kingdom, the Federal Republic of German (West Germany), Italy, and Mexico. The government's Cinema and Photo Section produced a limited number of newsreels on local subjects, but the majority were imported from France. The introduction of filming facilities for television broadcasting was expected to stimulate local film production in the 1970s.

SECTION III. ECONOMIC
CHAPTER 12
CHARACTER AND STRUCTURE OF THE ECONOMY

As the country entered the 1970s, the rapid growth of population was beginning to exert growing pressure on available resources, to strain traditional economic and social institutions, and to pose fresh challenges for the management of the national economy. A poor country with per capita income variously estimated at the equivalent of US$95 to US$120, the Malagasy Republic had hitherto been basically self-sufficient in staple foodstuffs. It had also produced a variety of tropical export crops and small quantities of two or three minerals in some demand on world markets, and had been able to finance its import requirements of manufactures, fuels, and matériel with the help of a large amount of foreign grant aid but without incurring burdensome foreign or domestic indebtedness.

The economy was essentially agricultural, and most of the population was dependent on cultivation except in a few cattle-herding districts of the south and middle west. About 80 percent of the cultivators were engaged primarily in subsistence cultivation of rice, although there were very few who did not sell some portion of their crop. The Malagasy rural population had taken over most of the production of export crops introduced by French planters, and foreign-owned plantations now occupied only a small fraction of the arable land under crops. There were no serious tenure problems, although the average Malagasy holding was uneconomically small, and mounting population pressure in some districts had given rise to fragmentation and soil depletion.

Although disadvantaged by irregular rainfall, recurrent destructive cyclones, a severe problem of erosion, and poor soils over much of its land area, the country had enough arable land, pastureland, and irrigation potential to permit a considerable expansion of agricultural production through resettlement projects in the western river basins and the north. It had a valuable advantage in the regional diversity of its climate and of its pockets of arable soil. In comparison to many developing countries, it had a relatively high rate of literacy, and the population possessed a high level of artisan skills and had shown alacrity in learning (see ch. 7).

A small but growing industrial sector, engaged chiefly in the processing of domestic agricultural products, was beginning to replace a portion of imports of manufactures. There was a mixed economy in which private enterprise and foreign private investment were encouraged. The privately owned portion of large-and medium-scale commerce and industry was largely in the hands of French firms or those of a few Asian residents, and small-scale retail trade was also dominated by Indians and Chinese in many regions. Wealthy Malagasy tended to put their savings into investment in real estate. In addition to operating the railroad and public utilities, the government participated directly in enterprises of mixed economy in agriculture and industry to make up for the deficiency in private investment or to represent the national public interest.

Politically independent since 1960, the country remained dependent on France for a large share of development expenditure, technical assistance, and management expertise in industry and commerce and for a portion of the current operating expenses of government. The close economic ties to France had become increasingly unpopular among students and urban dwellers in the early 1970s (see ch. 9). At the same time, the government's efforts to find alternative means of financing the development effort by the mobilization of domestic resources were by no means popular. Critics of the government demanded more, not less, state ownership of industry and commerce, but the rural population had grown restive under the burden of taxation. It constituted the nation's only broad tax base, and the head tax and cattle tax that were the chief targets of its resentment were broadly in line with the standard recommendations of international organizations for mobilizing the development effort. Collection at the local level had given rise to abuses, however, and an excess of zeal in collecting the cattle tax was said to have set off the active revolt that broke out in the south in early 1971 (see ch. 9).

When the new government of General Gabriel Ramanantsoa took power in mid-1972, it was faced with the difficult task of reconciling these conflicting demands for greater economic independence from France, increased government participation in commerce and industry, and relief from the burden of direct taxes. In early moves, the new government raised the minimum wage, suspended the head tax and cattle tax, imposed strict foreign exchange controls to prevent capital flight, and sought to tighten direct controls on the rising level of domestic consumer prices. It announced that it would continue to welcome foreign aid and provide incentives for foreign investment but that it would revise its economic agreements with other countries and insist that foreign firms maintain subsidiaries registered in Madagascar. It launched a crackdown on corruption in the administration, cut government ministers' wages, and accelerated the previous government's austerity program to reduce operating expenditures and to curtail civil service jobs. It adopted decrees concerning the return to the state of unutilized lands formerly distributed to private firms and individuals. In an early speech, Ramanantsoa castigated the lack of economic progress in the twelve years since independence, asserting that economic growth had been swallowed up by the rapid increases in population and in prices, profiting a minority at the expense of the mass of the population and creating a growing gap between the rich and the poor and between town and country dwellers.

The rate of economic growth in the 1960s had been somewhat slow, owing partly to a modest rate of investment and partly to priority investment in economic infrastructure such as roads—a type of investment that has little direct impact on output. Manufacturing had been relatively dynamic, but investment and production had failed to meet the targets of the ambitious First Five-Year Plan (1964-68), and the growth of population and per capita consumption had created recurrent local food shortages and necessitated rice imports. An interim plan known as the Program of Major Operations (1968-69) had boosted investment in agriculture, but it was thought that the total impact of these development efforts would not be felt until the following few years. The Second Three-Year Plan (1972-74) was introduced in January 1972 and aimed at a growth rate only slightly higher than that achieved under the First Five-Year Plan.

STRUCTURE OF OUTPUT AND EXPENDITURE

Gross domestic product (GDP) in 1970 was estimated at FMG247.7 billion (for value of the Malagasy franc—see Glossary). Population estimates varied, ranging from 6.75 million to 7.2 million. Using the 7.2 million population figure, per capita GDP would be FMG36,696. At the current official exchange rate in 1972 (which need not reflect relative purchasing power) it would be equivalent to US$102. Other per capita product estimates for the period ranged from the equivalent of US$95 to US$120. The average, however, concealed an important divergence in living standards between the urban and rural population (see ch. 6). In 1966, the latest year for which detailed national product calculations were made, the average per capita GDP for the country as a whole was placed at the equivalent of US$110. Incomes of foreigners resident on the island substantially raised the average, however. The per capita average for the Malagasy population alone was about US$90; urban incomes averaged about US$160, and rural incomes, only about US$80. If the subsistence consumption of the rural population was calculated at urban market prices instead of at farm prices, however, then the average rural income would have been equivalent to three-fourths of the urban average instead of only half.

Despite the high proportion of the population engaged in agriculture, only about 30 percent of GDP in 1970 was thought to consist of incomes generated in the primary production sector of agriculture, forestry, and fishing (see table 8). The share originating in forestry and fishing was negligible. More than half of the value added generated in agriculture was in the subsistence sector. Cash income from agricultural activity represented only about 20 percent of total money income. The farmers derived about 55 percent of their cash income from sales on the domestic market and 45 percent from export crops. Despite the rapid growth of industry from its very low base in the 1950s, only about 15 percent of GDP in 1970 consisted of value added in manufacturing and construction, and about 2 percent came from mining and electric power. Nearly half of total product consisted of factor incomes in the tertiary sector: commerce, transportation, government, and other services.

Services were thought to provide as much as 60 percent of money income in 1966: about 25 percent from activity in trade and transport, 13 percent in education and health services, and 22 percent in government administration (including French technical assistance). The disproportionately high share of services—as opposed to commodity production—in domestic product means that the country must depend upon imports for a large share of its commodity resources.

In 1966 an estimated 26 percent of the total supply of resources in goods and services for utilization in the monetized (nonsubsistence) sector of the economy consisted of imports, including the value of insurance and freight. At internal market value, including local transport costs, wholesale and retail markups, and indirect taxes, imports constituted 42 percent of total supply. In the supply of commodities alone, the share of imports at final market price was as high as 51 percent. This high dependence on imports can be attributed in part to the disproportionately high expenditures of foreigners resident on the island. The First Five-Year Plan estimated that about 20 percent of monetary consumption expenditures in 1960 came from about 50,000 foreigners, whose per capita expenditure was some twenty times the average for the Malagasy population. Assuming that these foreigners spend about 80 percent of their consumption on imports, the share of imports in the cash consumption expenditure of Malagasy would then be about 32.5 percent at internal market prices and 17 percent at port prices.

GDP includes income earned in the country but remitted abroad, such as the savings from salaries of management or technical assistance personnel working in the country, the unreinvested profits of French firms trading or producing in the country, and flight capital. These remittances, known in the statistics as net factor payments to abroad, must be deducted from GDP to show gross national product (GNP), a more accurate measure of the share of product actually accruing to the country. Madagascar does not publish estimates of GNP. International statistics estimated net factor income to abroad as 6 percent of GDP in 1968. This would indicate a per capita GNP of only about FMG30,108 compared to per

Table 8. Estimated Origin and Use of Gross Domestic Product,
Malagasy Republic, 1966-70
(in billion Malagasy francs at current prices) [1]

	1966 Subsistence Economy	1966 Total	1967	1968	1969	1970
Origin:						
Agriculture, forestry, and fishing	29	55	59	61	65	74
Industry:						
Mining and energy	--- [2]	2	3	3	4	5
Manufacturing	--- [2]	20	21	23	25	29
Construction	2	7	7	8	9	9
Services:						
Transportation	--- [2]	12	13	14	16	17
Commerce	--- [2]	24	28	30	34	35
Government wages	--- [2]	29	31	33	35	36
Other	6	22	23	24	26	29
Import taxes	2	11	8	11	11	13
Gross domestic product	37	182	193	207	225	247
Net imports of goods and nonfactor services	... [3]	12	11	14	18	8
TOTAL RESOURCES	... [3]	194	204	221	243	255
Utilization:						
Private consumption	n.a.	131	135	143	156	166
Public consumption	n.a.	39	42	44	47	49
Gross fixed investment	n.a.	22	25	30	33	35
Change in inventories	n.a.	2	2	4	7	5

n.a.—not available.
[1] For value of the Malagasy franc—see Glossary.
[2] --- means nil.
[3] ... means not applicable.

capita GDP of FMG32,030. This estimate may be too high, however, since according to one source official data do not reflect the true level of incomes leaving the country, which are concealed by the operation of franc area monetary arrangements.

The resources available for investment and consumption in a given year consist of domestic product supplemented by net imports of goods and nonfactor services (imports of goods and services minus exports and minus factor incomes remitted abroad). In 1972, for the first time, the submission of the government's fiscal budget to Parliament was accompanied by an economic budget designed to project the utilization of total resources for the coming year and thus avoid an inflationary gap between aggregate demand for goods and services for investment and consumption on the one hand and aggregate resources available on the other. The basic target of this 1972 economic budget was a growth rate in constant prices of close to 5 percent.

In the late 1960s the mounting pressure of aggregate demand on available resources had created a somewhat inflationary trend that was aggravated by a long-term deterioration in the terms of trade (the ratio of export prices to import prices). Private consumption accounted on the average for about two-thirds of total expenditure (see table 8). Public consumption (the government's current operating expenditures) was also increasing during this period. Nevertheless total consumption was expanding at a somewhat lower rate than GDP in current prices, so that there was some growth in domestic savings. This permitted an increase in fixed investment, but it remained a relatively modest proportion of total expenditure, increasing from about 11.2 percent in 1966 to 13.7 percent in 1970. Less than 60 percent of investment was of domestic origin. Foreign aid provided more than one-fourth; and foreign private investment, the remainder.

Government policy to influence the components of aggregate expenditure was not applied very flexibly in the 1960s. Restraint on private consumption expenditure consisted chiefly of maintaining ceilings on short-term credit from the central bank to the commercial banks between 1967 and 1969; but credit to the private sector nevertheless rose at a rate of about 12 percent a year, and there were heavy speculative imports of consumer goods in late 1968 and early 1969 by merchants anticipating imposition of a new transactions tax and devaluation of the French franc.

Government spending also had an expansionary impact beginning in 1968. Until 1967 the government had followed a relatively conservative fiscal policy, which generated public saving in the form of a surplus of current revenues over current operating expenditure on the budget, which was used to meet a portion of planned investment requirements in agriculture, industry, and transportation infrastructure. In the mid-1960s, however, it became evident that the growth of rice production was lagging considerably behind the rate of population increase, and the government was obliged to launch an intensified improvement program in rice production that required the mobilization of substantial financial resources, not only from foreign assistance but from domestic sources as well (see ch. 13).

As a result of the government's Program of Major Operations, public fixed investment expenditure increased sharply, and public spending had an expansionary impact in 1968 and 1969 (see Public Finance, this ch.). As investment expenditures increased, so too did consumption demand in the private sector, adding to the rapidly rising demand for imports. The trade deficit and the deficit on the current balance of payments increased correspondingly (see Foreign Economic Relations, this ch.). Price movements abroad and the revaluation of certain foreign currencies increased the pressure on the domestic price level.

Mounting government expenditure resulted in some drain on the Treasury's liquid assets, and the government introduced a policy of austerity in its current spending. In the second half of 1970 the Treasury liquidity position improved and had a contractionary effect on the economy—the expansion of domestic credit supply lessened by the first half of 1971. In 1970 a good harvest and a favorable trend in export prices resulted in a surplus on the current balance of payments. Although export earnings were maintained at the same level in 1971, the heavy pressure of import demand for consumer goods, investment goods, and raw materials meant that the trade deficit was the largest since 1960.

The government's proposed budget for 1972 was again expansionary. Imports were reportedly mounting. As a result of the inflow of foreign grant and loan aid, however, the country's foreign exchange position as recorded in official statistics appeared far from alarming. Official foreign exchange reserves in mid-1972 were equivalent to about nine months of imports at the high 1971 level.

Nevertheless, the Ramanantsoa government in mid-1972 expressed concern at the precarious situation of the country's finances. It promised to pursue an austerity regime in order to mobilize savings for development use. Foreign exchange controls were applied to all transactions, including those with the franc area.

Data on real economic growth are highly uncertain because of the lack of production indexes and of appropriate price deflators for GDP estimates. It was evident, however, that during most of the 1960s growth was at a fairly modest rate in real terms—that is, if the rate at current prices is deflated by a crude estimate of price trends. Such an estimate would indicate stagnating production and declining per capita income up to 1965 and an average real growth rate of about 4.5 percent a year at constant prices between 1965 and 1969. In 1970 record crop harvests and favorable world market prices for most exports resulted in rapid growth at an annual rate of about 7 percent in real terms. In 1971, however, there was once more a slowdown in the tempo of economic activity, chiefly because of a decline in agricultural production owing to cyclone Felicia. Activity in mining was also depressed, but manufacturing continued to expand despite setbacks in raw material delivery that resulted from the drop in crop output. Both private and public investment rose substantially during the year.

These data suggest a decline in real per capita income for the population as a whole—including foreigners—from 1962 to 1965 and a very moderate increase to slightly above the 1962 level by 1969. Production was thought to have increased on the average by 2.7 percent a year between 1962 and 1969, but the concurrent growth in population was estimated at 2.2 percent a year, leaving little per capita increase.

LABOR

Statistics on the labor force, and on unemployment in particular, are lacking or are unreliable, so that presented data represented rough estimates. In the early 1970s a series of labor surveys are to be undertaken with the assistance of the International Labor Organization. A survey of wage earners was scheduled for 1972; a survey of civil servants, for 1973; and an overall survey of employment and unemployment, for 1974.

In the late 1960s wage earners still constituted less than 9 percent of the active population (see table 9). The disproportionate expansion of the services sector emerged from the fact that 63 percent of all wage earners in the modern economy were engaged in services— commerce, banking, domestic service, government, and other services. Government employed only 17 percent of the 287,000 workers in the modern economy—not an unduly high proportion among French-speaking African countries. According to a 1966 source, nearly half of all wage and salary earners were working in the two coastal provinces of Tamatave and Diégo-Suarez. In the late 1960s the government had been hiring at a more rapid rate than other sectors, and a high proportion of graduates from secondary schools, technical colleges, and the University of Madagascar entered government employment. In 1969 employment increased in all sectors of the economy, but in 1970 there was a decline in the number of wage earners in commerce and banking and a leveling off of employment in construction. In 1970 the government claimed some net decline in unemployment.

*Table 9. Economically Active Population, Malagasy Republic, 1968, 1969, and 1970 **

	1968	1969	1970	Percent of Total 1970
	(in thousands)			
Private Sector:				
Industry	44	45	47	1.4
Agriculture (plantations)	39	41	42	1.3
Commerce and banking	44	46	45	1.4
Domestic service	38	40	41	1.3
Construction	15	16	16	0.5
Services	42	44	47	1.4
Subtotal	222	232	238	7.3
Government employees	41	45	49	1.5
Agriculture (independent and farmhands)	2,747	2,820	2,885	88.8
Other (including unemployed)	86	80	78	2.4
TOTAL	3,096	3,177	3,250	100.0

* Official estimates.

The national Labor Code of October 1, 1960, established a guaranteed minimum wage, accident insurance, maternity benefits, family allowances, medical care, and retirement pensions (see ch. 6). It also asserted the right of wage earners in private enterprise and of unskilled government workers to participate in the formulation of rules governing working conditions. The guaranteed minimum hourly wage was raised in 1963 and again in mid-1971 and early 1972 by the government of Philibert Tsiranana. The minimum wage was raised once more by the Ramanantsoa government shortly after it came to power in mid-1972.

Underemployment in agriculture is thought to be extensive, and rising migration to the urban areas is contributing to a growing problem of urban unemployment (see ch. 3). Part of the migration to the towns consists of young people who leave the countryside after the crop season is over, and they often return when they fail to find employment in town. The unemployment problem was expected to mount during the 1970s, and the problem of finding employment for school leavers reluctant to return to agriculture will be particularly acute.

In 1971 the government had started a training program called Workers' Action (l'Action Ouvrière) to increase employment possibilities for Malagasy nationals by improving the skills of those in the active labor force. It was also preparing several other programs. One would provide on-the-job training for adults in various enterprises to help them acquire special skills, including office skills. Another would teach managerial skills to small- and medium-scale entrepreneurs. A third program was being prepared to provide training for people who had not yet found employment.

DEVELOPMENT PLANNING AND INVESTMENT

Some form of centralized government investment planning has been applied to the island's economic development for more than forty years. Under French rule, most of the public investment undertaken came from French funds, often with the conscription of Malagasy labor for public works (see ch. 2). Between the two world wars, the Sarraut economic plan for the French Empire as a whole was applied in Madagascar. Designed primarily to promote the interests of the mother country and of French colonists, it nonetheless helped to cushion the worst effects of the worldwide depression of the 1930s on the island. A 1937 economic plan was disrupted by the outbreak of World War II.

Between 1949 and 1972 there were six successive plans, or, perhaps more accurately, five and one-half. Two preindependence plans under French auspices were followed by an interim plan prepared by the autonomous preindependence government.

In the preindependence period of French planning, a ten-year plan was first drawn up in 1949 but was converted to two shorter plans. The first of these shorter plans, for the years 1949 through 1953, was devoted to developing infrastructure, notably roads and ports. The next plan, drawn up in 1953, devoted only 43.4 percent of investments to infrastructure; 40.7 percent, to primary production; 0.5 percent, to industry; and 15.3 percent, to social investment.

An interim plan followed for the 1959-62 period, which permitted the incoming autonomous Malagasy government to break with the tradition of annual investment allocations that were no more than a list of operations to be financed by the government. It permitted the government to introduce a system of more comprehensive planning that established priorities for the economy as a whole.

As is the usual practice in independent African nations, the nomenclature of the national development plans began afresh from the date of independence, so that the two major postindependence plans effected since 1964 were entitled, respectively, the First Five-Year Plan (1964-68) and the Second Three-Year Plan (1972-74) being numbered consecutively without regard to the number of years comprised. In 1967, however, before completion of the period of the first plan, it became evident that plan targets were not being attained. The government accordingly launched a short-term interim booster plan entitled the Program of Major Operations (1968-69). It was not counted in numbering the plans, however. The second plan was originally intended to be a five-year plan, but unavoidable delays led to its being curtailed.

In July 1960, after independence, President Tsiranana appointed a general planning commission to coordinate the execution of projects by the various ministries involved. In June 1962 it issued the *Survey of the Malagasy Economy, Evolution 1950-1960*, taking inventory of the island's development resources; and the First Five-Year Plan was submitted to Parliament in early 1964. Its purpose was to determine by means of an elementary economic model the level of investment required to achieve the desired rate of growth and to compare these targets with the expected availability of financial and material resources. It also outlined investment priorities and production targets by sector, but it presented essentially a review of aspirations and priorities rather than specific development projects. As is often the case with plans of this nature, only a portion of the required financing proved to be forthcoming, so that actual investments and achievements under the plan fell somewhat short of its ambitious targets. The failure to complete more thorough economic analysis of proposed investment projects was owing partly to the plan's heavy dependence on foreign grant aid; it was felt that the choice of projects might ultimately be determined from abroad. Beginning with the Second Three-Year Plan, there will be greater use of domestic and foreign loan financing, and more detailed project-by-project analysis is being undertaken.

Among the anticipated sources of investment, foreign official assistance came closest to meeting the targets set in the plan. During the entire 1964-68 period of the first plan foreign aid amounted to the equivalent of US$50 million to US$55 million a year. The shortfall was greatest in private investment, which consisted mostly of foreign investment in industry; such scarce domestic capital as was available did not follow plan investment priorities. Total investment expenditure under the First Five-Year Plan finally amounted to between FMG90 billion and FMG95 billion, about 60 percent of target.

Parliament opposed approval of the increased taxes with which the government had hoped to finance a portion of first plan expenditure, so that reliance on foreign assistance had to be greater than anticipated. Despite the creation of new institutions to mobilize domestic savings, the contribution of domestic private investment to the plan was negligible. By 1967 it was evident that investment and production were well below first plan targets, and the government decided to take remedial action by launching its interim Program of Major Operations (1968-69). Its main feature was a shift in emphasis from investment in infrastructure to investment in the productive sectors, notably agriculture. The First Five-Year Plan had somewhat overemphasized infrastructure development. As a result of the new program, public sector investment rose from an average of FMG11 billion in the three-year period from 1964-1966 to FMG13 billion in 1967 and FMG17 billion in 1968.

Investment targets were almost achieved in manufacturing, and the shortfall in agriculture and in mining was relatively small. The actual allocation of resources may have been more efficient than that projected in the plan: only about 50 percent of the high target set for investment in transport and social infrastructure was actually met. The first plan's targets for road construction had probably exceeded the immediate traffic requirements. All in all, the level of investment achieved under the plan was not a bad one, although some of the investments undertaken turned out to be unduly costly or poorly coordinated.

Most of the crop production targets in agriculture were realized—notably in rice, sugar, coffee, vanilla, and pepper production. There were conflicting assessments of how much importance projects under the first plan had had in bringing this about, and some observers felt that the improvement might not be permanent. Moreover, the plan had not anticipated the growth in population and in per capita food consumption, which absorbed most of the gains in food production (see ch. 13). The value of industrial production reached only FMG25 billion in 1968, instead of the target figure of

FMG34 billion. This was not too disappointing a ratio, given the essentially indicative nature of the plan. Moreover, a number of projects initiated under the plan were still in their gestation period in 1972, and their impact on economic development might not be evident until the ensuing few years.

The planners had seriously underestimated import requirements during the first plan period. The value of imports projected for 1973 had already been reached by 1969. The planners had anticipated the steep rise in imports of capital equipment but not the concurrent increase in imports of raw materials and intermediate goods for industry. Exceptionally large imports of rice in 1969 also confounded expectations. The pressure of mounting consumption on the price level was apparently an unforeseen factor.

There had been some criticism of the planning procedure for not being sufficiently open to discussion by all elements of the population and political party spectrum. When the Second Three-Year Plan was prepared, its general outline of priorities was based partly on the recommendations of the National Days of Development Planning convention held in April 1971, at which representatives of the Party of the Congress for the Independence of Madagascar (Ankoton'ny Kongresi'ny Fahaleovantenan Madagaskara—AKFM), the only opposition party represented in Parliament, participated with representatives of the government. In December 1971 the government secured parliamentary adoption, despite AKFM opposition, of the new Charter of Development, which outlined general strategy for future economic plans and emphasized such objectives as the achievement of national economic independence, the accumulation of national capital, and the rapid promotion of Malagasy to decision-making positions and to management of production. Other major goals stressed were the improvement of living conditions and the achievement of full employment. This strategy was presumably followed in formulating the Second Three-Year Plan.

Some critics of the Tsiranana government also maintained that the greatest setback to execution of the First Five-Year Plan was the government's failure to enlist the active support of the rural population (see ch. 13). The voluntary labor feature of the village-level public works program under the plan was in fact far from voluntary and was resented and associated in the popular mind with forced labor under the prewar French administration. The peasants' growing recalcitrance in paying their taxes was said to be symptomatic of mounting distrust of the authorities.

The second development plan was originally intended to run from 1970 to 1974, but its preparation was considerably delayed because of the difficulty of drawing up specific, economically well-justified projects called for by the new procedure. During the first plan, only the Ministry of Public Works had prepared such projects, and the result was that a disproportionate share of projected (but not actual) financing was allocated to infrastructure or public works as opposed to projects in the productive sectors, which were to have been prepared by the ministries concerned with industry and agriculture. Another problem was that of keeping the projects fairly equitably distributed among the different regions, some of which lent themselves far better to development projects than others.

As finally discussed by the cabinet in November 1971 and again in January 1972 and submitted to Parliament in February, the second plan had evolved into an interim three-year plan to cover the 1972-74 period. Its goal was an annual rate of growth in constant prices of 4.6 percent. The First Five-Year Plan had aimed at an annual growth rate of 5 percent but achieved a rate of only about 4.5 percent. The Second Three-Year Plan is more detailed than was the First Five-Year Plan and contains a large number of specific projects, most of which already had been begun under the first plan or the Program of Major Operations or had been under study. It is therefore unlikely that the priorities established for the allocation of resources under the plan can be greatly changed before 1975.

The Second Three-Year Plan places greatest emphasis on developing production in food supply and export crops. It hopes to complete important projects for cattle ranching and slaughterhouse construction launched under the Program of Major Operations, and it also hopes to boost meat exports. The eastern and western regions are to be devoted to export crops: the east, to vanilla, coffee, cocoa, pepper, cloves, bananas, and oil palms; and the west, to cotton, tobacco, groundnuts, and stockraising. The Central Highlands will be the center for the development of food-processing industries. Basic objectives are to attain a higher degree of domestic processing of raw materials and to place more of the economic decisionmaking power in business and government in the hands of Malagasy.

PUBLIC FINANCE

The country's budgetary system has proved quite efficient in regulating government expenditure. As in most developing countries, however, the inadequate tax base has led to heavy reliance on customs duties and other indirect taxes, and the pressure of public expenditure has made the budget rather inflexible as an instrument to moderate the business cycle or to redistribute income.

The Malagasy fiscal year coincides with the calendar year. Capital appropriations may be carried over to the following year, but current appropriations may not. All revenues must be collected by January 31 of the following year, when the budgetary accounts are closed. Near the middle of the following year a revised or supplementary budget is drawn up with new estimates of revenue and expenditure. Estimates for expenditure are submitted by the appropriate governmental departments to the Ministry of Finance, which draws up and executes the general budget. It is then approved by the government and promulgated before the end of December.

The general budget includes current revenue and expenditure of the central government and the capital expenditure budget, part of which is financed by the surplus of current revenue over current expenditure. It also includes the annexed budgets of seven autonomous public agencies and certain special accounts of the Treasury. The seven autonomous agencies are: the Malagasy National Railroad, the Malagasy National Radio and Television System, the Post Office, the National Printing Office, the Government Garage, the Public Works Department Workshop, and the Harbor Authority. Under consideration in late 1971 was a measure to grant some of these agencies separate financial status so that they would be less of a burden on the budget and could carry out a more flexible pricing policy. The Treasury accounts in the general budget include commercial accounts, such as the tobacco and match monopoly, the National Lottery, and government purchasing funds.

The six provincial governments have separate budgets, under the control of the Ministry of Finance and the Ministry of Interior. Most of their spending is on primary schools and local health centers and hospitals. Their revenues formerly came chiefly from the head tax and the cattle tax. These taxes were abolished by the Ramanantsoa government in June 1972 and were expected to cause an estimated loss of FMG1.5 billion in revenues. It was not clear what would be used to replace them in supporting the provincial budgets.

The separate budgets of the forty-one urban municipalities and the 735 rural municipalities are not included in the consolidated general budget. They are only partly supervised by the Ministry of Interior. Most of the expenditures of the municipalities are for local administrative services, road maintenance, and participation in primary education. Municipality revenues came from special levies, such as a surtax on the head tax (before 1972), and from central government subsidies.

Control over public expenditure is monitored by a branch of the Supreme Court (see ch. 8). Administrative control is exercised by a directorate under the office of the president having delegates at the different governmental departments. The Treasury then determines whether administrative control has been carried out. This system has operated relatively well over the years to keep expenditure within the limits of appropriations.

More than two-thirds of the revenues and expenditures in the consolidated budget are derived from the central government, which determines the overall fiscal position of the public sector (see table 10). A law of 1963 created a special budgetary fund called the

National Development and Investment Fund, through which all capital expenditures must be channeled, whether financed by fiscal resources, by borrowing, or by Treasury resources. Projects that are financed entirely by grants from abroad are not included in the budget. The law provided that capital expenditures under the fund must amount to a given proportion of total domestic fiscal receipts plus the French budgetary contribution and that this proportion must increase by at least 2 percentage points each year. The rise of capital expenditures has been paralleled by a steady increase in

Table 10. *Consolidated Budgets, Treasury Operations, and Financing of the Deficit, Malagasy Republic, 1967-71.* [1]
(in million Malagasy francs) [2]

	Actuals				Budget Submission
	1967	1968	1969	1970	1971
Direct taxes	10,244	10,604	10,623	11,657	11,835
Indirect taxes	19,647	22,909	27,853	28,474	31,687
Nontax revenues	8,900	9,757	9,143	11,194	10,078
A. Current revenues	38,791	43,270	47,619	51,325	53,600
Public debt	639	1,092	1,267.	1,627	1,929
Administration	11,114	11,627	12,395	12,626	13,398
Education	5,768	6,388	7,150	7,616	8,706
Social services, other	4,059	3,972	4,653	4,713	5,141
Economic services	7,252	7,948	8,469	8,096	8,908
Industrial services	5,083	5,029	5,720	6,011	6,321
Other	2,025	2,863	2,234	2,545	3,357
B. Current expenditures	35,940	38,919	41,888	43,234	47,760
C. Current surplus (A minus B)	2,851	4,351	5,731	8,091	5,840
D. Capital expenditure [3]	5,952	10,403	12,534	12,698	9,607
E. Overall deficit (A minus B and D)	−3,101	−6,052	−6,793	−4,607	−3,767
F. Treasury net lending	−2,069	−885	−251	−1,784	−780
G. Overall treasury deficit (E plus F)	−5,170	−6,937	−7,044	−6,391	−4,547
Financing of G					
French budget subsidy	1,650	1,600	1,264	1,022	1,265
External borrowing	567	1,209	2,345	3,780	1,890
Domestic borrowing	326	98	589	674	500
Changes in correspondents' deposits [4]	386	251	19	5,159	892
Change in liquidity position (increase minus) [5]	2,241	3,779	2,827	−4,244	---[6]

[1] Consolidated budgets refer to: central government budget; provincial government budget; and annexed budgets of the seven autonomous agencies.
[2] For value of the Malagasy franc—see Glossary.
[3] Does not include projects wholly financed by foreign grants.
[4] Chiefly post office and commodity stabilization funds.
[5] Currency held by the Treasury; rediscountable customs duty bills; deposits with the Malagasy Institute of Issue (Institut d'Emmision Malgache); and deposits with the French *caisse des dépôts* (deposits office).
[6] --- means nil.

current expenditures on administration and economic services, so that despite the increase in revenues the overall budget deficit has worsened since the mid-1960s. Much of the rise in capital expenditure had to be met by external borrowing, and the foreign public debt had reached the equivalent of US$95 million by the end of 1970.

Central government revenue has come mostly from taxes, and in most years the revenue from indirect taxes has been at least twice that from direct taxes. Direct taxes include: a general income tax, which in 1970 was levied progressively on personal incomes above FMG90,000 a year, using a maximum rate of 40.5 percent for income of more than FMG3 million; a tax on profits, which applied to all income except from wages and salaries; a tax on capital (mainly on dividends); and business fees. Before 1972 more than half of direct tax revenues in the consolidated budget were coming from taxes on incomes, profits, and dividends. One-third came from the head tax. Receipts from the head tax and the cattle tax (applied to all livestock) went primarily to the provinces, but a portion went to the central government and the municipalities. The head tax was levied on males over twenty years of age and ranged by municipality from FMG3,225 to FMG3,450 per head. Both the head tax and cattle tax were substantially reduced by the Tsiranana government in mid-1971 and were abolished by the Ramanantsoa government in mid-1972. Real estate taxes on buildings and unimproved land went to the provinces and the urban municipalities; a tax on vehicles was shared among the central government and urban and rural municipalities.

The indirect taxes include: duties on imports and exports; excise duties on both imports and domestically produced goods; a liquor license tax; and a tax on value added (turnover tax). Import customs duties and the import tax yielded about one-third of total tax receipts. During the 1960s they were levied primarily for revenue reasons rather than for economic protection. Imports from franc area countries and the European Economic Community (EEC, known as the Common Market), which constitute the largest share of imports, are exempted from customs duties but not from the import tax, which ranges from 3 percent to 50 percent ad valorem and 135 percent on liquor. Export duties are levied on coffee, vanilla, cloves, pepper, and meat. Excise tax rates are low on essential items, such as sugar and matches, but high on luxuries such as liquor.

Since 1969 the value-added tax has been levied at a rate of 12 percent, applied only to the value added by the seller. The rate has been reduced to 6 percent for certain products—including fertilizers, machinery, and some vehicles—and for the services of construction, electricity, transportation, banking, and insurance. Exempted altogether are essential goods, including rice, salt, milk, fish, meat, vegetables, and liquid fuel; all exports; and certain transactions of small enterprises and cooperatives. The introduction of the value-added tax further increased the government's reliance on indirect tax revenue—from 66 percent of tax revenues in 1967 to 71 percent in 1970.

Current operating expenditures as a proportion of total government expenditure in the consolidated budget fell from an average of 86 percent in the 1965-67 period to about 79 percent in 1969 and 77 percent in 1970, as the government stepped up capital expenditure under its Program of Major Operations. After expanding by about FMG3 billion in both 1968 and 1969, current expenditures were somewhat restrained in 1970 under the government's selective austerity program. The hiring of new government personnel was limited to the filling of vacancies, and subsidies leveled off. The growth in capital expenditure was also significantly reduced. The overall budget deficit was appreciably curtailed, and the Treasury's liquidity position was greatly improved. Although the French budget subsidy had been reduced, the inflow from foreign loans was large, notably from the International Bank for Reconstruction and Development (IBRD, known as the World Bank) and the International Development Association. Correspondents' deposits with the Treasury increased to a record level because favorable export prices and harvests had caused large surpluses to be realized by the stabilization funds for coffee, cloves, and vanilla.

According to preliminary estimates, the overall budget deficit was further reduced in 1971 but, as the inflow to the Treasury from external borrowing and from stabilization fund deposits was much smaller, the Treasury's liquidity position deteriorated somewhat. The 1972 budget, prepared in late 1971, was quite expansionary. Current expenditure was expected to run about FMG2 billion above 1971, and development expenditure would be increased by FMG3 billion.

An economic budget was drawn up for the first time in 1972. Whereas the fiscal budget projects the government's receipts and expenditures, the economic budget projects the national accounts for the coming year, including the probable growth in GDP, total resources, and total demand for use of resources for consumption or investment. Probable fiscal revenues were then estimated on the basis of the expected expansion in industrial activity, domestic demand, investment, and imports. An increase of 15 percent in government expenditures was designed to stimulate the general expansion. Public and private investments were expected to expand by about 20 percent.

MONETARY AND BANKING SYSTEM

The country is a member of the French franc area. It has its own currency, the Malagasy franc, and its own central bank, the Malagasy Institute of Issue (Institut d'Emission Malgache—IEM). In other respects, however, its status is the same as that of French-speaking African countries within the franc area. The Malagasy franc is equivalent in value to the CFA franc of the African Financial Community (Communauté Financière Africaine—CFA), which served as Madagascar's currency until 1963. The Malagasy franc remains tied to the French franc at a fixed parity that can be changed only by mutual agreement with France.

The republic's status as a member of the franc area is regulated by the economic and financial cooperation agreement with France of June 27, 1960, elaborated in a separate convention of March 1963. Full freedom of transfers is maintained between the two countries. France guarantees full convertibility of the Malagasy franc into French francs. The IEM must hold its exchange reserves exclusively in French francs in its operations account with the French Treasury. Operations in other currencies must be converted on the Paris exchange market. When the French authorities decide to devalue the French franc, they must consult with the Malagasy Republic and negotiate to protect its legitimate interests. The IEM has the right to unlimited overdrafts on its operations account with the French Treasury but by the end of 1970 had not been obliged to use its overdraft facilities. France and the Malagasy Republic each have four members on the board of directors of the IEM; the board elects the IEM president in agreement with the French and Malagasy governments.

Details on the precise operation of franc area financial arrangements are not generally available. Press reports consequently contain a certain amount of speculation. Before the abolition of French exchange controls in 1967, member countries may have pooled their foreign currency assets in an exchange stabilization fund managed by the Bank of France (Banque de France) and negotiated their non-franc import programs with the French authorities on a year-to-year basis. Since 1967, however, arrangements have become more flexible. On the other hand, franc area exporters have lost their tariff protection and price supports on the French market, and the reduction of the common external tariff of the EEC has also exposed them to increased competition. France probably retains some advantage in franc area import markets.

After the civil disturbances and the change of government in mid-1972, there was mounting pressure for revision of the 1960 cooperation agreement with France. This was the theme of an article in the Roman Catholic socialist weekly *Lumière* in July 1972 (see ch. 11). It asserted that, as the IEM was merely the executor under the close supervision of France, all monetary policy on the island was dictated from abroad through the structure of the board of directors and management of the IEM; through the institution of the Joint French-Malagasy Commission on Trade and Currency; and especially by means of the IEM's connection with the French Treasury through the operations account agreement. It averred that the operating rules of the franc area, especially the pooling of foreign exchange resources and the application of a single regulation for financial relations with foreign countries, were not applied in a manner that served the interests of the Malagasy internal economy but were oriented toward foreign interests.

In his speech of July 27, 1972, Prime Minister Ramanantsoa reaffirmed that all agreements with other countries would be revised and that all elements of the agreements apparently opposed to national objectives would be renegotiated to conform to the country's real interests. There was no question of systematically denouncing all the existing agreements but merely of making them coincide with Madagascar's needs. In his policy statements, however, the prime minister appeared to take a very positive attitude toward French assistance.

Besides the central bank, the country's banking system includes a development bank—the Malagasy National Development Bank (Banque Nationale Malgache de Développement—BNM); an industrial investment bank—the National Investment Company (Société Nationale d'Investissement—SNI), whose functions were under review in 1972; the Savings Bank (Caisse d'Epargne); a postal checking and savings system; and four commercial banks. The commercial banks are largely owned by foreign interests, mostly French, but the Malagasy government owns 35 percent of the subscribed capital of the Malagasy Credit and Discount Bank (Banque Malgache d'Escompte et de Crédit) and 12.5 percent of the subscribed capital of the Bank of Madagascar and the Comores (Banque de Madagascar et des Comores).

The development bank succeeded earlier investment banks in 1963. The Malagasy government holds FMG650 million of its share capital of FMG1 billion; the remainder is held by the French Central Economic Cooperation Fund (Caisse Centrale de Coopération Economique—CCCE), the chief foreign aid fund. Eight members of its managing council are appointed by the Malagasy government; and four, by France. The bank's financial resources come mostly from long- or medium-term borrowing from the CCCE or from the Malagasy Treasury, and it is authorized to extend short-, medium-, and long-term loans to individuals, firms, or public institutions for any development purpose but especially for agricultural development.

Monetary policy is formulated by the board of directors of the IEM. There is also a national credit council, but it meets rarely. Its twenty members are mostly civil servants. To regulate commercial bank activities, there is the banking Control Commission, consisting of the chairman of the board of the IEM, the director of the Treasury, a counselor of the Supreme Court, and the president of the banking association.

The country's monetary policy is carried out by means of five principal instruments: ceilings on commercial bank lending; ceilings on government borrowing; prescribed liquidity ratios (ratio of a commercial bank's readily convertible assets to its total holdings); rediscount ceilings (ceilings on the amount of its lending that a commercial bank may transfer to the central bank); and changes in the rediscount rate (the cost to the commercial banks when they transfer their lending to the central bank). Rediscount rate adjustments were little used until 1969. After a period of expansionary domestic credit supply in the 1965-67 period, the rate of increase was reduced slightly in 1968 and 1969 and slowed appreciably in 1970. During 1968 and 1969 importers were building up inventories in anticipation of further price increases in France. The rate of private credit expansion was restrained by stricter control of rediscount ceilings, selective adjustments in the rediscount rate, and the imposition of liquidity ratios on the commercial banks. By applying selective credit ceilings, the central bank was able to restrain commercial bank short-term credits to the import and commercial sector but allow credit to agriculture, industry, and exports to expand.

Long-term credit to the private sector is granted exclusively by the development bank. Until 1969 most medium-term loans were also made by the development bank. Measures were then successfully introduced to encourage greater participation by the commercial banks in medium-term operations. Medium-term credit to the private sector is extended mostly for investments in industry, agriculture, and housing construction. Short-term credit from the central bank to the banks was effectively restrained between 1967 and 1969, but medium-term credit was allowed to expand, notably in 1970, when short-term credit for export financing was also measurably increased.

The public sector had an expansionary impact in 1968 and 1969 as the government drew down its previously accumulated deposits to finance the deficit resulting from the Program of Major Operations. By the end of 1969 the government had become for the first time a net borrower from the banking system. In the second half of 1970, however, the public sector again became a net creditor, and it had a very strong contractionary impact as the Treasury's liquidity position improved (see Public Finance, this ch.). Consequently, domestic credit expanded by only 7 percent in 1970. The trend of the second half of 1970 continued into the first half of 1971.

Ceilings on credit to the government provide that the total amount

216

of short-term credit through advances and Treasury bill operations must not exceed 15 percent of the government's fiscal receipts during the preceding year. Also, the total amount must not exceed 10 percent of average private deposits with the banking system and the Treasury during a twelve-month period.

The impact of credit expansion on money supply throughout the 1968-70 period was partially offset by continual reduction of the banking system's foreign assets and also by appreciable increases in time deposits. Interest rates were continually adjusted upward to keep them higher than those in France, and the result was a spectacular growth in time and savings deposits, especially in 1969 and 1970.

There are no overall price statistics for the island as a whole. The consumer price indexes published for the city of Tananarive indicate that the price level was fairly stable between 1965 and 1968 but began to rise sharply in the first half of 1969 as a result of retailers' markups in reaction to the introduction of tax on commercial value added. After the government revised the tax and exempted some more essential items, the price index for lower income families declined. After the devaluation of the French franc and the Malagasy franc in August 1969, the Malagasy price control authorities ordered a general price freeze, which was lifted in early 1970 and replaced by prescribed profit margins. These measures were effective in restraining price increases in the second half of 1969 and 1970, but by June 1971 the index for a lower income family had increased by 5 percent over the index of a year earlier, and that for a higher income family had increased by 7 percent. A new selective price freeze was introduced in mid-1971.

FOREIGN PARTICIPATION IN THE ECONOMY

In the early 1970s economic power was in the hands of ethnic Malagasy only at the upper level of government and at the grassroots level of traditional crafts, open-air trading, and small-scale agriculture for subsistence or export. Between these two extremes, French firms and technical assistance personnel or Malagasy citizens of Asian extraction still exercised considerable influence on economic decisions. The implications of this influence for major options in economic policy tended to be greatly exaggerated, however, by elements of the press and political parties, which frequently blamed many or all of the island's economic ills on foreign dominance in the economy. The effort to replace middle-level foreign manpower with educated or trained Malagasy management personnel had been progressing successfully under the Tsiranana regime and was an important part of the program of the new Ramanantsoa government.

Malagasy participation in ownership of industry or commerce, however, continued to be restricted by lack of a commercial tradition, by the scarcity of domestic savings, and by the traditional preference for nonproductive uses of savings in the acquisition of housing, real estate, and cattle or in ceremony or display (see ch. 5). To fill this vacuum, the government had been taking an increasingly active part since independence in the ownership, if not always the active management, of private industry and agriculture by participation in companies of mixed economy (see ch. 13).

In agriculture, French farmers and trading firms retained a dominant role in the production of certain export products, notably sugarcane grown in the northwest, sisal in the Mandrare valley of the south, and tobacco in the river basins of the western coast. Cotton was still being grown on private French plantations, but government-operated projects were playing an important role in increasing production of cotton. Most of the other export crops, as well as all subsistence crops, were grown predominantly by small-scale Malagasy farmers, but the French portion of the Alaotra ricegrowing project made an important contribution to commercial rice production (see ch. 13). Most of the coffee, clove, and vanilla growers were Malagasy, but trade and processing of these export specialties had been controlled by French or Asian interests through the 1960s. In the early 1970s it was not yet clear to what extent the government had succeeded in taking over direction of collection, pricing, and trade in these and other important exports.

In mining, a few of the older companies were under wholly French ownership, but the more important enterprises were companies of mixed economy in which the Malagasy government participated. The government owned 29 percent of the Andriamena chromite mine and was participating with a French firm in the bauxite survey.

In keeping with the French tradition, the government operates the railroad, the tobacco and match monopolies, and the explosives monopoly. It plays a predominant role in electric power production, in which French private interests also participate. Before the loss of tariff protection and price support on the French market, private French ownership was heavily predominant in other branches of industry, but since independence there has been more participation by foreign investors from other European countries, the United States, and Japan. Greek and Indian residents of the island have also participated in industrial investment, although for the most part they prefer commerce.

Import trade has been dominated by three large French private firms: the Compagnie Marseillaise de Madagascar, the Societé Industrielle et Commerciale de l-Emyrne, and the Compagnie Lyonnaise de Madagascar. Their virtual monopoly has sometimes been blamed for the high cost of living and production on the island. The Chinese on the eastern coast, the Indians or Pakistanis on the western coast, and the Greeks in Tananarive serve as middlemen and retail traders. As a rule they have been resident on the island for a long time, and many have acquired Malagasy citizenship. More and more Malagasy have been entering trade, although they have no commercial tradition. Merina from the highlands have long been active in retail trade in the coastal regions. The government has fostered the growth of consumer cooperatives and producers' cooperatives for trading purposes (see ch. 13).

Small taxi and transport companies are operated by Malagasy, Chinese, and Indo-Pakistanis, but most transport enterprise is in the hands either of the government or of private French firms. In addition to the railroad and the telephone and telegraph services, the government operates a number of bus lines. Air Madagascar and a large shipping line are operated by the government in close cooperation with French firms. The largest trucking firm is under French ownership.

DOMESTIC TRADE

Interregional trade is limited in scope. In the mid-1960s it absorbed about 30 percent of aggregate production. It consisted chiefly of trade in staple foods between regions that produce rice, sugar, or other foods surplus to their own needs and those regions, such as the south and the eastern coast, that have a deficit in food supply (see ch. 13). There is also considerable trade in cattle on the hoof from the south and the mid-west to the Central Highlands and the eastern coast. Prices on locally produced goods may vary by as much as 300 percent from one region to another for certain agricultural products, and there is also a wide range among profit margins on different categories of imports and local products.

Much trading takes place at village level—some of it on a barter basis. Altogether about 55 percent of agricultural production enters internal trade. A large proportion of internal trade consists of provisioning the towns, but most of this comes from the adjacent countryside.

In July 1972 Prime Minister Ramanantsoa announced that the government would intervene to streamline the circuits of trade. For certain key products such as rice, the government would take direct charge of the marketing. For other products it would "set limits to the role played by existing structures, governmental as well as private, within the marketing system as a whole." The objective would be to reduce the charges that weigh heavily on prices, injuring both producers and consumers.

The trading system, which Ramanantsoa denounced as "anarchic and poorly adapted," was composed of a few near-monopolies at the import-export end of the system and a multitude of tiny units at the other, serving both as collection points for export crops and as retail outlets for imports, as well as a storage point for locally produced foods (see ch. 13). This system weighed heavily on prices and gave rise to numerous abuses. In the bush and at the village level the collection system was essentially one of barter and usury. In most of the country, the portion of the crop sold was just sufficient to pay the head or cattle tax and to secure the most essential goods, such as tools and clothing. The peasants were obliged to spend too high a proportion of their cash income on imports. Imported goods were sold in town and village in tiny quantities, a system that tends to raise prices. The poorest consumers were those who had to pay the highest price.

In the 1960s the government was already intervening in the field of marketing through its commodity stabilization boards and its sponsorship of marketing and purchasing cooperatives and village unions (see ch. 13). Through the National Investment Company, the government also participated in the operation of a chain of department and variety stores scattered about the island and known as Magasins M., which was operated by a mixed enterprise, including the National Investment Company and private or philanthropic individuals. The company imported goods directly for its retail chain and thus competed with private outlets, but its prices were usually about the same as those in private stores.

FOREIGN ECONOMIC RELATIONS

After the disturbances and change of government in mid-1972, political rhetoric tended to place increasing emphasis on the disadvantages of the island's dependence on foreign trade and investment and of foreign dominance in the country's industrial and commercial enterprises. By the end of August 1972, however, the only major change actually effected in the orientation of foreign economic policy was the new government's rejection of economic rapprochement with the Republic of South Africa (see ch. 10). This policy change was expected to result in a reduction of planned investment in hotels and other tourist facilities and raised new uncertainty concerning investment in the Narinda tanker port and drydock project (see Transportation and Communications, this ch.). In other respects, it appeared that foreign economic policy might continue to follow the same basic orientation, perhaps with some diversification of trade ties and with increasing official acknowledgement of popular sentiment on the desirability of greater economic self-reliance.

In an economic policy speech of August 24, 1972, the minister of economy, commerce, and finances in the Ramanantsoa government rejected any suggestion that the country should, or could, attempt to move in the direction of economic autarky. He asserted that, on the contrary, the new government would be seeking a larger number of trade and economic partners abroad and that a country the size of

Madagascar could not expect to free itself from the forces that rule the world economy.

In the mid-1960s the country's imports of goods and services averaged about 20 percent of its GDP, and exports averaged about 15 percent. The public debt service ratio was less than 6 percent of imports of goods and services, excluding investment income. In this respect the country was relatively well off, as much of its debt had been incurred on fairly easy terms. Statements by members of the new government, however, emphasized the growth of the trade deficit since the 1950s, when investment and consumption expenditure were fairly low, and therefore exercised little pressure on imports.

Balance of Payments

The country's net foreign exchange position, as reflected in its balance of payments, may fluctuate from year to year, but over the long term foreign exchange earnings have not been able to keep pace with the mounting imports of goods and services generated by investment needs and consumer demand. The inflow of private capital has been limited, so that the deficit resulting from the exchange of goods and services had had to be covered either by official foreign aid grants (unrequited government transfers), by official loans (government nonmonetary capital), or in some years by drawing down the central bank's reserves of foreign exchange built up in more favorable years (see table 11).

At the end of August 1972 no comprehensive data were yet available for the balance of payments in 1971, but it was evident that the deficit on current account (goods and services) had not been kept down to the exceptionally low level achieved in 1970. Madagascar's balance of payments presentation differs from the norm in that freight costs are included in the merchandise trade deficit rather than as a debit under services. This tends to exaggerate the trade deficit somewhat but does not affect the balance on goods and services. On this basis, the 1971 trade deficit was the largest in absolute value since independence in 1960. Exports covered about 70 percent of imports, however, which was consistent with the average ratio during the 1960s. Higher prices for imports and rising freight rates were responsible for part of the rising deficit, introducing an important element of "imported inflation" into the island's domestic price level. The rise was accelerated by the impact of revaluation of certain foreign currencies, notably the West German deutsche mark and the Japanese yen. The volume of imports also increased heavily, however, as aggregate demand rose more rapidly than domestic output.

Only part of the rise in imports went to improve the country's productive capacity and economic infrastructure. Aircraft, trucks,

Table 11. Provisional Balance of Payments Estimates,
Malagasy Republic, 1968-70
(in billion Malagasy francs) [1]

	1968	1969	1970
Exports	28.61	29.15	40.22
Imports (including insurance and freight)	−42.02	−47.19	−47.34
Balance on merchandise trade	−13.41	−18.04	−7.12
A. Services (invisible):			
Transportation	0.83	1.04	0.16
Travel	−0.92	−0.37	−1.10
Investment income	−3.66	−3.44	−3.48
Government (not included elsewhere)	2.67	4.60	4.86
Other services	−3.34	−2.12	−2.93
Balance on services	−4.42	0.29	2.49
B. Current balance of payments (goods and services)	−17.83	−18.33	−9.61
C. Unrequited transfers:			
Private	2.20	2.35	2.81
Official	11.54	10.99	11.30
D. Capital (nonmonetary):			
Private:			
Long term	0.64	0.84	0.06
Short term	−0.33	−0.11	0.05
Official:			
Loan disbursements	2.05	1.74	2.34
Amortization	−0.48	−0.33	−0.59
E. Errors and omissions	−0.65	1.26	−0.58
F. Overall balance of payments (B through E)	−2.84	−1.57	5.76
G. Offsetting monetary movements (increase in reserves minus)			
Central bank holdings	2.97	2.25	−4.93
Commercial bank holdings	−0.13	−0.68	−1.70
Allocation of drawing rights with IMF [2]	--- [3]	--- [3]	0.87

[1] For value of the Malagasy franc—see Glossary.
[2] International Monetary Fund.
[3] --- means nil.

and industrial machinery and equipment were large items, but part of the increase was owing to large imports of rice, textile yarns, fabrics, clothing, and other consumer goods. A relatively poor crop year in agriculture was responsible for part of the deficit. Another factor was a month's shutdown for repairs at the Tamatave petroleum refinery, which necessitated some imports of refined petroleum products.

The fluctuations in agricultural crop production that have retarded medium- or long-term growth in gross domestic production and created recurrent problems in food supply also help determine the foreign exchange position from year to year. In 1970 both crop harvests and agricultural export prices were the best in many years, resulting in a small trade deficit and an actual surplus on the overall balance of payments. In 1971 agricultural production declined sharply, owing chiefly to damage from cyclone Felicia, which hit the island early in the year, but also to the fact that many crops were at the low point of their production cycle (see ch. 13). Marketed output of thirteen cash crops was about 9 percent below the exceptionally high 1970 level. Rice production was substantially unchanged, but the volume of such major export crops as coffee, cloves, and sugarcane was considerably lower. Producer prices for cloves, cotton, groundnuts, and pepper were raised, however, and the continuing favorable trend of export prices meant that export earnings maintained the high level of 1970.

In addition to its trade deficit, the country has a deficit on services (invisibles) resulting from the outflow of interest and dividend payments on foreign loans and also from remittances abroad by foreigners working in the country in technical assistance or business, who usually save part of their salaries and send it home to France or other foreign countries. These outflows more than outweigh the net inflow from expenditures in Madagascar by foreign military and other missions in the country.

The deficit on current account must be offset by net receipts under the remaining major headings of transfers, nonmonetary capital, and monetary movements. Unrequited transfers are grants received from foreign governments, international organizations, or private groups such as missionary societies. The salaries paid to foreign technical assistance personnel in the country, which appear as a debit under services, are offset by receipts from technical assistance donor countries under unrequited transfers. The balance on transfer account, as reported in the official statistics, is consistently favorable. Because there is complete freedom of banking trans-actions between Madagascar and France, however, a large portion of the receipts from public transfers may be offset by unrecorded private transfers of funds from salaries or commercial profits made by French nationals on the island.

Receipts of private capital in direct investment or other forms had been quite modest in the 1960s; and, short of unforeseen mineral discoveries, they were expected to continue to be quite limited despite the liberal tax incentives and provisions for repatriation granted under the investment code. Although in mid-1972 the new Ramanantsoa government had promised a complete revision of the investment code, there was no indication of any firm plan to reduce incentives materially. The new government declined to promise major nationalizations of foreign enterprise, and repeated statements stressed the importance of encouraging foreign investment in the economy as a means of providing increasing wage-earning and management jobs for Malagasy nationals.

An American economist who published a comprehensive survey of the country in 1971 saw considerable promise for the implantation of foreign investment and for development in the Malagasy economy. In his view the island offered a number of comparative advantages to large international enterprise, including proximity to new sea routes that would provide an alternative to use of the Suez Canal, and a large reserve of trainable manpower. Although skilled management personnel versed in the conduct of complex investment and commercial operations were rare, the literacy rate and the level of artisan skills were relatively high for a developing country. A tradition of school attendance was well developed, and the Malagasy had rapidly acquired facility, for example, as accountants, mechanical and electronic repair specialists, and machine operators.

After the disturbances in mid-1972, foreign investment commitments slowed, awaiting further developments. The government clamped tight foreign exchange controls on all transactions, including those with the franc area, to prevent the kind of capital flight that usually follows such upheavals. The outlook for development and investment appeared to continue to be favorable, however, on condition that heightened national self-awareness could find constructive expression in the 1970s and could enhance rather than defeat efforts to obtain foreign technical and financial assistance.

Transportation, irrigation, and other economic infrastructure required for development derives largely from official foreign aid, in the form of either grants (unrequited transfers) or official non-monetary capital. The inflow of foreign aid during the 1960s had been sizable, and the outlook for net official foreign borrowing seemed fairly good. Malagasy governments had for the most part followed a cautious policy of fiscal responsibility. The dogma of balancing the current operating budget was abandoned for the first time in 1968 in favor of deficit spending. Subsequent attempts to maintain an austerity program for government operating expenditures had not been entirely successful, but the Ramanatsoa government seemed committed to an intensification of anti-inflationary measures beginning in 1973.

Madagascar is among those countries that have received the largest amounts of foreign assistance per capita since World War II. Moreover, a very high proportion of official assistance received has been in the form of outright grants or technical assistance rather than in the form of loans. From 1964 to 1967, for example, 90 percent of official foreign aid was received in the form of grants. Before independence most of the country's capital investment, as well as budget subsidies and a portion of current government consumption expenditure, was financed from French government funds. It was estimated that from 1946 to 1960 official aid from France amounted to more than the equivalent of FMG60 billion. No comprehensive figure on aid received since independence was available. From 1964 to 1967 total foreign aid amounted to an average of FMG13 billion a year. After France, the Common Market has been the principal donor, contributing about FMG29 billion in the 1958-68 decade. In the mid-1960s support from the Common Market fund began to offset a portion of the gradual decline in aid from official French sources. Other donors have been the United Nations, Italy, the Federal Republic of German (West Germany), Israel, the Republic of China (Nationalist China), Japan, and Norway.

The largest portion of loan aid has been from the World Bank Group (see Glossary), which accords loans on relatively easy terms. Because the country's foreign debt burden was moderate, it may be able to procure more of its development financing from foreign loans in the 1970s, particularly from multilateral sources. In addition to the World Bank Group, France, the United States, West Germany, Italy, and Israel were furnishing loan aid in the late 1960s.

In years when net receipts from abroad of private or official transfers or capital have not been sufficient to cover the deficit on current account, an overall balance of payments deficit occurs and must be offset by monetary movements (see table 11). These consist of the drawing down of foreign exchange reserves held by the central bank and the commercial banks abroad and may be supplemented by drawing on the country's reserve rights with the International Monetary Fund.

Direction and Composition of Trade

In the second half of the 1960s the government was trying to reduce somewhat the country's heavy reliance upon imports from France. From almost two-thirds of total imports in 1967, France's share declined to 50 percent in 1969 and 55 percent in 1970. Imports from other Common Market countries were on the increase, owing largely to imports under mounting assistance from the Common Market's aid fund (see table 12). Other major import sources were the United States and Japan.

The merchandise trade deficit with France (including insurance and freight) was reduced from FMG17 billion in 1968 to FMG12 billion in 1970, but exports still covered only about half of imports from that source. At the same time the trade deficit with other Common Market countries almost doubled, and trade with Japan was brought almost into balance. Trade outside the franc area was not in deficit, chiefly because trade with the United States showed a growing export surplus. Exports to the United States showed the biggest gain, rising from FMG240 million in 1949 and FMG702 million in 1950 to FMG6,196 million in 1965 and FMG9,120 million in

Table 12. *Foreign Trade with Principal Countries,*
Malagasy Republic, 1967-70
(in billion Malagasy francs) [1]

	1967	1968	1969	1970
Exports:				
Common Market [2]				
France	9.43	9.58	10.56	13.76
West Germany	0.73	1.04	1.11	1.65
Italy	0.33	0.45	0.60	0.46
Netherlands	0.16	0.33	0.28	0.43
Belgium-Luxembourg	0.06	0.11	0.22	0.20
United States	6.32	6.43	6.91	9.12
Réunion	2.72	3.37	3.56	4.61
Malaysia	0.02	0.77	0.21	2.35
Japan	0.39	0.46	0.68	1.27
Senegal	1.16	0.93	0.94	0.61
Ivory Coast	0.35	0.42	0.46	0.62
Other countries	4.04	4.72	3.62	5.14
TOTAL	25.71	28.61	29.15	40.22
Imports:				
Common Market [2]				
France	23.21	26.42	23.95	25.89
West Germany	1.93	2.59	4.32	4.29
Italy	0.89	1.47	1.86	2.80
Netherlands	0.81	0.90	1.31	1.17
Belgium-Luxembourg	0.49	0.65	0.98	1.54
United States	2.46	2.11	3.97	2.69
Japan	0.96	1.03	1.15	1.30
Senegal	0.53	1.09	1.09	0.23
Ivory Coast	0.02	0.12	0.16	0.11
Other countries	4.58	5.64	8.41	7.33
TOTAL	35.88	42.02	47.20	47.35

[1] For value of the Malagasy franc—see Glossary.
[2] European Economic Community—EEC, known as the Common Market.

1970. The United States is the principal customer for the island's vanilla exports and also buys important coffee exports.

Agricultural products supply more than two-thirds of the island's exports. Most are exported in only lightly processed form; examples are dried coffee in the bean and cured vanilla. Of the eight leading agricultural exports, coffee has been consistently the largest foreign exchange earner, averaging about 28 percent of export value in the 1960s, and vanilla, rice, and sugar have vied for second place. The principal agricultural exports in the late 1960s were coffee, sugarcane, vanilla, cloves, export rice, live cattle, beef, sugar, sisal, cape peas (lima beans), and tobacco. Other export crops included essential oils for perfumery, pepper, raffia, tung oil, groundnuts (peanuts), and cassava products. There were exports of chromite, graphite, mica, hides and skins, wood products, and refined petroleum products.

The country is fortunate among developing nations in the diversity of its exports, but at the end of the 1960s they still had a very low processing content so that the value added domestically consisted in large part of commercial profits. Like many primary products, most of those exported by Madagascar were confronted in the 1960s with shrinking world markets and insecure or speculative foreign market prices. The protection and price support so long enjoyed on the French market had been lost. The overseas markets for several of the products, such as cloves, vanilla, cape peas, and essential oils for perfumery, were very limited, and cloves and vanilla had encountered severe competition from synthetic coal-tar derivatives.

The goal of the government planners is to reduce dependence on imported consumer goods. By the end of the 1960s some progress had been made in this direction (see table 13). By 1969, for example, domestic output of soap, cotton fabrics, and clothing had begun to replace a portion of imports, which are particularly heavy for textile products. Foodstuffs are an important component of consumer imports, making up about 10 to 12 percent of total imports in the 1960s. This is in part a reflection of French taste, which not only determines many of the purchases of the large foreign colony in Tananarive but also influences the consumption habits of higher income urban Malagasy (see ch. 6). It also results in part from setbacks in the development of the domestic dairy industry and production of fruits and vegetables. Primarily, however, it reflects the continuing failure to stabilize the growth of domestic rice production at a rate that can outstrip the growth of population and demand (see ch. 13). Food imports consequently fluctuate from year to year in response to the level of the domestic rice crop and to the demand generated by the earnings of export crop producers.

In 1970 consumer goods were replaced by raw materials and fuels for the first time as the largest import commodity group. The share of consumer goods in total imports, which had been 40 percent in 1967, had been reduced to 30 percent in 1970, and in the same period the share of raw materials and fuels increased from 25 percent to 34 percent, reflecting the growth of industry. Imports of capital goods increased from 24 percent to 34 percent, owing chiefly to imports of airplanes and other transportation equipment but also reflecting the impact of the government's Program of Major Operations.

TRANSPORTATION AND COMMUNICATIONS

Transportation is cumbersome and costly because of the island's distance from major world markets; its scarcity of natural deep-water ports; its topography, which divides the terrain into isolated

Table 13. Exports and Imports of Principal Products, by
Commodity Group, Malagasy Republic, 1968-70
(in billion Malagasy francs) *

	1968	1969	1970
Exports:			
Coffee	8.80	8.27	10.94
Cloves	1.96	0.41	4.70
Vanilla	2.53	3.01	3.61
Export rice	2.91	2.36	3.02
Sugar	1.58	1.66	1.55
Meat	0.58	0.66	1.22
Fish	0.28	0.46	0.85
Petroleum products	0.98	1.04	1.56
Chromite	0.00	0.21	0.85
Graphite	0.43	0.51	0.65
Other	8.56	10.56	11.27
Total	28.61	29.15	40.22
Imports:			
Foodstuffs	4.37	5.80	5.33
Other consumer goods	16.73	15.41	14.34
Capital equipment	9.51	12.59	11.18
Primary products	9.08	10.71	13.42
Other	2.33	2.69	3.08
Total	42.02	47.20	47.35

*For value of the Malagasy franc—see Glossary.

enclaves; and its climate, punctuated by torrential rains and periodic cyclones. Its soils are of a type of laterite that does not resist erosion by rain or heavy vehicles, so that the need for asphalt paving greatly increases roadbuilding costs. The country's area is relatively extensive in relation to its financial resources and potential traffic. The low density of population in many areas of the south and west does not repay investment in transport. The different modes of transport by road, rail, air, and water do not compete with one another, which would lower costs; instead, each serves a separate area.

Investment in transportation infrastructure absorbed a major proportion of government expenditure both under French colonial administration and under successive development plans since independence. Continuing improvement of the transport network is an essential prerequisite for private investment in industry and mining and for agricultural development, but this requires a high rate of capital investment with no immediate economic return and no visible impact on output and incomes. It is therefore heavily dependent on receipts of official foreign grants and long-term loans on easy terms from international organizations such as the World Bank.

In 1972 costly or inadequate transport connections between different parts of the island, particularly rural areas, were still a major hindrance to cash production and trade. Only about 1,850 miles of roads were hard surfaced, and between one-third and one-fourth of the road network consisted of all-weather roads (see ch. 3). There were no all-weather connections between the northern part of the western region and the rest of the country, and connections with the south were merely trails. Only the road from Tananarive to Majunga could take heavy trucks. The principal ports on the eastern and western coasts were linked with the national capital, but connections between smaller centers were erratic, and the lack of feeder roads encumbered the system of food supply and agricultural export. The 530-mile railroad constructed by the French connected the capital with the port of Tamatave on the eastern coast and with the vital rice production center of Alaotra and the chromium mine of Andriamena in the eastern highlands.

The state-owned railroad had very high maintenance costs because of its steep gradients and was obliged to maintain high rates. In the late 1960s it was making a profit on its current operations but could not finance investment and capital charges from its own resources; instead, they were covered in part by advances from the government and by borrowing. In 1969 the railroads carried about 2,099,000 passengers and 869,000 metric tons of freight. Traffic is unevenly distributed, and the only significant volume is on the Tananarive-Tamatave line. In order to maintain the volume of traffic on this line, the government has neglected maintenance of the parallel road connection between the capital and Tamatave, and the railroad makes special rate concessions to large-scale customers. This policy was under revision in the early 1970s, however, because its effect had been to increase already burdensome transport costs. The government was also considering the recommendations of a United Nations-financed study for consolidation of railroad service, reform of its organization, and revision of the rate structure in order to improve cost efficiency.

Under the First Five-Year Plan road development cost about FMG20 billion, or 20 percent of available investment resources. Nevertheless, a number of the scheduled engineering operations were put off because of delays in the international loan agreements and would not be completed until the period of the Second Three-Year Plan. This was true notably of the proposed links between Diégo-Suarez and the rest of the island and the construction of a permanent, yearround road the length of the east coast from Fort Dauphin in the south to Vohémar in the north.

Investments in the transport sector as a whole under the Second Three-Year Plan were initially expected to amount to about FMG41 billion, of which 60 percent would be for roads. The final allocation would depend, however, upon the availability of foreign loans. Urgent priority was to be accorded to improving the existing national routes to carry heavy transport trucks of up to twenty-five metric ton capacity and improving provincial routes for trucks of up to fifteen metric ton capacity. This would require grading of hills and curves in a number of places and the construction of a number of bridges. National routes are to be asphalt surfaced, but the provincial routes will be paved only in exceptional cases. The Second Three-Year Plan would also accord high priority to the construction of feeder roads in agricultural districts.

During the 1960s motor traffic on the national highways was increasing at a rate of more than 5 percent a year. On the more important routes, such as Tananarive-Majunga and Tananarive-Tulear, the rate was about 10 percent. During the period of the First Five-Year Plan the number of transport vehicles in use tripled. On January 1, 1970, there were 85,704 motor vehicles registered on the island, of which 50 percent were passenger cars, 34 percent were trucks, 3 percent were buses, 3 percent were other commercial vehicles, and the remainder were tractors, trailers, and motorcycles. One out of three motor vehicles registered for the first time during 1970 was assembled on the island.

Internal air service is good but costly. It was developed rapidly under government auspices to supplement inadequate surface transport and to link isolated outlying regions to the capital. Domestic air service is furnished exclusively by Air Madagascar, the national airline. The network of landing fields served by scheduled inland flights is dense (see ch. 3). It is supplemented by a large number of private landing strips and airfields not in regular scheduled use. In 1969, however, only seventeen landing fields had all-weather asphalt runways. Air traffic has not developed as rapidly as foreseen under the First Five-Year Plan. In 1971 it still consisted mainly of passenger transport; commercial cargo traffic was insignificant. In 1967 the domestic airline carried 113,115 passengers and 3,720 metric tons of freight.

Air Madagascar makes large profits on its international operations, which have more than offset its losses on domestic flights. International flights between Madagascar and Europe, Africa, and the Comoro Islands are chiefly operated by Air Madagascar and Air France under a pool arrangement for equal revenue sharing. Alitalia and South African Airways also operate flights to Madagascar. In 1969 international flights to and from the island carried 89,923 passengers and 3,108 metric tons of freight.

Of the island's twenty-three coastal ports, nineteen are simply open roadsteads without docking facilities, where ships must ride at anchor and freight must be transferred by lighter at considerable cost. Nevertheless, they play a very important role in internal trade because coastal shipping is the only means of moving goods between many areas on the island. At independence in 1960 international trade was inefficiently distributed among a number of coastal ports. Ships arriving from Europe spent an average of five weeks loading and unloading at seven or more ports around the island. An objective of the First Five-Year Plan therefore was to direct more of the island's foreign trade through the four main ports: Diégo-Suarez in the north; Majunga in the west; Tulear in the southwest; and Tamatave in the east (see ch. 3). The objective was partially realized. In 1968 these four ports were handling 85 percent of the island's foreign trade and 60 percent of its coastal traffic. Further concentration of international trade is to be pursued under the Second Three-Year Plan. Eventually, when a circumferential coastal road is developed, it is hoped to be able to concentrate coastal trade as well.

Tamatave, located near the export-crop regions of the eastern coast and having a rail connection to the capital, is by far the most important port. In 1968 it was handling 75 percent of imports, 35 percent of exports, and 20 percent of coastal traffic. After construction of the petroleum refinery at Tamatave and the opening of the chromium mine at Andriamena in 1969, the port's poor physical facilities were overstrained. In June 1970 the International Development Association approved a credit of US$9.6 million to Madagascar for improvement and enlargement of the port of Tamatave to handle the expected large increase in dry cargo and crude petroleum and products.

A proposed project to construct a drydock for oceangoing tankers at the Bay of Narinda, fifty-six miles north of Majunga on the western coast, had been under discussion for several years when the World Bank sent a team of financial experts to assess the project in mid-1972. Other potential backers of the project had included the United Kingdom, France, West Germany, and South Africa. It could result in important foreign exchange earnings for the island. A French consultant group had carried out a feasibility study for the project that indicated that, as long as the Suez Canal remains closed, the Narinda drydock would be assured of at least fifty vessels a year. This would probably depend, however, on the plans of South Africa, which had dropped a project for a drydock at Cape Town in favor of the Narinda plan. After the new Malagasy government reversed Malagasy policy toward South Africa in mid-1972, however, there was reported to be growing demand from South African shipping interests for the development of a drydock at Cape Town.

The Narinda venture was further jeopardized when Portugal announced, in August 1972, that plans were under discussion for the contruction of a giant drydock at one of three prospective sites on the coast of Angola. The project, said to have heavy financial backing and expertise, could reportedly be completed before either the Narinda or Cape Town ventures and could alienate prospective backing for the Narinda project. It was considered extremely doubtful that traffic around the cape could support two such drydock ventures.

There are five moderate-sized trucking companies: two operate out of Fianarantsoa to Tulear, Fort Dauphin, and Mananjary; two operate between Tananarive and Majunga; and one operates out of Tamatave. In addition, there are a number of truckowners' cooperatives, of which the largest, the Malagasy Transport Cooperative (Kooperative Malagasy Fitaterana), has a fleet of sixty to eighty vehicles. There are also a number of independent operators. Passenger transport vehicles range from company-operated forty- or fifty-seat buses along the major routes to brush taxis operated by cooperatives of individual entrepreneurs.

Despite its 4,000-mile coastline and the distant origin of much of its population, the island has no maritime tradition. The Malagasy merchant marine in the late 1960s consisted of two oceangoing ships that made regular runs to European ports; one ship of 1,900 gross register tons that operated between Madagascar and East African ports; six ships of more than 1,400 gross register tons engaged in coastal traffic and traffic with the Comoro Islands; six coastal ships ranging from 150 to 300 gross register tons; and six coastal oil tankers. In addition, there were some 300 dhows and schooners operating only between Tulear and Nosy Be.

Because of the well-developed domestic air service, the Malagasy postal system is rapid and reliable, even to outlying areas. The postal authorities also operate an efficient system of postal checking and savings. In the mid-1960s the telephone network covered some 28,000 miles, and there were about 27,000 instruments in use in 1970. There were five automatic telephone exchanges—in Tananarive, Tamatave, Majunga, Antsirabe, and Fianarantsoa. In 1967 the United Nations granted a sum of FMG19 million for further extension of the telephone system. New satellite telecommunications links between the island and France were officially inaugurated in April 1972. The telecommunications center had been built with French aid and was linked with the United States satellite, Intelsat-Four. The telephone system is supplemented by radio connections. The island also has a telegraph system and teletype and telex links.

CHAPTER 13
AGRICULTURE AND INDUSTRY

The productive sectors of the economy—agriculture, industry, and mining—generate only about half of the gross domestic product (GDP—see Glossary), the other half deriving from commerce and services. Agriculture is by far the dominant sector in size and output, but its growth has been slowed by the weight of tradition, by the deteriorating world terms of trade (export prices) for raw materials and foodstuffs, and by the disproportionate share of the commercial sector in agricultural earnings. Industry was the most dynamic sector during the 1960s. Activity in construction slowed during the second half of the decade, but manufacturing expanded from only about 5 percent of GDP at independence in 1960 to around 11.7 percent in 1970—a proportion that compares favorably with that in many French-speaking African countries. Nevertheless, several branches of manufacturing were operating below capacity in 1970 because of deficient raw material supply or other problems. Employment in manufacturing was still limited: an estimated 1.4 percent of the active population in 1970.

Government policy stressed the interdependence and complementary nature of industry and agricultural production on the island. Many of the newly created industries or those still in the planning stage were based upon domestic raw materials. In outlining the economic policy of his new government in a speech of July 27, 1972, General Gabriel Ramanantsoa emphasized that in the industrial sector priority would be accorded to enterprises that could add to the domestically created value of the products of the island's soil, whether agricultural or mineral.

Activity in mining was on the decline until 1969, as gold exports were reduced to a negligible quantity and shipments of minerals associated with nuclear energy—uranothorianite and monazite—ceased altogether. The island remained a leading world exporter of high-quality graphite, however, and exploitation of a chromite deposit of world importance was begun in 1969. Profitable commercial exploitation of other minerals was hampered for the present by the high cost of transport and the potential cost of installing industrial infrastructure in remote regions. In mid-1972 studies were underway on the feasibility of mining large deposits of bauxite and nickel.

Agriculture—the country's only important economic resource—furnishes the livelihood of more than 84 percent of the population and engages 90 percent of the active labor force. It contributes more than 80 percent of export earnings and is a major source of government revenue.

Cultivation is the dominant form of activity and provides most of the national diet as well as the bulk of exports. Stockraising is the chief activity in parts of the southern and western regions but, because of its low productivity, it is of more limited economic importance. Even where it predominates as a way of life or as an incentive to acquisition, herding rarely furnishes the major share of the daily diet.

Rice is the dietary staple throughout most of the island and occupies more than one-fourth of the cultivated land area. Wherever conditions permit, it is grown in small-scale irrigated paddy fields on the oriental model. Where water is lacking or the terrain precludes irrigation, it is sown on hillsides cleared by the destructive slash-and-burn method, which is illegal but still widely practiced. The first large-scale, mechanized rice-growing project celebrated its tenth anniversary in mid-1971.

The country is basically self-sufficient in staple foods but, as population increases at a rapid rate, imports of rice sometimes exceed the growing exports of special high-quality rice. Government programs aimed at increasing food production under the First Five-Year Plan (1964-68) were stepped up during the Program of Major Operations (1968-69) and were to receive number one priority under the Second Three-Year Plan (1972-74) (see ch. 12). In December 1971, however, a government spokesman, replying to criticisms in the Senate, averred that rice production had not attained the projected targets and that a steep increase in per capita rice consumption, as well as the rise in population, was making recurrent local food shortages a chronic feature of the island's economy.

Although tradition makes it heavily reliant on rice for its food supply, the island's variety of soils and climate permits a range of agricultural products of unusual diversity by African standards. Unlike many tropical developing countries, Madagascar is not dependent on one or two raw material exports but furnishes a spectrum of more than fifteen products in some demand on world markets. Most of them are subject to strong competition, however, and are vulnerable to periods of oversupply and frequent fluctuation in price. Moreover, they are grown predominantly in the northern and eastern regions most subject to periodic devastation by cyclones and other windstorms. Coffee leads the list of exports by an appreciable margin; but vanilla, specialty rice, cloves, cane sugar, essential oils for perfumery, sisal, and a variety of other products make a significant contribution to annual export earnings (see ch. 12).

STRUCTURE OF AGRICULTURAL PRODUCTION

An estimated 56.6 percent of crop production and 73 percent of livestock production is for subsistence consumption. About 80 percent of the nation's cultivators are engaged primarily in subsistence production, but there are very few who do not sell some portion of their crop for cash. Such sales may be required to pay the head tax; to meet minimal needs for consumer goods, such as cloth, salt, tea, or cooking utensils; or to acquire cattle for marriage or ceremonial purposes (see ch. 5). Very often such sales may be a form of deferred subsistence, as grain or other food must be obtained from the stores of the local merchant at high prices during the period of shortage and repaid with interest at harvesttime.

Small-scale farming predominates. Plantations run by settlers from France or Réunion were responsible for launching a number of the commercial and export crops. By 1970 such plantations occupied only about 100,000 acres. They produced all of the island's sisal, most of the sugarcane, and a substantial share of the tobacco, bananas, and cotton. Staple food crops and a growing share of the export and cash crops are produced by independent Malagasy on a very small scale. Those people who do not have land to cultivate, mainly migrants, seem to show a preference for sharecropping rather than working for wages. Only about 5 percent of the land under cultivation in 1960 was worked by sharecroppers: about 1 percent for European or Creole plantations; the remaining 4 percent for small Malagasy landholders.

Farming methods are often relatively advanced by African standards, in that they involve cultivation of a variety of crops and use of the long-handled hoe rather than the short-handled African type. Techniques are most advanced in the Central Highlands where cattle are often kept for manure and for trampling of the ricefields. Terracing and irrigation may be quite complex, and rice seedlings are often transplanted from seedbeds rather than sown broadcast. The use of ox-drawn plows is still the exception rather than the rule, however, and mechanization has been introduced only on the large-scale farms of the western river basin and the Lake Alaotra ricegrowing project in the highlands.

The methods commonly used do not permit the cultivation of more than an average of about 2.5 acres to support a family of five, and kin or even neighbors must be recruited for sowing and harvesting operations. In the more densely populated districts the ratio of land to cultivating families may be lower. Yields per acre are relatively low compared to the more intensive cultivation of the Far East. Where export crops are cultivated, food output does not suffice for the local population.

Government plans stress the need to extend the acreage cultivated by each family, and sizable areas of unoccupied arable soils are theoretically available for resettlement. Despite the historical tradition of migration, however, exisiting ethnic differences and cultivation customs adapted to specific types of terrain tend to impede rapid resettlement. The long-term solution to the problems of food supply and agricultural earnings is therefore thought to lie in the gradual intensification of cultivating methods and the improvement of yields.

LAND USE

Of the island's total land area of about 145 million acres, about 30 million acres (or 20 percent) are wooded, and 12 million acres (9 percent) are unusable. Nearly two-thirds of the land area, or 91 million acres, consists of grazing land. The remaining 9 percent, about 12 million acres, is thought to be readily arable without costly reclamation measures, but of this only 7 million acres were under cultivation or were fallow in 1968. The land classified as arable includes alluvial plains and basins, river-bottom land, and volcanic soils (see ch. 3). In addition, portions of the areas classified as grazing land could probably be rendered suitable for cultivation, but at some cost, by construction of dams, reservoirs, or wells, and by conservation measures. Some recent estimates put arable land at as much as 15 percent of the total land area.

In 1965 it was estimated that about 35 percent of the land in cultivation was fallow; 25 percent, under irrigated crops (primarily rice, but also sugar and cotton); 10 percent, under tree crops; and 30 percent, planted to other crops (the so-called dryland crops, such as mountain rice, cassava, maize (corn), groundnuts, sisal, and tobacco).

The tree crops are grown primarily in the east and in the north, and the irrigated crops, in the Central Highlands and the west (see fig. 9). The dryland crops are more evenly distributed among regions, accounting for 37 percent of cultivated area in the east, 46 percent in the highlands, 53 percent in the north, and 58 percent in the west.

The total number of farms on the island was estimated at about 940,000 in 1971. In the 1966 census some 845,000 men and 127,000 women were reported as independent farmers. Another 1,370,000 persons were family workers in agriculture. There were only about 37,000 sharecroppers and 17,000 agricultural wage workers.

The average holding supports five people and has been variously estimated at from 2.5 acres, excluding forest and right of way, to 4.3 acres in all. This mean size does not vary much from one geographic region to another. Only 3 percent of all holdings exceed ten acres; 35 percent are less than 1.2 acres in size; 30 percent, between 1.2 and 2.5 acres; and 15 percent, between 2.7 and 3.7 acres. Moreover, even where land is plentiful, most family holdings are divided into a number of separate fields or plots: for example, a rice paddy, a field for dryland crops, and a kitchen garden. Pastureland is usually communal.

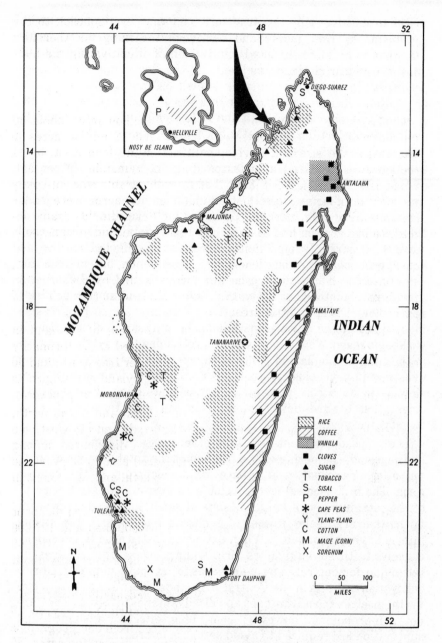

Figure 9. Areas of Maximum Crop Production, Malagasy Republic, 1967

When the population of a village outgrows the available land, satellite villages will usually be formed to cultivate new fields (see ch. 3). Tradition compels many groups, however, to continue cultivating only the traditional kind of land by the customary

237

methods sanctioned by the ancestors, endorsed by the community, and tested by time (see ch. 5). Although the government is attempting to promote increased cultivation of adjoining districts of unused or grazing land, as well as the sometimes marginally productive land on the hillsides known as *tanety*, the effect of population pressure in a number of areas has been reflected in increasing fragmentation of land and reduction of fallow, resulting in declining soil fertility and deterioration of yields.

Assessing the size and development potential of units of farm production on the island, a professor of agronomy at the University of Madagascar estimated in 1971 that from 90 to 95 percent of the total number of farms are very small units in a more or less stagnant stage and have only marginal potential for development. Many of them are one acre or less in size and cannot yield a significant crop surplus for market. From 75 to 95 percent of their production goes to subsistence consumption. There is consequently no margin for reinvestment and, because of lack of adequate credit and extension services, the methods of cultivation have not been improved. Yields remain low. There is little incentive to, or interest in, progressive investment of the cultivator's labor, the only form of investment within his reach. Nevertheless, it was concluded that gradual change in the total economic and political environment may be effecting an evolution in psychological attitudes at this level. This change is so slow as to be barely perceptible but permits hope of an effective orientation toward development over the long term of five to twenty-five years.

The same source identified three other classes of farm enterprise on the island, composing only a fraction of the total number of units but offering the only viable base for development in the shorter term. The first such category, including an estimated 3 to 8 percent of the total number of units, consists of small, independent peasant farms that are in the process of evolution but without any strong internal dynamic impetus. When extension instruction is effectively conceived, these cultivators are willing to accept changes in technique demonstrated from above, as for example in improved rice cultivation projects in the Central Highlands. They are able to judge for themselves the advantages and disadvantages involved. They are not self-propelling, however; continuing effective guidance and supervision are required to avoid setbacks in progress. Among such units, the share of production consumed for subsistence requirements falls to between 40 and 70 percent. A marketable surplus is available to permit repayment of the modest investment credits required and, in some instances, there is an increased investment of effort on the part of the owner-cultivator.

A second class consists of peasant cultivation units created by the government on land that has been specially prepared for the purpose. The number of such farms was still limited in 1971, but they had thus far shown good results. The size of such units ranged from five to fifty acres, depending on such factors as the crop involved, the quality of the soil, the size of the family, and the target income sought. The state furnishes the required investment inputs but is repaid wholly or in part out of the proceeds of the harvest. On such projects supervision is close and may be rather authoritarian in some cases, as on the cotton projects. Participation may at first be minimal, but the units have rapidly attained an average income level of FMG150,000 to FMG400,000 (for value of the Malagasy franc—see Glossary), which provides an appreciable incentive to progress. In some instances, as in the Lake Alaotra projects, the participants are grouped in an organization of their own that gradually takes over some of the tasks of extension instruction and supervision.

Among the peasant farms receiving assistance and guidance from the government or quasi-governmental organizations, there are a few isolated cases in each small subregion that may be said to have reached the self-perpetuating stage. These serve as experimental models for the extension personnel in testing the viability of new techniques, although they have not yet inspired emulation among the surrounding peasant cultivators. These more advanced farmers are ready not only to adopt suggestions that can improve their output and income but also to devise new solutions to their problems. In a few cases, notably in the area surrounding Tananarive, these farms have attained their technical optimum and can proceed to perfecting the economic management of the farm. Because they have rapidly increased productivity, such farms are able to increase their level of subsistence consumption and at the same time market from 80 to 95 percent of their output, earning a surplus that can be immediately reinvested in the operation.

Finally, there are the large-scale state farms and privately owned plantations, small in number and in their share of total cultivated acreage but having an important impact on increasing production for market and for export. Of these, the private corporations are the most dynamic and profit oriented. The state farms, numbering fifteen in 1971, concentrated on augmenting aggregate output as rapidly as possible and sometimes neglected considerations of economic viability. Both types of large-scale enterprise systematically employ wage labor and sharecroppers. There has been a gradual effort, which by 1971 had not made much progress, to terminate the system of sharecropping. In the case of the state farms, it was hoped that workers and sharecroppers would learn improved methods that they could in turn apply on their family holdings. This has not worked out in practice because they do not have access to savings or credits and their own holdings are not large enough to apply the mechanized techniques and economies of scale practiced on the state farms and plantations.

239

TRADITIONAL CULTIVATION PRACTICES

Systems of land use vary from one ethnic group or locality to another in accordance with such factors as density of population, climate, water supply, and the character of terrain and vegetation. The most intensive cultivation is practiced among the Merina and Betsileo of the Central Highlands, where the ricefields support the greatest density of population. At the other extreme are the extensive slash-and-burn methods of bush clearance and shifting cultivation practiced in the south and east, which use about 15 percent of the ground under rice to produce only about 5 percent of the annual crop.

The Betsileo, inhabiting the southern portion of the Central Highlands, concentrate most of their efforts on their ricefields. Supplementary crops are decidedly of secondary interest and are used primarily for home consumption. The rice paddies are constructed on narrow terraces ascending the sides of their steep valleys, creating an intricate manmade landscape reminiscent of parts of the Far East. The system of irrigation is minutely adapted, utilizing every available source of water and using small canals to carry the flow for considerable distances. Some of the rice paddies may cover no more than a few square yards. Only those surfaces that cannot be irrigated are planted to dryland crops.

In parts of the Central Highlands two rice crops a year may be grown, but not on the same plot. The Betsileo use a variety of local species that can be sown at different times, using irrigation to grow some varieties in the dry season and awaiting the rainy season for others. Because the aid of kin or neighbors is required for a number of the operations, the fields surrounding a village may exhibit a checkerboard of tiny plots in different stages of the crop cycle.

The cultivation cycle begins with repair of the irrigation and drainage channels and plowing of the fields. Among the Betsileo plowing is usually done with the long-handled spade or hoe; the plots are usually too narrow for use of the ox-plow. Manure or fertilizer may then be spread on the field. Often artificial fertilizer is regarded as too costly, and the supply of manure is limited; then only the seedbeds will be manured.

On a day fixed well in advance, a large group of kin and neighbors—perhaps thirty or more—is invited for the trampling, a festive occasion greatly enjoyed by all and followed by a feast. A dozen or more head of cattle are brought in and driven about the field by the young men to trample the mud. This operation may resemble a kind of impromptu bullfight and is often regarded as a test of valor. The older men in the meantime repair the small dikes between the terraces as they are trampled down. Sometimes preliminary plowing is dispensed with altogether, and trampling has to suffice.

If the rice is to be sown broadcast, it may be done the same day by a senior man followed by relays of women with baskets of seed. This method of sowing is used primarily in the less advanced areas or where land is relatively plentiful. Elsewhere in the highlands the seedlings are usually grown in protected seedbeds and transplanted to the paddy field on the day after the trampling. This is the task of the women.

Trampling and sowing or transplanting are the operations requiring the largest number of people. The minimal work force during the crop cycle usually consists of about five people—two adult men, a responsible boy to look after the cattle, one adult woman, and a girl for the household tasks and kitchen garden and to help on certain cultivation tasks. A larger family may result in land being subdivided; a smaller unit usually means that kin must be attracted to the household. Plowing and digging may be performed by two adult men, and weeding, by one or two adults. After the transplanting, little is done until the harvest, which requires ten or fifteen men using straight sickles or serrated knives. Threshing is done against a stone or with a flail, often by a group of six or ten men and women. Elsewhere the cattle of the household may be driven around the threshing floor to separate the rice from the straw.

Rice cultivating techniques among the Merina of the Central Highlands closely resemble those of the Betsileo but are usually somewhat less advanced and intensive, since the population pressure on available land is more consistent in the Betsileo region. The Imerina includes a few areas where land is relatively plentiful and there are more broad valleys permitting less laborious means of irrigation or terracing. About 50,000 ox plows were in use in the mid-1960s. Although rice is still the most important crop, more dryland crops are grown in the Imerina than in the Betsileo country, and greater use is made of the dry hillsides and the adjoining grasslands.

In the forest region of the eastern coast, the Betsimisaraka and Tanala peoples also practice irrigated rice culture wherever possible, as do the groups of Betsileo settlers who have emigrated from the highlands (see ch. 4). The dominant form of land use here, however, is shifting cultivation by the slash-and-burn method, known on the island as *tavy*. The smaller trees and brush are cut down and left to dry, then fired just before the rainy season. The clearning thus created is sown, usually to mountain rice and maize. After two or three years of cultivation the field is left fallow and is gradually covered by a secondary vegetation known as *savoka* (see ch. 3). After an interval of between ten and twenty years, it may be planted again.

Because the slash-and-burn method produces low yields, devastates the forests, destroys other vegetation cover, and promotes erosion, it has been made illegal on the island, and those who practice it are subject to fine or imprisonment. Government assistance is given to those east-coast cultivators who undertake to prepare irrigated rice paddies instead. Ricefields in the valley bottoms of the eastern coast are subject to periodic destruction by flash floods, and terracing on the Betsileo model could raise them above flood level. The experts have concluded that terracing could also permit more effective utilization of the slops of the foothills.

Despite the penalties, *tavy* continues to be widely practiced, and even those who have constructed irrigated rice paddies will often practice *tavy* on the side. Those who do not may be regarded as deficient in their lineage responsibilities, for the crop cycle for *tavy* rice is shorter than for irrigated rice; generations of experience have taught that it may therefore be the only insurance against famine in the droughts that occur in the eastern region every third year. Moreover, the precipitous slopes and heavy, irregular rains make it difficult for the cultivators of the forest belt to maintain irrigated paddy fields except near the valley bottoms. The streams of the eastern region tend to be dry during the rice season, and during the rainy season they are often too swift to be safely regulated by the traditional hand-constructed irrigation channels and mud dikes. For all these reasons, irrigation often tends to be too costly for the east-coast cultivators to afford from their own very limited resources.

A similar system of shifting cultivation, known as *tetikala*, is practiced in the arid, sparsely populated regions of the extreme south and southwest by the Mahafaly and the Masikoro peoples. The dry bush or grassland is burned off, and drought-resistant sorghum or maize is sown in the ashes. In the Androy and Mahafaly districts, however, the main staples of subsistence—cassava, maize, beans, and sorghum—may be grown around the villages in permanent fields enclosed by hedges.

Dry-season cultivation in empty streambeds is practiced largely on the western coast and in the southwest and is known as *baiboho*, meaning cultivated plot. In these regions most of the streams are active only during the rainy season, and crops may be sown after the last rising of the waters and grown during the dry season. The fertility of the soil is renewed each year by fresh alluvial deposits. Lima, or butter, beans (known on the island as cape peas) are raised by this system in the delta of the Mangoky River on the western coast, and tobacco and a number of newer crops are also grown by the *baiboho* method.

AGRICULTURAL DEVELOPMENT PROGRAMS

The introduction of plans for agricultural improvement in Madagascar goes back some forty years, and efforts at rural development have been considerably intensified since 1950. As in many of the former French territories, a variety of technical

242

agencies, organizational structures, and programs of *encadrement* (framing) have succeeded one another over the years, giving rise to an endless list of acronyms representing the successive funds, societies, mixed companies, agencies, and projects involved (see table 14).

The French concept of *encadrement* is somewhat vague in its exact implications but involves primarily the ordering of agricultural production within the scope and overall supervision of the relevant authorities. This process usually begins with the demarcation of limited districts or crops for which minimal extension services and supervision are to be provided; at its most intensive it may take the form of resettlement on government-cleared land or of a government-managed development project or state farm. Thus *encadrement* represents the antithesis of the haphazard traditional subsistence production that often eludes supervision and statistical survey, taking place largely without the knowledge of the authorities.

An official French aid publication in 1971 differentiated between *encadrement souple* (flexible framework), as exemplified by the regional extension centers, and *encadrement lourd* (heavy framework), represented by the various companies of mixed economy for agricultural development. Some of these companies and their major land development projects have also been termed authoritarian because participation and compliance with the improved planting schedules and methods of cultivation involved are compulsory.

The diversity of climate, soils, and crop potential that preserves the island from excessive reliance on monoculture or on one or two export crops has in another sense been a partial handicap, in that it has given rise to dispersal of development efforts among a succession of crop experiments and extension programs over the years. In the preindependence period between 1950 and 1960, for example, efforts were focused first on one promising commercial or export crop, then on another: a rice campaign was succeeded in turn by equally enthusiastic hopes for coffee, sugarcane, and cotton. All these commercial crops have been successful in the long run, but each suffered serious setbacks as limited funds and personnel were transferred from one crop to another, and the participating peasants were abandoned for a time to their own inadequate devices. Several of these crop improvement programs had subsequently to be resumed virtually from nothing (see Crop Production, this ch.).

The 1950s also provided much experience of trial and error in the creation of peasant cooperatives and other organizations for the use of equipment credits and marketing and agricultural improvements. The various attempts to create development structures at the local level, which bore three or four successive titles between 1951 and

Programs	Organizations
1. *Travaux au ras du sol* (small public works projects at village level—literally "at ground level"). Always involve unpaid village labor. May involve clearing new land for crops or digging irrigation channels. Other simple investments to facilitate mass operations. Initiated by *e.* with support of *d.*	*a.* Ministry of Agriculture; Ministry of Interior; president's office; relevant secretariats and commissariats. *b.* Prefecture. *c. Unité régionale d'expansion rurale* (regional extension center).
2. *Actions de masse* (mass operations) to introduce methods and boost yields. Carried out by extension agents of *a.* and by foreign technical assistants assigned to *c. Examples:* Rice Productivity Campaign; coffee-pepper productivity campaign on east coast.	*d. Syndicats de communes préfectoraux à vocation économique* (organization of communes of a prefecture with economic competence). Responsible to *b*; groups delegates from *e.* *e.* Commune Conseil de Commune (Communal Council) Conseil Rurale de Développement (Rural Development Council).
3. *Aménagement de grandes périmètres* (major large-scale land development projects). Operated by *h.* In some cases, preliminary land clearance or early operation may be undertaken by *g.*	*f.* Rural cooperatives at village level. *g.* Caisse d'Equipement Agricole et de Modernisation de Paysannat— CEAMP (Fund for Agricultural Equipment and Modernization).
4. *Aménagement de moyens ou petits périmètres* (medium- or small-scale land development projects). Generally managed by *g.*	*h. Sociétés d'aménagement à économie mixte* (companies of mixed economy for agricultural development). SOMALAC, for Lake Alaotra; SAMANGOKY, for lower Mangoky; SOMASAK, for Sakay; SEDEFITA, for Fiherenana and
5. *Animation rurale* (diffuse information campaign designed to engage initiative and support of rural population for development). May involve literacy, education in agricultural techniques, and participation in rural public works. Operated by *a.*	Teheza; MOYEN OUEST, for the Middle West; BAIBOHO, for the western river basins; COMEMA, for Marovoay; and SODEMO, for Morondava.
6. *State farms* Capital furnished by state. Operate as experimental stations or pilot farms. Some managed by *g.*	*i.* Producers' groups Association of Rural Interests to improve production, marketing, and credit; mutual credit societies; producers' cooperatives (for groundnuts, coffee, bananas, vanilla, and others nationwide).

Programs	Organizations
	j. Applied research institutes For tropical agronomy; for citrus and tropical fruits; for cotton and textiles; for coffee and cocoa; and for oilseeds and oils.

Source: Adapted from France, Secrétariat d'Etat aux Affaires Etrangères, *Economie et Plan de Développement République Malgache*, Paris, 1969, pp. 114-120, 231.

1962, were criticized for not being sufficiently representative of the interests and wishes of the local population and for failing effectively to enlist the support and participation of the villagers.

After independence, the government of President Philibert Tsiranana stressed a socialist ideal of development through peasant participation in the rural commune and the agricultural cooperatives at village level. After 1962 the rural commune was rapidly developed as an instrument of economic development. Besides its Communal Council, each commune was to create a Rural Development Council designed to associate the peasants with the discussions of the Communal Council whenever development measures were being discussed. The rural communes in turn were represented at prefectoral level in associations of communes having economic competence (*syndicats de communes préfectoraux à vocation économique*). These are authorized to function as industrial and commercial enterprises, whose management was to be independent of administrative control, to create or encourage projects of production, marketing, or small-scale industry. They may intervene at various stages in the collection, marketing, or processing of a range of products, including groundnuts, cape peas, maize, and potatoes.

The local formula particularly favored by the government after 1962 was the encouragement of agricultural cooperatives for production, marketing, and consumption. Lack of funds and, more particularly, lack of qualified management personnel retarded the formation of viable cooperatives and led to a number of failures and disappointments. There has been considerable debate and a prolific periodical literature on the best means of promoting cooperatives as a spontaneous outgrowth of the national tradition of peasant self-help or mutual aid, rather than as an arbitrary administrative formula based on a European model and imposed from above.

When the cooperative ideal was revived as a Malagasy concept, some felt that the earlier French-sponsored associations had failed in part because they tried to replace the traditional socially oriented links of mutual aid based upon kinship and common ancestry by new, economically oriented groupings based upon market relationships foreign to village concepts (see ch. 5). Instead of imposing a readymade European-style cooperative framework, the new school of thought advocated forming precooperative groups on the basis of traditional village associative structure.

An important feature of traditional associative groupings was the absence of hierarchy and of delegated authority. The necessity of having decisionmaking management personnel in the European-style cooperative organizations and other new rural structures led the peasants to reject them all as authoritarian. Another major obstacle to participation was the need to levy dues of membership and to meet costs and investment needs from a portion of the sum realized on sale of the harvest. The peasants often preferred to deal with private usurers who could meet their immediate needs even at a far higher ultimate cost. At the time of the revolt in the south in April 1971, one of the major grievances cited was that the peasants had been obliged to sell their groundnuts to the cooperative—an organization that they did not understand—and received in return only a paper, having to wait six months for payment. They then received only FMG15 per kilogram (1 kilogram equals 2.2 pounds) instead of FMG25, the difference being used for expenses.

After a long period of experiment, trial and error, and resistance from villagers, the system of rural and consumer cooperatives was reported in 1970 to be more solidly organized and ready to get off the ground. The system had been entirely reorganized in 1967 under the Commissariat of Cooperation. Altogether there were about 510 cooperatives of various types on the island, of which 242 were agricultural, two were for cattle raising, and twenty were consumers' cooperatives.

Since the mid-1960s there has been increasing emphasis in the government's agricultural development programs upon direct state intervention in the production and marketing processes and also upon large-scale units of public or semipublic ownership that rely more heavily upon wage- and salary-earning employees than upon independent producers. This emphasis has been intended primarily to increase cash production, marketing, and export of farm commodities more rapidly than can be effected by the village-level programs involving independent traditional producers.

Nevertheless, the ultimate goal of such programs is independent rather than collective farming. Both on some of the state farms and on the regional development programs managed by companies of mixed economy, there are arrangements for eventually transferring some of the newly improved land to those at present working as tenant farmers or wage earners on the projects, once they have

246

acquired improved cultivation techniques. The interim concentration on large-scale sectoral programs designed to boost production more rapidly in the near term was inspired by the setbacks in food supply encountered in the mid-1960s.

Rice Productivity Campaign

Conducted by various agencies, the Rice Productivity Campaign initiated in 1962 is the foremost example of a mass development operation. In principle it has been under the aegis of the Ministry of Agriculture, Rural Expansion and Food Supply, and numerous Malagasy extension agents from this and other ministries were assigned to the program. Regional extension centers were established in each project region. The French technical assistance agency, however, has provided technical supervision and a large number of foreign technical assistants. Of the FMG3.9 billion spent on the program by 1968, FMG2.6 billion came from France and the European Economic Community (EEC, known as the Common Market). Some 110,000 Malagasy farmers had been involved, and production had increased by an estimated 85,000 metric tons. Fertilizer use had expanded from nothing in 1956 to around 8,000 metric tons in crop year 1968 / 69. Satisfactory as these tentative results might appear, however, by 1971 the authorities were still expressing disappointment with the progress of productivity efforts in the context of rising demand, and the campaign was scheduled to continue beyond 1974.

Conditions in the Central Highlands are such that rice cultivation might be able to approximate the Japanese model of development. The Japanese obtain yields of twenty to twenty-five metric tons an acre on fields of three to five acres. Cultivators on the same scale in the Tananarive plain had improved their yields by 1970 to as much as two or three metric tons per acre, but the average for the district was only 1.7 metric tons per acre. In the large-scale mechanized Alaotra project, yields up to 3.6 metric tons an acre had been attained by the mid-1960s. For the country as a whole the average of about 0.7 metric tons an acre had not measurably improved by 1970. Rain-fed rice production was yielding only 0.5 metric tons an acre, and the *tavy* method, about 0.6 metric tons.

The techniques advocated by the productivity campaign included some that had long been practiced by the more advanced or more prosperous farmers of parts of the Central Highlands, such as transplanting the rice seedlings from nursery beds that have been manured or trampling the fields before planting (see Traditional Cultivation Practices, this ch.). The innovation that aroused the most resistance was the requirement for transplanting in straight rows. Transplanting is customarily performed by the women, and there is a traditional rivalry as to who can plant most rapidly. Planting in rows slows the rhythm of the entire line of workers to the pace of the slowest one, although it subsequently facilitates weeding and harvesting and permits a higher yield. In many villages transplanting had to be taken over by the men because of the refusal of the women to plant in rows; there have even been a few instances of divorce over the issue. Other requirements are wider spacing of plants and the planting of only one or two shoots at a time, instead of a whole tuft, so that the plants need not compete for nourishment. This is the most discouraging stage of the innovation for the cultivator: during the first few weeks the field looks pitifully sparse and unhealthy in contrast to the thickly planted paddy of nonparticipating neighbors.

The requirement for sparser sowing of seed in the nursery seedbed also puzzles the unaccustomed peasant: how to obtain more rice from less seed? The improved seed varieties introduced from the experimental stations of Marovoay or Alaotra also bring new problems. They are more fragile and vulnerable to sun and wind and tolerate less margin of error in meeting the fertilizer needs of the soil; without enough manure, their yield may actually be lower than the old varieties. Worst of all, the recommended Ali Kombo variety requires a mechanical thresher, which may be rented in some localities but is not always easy to afford.

At least one peasant in three in the Central Highlands has no cattle. Trampling of the paddy field requires numerous cattle, either owned or borrowed from kin or neighbors. The trampling exhausts the animals, whose mortality rate always climbs during the trampling season. To obtain enough natural or artificial manure for 2.5 acres of paddy, the cultivator requires 3.6 acres of rice straw or twelve acres of grass, which is more commonly used than straw. The shortage of grassland in the Central Highlands is the factor limiting the number of oxen that can be kept there. The shortage of manure and the high cost of fertilizer mean that not all cultivators can afford to manure the nursery seedbeds and that even fewer can hope to supply the recommended amount of nutrients for the ricefields. If the improvement effort is confined to the seedbeds rather than extended to the fields, the best that can be hoped for is an increase in yield of about 0.75 metric tons per acre.

Similarly, not all peasants can afford the cash to acquire the improved small-scale equipment recommended by the program. The average monetary income of a peasant in the Central Highlands in late 1968 was about FMG25,000 to FMG30,000. A harrow, for example, cost FMG6,000. A bullock-drawn plow sold for FMG8,000 to FMG10,000, and a pair of oxen to pull it cost from FMG12,000 to more than FMG15,000. Planting in rows permits the use of a mechanical weeder, which cost FMG2,000 to FMG3,500 and was operated by men, whereas weeding had traditionally been the task of women.

In order to attain the target increase in rice yields on the small irrigated rice fields of the Central Highlands, the entire improvement program in each of its recommended aspects from seedbed to harvest would have to be introduced. The authorities have recognized in some instances, however, that this ambition is unrealistic for the immediate term and since 1964 have compromised by applying the improved methods to the traditional seed varieties or by confining the immediate effort to the seedbeds and leaving the fields for a later stage.

Major Land Development Projects

With two important exceptions, the principal large-scale agricultural projects of the 1960s were located in the sedimentary river basins of the west coast (see table 14 and fig. 10). Traditional cultivation is difficult in the west because most of the streams disappear in the dry season, when crops can be grown only by means of irrigation. Because of their alluvial soils and low density of population, however, the river basins of the west are considered the most promising areas for migration, resettlement, and the rapid increase of production with improved agricultural methods.

There were originally twelve special rural development areas—immense areas coinciding in part with former or existing areas of French settlement and subject to special legislation under which access to land, either private or collective, is made conditional upon its improvement and utilization in conformity with development planning objectives. A number of these regional projects were initially private French agricultural ventures or official French projects for the settlement of French farmers. As independence approached, there was some pressure from the government's opposition for outright expropriation of all French-owned concession lands. The government, however, consistently maintained that drastic measures to confiscate land and to eliminate usury and sharecropping—two other measures demanded by the opposition—were not required, since ample reserves of arable land were available to permit settlement of Malagasy migrants and gradual reform of the land tenure system. In August 1972 the new Ramanantsoa government adopted decrees to return to the state those portions of land formerly distributed to private firms and individuals that had been left undeveloped.

The Companies of Mixed Economy

Most of the major land development projects were being operated by companies of mixed economy, a formula first devised in 1960 to improve and distribute some of the unoccupied public lands that the Malagasy government had inherited from the French ad-

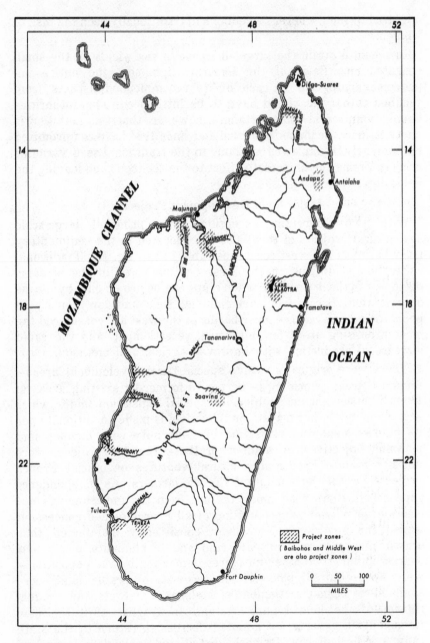

Source: Adapted from Andre Guilcher and Rene Battistini, *Madagascar: Geographie Regionale*, Paris, 1967.

Figure 10. Major Agricultural Development Projects, Malagasy Republic, 1970

ministration. The government has majority ownership of the companies, but critics and opponents of the government in the late 1960s and early 1970s averred that real control and management remained in the hands of the French technical assistance agencies or, in a few cases, of the participating French private firms. One European observer commented that the creation of companies of mixed economy appeared to be a clever move by the private firms to attract capital from the French aid funds and the Malagasy government and to avoid the confiscation of unutilized land. There were also some complaints that by independence the French companies or settlers had already monopolized the best lands and those having the most costly improvements, notably in the Aloatra basin and in the Sakay area (see fig. 10).

By mid-1972 there were as yet no aggregate data on how much new land had been brought into production by means of these large-scale development projects. Ambitious goals for six of the companies of mixed economy had been outlined by the planning authorities in terms of projected investment levels, acreage to be improved, and number of peasant families to be settled by 1968 in the first phase and by 1973 in the second. There was no indication of whether the 1968 target of 104,000 acres for the first five projects had actually been met.

The largest share of investment under the first plan was allocated to SAMANGOKY, the name of a company of mixed economy for development of the lower Mangoky delta cotton-growing project (see table 14). By 1973, however, the most massive investment was expected to have taken place in the Lake Alaotra rice project and in the Middle West program for mixed farming and forestry. By 1973 the Lake Alaotra project was expected to involve some 5,600 Malagasy families and to cover some 75,000 acres; the Middle West program, 4,000 families and 1.08 million acres. The 1973 targets for the five other major projects were: Mangoky (cotton), 5,000 families and 23,500 acres; Sakay (mixed farming), 2,570 families and 47,700 acres; Fiherenana (rice, cotton, and vegetables), 2,500 families and 10,870 acres; Teheza (rice, cotton, and vegetables), 1,800 families and 10,730 acres; and the Baibohos of the west coast (cotton and groundnuts), 2,300 families and 11,120 acres.

In most instances the eventual goal of the projects is to set up the participating Malagasy as independent farmers trained through work on the project to employ modern methods of cultivation and soil conservation. In the short term, however, the profit motive or the government's concern for boosting production as rapidly as possible has dictated, on certain of the projects, the use of mechanization and other devices beyond the reach of the independent peasant. Some critics of the projects therefore fear that Malagasy trained as wage earners on the large-scale projects will tend to seek salaried government employment or will lapse into traditional habits of cultivation and economic activity.

In mid-1971 the Lake Alaotra ricegrowing project, after ten years under Malagasy auspices, appeared to be proceeding on schedule and afforded an example of a large-scale project that had had considerable success in distributing improved lands among independent cultivators and increasing rice yields. The best drained soils of the basin and surrounding terraces had first been developed by French colonists under government sponsorship after 1950. Subsequently dams have been constructed, and costly improvement operations have been undertaken to harness the Maningory River for irrigation and to utilize the vast swampy areas to the west of the present lake. Since 1960 massive French aid and contributions from the European Economic Community development fund, the International Bank for Reconstruction and Development (IBRD, commonly called the World Bank) and the United Nations have financed the irrigation infrastructure and other improvements required for the newer lands of the basin involved in the SOMALAC project. The Malagasy government owns FMG171 million of SOMALAC's capital of FMG200 million. Other participants are the French government's Central Economic Cooperation Fund, the Malagasy National Development Bank, and SCET International, a Paris-based engineering and development consultant firm.

By mid-1971 the company had reclaimed 42,980 acres of ricefields distributed among 3,889 families of Malagasy cultivators. The extension of the ricefields was proceeding at the rate of about 7,400 acres a year; average yields on the Malagasy holdings had been raised to about 1.2 metric tons per acre. The average annual income of participating families had been increased from about FMG35,000 to FMG207,000. In addition to the ricegrowing operation, a diversification program had encouraged the raising of dryland crops, cattle, pigs, and poultry. The Lake Alaotra region also grows large quantities of groundnuts and cassava for industrial processing.

Another company of mixed economy, the Committee for the Economic Expansion of Marovoay (Comité d'Expansion Economique de Marovoay—COMEMA), was created with majority government ownership in 1964 to continue the development of rice production initiated by French firms in the Marovoay Basin on the western coast. The ricegrowing area extends over 58,800 acres of the basin; of this area, 15,550 acres are the property of COMEMA, and 43,250 acres belong to the government. The Malagasy sharecroppers working for COMEMA must give one-fourth of their crop to the company: after deduction of the costs of operation, the sale price of this portion is credited to the account of the sharecropper against the eventual purchase of a parcel of the riceland on the left bank of the river. This system should permit most of the sharecroppers to take over their own land by 1974 or 1975, when the land on the left bank will have been made ready for cultivation.

In July 1972 the republic received a sizable credit from the International Development Association to finance another large-scale irrigation and rural development project on 23,000 acres in the Morondava River basin on the western coast. The credit was to provide 57 percent of the financing for the project, which was to be carried out by the Company for Economic Development of the Morondava Region (SODEMO). It was to include the construction of dams and canals, the building of roads and villages, the irrigation and drainage of 16,000 acres, and the resettlement of 2,100 cultivating families in addition to the 1,200 families already living there. A health project was to establish dispensaries and provide means to combat schistosomiasis (snail fever), which is endemic in the region (see ch. 6).

CROP PRODUCTION

In the early 1970s the level of national output of both food and export crops remained highly vulnerable to year-to-year fluctuations resulting from external influences, such as weather conditions and cyclical variations in overseas demand. The overwhelming majority of Malagasy cultivators were still operating at subsistence level and employing traditional techniques that did not permit the cultivation of an adequate land area or the production of an adequate surplus. Storage and transport facilities had not yet reached a level that would facilitate stockpiling and internal exchange. Both as producers and consumers, most rural villagers remained too much at the mercy of shopkeepers and other middlemen; they were not sufficiently organized to protect their interests, to accumulate a surplus for investment, or to stabilize the impact of seasonal variations in supply and demand on prices.

Data on crop production levels were somewhat uncertain because of the difficulty involved in measuring subsistence production. Consequently conflicting data were found in different sources, as well as conflicting assessments of the progress of government efforts to boost crucial production of staple food crops, particularly rice. Official crop production statistics going back to 1964 were published for the first time in February 1971.

Food Supply

Rice is the primary food in most of the country and the mainstay of the subsistence economy (see table 15). Even in those parts of the island best known for their tree crops or plantation crops, paddy fields or mountain rice will appear wherever conditions permit any hope of a harvest. Only where conditions are too arid, as in most of the south and southwest, will rice be replaced as a staple by sorghum, maize, or tubers. Cassava is frequently grown as a dietary supplement in rice-producing regions; it also serves as a substitute where rice cannot be grown and as a last resort in periods of food shortage or famine. Government efforts to achieve a rapid increase in food production have included the planting of dryland cassava, maize, and sorghum on the marginal slopes of the *tanety* or hillsides.

Of the island's ninety-six subprefectures in 1962, only four were producing a substantial quantity of rice surplus to their own consumption needs (see fig. 11). In 1971 a parallel situation existed despite the overall rise in rice production: a number of the more populated areas of the island still had a chronic deficit in food supply. World tables published by the World Bank showed the island's food production increasing by an annual average growth rate of 3.5 percent in the 1951-60 period, 2.6 percent from 1961 to 1967, and 1.6 percent in 1968, but decreasing by 2.4 percent in 1968 and by 8.9 percent in 1969. Because population grew at an average rate of 2.4 percent during these years, the increase in per capita food was only 1.1 percent in the 1951-60 period and was static or declining after 1961.

Early official estimates indicated that, from about 750,000 metric tons in 1949, rice production had increased steadily to the vicinity of 1,320,000 metric tons in 1964. Because of the rapid growth of population in the same period, however, it had become apparent that the growth of rice output did not afford a sufficient margin of safety to allow for climatic or other reverses in poor crop years. When weather conditions caused production to drop off in 1965, some 78,000 metric tons of rice had to be imported.

Accordingly, the First Five-Year Plan (1964-68) placed considerable emphasis on increasing rice production, and the effort was further intensified under the Program of Major Operations (1968-69), which allocated much of its resources to efforts to improve the conditions of subsistence production and to guarantee food supplies to local and urban markets. By 1970 there had been some increase in area planted to food crops, and rice production in the island as a whole had shown a measurable increase. Government spokesmen warned, however, that the good crops of 1970 were attributable in large part to favorable external and weather conditions and that food production must therefore once again receive highest priority under the Second Three-Year Plan (1972-74).

Preliminary crop forecasts in July 1971 were generally favorable (see table 15). Revised assessments published in June 1972, however, indicated that 1971 crop results had been generally more disappointing than the preliminary forecasts had predicted.

During the annual period of shortest supply in September and October 1971, the Consultative Committee on Food Supply (Comité Consultatif du Ravitaillement) noted that the rice shortage had been caused in part by an improvement in purchasing power among east-coast peasants as a result of favorable harvests and favorable prices for export products—notably coffee, which had benefited in price

Table 15. *Area and Production of Principal Crops, Malagasy Republic, 1964-71*

	Area (in thousand acres)				Production (in thousand metric tons)			
	Average for 1964-68	1969	1970	1971*	Average for 1964-68	1969	1970	1971*
Food Crops:								
Rice (paddy)	880	913	930	951	1,739	1,858	1,869	n.a.
Maize (corn)	133	138	105	109	137	143	108	115
Beans	43	45	43	44	32	35	35	35
Cape peas (lima beans)	19	18	21	22	17	21	21	17
Cassava	171	184	185	192	1,072	1,253	1,218	1,291
Potatoes and sweet potatoes	69	72	72	75	455	464	427	448
Export and Industrial Crops:								
Coffee	198	202	205	206	70	64	69	44
Cloves	29	n.a.	n.a.	n.a.	5	5	14	4
Vanilla	6	n.a.	n.a.	n.a.	1	1	2	2
Sisal	24	24	23	n.a.	28	30	26	n.a.
Raffia	10	10	n.a.	n.a.	12	14	n.a.	n.a.
Pepper	11	n.a.	n.a.	n.a.	2	3	2	2
Tung	4	5	4	4	8	5	5	4
Cocoa	2	2	3	3	1	1	1	1
Sugarcane	19	20	n.a.	n.a.	998	1,113	n.a.	n.a.
Groundnuts (peanuts)	41	42	37	37	40	44	37	33
Castor beans	6	6	6	6	1	1	1	1
Tobacco	6	6	5	6	5	6	5	5
Cotton	5	10	10	12	8	17	19	24

n.a.—not available.

*Forecasts as of July 1971. Revised assessment of June 1972 stated several crops below forecast.

255

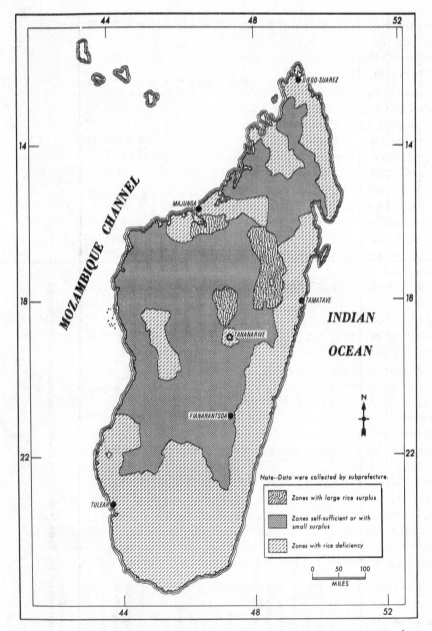

Source: Adapted from Patrick Francois, *Budgets et Alimentation des Ménages Ruraux en 1962*, Vol. 3, Paris, 1958.

Figure 11. Rice Production Balance, Malagasy Republic, 1962

from the blight in Brazil. This turn of events had upset all prior predictions concerning food supply for the island as a whole, and some 60,000 metric tons of paddy had to be imported in 1971. The steep increase in consumer demand for rice was expected to continue during the 1972 / 73 season, while the harvest was expected to decline in the same period because of unfavorable weather in certain production zones.

Rapid population growth since World War II has worked in three principal ways to affect food supply: first, by increasing the number of mouths to feed; second, by increasing the pressure on available riceland and, in some localities, producing land fragmentation and the pauperization of cultivators; third, by disrupting the traditional equilibrium by which cultivation techniques were carefully adapted to local conditions.

The effort to diffuse improved agricultural methods is rendered more difficult by the impact of population growth on the size of exploitations, the length of fallow periods, the disappearance of grazing and other vegetation cover, the consequent erosion of marginal farmland, the deterioration of livestock productivity, and the reduction of crop yields. The progressive pauperization of marginal cultivators in overpopulated districts results in the spread of indebtedness and usury and makes it more difficult for the peasant to afford improved tools or improved inputs of seed or manure, much less fertilizer or pesticides.

Moreover, traditional methods have been minutely calculated over the years to make the most of the alternation of good and poor crop years to achieve a tolerable mean of subsistence. The population increase had disrupted this process and made traditional methods obsolete. The resulting problems in many instances may be compounded by attempts to introduce innovative techniques without sufficient preliminary preparation. These techniques usually take hold effectively only where a new situation radically different from that of tradition exists. Numerous exceptions to this rule, however, have been noted in the existing development literature of the country, particularly, where emigration from the overpopulated districts to areas of greater potential has resulted in the transplanting of more advanced techniques (see ch. 4).

The consensus of modern nutritionists is that rice plays too great a part in the average Malagasy diet (see ch. 6). Per capita rice consumption on the island was thought to be the highest in the world in the mid-1960s and has been increasing steadily since that time. Although higher average consumption of vegetables, fruits, and animal proteins would undoubtedly represent an improvement, the Malagasy are doubtless more fortunate than many of the world's peoples in the total caloric value of their daily diet. Moreover, in seeking higher rice production, the authorities are proceeding on the assumption that it should prove far easier to attain than would increased production of nutritionally superior fruits, vegetables, and animal products because of entrenched habits both of consumption and of cultivation. In existing circumstances, the probable alternative to rice in periods of shortage is greater reliance on nutritionally inferior cassava. Maize, sorghum, and millet grown in the south and west, however, are nutritionally somewhat preferable to rice.

Rice Cultivation

Rice is grown by about 80 percent of the country's cultivators on an estimated one-fourth to one-third of the total cultivated land area, perhaps more than one-half of total land actually under field crops. It accounts for 40 to 50 percent of the annual value of agricultural production. In 1965 about 85 percent of riceland was thought to be in irrigated paddies, and 15 percent was rain fed or cultivated by the *tavy* method of slash-and-burn. About half of the country's irrigated rice production is grown in the Central Highlands, including the Alaotra basin. Because rice is grown on most of the island under varying climatic conditions and because the varieties of seed used mature at different rates, both the planting and harvest are spread throughout the calendar year. The peak harvest for the island as a whole occurs from April through June, and the period of shortest supply comes in September and October.

Four subprefectures produced a substantial quantity of rice surplus to their own needs in 1962. Three were in the Central Highlands; of these, two were in the Alaotra basin, and one, on the Tananarive plain. The fourth was on the swampy Marovoay plain along the Betsiboka River on the western coast, a traditional granary area where a modern agricultural station and a large-scale French private firm had been promoting the cultivation of high-quality rice varieties for export to France and Réunion. Of the densely populated areas, the Imerina and Betsileo portions of the highlands were among the areas where rice production and consumption were roughly in balance in 1962. Consumption, however, has since been increasing at such a rate that there is a deficit in some years, and the Betsileo can no longer be relied upon to supply the central and southern east coast.

Other subprefectures having an approximate balance between rice production and consumption were largely in areas that had a relatively low population density or a strong production of export crops, such as the north-central region and the sedimentary riverain areas of the western coast. Some forty of the ninety-six subprefectures in 1962 were unable to produce enough rice for their own needs; but nine or ten of these were in the south and extreme southwest, where rice is not the staple of diet. The north has the potential to grow its own rice supply, if transport links and storage can be improved. The remaining food-deficit districts are predominantly on the east coast, where population density, cultivation habits, floods, and rainstorms make it probable that, despite official rice improvement programs, a continuing chronic food deficit will have to be met by imports from other parts of the island and by the migration of surplus population to the west.

Other Food Crops

Cassava (manioc) is the second food crop in terms of area planted and probably in quantity consumed, although it rates low in consumer preference. In the 1960s it was grown in every part of the island except the interior grazing lands of the west and the uncultivable mountain ranges of the east. Production was greatest in the far south, where it is the staple of subsistence consumption, and around Lake Alaotra and the Sambirano River, where it is grown for industrial processing into tapioca, starch, and flour at the chief processing centers in the provinces of Tananarive, Majunga, and Tamatave. Exports were on the decline in the late 1960s and were not thought to have much potential. The flour is used locally in bread in the proportion of about 10 percent, and the other processed products are also consumed domestically.

According to the 1962 consumption survey, about 100,000 metric tons of cassava, out of total production of about 327,000 metric tons, were fed to livestock—particularly in the Central Highlands, where it is often used as fodder for penned cattle. Elsewhere it may be used primarily as a reserve against famine, so that potential resources in cassava in an average year are thought to be about double the amount actually consumed for subsistence or marketed. A plot of cassava may be left unharvested as a sort of domestic larder, either because commercial demand and prices are too low in the locality or because subsistence consumption is directed by preference to rice and vegetables—often for both reasons. The sweet varieties are most often cultivated for the roots, especially in the south; but the bitter varieties are sometimes grown, and the leaves are cooked as greens, particularly in the Central Highlands.

The planners do not favor any increase in the acreage under cassava. Most villagers do not need encouragement to plant cassava as a famine reserve. Instead, better utilization of some of the acreage under cassava may be sought in connection with the programs for other crops.

A variety of other roots and tubers enter into the Malagasy diet; sweet potatoes and potatoes rank second and third in importance to cassava. Wild roots and tubers are also gathered to supplement the cultivated varieties; consumption of these was thought to amount to about 20,000 metric tons in 1962, compared to 137,000 metric tons of sweet potatoes, 62,000 metric tons of potatoes, 300,000 metric tons of cassava, and 26,000 metric tons of taro.

Estimated consumption of maize in 1962 was only about 21,000 tons; and sorghum, 2,500 tons. Sorghum was grown only in the coastal region of Androy, and maize was the staple of diet only in a few subprefectures of the southern region. Maize is also grown, however, in the Central Highlands and from Tulear up the western coast to Diégo-Suarez in the north. It is used both as a vegetable for human consumption and sometimes as an animal feed, although its use in mixed farming has not yet been highly developed.

A variety of other food crops is grown as a supplement to the main staples of diet. These include groundnuts (peanuts), peas, beans, bananas, and other fruits and vegetables. Except for cape peas, production is largely for domestic consumption. Price stabilization agencies exist for the marketing of some of these crops, including groundnuts, but they were not yet very active in the late 1960s.

Export and Industrial Crops

The list of the island's export crops in the 1960s was long and diversified, but the value of many of them was rather small. In the mid-1960s rice, including domestic consumption, accounted for about 40 percent of the value of agricultural production. The seven leading export products—other than export rice—amounted to another 40 percent by value, and the remaining agricultural products amounted to only 20 percent. The principal agricultural exports in the late 1960s were coffee, sugarcane, vanilla, cloves, export rice, live cattle, beef, sugar, sisal, cape peas, and tobacco. Other export crops included essential oils for perfumery, pepper, raffia, tung oil, groundnuts, and cassava products. There were plans to develop exports of cocoa, palm oil, bananas, cashew nuts, paka, and pyrethrum.

Among the major exports a number were facing shrinking world markets or falling price trends. Coffee and sugar, two of the leading export crops, had lost their protection and price supports in France after the introduction of the common external tariff for the European Economic Community countries. Cloves, vanilla, cape peas, and essential oils all had too narrow an overseas market to permit any significant future expansion of exports. Cloves and vanilla faced severe competition from synthetic coal-tar derivatives.

Although many Malagasy peasants grow sugarcane on a subsistence basis, export production comes largely from the northern and west-coast plantations of subsidiary firms of the French Compagnie Marseillaise de Madagascar and of French banks. Sisal production is entirely in the hands of French companies, and production of Macassar oil for perfumery from ylang-ylang on the island of Nosy Be is also a French enterprise.

Tobacco plantations in the river basins of the western coast were run by French settlers, formerly under the French but now under the Malagasy government tobacco monopoly. They have long employed Malagasy sharecroppers, and some Malagasy family

260

cultivators also grow tobacco. Tobacco has lost its protection on the French market, and future exports will depend on thorough reconversion to higher quality, more carefully handled leaf to meet quality standards of the European Economic Community. Some of the settlers have switched to cotton. The government program is supervised by the institutes of research and by extension agents.

Cotton is grown on the alluvial flood plains of the west-coast river basins, by large-scale state farms and French estates under the Compagnie Française du Textile, and on the lower Mangoky land development project. By 1969 production of seed cotton had reached 16,300 metric tons and was one of the successes of the First Five-Year Plan. Exports of cotton had ceased, and the domestic market was beginning to absorb the production for industrial processing, according to plan. Imports of cotton yarn had been virtually eliminated, and it was hoped that the country might soon become self-sufficient in cotton fabrics and clothing.

Two kinds of coffee are grown—Robusta, the hardy variety more usually grown in Africa, and Arabica, otherwise grown chiefly in Latin America and Ethiopia. Arabica is produced in the highlands in very limited quantity and is mostly consumed domestically, but the Robusta variety is exported. Robusta coffee has long been the leading export, averaging about 28 percent of export value, 10 percent of agricultural income, and 50 percent of government export revenue. French firms and settlers from Réunion own the best coffee land and export the highest quality product, but 85 percent of production comes from very small scale Malagasy stands. Coffee is the chief economic resource of the peoples of the east-coast region.

In the late 1960s coffee exports were still being handled by the large French trading concessions. A barrier to progress was the system of collection and marketing through local Chinese storekeepers on the eastern coast. The small-scale grower had little or no bargaining power and was confused by the drastic year-to-year fluctuations characteristic of coffee prices. The merchants did not scale their prices to the grower according to quality or grade, so that there was little incentive to improve the care of trees or handling of the crop.

Because of world oversupply, the island's export quota in the 1960s was only 50,000 metric tons, but some 10,000 additional metric tons could be exported to nonquota destinations. In the mid-1960s the quota had not been filled for some years because of low average yields resulting from the age and neglected condition of many of the small-scale stands. The authorities therefore launched a coffee improvement and diversification program to improve yields, processing, and distribution of the product of small-scale Malagasy growers. It received assistance from the European Economic Community aid fund, the diversification fund of the International

Coffee Organization, and the government of the Federal Republic of Germany (West Germany). It sought to replace older trees with select young stock of high yield and to teach better care of coffee planting.

In 1971 the program was still in its preliminary phase, and the young trees had not yet reached bearing age, but harvesting and sale of coffee had greatly increased in response to rising export prices. Because long-range expansion of exports was blocked by the quota system, the program included diversification of coffee in the northern and northeastern regions, where most of the large estates were situated. They were to be converted to cocoa, vanilla, and oil-palm production, as were some of the small-scale east-coast growers. The area of maximum coffee production would thereafter be confined to seven subprefectures in the central portion of the eastern region, where Malagasy villagers had become strongly dependent on earnings from the coffee crop.

Although cocoa suffers on the world market from even greater swings in demand, price, and oversupply than does coffee, the Malagasy growers do not expect to be affected. Their *criollo* variety is considered superior to the *forastero* bean grown in most African countries and commands a ready market in Europe. Most of the cocoa has hitherto been grown by two foreign concession firms, but the authorities are encouraging its extension among small-scale Malagasy cultivators in Sambirano and in the northeast and are establishing pilot farms on the eastern coast to supply domestic demand and the chocolate factory at Tananarive.

By the mid-1960s 90 percent of the island's vanilla was being grown on a small scale by Malagasy, who constituted about 85 percent of the 3,000 growers. The painstaking task of preparing the vanilla for export, however, as well as the collection of the harvest were in the hands of Asians or Réunionnais Creoles. The small-scale grower was often in debt to one of the local Chinese storekeepers of the eastern region, who ended up owning an estimated 80 percent of the harvested crop. Antalaha, on the northeastern coast, is the center of the vanilla trade, and the surrounding province of Diégo-Suarez is the chief producing region.

Vanilla has traditionally been a highly speculative product; a few New York buyers have controlled the overseas market, and the sellers in Antalaha engage in annual operations to boost the price. The demand tends to be inelastic; and the supply, too elastic (responsive to price). The small grower will often grow too much and harvest it too carelessly in a season that follows a high price. The result is an oversupply of poor-quality vanilla and a drastic price drop.

The island produces more than two-thirds of the world's supply of Bourbon vanilla, as the natural product is called, but there has been

262

strong competition from artificial vanillin, distilled from clove extract. In recent years both these Malagasy exports have been rivaled by synthetic flavorings derived from coal tar.

Since the mid-1960s the government has enacted more strenuous measures to rationalize the marketing of vanilla and to combat speculation. Stockpiles equivalent to one year's exports are maintained, and excess stocks are destroyed when required to maintain prices. The price of both green and prepared vanilla is now fixed by government decree each year after consultation with the Professional Vanilla Association, formed of planters, preparers, and exporters on the island. Export quotas and prices are agreed upon annually with United States and European importers.

Spice plants grown on the island include nutmeg, saffron, and ginger, but cloves and pepper make the most significant contribution to export earnings. The country ranks as a major clove producer. Cloves are subject to damage from the cyclones and wind storms of the eastern coast, and yields tend to fluctuate in a cycle of one good crop year followed by two poor crops. Because the harvesting season coincides with the time for hand-pollinating the vanilla vines, the cloves may not be picked when the price is low. The world market has been stagnant for some years because of competition from synthetics and balance-of-payments difficulties in Indonesia and Malaya, the principal consuming countries, where cloves are used in the processing of tobacco. Exports depend upon market negotiations with these countries and on price negotiations with Tanzania, a serious competitor.

LIVESTOCK

Despite the many problems impeding scientific stockraising on the island, average per capita meat consumption is relatively high for a developing country: 53.6 pounds a year in the mid-1960s (higher than the rate in Italy or Greece). It varies considerably by region, however. The meat consumed is mainly beef, and the main cattle-producing zones are the provinces of Tulear and Majunga in the south and west and the prefectures of Alaotra, in the Central Highlands, and Vohémar. From the northeastern port city of Vohémar cattle are shipped to the Mascarene Islands. These producing zones have two-thirds of the national cattle herd and a surplus production of calves of 11 to 13 percent; this surplus supplies the country's slaughterhouses and canneries and furnishes the herds in the rest of the island.

In the south and west, almost every inhabitant owns some cattle, but they are given so little care that the practice hardly conforms to the usual definition of stockraising. The Bara, Sakalava, and other cattle-herding peoples allow their animals to roam and graze more or less at will, providing only minimal guard against the popular custom of cattle stealing. They burn off the dry grass to promote the growth of new vegetation. In principle, animals are slaughtered only upon ceremonial occasions, but these are so frequent that per capita meat consumption in the west averages about sixty-six pounds a year. An estimated 75 percent of the country's disposable surplus of livestock is consumed by the herders, who generally slaughter the older animals. Contrary to the prevalent impression, a survey by livestock experts concluded that the annual rate of takeoff from the national herd exploits nearly all the animals available for slaughter. By improving the breed and intensifying stockraising methods, however, both male and female stock could be slaughtered at an earlier age, and production could be increased by about 50 percent.

The zone of cattle utilization, consisting of the Central Highlands and the eastern region, has less than one head of livestock per inhabitant. There would be little available for meat production if it were not that 8 to 12 percent of the herd in these regions is imported every year from the producing zones. Per capita meat consumption is twenty-five pounds a year in the Central Highlands and only 9.4 pounds a year in the eastern region. In the Central Highlands the peasants are cultivators who need cattle to trample the ricefields, provide manure, and furnish traction. Fewer than two in three can own their own cattle, however. Grazing is short, and farmwork exhausts the animals and makes them more susceptible to disease; an estimated 100,000 head are thus lost every year from the national herd.

On the eastern coast, the growers of coffee, vanilla, cloves, and other crops purchase cattle from the productive zones for their meat consumption and to trample the ricefields. Because the climate is unhealthy for cattle, about 75,000 to 150,000 head have to be imported into the region every year; the level of purchases depends on how well the export crops are selling that year.

An intermediate zone, including the northwest and middle west, includes small regions with a livestock surplus and others with a deficit. In the former, cattle are grazed more intensively and are systematically fattened for slaughter.

The national herd consists largely of zebu cattle, which are well adapted to conditions on the island and yield relatively good quality meat, although not until an age of six to eight years. The cows yield little milk, and milk consumption on the island is generally deficient, although a dairy industry has been developed in the vicinity of Tananarive. Dairy products are imported in some quantity. Imported cattle breeds, when raised under traditional conditions, give no better yields than the zebu. The government is therefore obliged to undertake most of the selective breeding on its own ranches or experimental stations, and improvement of the national herd is a slow and time-consuming process.

Livestock production makes up about 10 percent of the country's gross domestic product (GDP) and 7 or 8 percent of exports; yet only about one-fourth of all livestock output enters the money exchange economy, the remaining 75 percent being consumed for subsistence. About 70 percent of all livestock production in the 1960s was derived from cattle herding. Estimates of livestock numbers are highly uncertain because of widespread evasion of the cattle tax. Official data for 1969 include an allowance for probable tax evasion (see table 16). The increase in the herd in the ten years from 1960 through 1969 was thought to be only moderate, but the potential for expansion is good. Despite erosion, excessive burning of grassland, and regrowth of inferior secondary grasses, the country still possesses extensive grazing lands, notably in the west and midwest; the herd is free of serious diseases.

Investment in livestock improvement projects under the First Five-Year Plan fell drastically short of projected targets, but programs began to get underway in the early 1970s. Government cattle-ranching stations and the building of slaughterhouses were important projects under the Program of Major Operations, and the Second Three-Year Plan also assigned high priority to improvement of the livestock sector through ranching in the west and improved facilities for slaughtering, distribution, and marketing. The planners want to increase domestic consumption of meat other than beef to permit the development of beef exports. Quality and veterinary standards are to be improved so that meat exports may find a wider range of overseas markets.

FISHING

In the late 1960s the island had no professional fishermen despite its long coastline and nineteen sizable lakes. Fishing was largely an occasional practice of cultivators or herders, and the catch was used as a supplement to the subsistence diet. Fish for the most part were consumed only by those who lived within ten miles of a lake or the coast. Because of poor transport from the coast, prices of marine products in Tananarive were higher than the price of meat or of freshwater fish. Fishing was thought to contribute less than 1 percent of GDP. Of the estimated 1970 catch of 50,000 metric tons, more than two-thirds consisted of freshwater fish consumed domestically. The sea catch, including shrimp, lobster, and crab, was largely for export.

Because of the strong winds, conditions off the coast are generally too rough to encourage much fishing with the crude outrigger canoes and nylon lines that are the only equipment that most of the part-time fishermen can afford. Nylon or cotton nets were still the exception in the late 1960s. The Japanese had been fishing for tuna and other varieties off the island and were considering the construction

Table 16. Estimated Livestock Population and Production, Malagasy Republic, 1969

	Unit of Quantity	Cattle	Pigs	Sheep	Poultry
Livestock population	thousands	10,400	430	1,200	15,000
Number slaughtered	---do---	950	300	255	23,200
Unit weight	metric tons	0.1275	0.06	0.013	0.001
Total weight	thousand metric tons	120.9	18	3.3	22.5
Domestic consumption	---do---	109.2	18	3.3	22.5
Available for export	---do---	11.7	---	---	---

--- not applicable.

266

of a freezing plant or other facilities. The potential for industrial deep-sea fishing from the island was under study by two mixed French-Malagasy companies, one concerned with tuna and the other with shrimp. A government expansion program for deep-sea fishing was to include the improvement of port facilities and the purchase or conversion of seagoing fishing boats. The initial phase of the program was expected to take about four years.

The introduction of tilapia fish to the island from the African continent in 1950 gave a great boost to freshwater fishing both in the lakes and in the rice paddies. Since that time, carp, black bass, and trout have been introduced with equal success. By 1969 it was estimated that 85,000 family fishponds were on the island, almost all in the Central Highlands. The breeding of fish in the ricefields requires expert control of the water supply, and poaching, dynamiting, and poisoning have been chronic problems. In 1972, despite the progress in stocking new freshwater varieties, the country had scarcely begun to exploit its real fishing potential.

MINING

The only minerals being actively exploited in mid-1972 were chromite, graphite, beryl, certain stones for ornament or for electrical geodes (such as quartz and celestine), and a tiny quantity of gold. There was an important bauxite deposit, and plans were underway for its exploitation. Nickel deposits were promising, but access to them was difficult. Favorable world demand for nickel, such as prevailed in 1972, might make it feasible to extract and ship the ore, and nickel prospecting was continuing. Oil exploration had taken place since the early 1900s and was intensified—chiefly offshore—after the closing of the Suez Canal. By mid-1972 this activity had yielded only dry wells, and a few traces of oil and gas.

Pending eventual exploitation of bauxite and nickel, chromite was the most important mineral export. The mine at Andriamena in the Alaotra region was operated by the Andriamena Mining Company (Compagnie Minière d'Andriamena—COMINA). Mining began in mid-1969, and in 1971 exports amounted to around 114,000 metric tons valued at FMG915 million, of which 96,000 metric tons went to the French steel mills of the Ugine-Kuhlmann company, promoter of the Andriamena chromite mining venture and owner of 55 percent of the stock. Other stockholders included: the Malagasy government, with 29 percent; the French firm Pechiney (which merged with Ugine-Kuhlmann in 1971 to form Europe's largest stainless steel concern), with 10 percent; and the French Overseas Finance Company (Compagnie Financière d'Outremer—COFIMER), with 10 percent. COMINA was unable to market any more than three-fourths of its output in 1971 and had to stockpile some 68,000 metric tons, immobilizing FMG400 million. Consequently, output in the ensuing years was to be curtailed to below capacity.

The island is seventh among world graphite producers. There were six graphite mines in operation in 1972; five of them were French owned, and the sixth had some Malagasy government participation. They were located in a strip about 200 miles inland from the eastern coast running from Vatomandry in the south to Tamatave, the exit port, in the north. Output increased from 17,114 metric tons in 1969 to 20,025 metric tons in 1971, valued at FMG650 million. It went principally to the United States, the United Kingdom, France, West Germany, and Japan. The mines have difficulty with delays in shipment, with washed-out east-coast roads during the rainy season, and with acute labor absenteeism during the east-coast harvesting seasons for coffee and cloves.

The bauxite deposit of Manantenia, located along the southeastern coast north of Fort Dauphin, was under survey in 1972 by a joint company created by the Malagasy government and Pechiney. The World Bank was considering financing construction of the required infrastructure. The crude ore reserve was tentatively assessed at 500 million metric tons; and the reserve of concentrated bauxite, at 125 million metric tons. If extraction averages 5 million tons of crude bauxite a year, the mine's estimated minimum life would be about twenty-five years. Investment of several billion Malagasy francs would be required either to construct a wharf near the mine or to develop the existing port of Fort Dauphin to ship the ore.

All zones with possible petroleum potential were being fully explored in 1972, and more than FMG6 billion was invested in exploration undertakings. The ten firms given exploration concessions included the Compagnie des Pétroles Total de Madagascar, a subsidiary of the French petroleum company Total; the Italian petroleum enterprise AGIP; and five United States oil firms.

MANUFACTURING

In the early 1970s manufacturing was generating about 12 percent of GDP, having increased from only 5 percent at independence in 1960. In 1970 it employed an estimated 47,000 persons, about 1.4 percent of the active population. Artisan activity, which is relatively important on the island, was thought to generate another 12 percent of GDP. Manufacturing activity had been developed largely since World War II and was based for the most part on the processing of domestic agricultural or forest products (see table 17).

Since independence the government had taken an active role in promoting industrialization by legislating a basic code of investment and by creating a national investment fund in 1962, a multisectoral development bank in 1963, and an agency for the promotion of industrial development in 1966. Because private investment was scarce and not all infant industries could be remunerative in the immediate term, government investment was channeled into an increasing number of medium- and small-scale industrial firms. The protection accorded by tariffs was only moderate as of 1970, however. The tariff system was designed primarily for revenue purposes rather than for protection of infant industry.

Table 17. Manufacturing Production, Malagasy Republic, 1968-70

Industry Group	Unit of Measure	1968	1969	1970
Food Processing:				
Tapioca	thousand metric tons	5.3	5.6	3.7
Starch	-do-	1.7	1.6	1.9
Cattle slaughtered for processing	thousand head	67.5	67.6	85.7
Pigs slaughtered for processing	-do-	4.1	4.9	8.5
Canned beef	thousand metric tons	9.7	9.5	12.1
Canned pork	-do-	0.3	0.4	0.8
Sugar	-do-	98.6	98.0	101.6
Edible oils	-do-	6.2	6.2	7.0
Tobacco and cigarettes	-do-	2.1	2.3	2.6
Beer	thousand US gallons	1,793.8	2,118.7	2,451.6
Textiles:				
Cotton fabrics	thousand metric tons	4.5	4.1	6.0
Sacks	-do-	4.4	3.8	4.2
Blankets	-do-	1.0	1.2	1.2
Sisal products	-do-	0.4	0.5	0.7
Metalworking:				
Corrugated sheet metal	thousand metric tons	8.4	9.0	8.2
Nails	-do-	1.4	1.5	1.6
Construction materials (cement)	thousand metric tons	66.9	77.1	75.2
Chemicals:				
Soap	thousand metric tons	2.0	4.1	6.4
Petroleum products .	thousand cubic yards	648.3	670.2	867.1
Matches	million boxes	48.1	60.1	74.9
Paper:				
Paper pulp	thousand metric tons	4.7	5.5	6.2
Paper	-do-	4.8	4.9	5.7

Under the successive development plans, emphasis was being placed upon plant installation or expansion that could effect savings in foreign exchange, such as refining of imported crude petroleum and more advanced manufacture of cotton textiles and clothing. By the late 1960s the largest industries were those producing sugar, meat, beer, cement, and textiles. Of the value added in manufacturing in 1966, the year of the first industrial census, fully half was derived from food-processing industries. Another 25 percent was from textiles and clothing; 7 percent, from tobacco manufacturing (including excise tax); 5 percent, from construction materials (largely cement); 4 percent from metalworking and vehicle assembly and repair; and 3 percent, from processing of wood and paper.

Under the First Five-Year Plan investment in manufacturing fell short of target by only about 9 percent, but the rise in manufacturing production and employment during the plan period came to only about 50 percent of the desired target, mainly because of stagnation or inadequate growth in the food industries and a shortfall of anticipated investment in the mechanical and electrical industries. Investment under the plan was chiefly in textiles, leather, and clothing; wood and paper; petroleum refining; and food processing. In the 1968-72 period manufacturing made satisfactory gains in output, averaging more than 10 percent a year. The most rapid gains were in production of beer, textiles, cement, and refined petroleum products. By the end of the period the cement, sugar, and match industries were supplying the whole of current domestic demand, and production leveled off near capacity. New manufacturing capacity being introduced near the end of the period included French automobile assembly, a tannery, and important new textile capacity.

The usual problems of infant industry in developing countries have been encountered: the high cost of transport, erratic supply of raw materials and power, and shortage of skilled labor and management personnel. A large proportion of manufacturing capacity was owned by French, Asian, or other foreign nationals. Before the coup of May 1972 the government had expressed satisfaction with the progress of the use of Malagasy personnel in foreign-owned firms, and further progress along this line was an important goal under the Second Three-Year Plan. It appeared that agitation against foreign predominance in industry and commerce might mount after mid-1972.

Despite the improvement in industrial output, several of the manufacturing firms financed by the agency for the promotion of industrial development were operating at a loss after the payment of the required 4-percent dividend to private shareholders, and the fund had to be subsidized from the national treasury. It was difficult to raise private domestic capital, and the inflow of foreign capital for manufacturing had also disappointed the planners' expectations. The authorities were hopeful that growing public and foreign aid investments in transport, communications, and power facilities, along with more thorough preparation of proposed investment projects, would help to attract more future industrial investment. The incentives offered were quite favorable to foreign industrial firms.

Attention was given under successive plans to appropriate decentralization of industrial plants to provide employment in manufacturing or raw material supply in the respective economic regions. The petroleum refinery was located at Tamatave on the eastern coast; the major textile capacity was at Antsirabe; and other important industrial establishments were at Diégo-Suarez in the north and Majunga on the western coast. Smaller plants were formed at a number of other regional centers (see fig. 12). There was some danger of excessive dispersion of capacity resulting in higher unit costs. Because of the island's topography, heavy rains, poor roads, and dearth of other infrastructure, export industries could be most efficiently located near the ports, and other industries could be near the principal centers of population or raw material supply. Under the Second Three-Year Plan investment was to be increased in food-processing industries in the Central Highlands, which offered combined advantages of markets, manpower, and crop production.

Artisan activity is highly developed and has not atrophied as much after the introduction of imported manufactures as has been the case in many African countries, although it suffers from many of the same problems of high unit costs and limited capacity. The number of artisan workers is unknown; estimates range from 35,000 to 150,000. Artisan activity is not confined to arts and crafts but proliferates in both the service and production sectors and in the woodworking, cabinetmaking, clothing-making, and other branches. Government policy accords an important role to the artisan sector in the development process. The Economic and Technical Center for the Artisanate (Centre Economique et Technique de l'Artisanat) is in charge of facilitating credit and promoting the rationalization of production and the formation of artisan cooperatives for raw material supply and marketing. By 1969 twenty-nine such cooperatives had been formed. Government projects had affected weaving, shoe manufacture, agricultural tools, dairy products, and the working of wood and aluminum.

ELECTRIC POWER

The island has a large potential for hydroelectric power development, which had been only partially exploited by 1972. In 1970 installed electric power generating capacity was 85,900 kilowatts, of which 58 percent was hydroelectric capacity. Electric energy generated had increased by about 10 percent a year in the 1965-70 period to reach 178 million kilowatt-hours. Plans for electric power development under the Second Three-Year Plan included: expansion of the hydroelectric station at Mandraka, forty-three miles east of Tananarive; construction of a high-tension line between Tananarive and Antsirabe; and construction of a new hydroelectric plant at Rogez, using the falls of the Vohitra stream. The Rogez plant would be located near the town of Moramanga, on the road east from Tananarive to Brickaville. The government has ambitious plans for

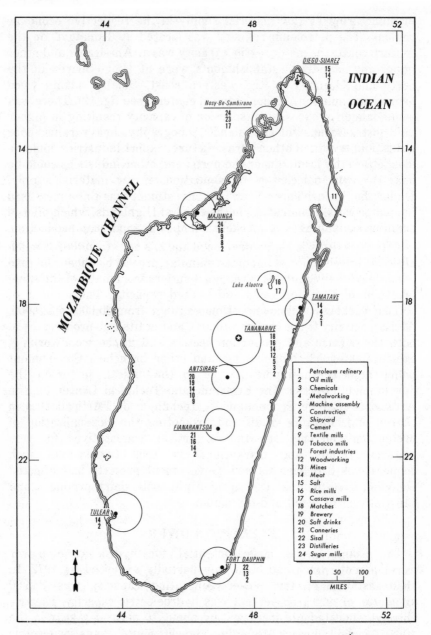

Source: Adapted from Georges Bastian, *Madagascar: Etude Géographique et Economique*, Tananarive, 1967.

Figure 12. Location of Industry, Malagasy Republic, 1966

eventually creating industry in the vicinity, including a possible ferrochrome installation. The plant will also permit the electrification of the Brickaville-Tananarive and Antsirabe-Tananarive axes.

SECTION IV. NATIONAL SECURITY
CHAPTER 14
NATIONAL SECURITY

Upon gaining independence in 1960, the republic established its own military force by transferring Malagasy soldiers who had been serving in the French colonial forces in Madagascar. A close military relationship with France continued during the 1960-72 period, in which the French supplied military aid, technical training, and other support. Malagasy government leaders apparently felt the need for a continuing association with a major power that would discourage intrigue, subversion, or attack by other nations. Meanwhile, the regular military forces of the country, consisting of about 4,000 men in 1972, remained relatively small in relation to the total population and the extent of the nation's land area and coastlines.

Most Malagasy were accustomed to accepting the authority of family elders and were apparently prepared to accept a strong central government. Customary law was handed down from the highly structured Merina-dominated society of the eighteenth and nineteenth centuries (see ch. 2). Nevertheless, the Penal Code promulgated by the government in 1962 was based primarily on the French Penal Code; some adaptations were made to allow for traditional Malagasy law. Judicial processes, punishments, and protections for the accused were generally similar to those in the French system of justice.

The highly trained, mobile paramilitary National Gendarmerie (Gendarmerie Nationale), having a strength of about 4,000 men in 1972, was the government's primary instrument for maintaining public order and internal security. It was assisted in the towns and smaller communities by several thousand civil police.

After ten years of relative stability, marked by the absence of serious external or internal security problems, internal tensions began to surface in 1970. Several demonstrations or minor strikes by students in 1970 and 1971 were essentially nonviolent, but they also brought little response from the government or progress toward their goals, which included modernization of education and a reduction of French influence (see ch. 7; ch. 9).

Meanwhile, in April 1971 a widespread demonstration that extended to a number of towns in the southern province of Tulear was apparently conceived as an attempt to draw the attention of the government to local problems of poverty, which had been compounded by droughts and hurricanes. Although the so-called uprising had been restrained and there had been no bloodshed in most towns, the government responded by initiating a violent and prolonged counteraction by the National Gendarmerie and other security forces.

In the capital city of Tananarive the dissatisfactions of students and other urban dwellers led to demonstrations and strikes between March and May 1972. President Philibert Tsiranana exacerbated the crisis by sending units of the Republican Security Force (Force Républicaine de Sécurité—FRS), his personal security force, against the growing street crowds. Undisciplined tactics by the FRS resulted in bloodshed and broadened public resistance, which led to major changes in the national government.

In May 1972 President Tsiranana asked his senior military officer, General Gabriel Ramanantsoa, to restore order and to take control of the government, thus bringing the military to power—a move that had been sought by the demonstrators and was generally approved by the population. Under Ramanantsoa as prime minister, five of the ten cabinet-level positions in the reorganized government were filled by military officers, and others were appointed as governors of all six provinces.

THE SECURITY FORCES

Military Traditions

During the early nineteenth century, as the Merina kings extended their control throughout most of Madagascar, the royal army was their primary instrument of power (see ch. 2). The core units were a small permanent force of career soldiers. They were augmented by periodical levies of freemen, who shared in the spoils of war as the Merina expanded and consolidated their control.

During the 1820s the strength of the army increased to about 14,000 professional soldiers, and fewer conscripts were inducted. Great Britain was attempting to oppose French influence in Madagascar at that time, and the British provided new weapons, ammunition, uniforms, and guidance. They helped reorganize the army and provided instruction in new tactics and techniques, which the Merina retained and used to advantage long after British influence declined during the latter half of the century.

In theory, service in the nineteenth-century Merina military units was obligatory, although the application varied. The sons of members of the ruling class were excused, and slaves were not allowed to enlist. Warriors therefore were mostly free commoners.

Under the French, who controlled Madagascar from 1896 to 1960, the Malagasy could be conscripted for service in the colonial forces, and they sometimes served with Comorians, Creoles from Réunion, or soldiers from western and central Africa. In world wars I and II several thousand Malagasy served in France, North Africa, and other combat zones along with troops from other French colonies.

As independence was attained and Malagasy-born troops were transferred from French to Malagasy control to form the nucleus of a national army, government leaders also prepared a conscription law, promulgated in September 1960. The law, making all men from twenty to fifty years of age subject to call, provided the legal basis for conscripting men as needed and provided for an initial period of service of eighteen months.

The military forces remained relatively small between 1960 and 1972. The formerly warlike Merina reportedly had developed a dislike of military service during the colonial era but, because the services offered a degree of security and opportunity, volunteers from coastal ethnic groups entered the army or the National Gendarmerie voluntarily, diminishing the need to use the draft system.

Foreign Influence

After World War II the Malagasy desire for independence intensified, and veterans of wartime service in the French forces were among the leading groups in the drive for an end to colonial status. They were active in the revolt of 1947, which was firmly put down (see ch. 2).

As it became more likely that there would be changes in the colonial status of Madagascar, French administrators and military leaders maintained order and arranged to retain the right to the future use of areas such as Diégo-Suarez as strategic outposts of France. This excellent natural harbor at the northern end of the island of Madagascar had the potential for development into a much larger naval base, if that should ever be desirable. Meanwhile, it was to continue to support a small number of French naval vessels, permitting France to maintain a naval presence in the Mozambique Channel and the southwestern Indian Ocean.

In 1949 the collective defense of French holdings in the southwestern Indian Ocean—the island of Réunion, the Comoro Islands, and Madagascar—had been assigned to the senior French commander in Madagascar. Great Britain also controlled a number of islands in the Indian Ocean, as well as a large area of East Africa, and her representatives joined in discussions of mutual defense interests in the area.

Between 1946 and 1972 French interests in Madagascar were not seriously challenged by other major powers. The closure of the Suez Canal from 1956 to 1957 and again in 1967—with little prospect for an early reopening—caused tankers to use the ancient route past the island and around the southern tip of Africa to deliver Middle East petroleum to Western Europe or elsewhere in the Atlantic Ocean area. Although this may have led to a modest boost in the importance of Madagascar as a base for the protection of strategic sea lanes, major power relationships and interests in the general Madagascar area remained relatively unchanged both before and after the Malagasy Republic was established.

An accord dated June 27, 1960, the day after the formalization of Malagasy independence, called for France to provide strategic protection for the new republic and allowed French military bases on Madagascar. In 1972 the naval base at Diégo-Suarez on the northern peninsula and Ivato airfield near Tananarive—also used by civil aircraft—were the major French military installations.

The 1960 agreement gave France freedom of movement in the island's airspace and coastal waters. The republic was technically responsible for its own defense, but it was empowered to call for assistance from France, especially in the form of equipment and training. Mutual military interests were managed by a joint Franco-Malagasy defense command consisting of the president of the republic, the French ambassador, and the commander of France's Third Overseas Zone, the southwestern Indian Ocean area.

As Malagasy political leaders moved toward independence between 1958 and 1960, they wanted a national army as an affirmation of sovereignty for the new republic. They had only a small pool of veterans with some knowledge of modern military skills, but thousands of Malagasy citizens were serving in the French forces. By agreement with France, about 4,500 of these men were transferred to the new Malagasy military service.

These troops retained French military philosophies as well as local military traditions surviving in the myths of the local nineteenth-century kingdoms, which had been dominated by the Merina. They used French weapons and equipment and occupied the former French garrisons. They were under the command of a Malagasy colonel (promoted to brigadier general in 1961) who was a graduate of the St. Cyr Military Academy in France. Twenty-seven other officers of Malagasy origin, seven of them St. Cyr graduates, had also transferred to the national army. During the first five years of independence France provided military aid at an equivalent rate of approximately US$5 million annually, including technical assistance, training, and practically all of the arms and equipment for the Malagasy services. The National Gendarmerie also retained traditions and operational methods learned from French administrators and instructors, even though many of the gendarmes were not necessarily fluent in the French language.

The essentials of the 1960 Franco-Malagasy security agreements continued in force in 1972. France maintained 4,000 of her own troops in Madagascar—up from less than 2,500 before 1967—under the command of a general with the title of Senior Commander of French Forces in the Southern Indian Ocean. His command also included

French forces on Réunion and in the Comoro Islands. His forces reportedly included a marine parachute regiment, a foreign legion regiment, and units with special training in the management of civil unrest. French air units in the Malagasy Republic had helicopters and transport aircraft, and navy units operated escort ships and other naval vessels at Diégo-Suarez.

In addition to the tactical units operating from Diégo-Suarez, in early 1972 France also had three destroyer-size vessels, a tanker, and a logistical support ship operating near Madagascar to study operational problems and future needs in the area. Unconfirmed reports indicated that French naval units operating from Diégo-Suarez would be increased and that a small strategic naval intervention force would be based there.

Close military ties with France continued in 1972 and influenced the Malagasy defense structure in many ways. France continued to furnish most of the equipment and technical training for the Malagasy security forces. French officers served in the Malagasy army—many of them in some of the most authoritative or sensitive positions—in the upper levels of the National Gendarmerie and other security services. Gradually the senior positions in the military and security services were being filled by Malagasy officers, and more Malagasy junior officers were becoming available from a national military academy established in 1966.

Malagasy Military Structure

The Malagasy armed forces have a twofold mission. Under the terms of the 1960 defense agreement with France, they are responsible for the defense of the republic against external attack, but the government may request assistance from France. As a secondary mission, the military units assist the National Gendarmerie and the civil police in maintaining public order and safety.

The defense establishment, as organized in 1972, was composed principally of ground force elements having a primary emphasis on infantry. Of approximately 4,000 men in uniform, all but about 400 were members of the army. Ground force elements consisted of two infantry units (nominally regiments but actually about equal to two battalions); one parachute company; an armored squadron; an artillery battery; and an engineer regiment (also actually battalion size). Once their structures have been established and key personnel have been trained, such units could be expanded by conscription.

Similarly, the much smaller air and naval elements were little more than cadres gaining experience for use in a possible future expansion of these services. The air unit, known officially as the Malagasy Air Flight, was organized around a nucleus of about 200 men, reportedly including approximately ten Malagasy pilots. The flight operated a small inventory of aircraft that included eight light and medium transports, several small liaison aircraft, and a few helicopters. Essentially a supporting element for the army, the air arm did not have a tactical combat capability.

The navy consisted of about 200 men, including a small unit of naval infantry, and was engaged primarily in training. The Malagasy fleet consisted of several small patrol craft acquired from the Federal Republic of Germany (West Germany), a training ship, and a small tender. Probably not more than two of the patrol craft were operable in 1972.

The armed forces were directed by three Malagasy generals. Most other officers were French-trained Malagasy. In early 1972 the key military advisory staff in the offices of the Malagasy president consisted of six French colonels. General Ramanantsoa, who became prime minister in May 1972, was a graduate of the French Military Academy at St. Cyr. As an officer in the French army before the Malagasy Republic was established, he had had combat service in several areas, including Indochina and North Africa, and had risen to the rank of colonel (see ch. 9).

Rank structures, regulations, customs, and supply and support systems were adopted from the French military services. French officers and technical specialists served in the Malagasy forces, usually in Malagasy uniforms and insignia. A few units included both Malagasy and French components, providing members of the two national services the opportunity to develop full cooperation and integration of command and control functions.

Government publications indicate that regular military personnel also assisted in development work near their garrisons, including reforestation and farm activities. Engineer units worked on improvements to roads, bridges, and canals and provided aid to disaster areas.

Paramilitary Forces

The National Gendarmerie

Developed from colonial origins, the National Gendarmerie is the primary Malagasy organization responsible for the maintenance of public order. About 1,900 gendarmes, trained and equipped by the French, were on duty in the mid-1950s. As Madagascar became independent the government—by a decree of January 25, 1961—placed this organization directly under the office of the new president.

The gendarmerie provides police services outside the municipalities throughout the country. Its equipment inventory includes automatic weapons, armored cars, and aircraft, and its units are connected with gendarmerie command centers by a modern system of radio communications.

Under President Tsiranana, most of the new gendarme recruits were *côtiers* (see Glossary). The force expanded from about 3,000 during the mid-1960s to approximately 4,000 in 1972. This increase to a size comparable to that of the armed forces suggests that the Tsiranana government viewed the gendarmerie as a counterforce that would discourage dissidents within the army from attempting to usurp power.

The gendarmerie is regarded as part of the defense establishment, but its command structure is entirely separate from that of the army. After the government reorganization in mid-1972, the force was directed by the minister of interior, an army lieutenant colonel who had been appointed by Prime Minister Ramanantsoa. Until 1971 French military technical assistants or instructors (numbering about 175 in 1970) either occupied most of the more important positions or functioned as direct advisers to Malagasy officers and supervisors.

The Republican Security Force

Another special form of security police, the Republican Security Force (Force Républicaine de Sécurité—FRS), was established by President Tsiranana as a presidential bodyguard and an antiriot unit, controlled through channels separate from those of the other security forces. The personnel strength of the FRS was estimated at about 1,000 men in 1972.

The FRS was reportedly less disciplined and trained than the National Gendarmerie or the army and as an institution was disliked by many citizens. During the strikes and rioting in May 1972, it was reported that the FRS was blamed for the deaths of student protesters, and by May 16 FRS members had been ordered to remain off the streets. The gendarmerie protected them from reprisal action by the rioters and began to restore order. Spokesmen for the protesters demanded that the Ramanantsoa government suppress the FRS, and the attitudes and policies of the new government indicated that such action probably would be taken (see ch. 9).

The Civil Police

The civil police maintained order in towns and smaller communities. They were transferred from French to Malagasy control in 1961. During the late 1960s they were reported to total about 3,000. The head of each subprefecture had at least a small contingent of them under his control. They provided the usual services of local police, helping to prevent theft, controlling small disturbances, and helping in natural disasters. They were important to their local communities, but they were not as well-trained, disciplined, or heavily armed as the paramilitary National Gendarmerie.

The Civic Service

The Civic Service (Service Civique) was, like the National Gendarmerie, a paramilitary force. It was a reserve element of the defense forces, and its leaders were military officers in uniform, but it was controlled directly by the head of the executive branch of government via channels separate from those of the armed forces or the National Gendarmerie. In its nonmilitary mission, it participated in economic and social development programs, which were being coordinated during the late 1960s by a commissioner general in the offices of the secretary of state for development. This arrangement may have changed when the government was reorganized in mid-1972, but few details on control channels have become available.

Its legislative bases included the National Service Ordinance issued in September 1960 and a decree in January 1963. The National Service Ordinance gave potential draftees an opportunity to serve in the Civic Service as an alternative to regular military duty and was designed to utilize unemployed or underemployed young people in achieving social goals as well as to increase the reserve of partially trained defense personnel. Young people entering the program are trained in practical mathematics, languages, agricultural subjects, and the organization of recreational activities, as well as in basic military organization and tactics. In the early 1960s a school for future junior officers or noncommissioned officers of the Civic Service was set up in an old military camp at Antsirabe. These cadre members received six months of training, and some received additional instruction at civilian schools or at a center in Tananarive operated by the army and the Civic Service.

After initial training, section or team leaders were sent to various rural areas to set up centers for the training of additional Civic Service leaders and workers. Others with appropriate training became practical nurses, literacy instructors, or rural artisan-teachers. Some Civic Service personnel farmed small plots of land and produced some of their own food. Meanwhile, they taught and demonstrated useful rural skills, such as improved farming methods and simple construction techniques. They worked in the "action zone"—the local community—as well as on their own land. The needs of each area were examined beforehand, and the programs were correlated with the provincial delegate from the Ministry of Agriculture. Service members were also prepared to help the victims of natural disasters.

The program expanded slowly during the 1960s. Ten companies of 100 to 125 persons each were active in 1969. Usually a company was divided into three sections; each section consisted of three teams. Trained personnel were reportedly teaching 4,000 children in sixty rural schools in school year 1969 / 70, and small agricultural villages had been established as self-help and demonstration projects. Government plannners expected at that time that eventually there would be an active company in each prefecture, consisting mostly of local young people—some volunteers and some draftees—trained to help to improve conditions in their own areas through education, military training, and service to their communities. Apparently because of a lack of funds, the 1972 strength of the Civic Service was reported to have increased only slightly—from less than 1,250 in 1969 to about 1,500 members.

Defense Costs

Annual defense budgets increased only moderately between 1966 and 1972, ranging from slightly over the equivalent of US$10 million in 1966 and 1967 to approximately US$12.2 million in 1969 and a similar amount in 1970. France financed about 85 percent of the military budget in 1968. There was little change in the size or mission of the armed forces in the 1970-72 period and probably no more than a modest rise in the military budgets for those years. In the early 1970s France continued to furnish military matériel and technical assistance at an estimated rate equivalent to about US$12 million per year, apparently continuing to cover most of the Malagasy government's military costs.

Postindependence foreign military aid had been provided mostly by France, and small additional amounts came from West Germany, the United States, and Israel during the 1960s. United States military assistance, which totaled less than US$3.5 million from 1960 to 1965, consisted primarily of communications equipment for the paramilitary National Gendarmerie. Israel had trained and equipped 500 police recruits and carried out the initial training program for the Civic Service. Practically all foreign military assistance ceased after 1969 except that which was a part of the continuing cooperation with France.

Training

With French assistance, the Military Academy (l'Académie Militaire) was established in 1966 at Antsirabe, a highland town eighty miles south of Tananarive, to train officers for the military forces, the National Gendarmerie, and the Civic Service. The first students entered in 1967. The three-year program was designed to provide a broad education in order to develop future officers as citizens and leaders in national development as well as in military affairs. Students chose a specialty either in letters or sciences. Each year a few places were assigned to student officers from other countries, usually from francophone countries in Africa.

The Military Academy was affected by the rebellion and student strikes against official policies in civilian schools, which led to violent clashes with the authorities in May 1972 (see ch. 9). Examinations were temporarily suspended by General Ramanantsoa soon after he was appointed prime minister. After discussions, government officials announced that questions raised by student officers, presumably concerning modernization of course material and educational policies, were to be settled by a committee. Reports in June 1972 indicated that tests and requirements for entry into the academy would also be reviewed. In addition to training officers at the local military academy, the government annually selected a small number of officer candidates to attend the French military academy at St. Cyr, filling places allotted by the French for this purpose.

Malagasy and French military units participate in joint annual maneuvers. Beyond this, little detail is available on training philosophies or schedules. Malagasy military forces are considered to be relatively well trained and, in conjunction with other security forces, capable of maintaining internal security.

Security Forces in National Life

The absence of information on the internal structure of the various security forces, and particularly on their investigative units, makes it impossible to evaluate their roles in detail. The actions of National Gendarmerie and FRS personnel and the public reaction to them allow tentative and generalized conclusions. Gendarmerie personnel were generally both disciplined and effective, but they were uncharacteristically brutal against the Antandroy in Tulear Province after the 1971 uprising. The FRS, already low in the esteem of the Malagasy citizenry, was blamed for the deaths of student demonstrators during the May 1972 crisis.

At least two intelligence organizations were reportedly operating under the Tsiranana government during the 1970-72 period; each was subject to different channels of command. One was in the National Gendarmerie; it was staffed by Malagasy personnel and had reported to Vice President Resampa until he began to fall into disfavor with the president in early 1971 (see ch. 9). The other organization worked under the supervision of Tsiranana's personal military staff of French officers. Information on roles and command channels of these units under General Ramanantsoa was not available in late 1972.

PUBLIC ORDER AND SECURITY

Development of Criminal Law

The criminal law prevailing in 1972 has developed primarily from French legal and penal codes and procedures, although it is somewhat influenced by Malagasy customary law. The Malagasy traditions were principally those of the former Merina kingdoms, which controlled nearly all of Madagascar for most of the nineteenth century (see ch. 2). Theirs was a highly organized society, in which rigorously enforced customs, taboos, and interdictions informed the citizens what behavior was accepted or discouraged.

Many customs and practices had in fact been organized into a written code by King Andrianampoinimerina (1782-1810) almost a century before the French gained control of Madagascar. Another code, containing 305 articles, was prepared by the Merina government in 1881. It provided that prevailing customs should be as fully represented in the settling of disputes as written law of French or colonial origin—a principle that was carried forward to independence and still had considerable force in 1972.

As they completed their conquest of most of the island during the early nineteenth century, the Merina had also replaced much of the local authority with a centralized system dominated by the Merina king. Conditioning toward the acceptance of a strong central authority has continued to be an important factor in law enforcement. Maintaining order and carrying out the directives of the central government were, however, local responsibilities assigned to a committee of the local elders—the *fokon'olona* (see Glossary) or community (see ch. 5; ch. 8). This included the power to arrest petty criminals.

From the beginning of the colonial period until World War II, French penal law and procedures were in limited use. After 1946 French officials began to enlarge the staffs and the number of French courts in order eventually to try all criminal cases in Madagascar under French penal law. The problems of conflict between the Malagasy and French systems and beliefs were increased by a shortage of trained magistrates during the years when the change to French procedures greatly increased the caseload of the courts.

In 1960, as the nation gained formal independence, Malagasy legislators set up a commission to review the French Penal Code, which continued to be in use in Madagascar for most of the first two years of independence. Recommendations were made concerning adaptations of the French system for incorporation into a Malagasy code. Only moderate revisions were made, and most of the provisions of the French Penal Code were adopted and promulgated in August 1962 under the name of the Penal Code of the Malagasy Republic (Code Penal de la République Malgache).

The Malagasy Penal Code

Under the seal of the new nation, the Malagasy penal code retained most of the French trial procedures as well as its legal principles. Probably the most fundamental difference between the French system and the ancient Malagasy customary law—a difference known to and long accepted by French-educated Malagasy leaders—was the redefinition of the law's purpose in establishing guilt. The French system, retained by the Malagasy in their own code, punished the wrongdoer or called for correctional treatment in an attempt to cause him to become law-abiding. The traditional Malagasy approach, which was being deemphasized or dropped, has emphasized redress for parties injured by the lawbreaker. More severe penalties were established for certain crimes that were considered especially heinous or troublesome in Madagascar, such as certain acts of sorcery, cattle theft, or the violation of burial sites (see ch. 8).

Another important change affected procedure. The previously used code of instructions for processing criminal cases was modified in an attempt to simplify the processing of relatively uncomplicated cases in which the facts appeared to be well established. A step in this direction had been taken two years earlier, with the publication of Ordinance 60-029 in May 1960. Magistrates were authorized by this directive to use a summary of information in certain cases in which a person had confessed to a crime or had allegedly been caught in the act. In effect the 1962 code extended the preexisting principle of *flagrante delicto* (obvious lawbreaking) to a greater range of cases. Still excluded were cases that could result in such extremely severe punishments as forced labor for life or the death penalty. The summary of information, used to hasten the processing of simple cases, was intended to reduce congestion in the courts.

Investigators and judicial assistants preparing a summary of information worked under the supervision of the Public Ministry, or staff of prosecutors, who decided whether to close or to continue investigations. The 1962 code also shifted more control over investigations and prosecutions to the magistrates (*juges d'instruction*) and away from local administrative officials, who henceforth were to be excluded from the supervision of the legal process in ordinary cases and were to play a role only in very serious or complex cases.

The 1962 code provided the accused most of the same rights and protections established in French and other Western penal codes. Punishments were usually prison sentences or fines more or less similar in severity to those passed down in courts in Western Europe or the United States. Removal of some or all of a convicted person's civil rights was authorized for some crimes.

Authorized punishments for the most serious crimes included the death sentence, forced labor for life, forced labor for a specified period of time, deportation or banishment, imprisonment, and withdrawal of specified civil rights. The death penalty was authorized for those found guilty of assassination, killing a parent or other family elder, or murder when accompanied by acts of barbarity or torture or when committed in association with another crime. Treason and certain related crimes, such as aiding a foreign power, were also punishable by death.

Other crimes against the state, such as serious violation of public peace and order, counterfeiting money, or breaches of public trust, could bring sentences as severe as forced labor for life. Abuses of authority were also heavily punished. For example, police or other officials convicted of false arrest could be given severe sentences, including forced labor, if the party unjustly arrested and sentenced had served more than a month in prison as a result of the improper arrest.

Attempting a serious crime could be as serious as the crime itself, and accomplices could be given the same sentences as the principal offender, except in cases where the law specifically ordered milder punishment. Penalties for second offenses were heavy, ranging from double the prison sentence for the first offense to forced labor for life, depending on the seriousness of the crime and other circumstances.

Minor offenses, more or less equivalent to some of the misdemeanors in United States codes, were known as contraventions. These were usually tried in administrative courts. Sentences were usually fines or jail sentences of less than one month, served locally. Minor violations could also be punished by withholding civil or family rights for a period of time, sometimes in conjunction with fines and short terms in local jails. Some village societies had a form of rehabilitation center, where local transgressors were given limited freedom of movement in some cases in order to allow them to make restitution to injured parties.

Prisons

Each province had a central prison for inmates serving sentences of less than five years. There were also, at the seats of various courts, at least twenty-five lesser prisons where terms of less than two years were served; prisoners awaiting trial were also remanded to these jails. Courts at the local (subprefecture) level also had jails, where lesser offenders served sentences up to six months in length. Women serving long sentences were kept in the Central Prison (Maison Centrale) in Tananarive.

Hardened criminals or others sentenced to terms longer than five years were usually sent to one of the prisons on small coastal islands. such as Nosy Lava or Nosy Be. Data on prisoners, prison conditions, and paroles or remissions of sentences for these and for the local prisons on Madagascar island were unavailable in 1972.

Security Issues, 1970-72

Alleged Antigovernment Plots

In June 1971 government allegations that Vice President André Resampa was plotting the overthrow of President Tsiranana became one of the major internal security issues of the republic's eleven years of independence (see ch. 9). Although political maneuvering was probably the primary reason for Resampa's arrest, unofficial news accounts suggested that rivalry between Tsiranana's two intelligence organizations may have been a contributing factor.

Resampa was never tried, a fact that led to speculation that the intelligence services had not developed a case that could be publicly aired. Instead he and about twelve other alleged plotters arrested at approximately the same time were held under supervision on Ile Sainte-Marie.

A second plot announced by government spokesmen in October 1971 involved the Office of Scientific and Technical Research Overseas (Office de la Recherche Scientifique et Technique Outre-Mer—ORSTOM), a French technical research organization. This plot came to be known as the ORSTOM or Roy-Regis affair. Two members, one of them French, were accused by the Tsiranana government of being implicated in a plot inspired by the communist philosophy of Mao Tse-tung. About thirty-eight Malagasy were also taken into custody.

On June 8, 1972, after Tsiranana had been shifted to a figurehead role in government, Resampa was released, and all his rights as a citizen were restored. All others involved in the two alleged plots were released in the amnesty declared by Prime Minister Ramanantsoa on June 26, 1972, the anniversary of Malagasy Independence.

Southwestern Revolt

A brief and unusual uprising took place on the night of April 1, 1971, instigated by the National Movement for the Independence of Madagascar (Mouvement National pour l'Indépendance de Madagascar—MONIMA) but initiated and carried out by local groups. The participants were motivated by regional interests and apparently sought to make a dramatic gesture to the government. Crudely armed but well-organized groups of fifty to 500 men seized all the government posts in a wide area of Tulear Province with an overwhelming show of strength and occupied a number of towns. Local police and National Gendarmerie stationed in the south were reported to have resisted in only a few places, and only three security force personnel were reported killed. The action was otherwise marked by restraint on the part of the MONIMA organizers and a minimum of violence.

The next day these groups, numbering thousands of men—a larger force than the national army—withdrew from all captured positions. No attempt was made to hold the towns or set up a rebel government. What they staged was a protest, either as a warning to the government to listen to their economic and tax problems or as an effort to drive away the hated government representatives (see ch. 9).

Nevertheless, the central government and its local representatives initiated a determined suppression drive. The participants were searched out by the local police, the National Gendarmerie, and the FRS; and indirect support was received from the military forces. Reports indicated that about thirty people were killed in the initial counteraction. As government forces continued an extensive campaign, 5,000 persons were arrested, and 600 were sent to the island prison of Nosy Lava. The leadership of the local Antandroy ethnic group, historically difficult to govern from Tananarive, was crushed. Local police and administrators continued the campaign of suppression in some areas well into 1972. In August 1972 a French journalist-observer estimated that 1,000 people had been killed in the south since April 1971. MONIMA leaders stated that the number of deaths was even higher and that thousands of others had suffered serious hardship.

Student Unrest and Urban Crisis

Actual or potential dissidence and related security problems in the early 1970s sprang from many of the same issues that affected other developing countries: demands by militantly nationalistic groups for removal of the last vestiges of colonialism and demands for better education, more health care, better wages, and a more equitable division of the national income. Nationalist anticolonial sentiments and the desire for liberalized and modernized education led to the students' demand for increased use of the Malagasy language in schools and a lessening of French cultural influence (see ch. 9).

The tensions and dissidence that were to climax in violent confrontations and the collapse of the government in 1972 began to surface in 1970, when a series of small strikes occurred after years of relative harmony. In January 1971 a bomb was set off at the Ministry of Public Works. More strikes occurred, and in April 1971 the University of Madagascar was closed temporarily after a relatively mild disturbance.

On the surface, the disagreements between the authorities and the students were relatively restrained until early 1972. Before and after the presidential inauguration on May 1, 1972, unrest and demonstrations in the urban centers increased. Three thousand students and other supporters demonstrated in Fianarantsoa on May 5. In Tananarive the situation became so serious that on May 12 Tsiranana ordered wholesale arrests. About 375 students and other citizens were taken into custody, and most were transported to the prison island of Nosy Lava. This action triggered larger demonstrations and a general strike.

On May 13 thousands of students marched to the presidential palace. Two days of rioting left thirty-four persons dead—mostly students and other strikers killed by the FRS, which had been ordered by Tsiranana to suppress the strikers. Another 170 persons were injured. The building that housed the National Statistics Institute, the Tananarive city hall, and the offices of the government newspaper *Le Courrier de Madagascar* were burned down.

The deaths at the hands of the FRS shocked the urban population and broadened the support for the demonstrators. The Tsiranana government moved to accept the demands of the demonstrators rather than ordering a further attempt to suppress by force the general strike and the growing street demonstrations. The FRS was ordered to remain off the streets, protected from angry strikers by units of the National Gendarmerie, which was generally respected by the citizenry.

On May 16 President Tsiranana moved to transfer power to a military government, as the students and other strikers had demanded. General Ramanantsoa, chief of staff of the Malagasy army—a highly respected veteran of many years in the French forces and in the independent Malagasy government—was appointed prime minister.

The new government immediately responded to a number of other student demands or promised future action on them. The demonstrators being held in Nosy Lava prison were immediately flown back to Tananarive and released. The National Gendarmerie restored order, and no further clashes or bloodshed were reported. Acceding to a specific demand by the students, Prime Minister Ramanantsoa agreed to disband the FRS, which had a reputation for roughness and lack of discipline long before the May 1972 crisis. When the immediate demands of the demonstrators were satisfied, tensions subsided and strikers began to return to work.

Subversive Activity

In late 1972 evidence of major action by subversive groups opposing the national government was extremely scarce. In retrospect, President Tsiranana's 1971 allegations of plots against his government lacked substantiating evidence.

Foreign intrigue and the activities of international movements apparently were also of minor importance in the Malagasy Republic during the 1960-72 period. Nevertheless, President Tsiranana had expressed concern over alleged dangers from international communism. He had declined formal diplomatic relations with all communist nations except Yugoslavia and Romania and had warned against subversion by the PRC (see ch. 10).

The principal communist nations, however, had shown little discernible interest in subverting the young republic. Whatever support or encouragement it may have received, the Malagasy Communist Party (Antoko Kaominista Malagasy—AKM) remained small and was reported to have only a few hundred members during the 1970-72 period and possible 2,000 to 3,000 nonmember sympathizers.

A larger number of people, who accepted communist political philosophies but who had not aligned themselves with the AKM, belonged to and often dominated the policymaking of the left-wing opposition of the Congress for the Independence of Malagasy (Ankoton'ny Kongresi'ny Fahaleovantenan Madagaskara—AKFM) (see ch. 9). In August 1972, after Tsiranana had relinquished his position as head of government, the AKFM and some Malagasy Communists urged all citizens to support Prime Minister Ramanantsoa for the sake of national unit.

Political Activism After the 1972 Crisis

Overt political action, rather than subversion, appeared to be more representative of the Malagasy temperament, and there was some evidence that politically active groups would have greater freedom of expression under the Ramanantsoa government. In late 1972 the most noteworthy activist group was the Joint Struggle Committee (Komity Iombonan'ny Mpitolona—KIM), an organization consisting mainly of students who came together after the May 1972 political crisis. The group appeared to be well organized and had chapters operating in several cities. Local views were communicated to the government through a coordinating group at national level.

The KIM supported Prime Minister Ramanantsoa, but with reservations. Its members favored far-reaching economic, political, and military changes, including the total abrogation of existing accords with France and the evacuation of French military bases at Diégo-Suarez and Ivato. Ramanantsoa had praised them and promised to study their policy demands. The KIM also was reported to have formed strike committees, despite a suspension of the right to strike that had gone into effect under the state of emergency declared when Ramanantsoa assumed power.

Social Attitudes and Public Order

The political activists of 1971 and 1972 were notable for their willingness to avoid excess, which appears to be an important facet of the Malagasy temperament. The Merina, who gained control of most of the other groups in Madagascar between one and two centuries ago, have sometimes been described by other Malagasy as aggressive. Also, members of the Sakalava ethnic group—who ruled a kingdom in the southwestern coastal area before the Merina ascendancy—have a similar reputation. Within limits, these views may be historically accurate, but there is also evidence of a predilection for political action rather than physical violence among most of the Malagasy. Instances of organized or large-scale violence, such as armed rebellions, are rare in the recent history of Madagascar.

The excesses perpetrated by veterans returning from World War II have been regarded by observers as rare exceptions. Wanton killings by veterans in 1946 were attributed to unique combinations of causes growing out of the war and its aftermath. In one case, for example, young Malagasy men were suddenly released after years of training and experience in the specialized arts of underground warfare practiced by French Resistance forces and after weeks of travel in the steaming troopships that brought them from France to Madagascar. Other returning Malagasy soldiers had endured four years in Nazi prison camps.

Similarly, the 1947 rebellion was regarded as atypical in its violence and is attributed to special postwar tensions. After the uprising and bloodshed began at Moramanga in March 1947, the nationalistic intellectuals and politicians who had been urging rebellion against the French denied having sponsored the attacks and described the violence as "odious."

Despite political tensions as the Malagasy moved toward independence and the problems of a decade of self-rule, there were practically no significant incidents of armed rebellion or organized violence between 1948 and the early 1970s. The southern uprising in April 1971 was not necessarily a significant exception, although it involved thousands of the Antandroy—one of the most independent groups in the nation. Their broad-scale action involved the capture and overnight occupation of the small security-force post in a number of towns in Tulear Province. Although a minority of member of MONIMA were known to favor violence (probably all of the participants had long-term grievances against local representatives of the central government), the thousands of crudely armed villagers avoided bloodshed in all but a few places.

In April and May 1972, the most politically troubled months since independence, the thousands of strikers and demonstrators in the streets of the capital city of Tananarive were peaceful until they were set upon by the FRS. The killing of more than two dozen protesters by the FRS shocked and angered the demonstrators, but only a handful of security personnel were reported to have died or suffered serious injury in the street clashes.

The FRS action was apparently regarded by the Malagasy people as such an excess that they put aside their traditional respect for authority and their preference for political maneuver. They directed their own violence primarily against the physical symbols of authority and burned several government buildings. Most significantly, they refused to accept what they apparently regarded as an overreaction and a violation of social norms. Besides its own critical importance, this use of force increased a general fear that President Tsiranana, a patriarchal figure among the urban electorate, was no longer providing balanced authority. Reaction to the use of force and, ironically, a feeling that the government had not been forceful enough in other matters brought on the collapse of the government.

The demonstrators demanded that the FRS be disbanded. Apparently desiring firm but restrained leadership and believing that General Ramanantsoa would provide it they approved a military takeover apparently representative of the Malagasy political temperament.

Nevertheless, the record of recent decades cannot be taken to indicate that the future will be peaceful. There undoubtedly have been many violent intertribal battles in the history of Madagascar. Of more immediate significance, security personnel killed fellow citizens, and police and administrators were engaged in fierce suppressive measures extending over many months after the relatively mild use of force in Tulear Province in 1971. These excesses may have sprung from exaggerated fear of the Antandroy, interethnic rivalry, and institutionalized approval of their actions by the Tsiranana government.

Unusual stresses may, of course, break down ordinary behavioral norms in any society, and instances of individual or group violence may occur. The events of the crisis year of 1972 indicated a general willingness among most of the population to avoid bloodshed, but they may also have indicated that social attitudes and behavioral norms were changing more rapidly than in the past.

BIBLIOGRAPHY

Section I. Social

Adriantsilaniarivo, E., and Abraham, Elie-Charles. "La littérature Malgache," *Revue de Madagascar* [Tananarive], XXVI, July 1946, 16-25.

"L'alphabetisation et l'éducation de base," *Bulletin de Madagascar* [Tananarive], XV, No. 231, August 1965, 715-730.

Althabe, Gérard. *Oppression et Libération dans l'Imaginaire; les Communautés Villageoises de la Côte Orientale de Madagascar.* Paris: Maspéro, 1969.

Andriamanjato, Richard. *Le Tsiny et le Tody dans la Pensée Malgache.* Paris: Editions Présence Africaine, 1957.

Andriamohy. "La personalité malgache," *Recueil Penant* [Paris], LXXII, No. 692, June-August 1962, 327-347.

Andrianarahinjaka, Lucien X. Michel. "Ramananato: Poète Betsileo du début du siècle," *Présence Africaine* [Paris], LV, 1965, 42-72.

Association Universitaire pour le Développement de l'Enseignement et de la Culture en Afrique et à Madagascar. *Informations Pédagogiques* (Report No. 10, AUDECAM.) Paris: 1971.

Bastian, Georges. *Madagascar: Etude Géographique et Economique.* Tananarive: Fernand Nathan, 1967.

Beidelman, T. O., with replay by Ruth Finnegan. "Approaches to the Study of African Oral Literature," *Africa* [London], XLII, No. 2, April 1972, 140-147.

Bloch, Maurice. "Decision-Making in Councils Among the Merina of Madagascar." Pages 26-62 in Audrey Richards and Adam Kuper (eds.), *Councils in Action.* Cambridge: Cambridge University Press, 1971.

— —. "The Implications of Marriage Rules and Descent: Categories for Merina Social Structures," *American Anthropologist*, LXXIII, No. 1, February 1971, 164-178.

— —. *Placing the Dead.* New York: Seminar Press, 1971.

— —. "Tombs and Conservatism Among the Merina of Madagascar," *Man* [London], Nos. 1 and 3, March 1968, 94-014.

Block, M. "Astrology and Writing in Madagascar." Pages 277-297 in John R. Goody (ed.), *Literacy in Traditional Societies.* Cambridge: Cambridge University Press, 1968.

Cadoux, Charles. *La République Malgache.* Paris: Editions Berger-Levrault, 1972.

"Cent ans de peinture malgache," *Afrique* [Paris], XLIV, March 1965, 56-57.

Chabeuf, M. "Les caractères physiques de sept populations

malgaches," *Bulletins et Mémoires de la Société d'Anthropologie* [Paris], IV, (Série XII), April-June 1969, 181-207.

Chamla, Marie-Claude. *Recherches Anthropologiques sur l'Origine des Malgaches.* Paris: Mémoires du Musée, 1958.

Colin, Pierre. *Aspects de l'Ame Malgache.* Paris: Editions de l'Orante, 1959.

Cotte, Paul Vincent. *Regardons Vivre une Tribu Malgache: Les Betsimisaraka.* Paris: La Nouvelle Edition, 1947.

Czarnecki, Jan. "Présence de la littérature malgache," *Christianisme Social* [Paris], LXVIII, No. 12, December 1960, 798-805.

Decary, Raymond. "L'art des tombeaux à Madagascar," *Tropiques* [Paris], LV, No. 400, November 1957, 48-53.

— —. *La Divination Malgache par le Sikidy.* Paris: Genthner, 1970.

— —. *Moeurs et Coutumes des Malgaches.* Paris: Payot, 1951.

— —. *La Mort et les Coutumes Funéraires à Madagascar.* Paris: Maisonneuve et Larose, 1962.

Deschamps, Hubert. *Histoire de Madagascar.* Paris: Editions Berger-Levrault, 1960.

— —. *Madagascar.* (Série "Que Sais-Je?" No. 529). Paris: Presses Universitaires de France, 1968.

— —. *Les Migrations Intérieures à Madagascar, Passées et Présentes.* Paris: Editions Berger-Levrault, 1959.

— —. "La notion de peuples," *Bulletin de Madagascar* [Tananarive], XI, No. 177, February 1961. 95-98.

Deschamps, Hubert, and Vianès, Suzanne. *Les Malgaches du Sud-Est.* Paris: Presses Universitaires de France, 1959.

Deval, R. *Le Particularisme Malgache.* Paris: France, Ministry of Foreign Affairs, 1967.

Dez, Jacques. "Les conflits entre la tradition et la novation," *Bulletin de Madagascar* [Tananarive], XV, Nos. 277-228, April-May 1965, 367-392.

— —. "La figuration humaine dans le Vakinankaratra," *Revue de Madagascar* [Tananarive], XXIX, No. 1, 1965, 45-50.

— —. "L'habitat traditionel," *Bulletin de Madagascar* [Tananarive] XIX, No. 279, 701-713.

— —. "Proverbes Betsimisaraka," *Bulletin de Madagascar* [Tananarive], CCLI-CCLII, April-May 1967, 349-379.

— —. "La société rurale Malgache face aux éxigences du développement agricole," *Bulletin de Madagascar* [Tananarive], XX, No. 295, 1970, 907-964.

Domenichini-Ramiaramanana, B. "A propos d'une chanson ou du vocabulaire et de la décolonisation linguistique à Madagascar," *Revue de l'Ecole Nationale Orientale* [Tananarive], II, 1965, 99-123.

Dominjoud, M. "Les impératifs de la magie dans la vie quotidienne des Malgaches," *Bulletin de Madagascar* [Tananarive], IX, No. 135, February 1959, 151-161.

Donque, Gerald. "Les minorités chinoises et indiennes à Madagascar," *Revue Française d'Etudes Politiques Africaines* [Paris], No. 26, February 1968, 85-103.

— —. "La Population de Madagascar," *Revue Française d'Etudes Politiques Africaines* [Paris], No. 40, April 1969, 32-46.

Donque, Gerald (ed.). "Tananarive," *Notes et Etudes Documentaires* [Paris], Nos. 3529 and 3530, October 28, 1968.

Dubois, H. M. *Monographie des Betsileo*. Paris: Musée de l'Homme, 1938.

Duvelle, Charles. *Musique Malgache*. Paris: Office de Coopération Radiophonique, 1965.

Enquête Démographique, Madagascar, 1966. Malagasy Republic, Ministère des Finances et du Commerce, Institut National de la Statistique et de la Recherche Economique, 1967.

"L'enseignement à Madagascar," *Revue Française d'Etudes Politiques Africaines* [Paris]. No. 52, Avril 1970, 57-76.

"Les étudiants malgaches aussi...," *Afrique Nouvelle* [Dakar, Senegal], MXC, June 27-July 3, 1968, 6.

Europa Yearbook, 1971. London: Europa Publications, 1971.

Faublée, Jacques. *La Cohésion des Societés Bara*. Paris: Presses Universitaires de France, 1953.

— —. "Les coutumes ancestrales et leur adaptation à l'évolution," *Afrique* [Geneva], IV, No. 1, 1965. 52-54.

— —. "Les coutumes ancestrales et leur adaptation à l'évolution," *Afrique* [Geneva], IV, No. 2, 1965, 52-64.

Faublée, Marcelle, and Faublée, Jacques. "Le costume à Madagascar, hier et aujourd'hui." *Tropiques* [Paris], LI, No. 356, December 1953, 67-73.

France. Secrétariat d'Etat aux Affaires Etrangères. *Economie et Plan de Développement: République Malgache*. Paris: 1969.

Francois, Patrick. *Budgets et Alimentation des Ménages Ruraux en 1962*. 3 vols. Paris: Ministère des Finances et du Commerce, 1958.

Frère, Suzanne. *Panorama de l'Androy*. Paris: Edition Aframpe, 1958.

Garrigues, A. "Problèmes de l'artisanat rural à Madagascar: Formation artisanale et entreprises artisanales," *Terre Malgache* [Tananarive], VII, January 1970, 171-193.

Gaussin, P. R. "L'Université de Madagascar," *Europe-France Outremer* [Paris], XL, No. 405, October 1963, 21-24.

Gendreau, F. "Quelques aspects de la recherche en démographie à Madagascar," *Cahiers ORSTOM* [Paris], (Office de Recherches Scientifiques et Techniques d'Outre Mer), VI, No. 4, 1969, 93-127.

Gernboeck, Lotte. "Beitraege zur Kenntnis der Ehe-und

Familiensitten in Madagaskar," *Mitteilungen der Antropologischen Gesellschaft* [Vienna], XCV, 1965, 49-54.

Godin, C. "L'art de Madagascar," *Revue de Madagascar* [Tananarive], XXXVI, No. 4, 1966, 49-60.

"Une grande île pour une grande nation," *Missi* [Lyon, France], 1970, 300-328.

Grandidier, Alfred, and Grandidier Guillaume. *Ethnologie de Madagascar.* Paris: P. Brodard, 1908-1928.

Guilcher, André, and Battistini, René. *Madagascar: Géographie Régionale.* Paris: Centre de Documentation Universitaire, 1967.

Hardyman, James-Trenchard. "La sculpture Sakalava," (Trans., H. Day.) *Bulletin de l'Académie Malgache* [Tananarive], XLI, No. 65, 1963, 51-55.

Hébert, J. C. "Le cycle légendaire de Tandrokomana," *Revue de Madagascar* [Tananarive], XXI, No. 1, 1963, 13-26.

Hébert, M. "La parenté à plaisanterie à Madagascar," *Bulletin de Madagascar* [Tananarive], VIII, No. 142, March 1958, 178-217.

– –. "La parenté à plaisanterie à Madagascar," *Bulletin de Madagascar* [Tananarive], VIII, No. 143, April 1958, 268-335.

Henriet, M. "The Malagasy Churches Under the Sign of 'All Things New'," *International Review of Missions* [Edinburgh] LVIII, No. 229, January 1969, 107-109.

Heseltine, Nigel. *Madagascar.* New York. Praeger, 1971.

Houlder, J. A., et Noyer, H. *Proverbes Malgaches.* Tananarive: Imprimerie Luthérienne, 1959.

International Monetary Fund. "Malagasy Republic." Chapter 3 in *Surveys of African Economies*, IV, Democratic Republic of Congo, Malagasy Republic, Malawi, Mauritius, and Zambia. Washington: IMF, 1969.

International Yearbook of Education, 1969. XXXI, Paris: United Nations Educational, Scientific and Cultural Organization, International Bureau of Education, 1970.

Isnard, Henri. "Disparités régionales et unité nationale à Madagascar," *Cahiers Internationaux de Sociologie* [Paris], IX, No. 32, January-June 1962, 25-42.

Isnard, Hildebert. *Madagascar.* Paris: Librairie Armand Colin, 1955.

Kent, Raymond K. *Early Kingdoms in Madagascar, 1500-1700.* New York: Holt, Rinehart and Winston, 1970.

– –. *From Madagascar to the Malagasy Republic.* New York: Praeger, 1962.

Kitchen, Helen (ed.). *The Educated African.* New York: Praeger, 1962.

Kottak, Conrad Phillip. "Cultural Adaptation, Kinship and Descent in Madagascar," *Southwestern Journal of Anthropology*, XXVII, 1971, 194-247.

– –. "Social Groups and Kinship Calculation Among the Southern

Betsileo," *American Anthropologist*, LXXIII, No. 1, February 1971, 78-193.

Laulainé, Henri de. "De l'économie de subsistance a l'économie d'échange dans le cadre de Madagascar," *Terre Malgache* [Tananarive], V, 1969, 67-85.

Lavondès, Henri. *Bekoropoka: Quelques Aspects de la Vie Familiale et Sociale d'un Village Malgache.* The Hague: Mouton, 1969.

Linton, Ralph, "Culture Areas in Madagascar," *American Anthropologist*, XXX, No. 3, 1928, 363-390.

— —. *The Tanala: A Hill Tribe of Madagascar.* Anthropological Series, XXII, Publication No. 317.) Chicago: Natural History Museum, 1933.

McLeod, Norma. "The Status of Musical Specialists in Madagascar," *Ethnomusicology*, VIII, No. 3, 1964, 278-289.

Malagasy Republic. *Madagascar: AN X de la République (1958-1968).* Tananarive: Ministère de l'Information, 1969.

Malagasy Republic. Institut National de la Statistique et de la Recherche Economique. *Population de Madagascar, Situation au 1er Janvier 1967.* Tananarive: Ministère des Finances et du Commerce, 1967.

— —. *Population de Madagascar, Situation au 1er Janvier 1970.* Tananarive: Ministère des Finances et du Commerce, 1971.

The Malagasy Republic, Hour of Independence. New York: (UN), Service de Presse, Embassade de France, 1960.

Mannoni, Octave. "La personnalité malgache: Ebauche d'une analyse des structures," *Revue de Psychologie des Peuples* [Le Havre], III, No. 3, July 1948, 263-281.

— —. *Prospero and Caliban: The Psychology of Colonization.* New York: Praeger, 1964.

Marden, Louis. "Madagascar: Island at the End of the Earth," *National Geographic*, CXXXII, No. 4, October 1967, 443-487.

Marquandt, W. "Das Bild der Bevoelkerung Madagaskars," *Afrika Heute* [Bonn], No. 1, January 1969, 1-8.

Massiot, Michel. *L'Organisation Politique, Administrative, Financière et Judiciaire de la République Malgache.* (Série les Codes Bleus Malagaches.) Tananarive: Editions de la Librairie de Madagascar, 1970.

May, Jacques Meyer. *Studies in Medical Geography.* VIII: The Ecology of Malnutrition in the French-Speaking Countries of West Africa and Madagascar. New York: Hafner, 1968.

Michel, Louis. *Moeurs et Coutumes des Bara.* Tananarive: Institut Scientifique du Madagascar, 1957.

— —. *La Réligion des Anciens Merina.* Aix-en-Provence, France: La Pensée Universitaire, 1958.

Millot, Jacques. "Depot d'une collection Malgache choisie," *Objets et Monde* [Paris], IV, No. 1, Spring 1964, 47-72.

Molet, Louis. "Bibliographie critique recente sur Madagascar," *Canadian Journal of African Studies* [Montreal], I, No. 1, March 1967, 51-63.

— —. "Esquisse de la mentalité malgache," *Revue de Psychologie des Peuples* [Le Havre], XIV, No. 1, January 1959, 25-40.

— —. *L'Expansion Tsimihety*. Tananarive: Institut Scientifique du Madagascar. Paris: Editions Berger-Levrault, 1959.

— —. "Les manuscrits arabico-malgaches," *Revue de Madagascar* [Tananarive] III, 1957, 53-57.

— —. "Nomenclature des groupes ethniques à Madagascar," *Bulletin de Madagascar* [Tananarive], VII, No. 129, February 1957, 162-169.

— —. "Les principales populations malgaches," *Revue de Psychologie des Peuples* [Le Havre], XIV, No. 1, 1959, 41-48.

— —. "La sculpture malgache," *Revue de Madagascar* [Tananarive], I, 1958, 35-38.

Mondain, G. "Note sur les tout premiers débuts de la littérature malgache avant l'arrivee des Européens," *Bulletin de l'Académie Malgache* [Tananarive], XXVI, 1944-45, 43-48.

Mountjoy, Alan B., and Embleton, Clifford. *Africa: A New Geographical Survey*. New York: Praeger, 1967.

Neri, Italo. "Educational Television in the Service of Development," *European Broadcasting Union Review* [Geneva], CVIIIB, March 1968, 16-21.

"La nouvelle université de Tananarive," *Afrique* [Paris], XXXIII, April 1964, 35-37.

Ottino. Paul. *Les Economies Paysannes Malgaches du Bas-Mangoky*. (Série l'Homme d'Outre-Mer No. 7.) Paris: Editions Berger-Levrault, 1963.

— —. "Le Tromba," *Homme* [Paris], V, No. 1, 1965, 84-93.

Pascal, Roger. *La République Malgache*. Paris: Editions Berger-Levrault, 1965.

Poirier, Jean. "Aspects de l'urbanisation à Madagascar: les villes malgaches et la population urbaine," *Civilisations* [Brussels] XVIII, Nos. 1 and 2, 1968, 80-109, 285-298.

— —. "Les origines du peuple et de la civilisation malgaches," *Bulletin de Madagascar* [Tananarive], XVII, February 1967, 171 192.

— —. "La recensement ethno-démographique," *Terre Malgache* [Tananarive] June 1965, 129-147.

Pollock, Norman C. *Studies in Emerging Africa*. London: Butterworth, 1971.

Rabearivelo, Jean-Joseph, and Razakandraina, Dox. "Poëtes de Madagascar," *African Arts / Arts d'Afrique*, III, No. 3, Spring 1970, 64-66.

Rabemananjara, Jacques. "A Unified Madagascar Looks Ahead," *Optima* [London], XVIII No. 4, December 1968, 174-185.

Rabiaza, P. "Le mariage malgache," *Recueil Penant* [Paris], LXXX, No. 728, April-June, 1970, 133-152.

Raharijaona, H., and Ratsirahonana, N. "Le droit malgache de la famille," *Recueil Penant* [Paris], LXXVIII, No. 722, October-December 1968, 433-448.

Raison, F. "Le catholicisme malgache: passé et present," *Revue Française d'Etudes Politiques Africaines* [Paris], No. 53, May 1970, 78-98.

Rakotarivelo, Jules-Valson. "Légende de Fito," *Revue de Madagascar* [Tananarive], XXVI, 1956, 62-63.

Rakoto, Ignace. *Parenté et Mariage en Droit Traditionel Malgache.* Paris: Presses Universitaires de France, 1971.

Rakotomavo, S. "Foundations of Agriculture Seen Shaky," *France Eurafrique* [Paris], July 1970, 6-8.

Rakotonirina, Manandafy. "Transformations sociales et actions de développement rural à Madagascar," *Terre Malgache* [Tananarive], No. 4, July 1968, 85-96.

Ralibera, Remy. *Vazaha et Malgaches en Dialogue.* Tananarive: Imprimerie Catholique, 1966.

Ratsifandriahamanana, B. "Analyse sociologique," *Psychopathologie Africaine* [Dakar], III, No. 2, 1967, 279-292.

Robequain, C. *Madagascar et les Bases Dispersées de l'Union Française.* Paris: Presses Universitaires de France, 1958.

Ruud, Jørgen. *Taboo: A Study of Malagasy Customs and Beliefs.* Oslo: Oslo University Press, 1960.

Sasnett, Martena and Sepmeyer, Inez. *Educational Systems of Africa.* Berkeley: University of California Press, 1966.

Savarolles, François Jacques. "Rabemananjara; de la littérature à la politique," *Afrique* [Paris], LII, February 1966, 40.

Segre, Dan A. "Madagascar: Example of Indigenous Modernization in the 19th Century," in K. Kirkwood (ed.), *African Affairs, III, St. Anthony's Papers,* XXI. London: Oxford University Press, 1969.

Southall, Aidan. "Kinship, Descent and Residence in Madagascar," *American Anthropologist,* LXXIII, No. 1, February 1971, 144-164.

Spacensky, Alain. *Madagascar: 50 Ans de Vie Politique.* Paris: Nouvelles Editions Latines, 1970.

Statistical Yearbook, 1970. New York: United Nations Educational, Scientific and Cultural Organization, 1971.

Stratton, Arthur. *The Great Red Island.* New York: Scribner's 1964.

"Tananarive," *Notes et Documentaires* [Paris], October 28, 1968, 63-64.

Thiout, Michel. *Madagascar et l'Ame Malgache.* Paris: Horizons de France, 1961.

Thompson, Virginia, and Adloff, Richard. *The Malagasy Republic: Madagascar Today.* Stanford: Stanford University Press, 1965.

United Nations Educational, Scientific and Cultural Organization,

"Functional Literacy Project in Madagascar," *UNESCO Chronicle* [Paris], XV, No. 7 / 8, July-August 1969, 271-272.

— —. *World Survey of Education.* IV. New York: UNESCO, 1966.

United Nations, Department of Economic and Social Affairs. *Population and Vital Statistics Report,* XXIV. April 1972, 6-7.

U.S. Department of Agriculture. Economic Research Service. *Indices of Agricultural Production in Africa and the Near East.* (ERS-Foreign 265. Washington: GPO, April 1972.

U.S. Department of Commerce. Office of Technical Services. Joint Publications Research Service—JPRS (Washington). The following items are from the JPRS series *Translations on Africa:*

"Educational Ministers Plan Various Reforms—Resolutions of the Conference of Ministers of National Education," *Le Courrier de Madagascar,* Tananarive, February 29 and March 2, 1972. (JPRS: 55,660, Series No. 1,141, April 7, 1972).

"Education Minister Outlines Reforms," *Le Courrier de Madagascar,* Tananarive, October 30-31-November 1, 1971. (JPRS: 54,615, Series No. 1,088, December 3, 1971).

"French-Malagasy Scientific Research Effort...French-Malagasy Cooperation in 10 Years More than 6 Billion Malagasy Francs Devoted to Applied Scientific Research," *Info-Madagascar,* Tananarive, August 2, 1969. (JPRS: 48,766, Series No. 812, 1969).

"Madagascar Press Comments on Medical School Closing," *Lumière,* Fianarantsoa, March 26, 1972. (JPRS: 55,689, Series No. 1,143, April 12, 1972).

"Madagascar Reports Educational Progress," Press Interview with Laurent Botockeky, Minister of Cultural Affairs. *Info-Madagascar,* Tananarive, August 9, 1969. (JPRS: 48,817, Series No. 813, September 13, 1969.

"Madagascar Students' Association Holds Meeting," *Lumière,* Fianarantsoa, May 25, 1969. (JPRS: 48,317, Series No. 795, June 30, 1969).

"Medical Students' Strike Discussed," by H. Rajaona. *Lumière,* Fianarantsoa, March 12 and 19, 1972. (JPRS: 55,689, Series No. 1,143, April 12, 1972).

"Need for Educational Reform Discussed," *Lumière,* Fianarantsoa, May 30, 1971. (JPRS: 53,503, Series No. 1,047, July 1, 1971).

"News Briefs: Malagasy Publications," *Le Moniteur Africain,* Dakar, August 7, 1969. (JPRS: 48,766, Series No. 812, September 8, 1969).

"Problem of Religious Instruction in Schools," *Lumière,* Fianarantsoa, September 14, 1960. (JPRS: 49,021, Series No. 824, October 9, 1969).

"Recent Student Unrest Analyzed," by Andre' Ravatomanga.

Lumière, Fianarantsoa, May 7,1972. (JPRS: 56,191, Series No. 1,168, June 6, 1972).
"Significance of Student Strikes Analyzed," by André Ravatomanga. *Lumière*, Fianarantsoa, April 30, 1972. (JPRS: 56,103, Series No. 1,162, May 25, 1972).
"Statistics on University Enrollment," *Lumière*, Fianarantsoa, January 23, 1972. (JPRS: 55,280, Series No. 1,122, 1972).
"Structural and Program Reforms Proposed for University," *Marchés Tropicaux et Méditerranéens*, Paris, February 25, 1972. (JPRS: L / 4106, Series No. 284, March 27, 1972.
U.S. Department of State. *Background Notes: Malagasy Republic.* Washington: 1968.
— —. *Madagascar Post Report.* Washington: 1970.
U.S. Department of State. Agency for International Development. Office of Statistics and Reports. *Africa, Economic Growth Trends.* Washington: AID, 1972.
Urfer, S. *Approche de la Civilisation Malgache.* Paris: Centre de Hautes Etudes Administratives sur l'Afrique et l'Asie Modernes, 1969.
Valmy, R. "Orfèvres et bijoux malgaches," *Revue de Madagascar* [Tananarive], II, 1958, 38-46.
Weiss, Louise. "Les tombeaux mahafaly," *Connaissance du Monde* [Paris], XIV, No. 75, 1965, 29-36.
Wislon, Peter J. "Sentimental Structure: Tsimihety Migration and Descent," *American Anthropologist*, LXXIII, No. 1, February 1971, 193-207.
World Health Statistics Annual for 1968. Geneva: World Health Organization, 1971.
The World of Learning, 1970-71. (21st ed.) London: Europa Publications, 1971.
World Survey of Education, V. Paris: United Nations Educational, Scientific and Cultural Organization, 1971.
Yearbook of International Organizations, 1968-69. Brussels: Union of International Associations, 1969.

Section II. Political

Ainslie, Rosalynde. *The Press in Africa.* New York: Walker, 1967.

Allen, Philip M. "Madagascar and OCAM: The Insular Approach to Regionalism," *Africa Report*, XI, No. 1, January 1966, 13-18.

— —. "Malagasy Non-Succession," *Africa Report*, XVI, No. 4, May 1971, 9-10.

— —. "Rites of Passage in Madagascar," *Africa Report*, XCI, No. 2, February 1971, 24-27.

— —. "Self-Determination in the Western Indian Ocean," *International Conciliation*, No. 560, November 1966, 5-74.

Althabe, Gérard. "Les manifestations paysannes d'avril 1971," *Revue Française d'Etudes Politiques Africaines* [Paris], June 1972, No. 78, June 1972, 71-77.

"L'attitude des églises Malgaches face à la situation politique," *Revue Française d'Etudes Politiques Africaines* [Paris], No. 72, December 1971, 85-89.

"Constitution of the Republic of Madagascar (Text of 27 December 1962)," *Constitutional and Parliamentary Information* [Geneva], Third Series, No. 61, 1965, 30-49.

Delacourt, A. "Les relations extérieures de Madagascar," *Revue Française d'Etudes Politiques Africaines* [Paris], No. 40, April 1969, 47-66.

Donque, Gerald. "Les minorités chinoises et indiennes à Madagascar," *Revue Française d'Etudes Politiques Africaines* [Paris], No. 26, February 1968, 85-103.

Donque, Gerald (ed.). "Tananarive," *Notes et Etudes Documentaires* [Paris], Nos. 3529-3530, October 28, 1968.

Dumon, F. *La Communauté Franco-Malgache, ses Origines, ses Institutions, son Evolution, Octobre 1958-Juin 1960.* Brussels: Institut de Sociologie Solvay, 1960.

Editor and Publisher International Yearbook, 1970. New York: Editor and Publisher, 1970.

"Evolution of Madagascar Since Independence," *Asian Review* [London], LVIII, No. 213, January 1962, 27-49.

Hachten, William. *Muffled Drums: The News Media in Africa.* Ames: Iowa State University Press, 1971.

"Jacques Rabemananjara: Madagascar n'est pas pauvre, mais en totale dépendence économique," (Interview with Malagasy Minister of Foreign Affairs.) *Jeune Afrique* [Paris], August 26-September 1, 1968, 22-24.

Leymarie, Philippe. "Madagascar—ce n'etait qu'un début...," *Revue Française d'Etudes Politiques Africaines* [Paris], No. 79, July 1972, 29-33.

— —. "Madagascar: La tentation Sud-Africaine," *Revue Française d'Etudes Politiques Africaines* (Paris), No. 48, December 1969, 22-25.

"Links Broken," *African Research Bulletin* [Exeter, England], IX, No. 6, July 14, 1972, 2406c.

"Madagascar an VIII," *Jeune Afrique* [Paris], No. 307, November 27, 1966, 36-51.

"Madagascar: Cutting Free from Mother France," *African Development* [London], August 1969, 24-25.

"Madagascar," *Europe-France Outre-Mer* [Paris], XLIII, July-August 1966.

"Madagascar," *Marchés Tropicaux et Meditérranéens* [Paris], XXVIII, No. 1,393, July 21, 1972, 2198-2199.

"Madagascar: New Member of the United Nations," *World Today* [London], March 1961, 123-124.

"Madagascar," Pages 148-157 in Colin Legum (ed.), *African Contemporary Record: Annual Survey and Documents, 1971-72*, London: Rex Collings, 1972.

Maestre, Jean C. "Aspects originaux de la fonction publique Malgache," *International Review of Administrative Sciences* [Brussels], XXXIII, No. 3, 1967, 185-226.

Malagasy Republic. *Madagascar: AN X de la République [1958-1968]*. Tananarive: Ministère de l'Information, 1969.

Malagasy Republic. Commissariat Général au Plan. *Inventaire Socio-Economique de Madagascar, 1964-1968*. Tananarive: Ministère des Finances et du Commerce, 1969.

Malembe, Paul. *Le Panafricanisme et le Regroupement des Etats Africans et Malgaches de Langue Française*. Louvain: Université Catholique, 1965.

Massiot, Michel. *L'Organisation Politique, Administrative, Financière et Judiciaire de la République Malgache*. (Série Les Codes Bleus Malgaches.) Tananarive: Editions de la Librairie de Madagascar, 1970.

Merrill, John; Bryan, Carter R.; and Alasky, Arvin. *The Foreign Press*. Baton Rouge: Louisiana State University Press, 1966.

Molet, Louis. "Sources et tendences du droit moderne à Madagascar," *Canadian Journal of African Studies* (Montreal), I, No. 3, November 1967, 123-134.

Pascal, Roger. *La République Malgache*. Paris: Editions Berger-Levrault, 1965.

Pautard, André. "Madagascar, une révolution ambigue," *Revue Française d'Etudes Politiques Africaines* [Paris], No. 78, June 1972, 3-6.

"Le poids de l'assistance technique," *Revue Française d'Etudes Politiques Africaines* [Paris], No. 78, June 1972, 64-68.

Rakotmalala, Paile-Robert. "La presse Malgache et les partis d'opposition," *Lumière* [Fianarantsoa], XXI, No. 1,514, April 11 and 15, 1965.

"Rapport sur Madagascar," *Temps Modernes* [Paris], XXVII, No. 301-302, August-September 1971, 87-121.

"Les relations entre l'URSS et Madagascar," *Afrique Nouvelle-* [Dakar, Senegal], No. 1,071, 1968, 6.

"La République Malgache," *Revue Française d'Etudes Politiques Africaines* [Paris], No. 78, June 1972, 44-118.

Richards, Audrey, and Kuper, Adam. *Councils in Action.* London: Cambridge University Press, 1971.

Ruud, Jørgen. *Taboo: A Study of Malagasy Customs and Beliefs.* Oslo: Oslo University Press, 1960.

Slawecki, Leon M.S. *French Policy Toward the Chinese in Madagascar.* Hamden, Connecticut: Shoe String Press, 1971.

Spacensky, Alain. "Dix ans de rapports Franco-Malgaches (1960-70)," *Revue Française d'Etudes Politiques Africaines* [Paris], No. 60, December 1970, 77-92.

— —. *Madagascar: 50 Ans de Vie Politique.* Paris: Nouvelles Editions Latines, 1970.

Thompson, Virginia. "Madagascar." Pages 449-464 in *Africa South of the Sahara, 1972.* London: Europa Publications, 1972.

Thompson, Virginia, and Adloff, Richard. *The Malagasy Republic: Madagascar Today.* Stanford: Stanford University Press, 1965.

United Nations Educational, Scientific and Cultural Organization. *World Communications: Press, Radio, Television, Film.* Paris: UNESCO, 1964.

U.S. Department of Commerce. Office of Technical Services. Joint Publications Research Service—JPRS (Washington). The following items are from the JPRS series *Translations on Africa:*

"Afro-Malagasy Telecommunications Union Meets," *Jeune Afrique* Paris, May 1969. (JPRS: 48,188, Series No. 789, 1969).

"AKFM Demands Freedom of the Press," *La Presse Malgache,* Tananarive, February 1972. (JPRS: 55,765, Series No. 1,147, 1972).

"Breaking Diplomatic Relations with United States Advocated," *Maresaka,* Tananarive, February 7, 1972. (JPRS: 55,372, Series No. 1,127, 1972).

"Commentary on Dialogue with South Africa," by Pierre Nassara. *Lumière,* Fianarantsoa, January 16, 1972. (JPRS: 55,183, Series No. 1,117, 1972).

"Commentary on Relations with China and South Africa," *La Presse Malgache,* Tananarive, March 3, 1972. (JPRS: 55,639, Series No. 1,140, 1972).

"Commentary on U.S.-Chinese Relations," *La Presse Malgache,*

Tananarive, March 8, 1972. (JPRS: 55,639, Series No. 1,140, 1972.

"Communiqué on International Affairs by AKFM," *Tananarive*, March 8, 1972. (JPRS: 55,803, Series No. 1,149, 1972).

"Concept of Full Powers," *Lumière*, Fianarantsoa, May 28, 1972. (JPRS: 56,369, Series No. 1,176, June 27, 1972).

"Demanding Break with U.S. to Remove Suspected CIA Activities," *La Presse Malgache*, Tananarive, June 16, 1972. (JPRS: 53,893, Series No. 1,061, August 24, 1971).

"Economies Realized Through Elimination of Ministries," *Maraina Vaovao*, Tananarive, June 7, 1972. (JPRS: 56,439, Series No. 1,198, 1972).

"Expulsion of Radio-Netherlands Demanded," *Hita Sy Re*, Tananarive, February 22, 1972. (JPRS: 55,765, Series No. 1,147, 1972).

"General Ramanantsoa's Address to the Nation," *Madagascar Matin*, Tananarive, July 28, 1972. (JPRS: 56,941, Series No. 1,209, 1972).

"Government Seizure of Newspaper Reported," *Basy Vava*, Tananarive, February 1, 1972. (JPRS: 55,482, Series No. 1,133, 1972).

"Improvement of U.S.-Malagasy Relations Discussed," *Basy Vava*, Tananarive, March 2, 1972. (JPRS: 55,803, Series No. 1,149, 1972).

"Indians Criticized for Amassing Wealth in Madagascar," by Gaby Ramananjato. *Basy Vava*, Tananarive, June 8, 1972. (JPRS: 56,439, Series No. 1,180, July 6, 1972).

"Information Minister Discusses Press, Television," Le Courrier de Madagascar, Tananarive, March 5, 1970. (JPRS: 50,238, Series No. 885, 1970).

"Madagascar Nears a Predictably Difficult Succession," by François Partant. *Le Monde Diplomatique*, Paris, February 1972. (JPRS: 55,457, Series No. 1,134, March 21, 1972).

"Malagasy Foreign Minister Discusses Negritude," by Rangers Latimer. An Interview with Jacques Rabemananjara. *Jenue Afrique*, Paris, July 7-13, 1969. (JPRS: 48,594, Series No. 806, 1969).

"Minister Discusses National Radio Chain Merger...Merger of Two Radio Chains—Cultural But Also Economic Measure," *Le Courrier de Madagascar*, Tananarive, 1970. (JPRS: 51,343, Series No. 940, 1970).

"Official Disappointed in Soviet Trip," *Le Courrier de Madagascar*, Tananarive, August 25, 1970. (JPRS: 51,236, Series No. 936, 1970).

"Opposition Newspaper Attacks U.S. Presence," *Imongo*

Vaovao, Tananarive, June 10, 1970. (JPRS: 51,046, Series No. 924, 1970).

"Paper Demands Freedom of Press," *Hita Sy Re*, Tananarive, February 1972. (JPRS: 55,482, Series No. 1,133, 1972).

"Press Association Protests Seizure of Newspapers," *Le Presse Malgache*, Tananarive, March 1972. (JPRS. 55,765, Series No. 1,147, 1972).

"Revision of French Cooperation Accords Urged," by Philippe DeCraene. *Le Monde*, Paris, July 22, 1972. (JPRS: 56,721, Series No. 1,198, 1972).

"SECES Communiqué Protests the Jailing of Two of Its Members," *Le Presse Malgache*, Tananarive, December 1971. (JPRS: 55,129, Series No. 1,114, 1972).

"Seizure of Independent Paper Denounced," *Maresaka*, Tananarive, January 1972. (JPRS: 55,482, Series No. 1,133, 1972).

"Student Crisis Discussed from Three Viewpoints," *Réalités Malgaches*, Tananarive, June 1-15, 1972. (JPRS: 56,414, Series No. 1,178, 1972).

"Survey of Madagascar's Foreign Relations," by Antoine Delacourt, *Revue Française d'Etudes Politiques Africaines*, Tananarive, April 1969. (JPRS: 48, 378, Series No. 797, July 9, 1969).

"Ten Years of Independence Assessed," *Lumière*, Fianarantsoa, June 28, 1970. (JPRS: 51,097, Series No. 928, 1970).

U.S. Department of State. Tracking Stations: Agreement Between the United States of America and the Malagasy Republic Amending Agreement of October 7, 1963 (U.S. Treaties...1963-69 L.B.J.). (Series No. 6,024, Treaties and other International Acts.) Washington: GPO, 1966.

U.S. United States Information Agency. Office of Policy and Research. *Communications Data Book for Africa*. Washington: USIA, August 1966.

Valette, Jean. *Malagasy Foreign Relations in the Nineteenth Century*. Tananarive: Imprimerie Nationale, 1965.

World Radio-TV Handbook, 1972. (Ed., J. M. Frost.) Hvidovre, Denmark: World Radio-TV Handbook. 1972.

Yearbook of International Organizations, 1968-69. Brussels: Union of International Associations, 1969.

Section III. Economic

Bastian, Georges. *Madagascar: Etude Géographique et Economique.* Tananarive: Fernand Nathan, 1967.

Cadoux, Charles. *La République Malgache.* Paris: Editions Berger-Levrault, 1972.

Combaz-Fauquel, André. "Situation et perspectives associatives de l'animation rurale malgache," *Développement et Civilisations* [Paris], XXXIX / XL, 1970, 132-145.

Deschamps, Hubert. *Madagascar.* (Série "Que Sais-Je?" No. 529). Paris: Presses Universitaires de France, 1968.

Dez, Jacques. "Les conflits entre la tradition et la novation," *Bulletin de Madagascar* [Tananarive], XV, Nos. 227-228, April-May 1965, 367-392.

— —. "A propos de la méthode ameliorée de riziculture," *Bulletin de Madagascar* [Tananarive], XIX, No. 273, February 1969, 170-180.

— —. "La société rurale malgache face aux éxigences du développement agricole," *Bulletin de Madagascar* [Tananarive], XX, No. 295, 1970, 907-964.

Eberle, Carmen-Maria. *Madagaskar als Wirtschaftspartner.* Cologne: Bundesstelle für Aussenhandelsinformation, 1970.

Europa Year Book, 1972. London: Europa Publications, 1972.

France. Secrétariat d'Etat aux Affaires Etrangères. *Economie et Plan de Développement: République Malgache.* Paris: 1969.

— —. *Madagascar 1969-1970: Dossier d'Information Economique.* Paris: Direction de l'Aide au Développement, August 1971.

François, Patrick. *Budgets et Alimentation des Ménages Ruraux en 1962.* 3 vols. Paris: Ministère des Finances et du Commerce, 1958.

Guilcher, André, and Battistini, René. *Madagascar: Géographie Régionale.* Paris: Centre de Documentation Universitaire, 1967.

Heseltine, Nigel. *Madagascar.* New York: Praeger, 1971.

International Bank for Reconstruction and Development. *World Tables, 1971.* Washington: IBRD, 1969.

International Monetary Fund. "Malagasy Republic." Chapter 3 in *Surveys of African Economies*, IV: Democratic Republic of Congo, Malagasy Republic, Malawi, Mauritius, and Zambia. Washington: IMF, 1969.

Koerner, Francis. "Les types de sociétés agricoles privées à Madagascar," *Cahiers d'Outre-Mer* [Bordeaux], XXI, No. 83, 1968, 276-297.

Laulanié, Henri de. "De l'économie de subsistance à l'économie d'échange dans le cadre de Madagascar," *Terre Malgache* [Tananarive], V, 1969, 67-85.

Legum, Colin (ed.). *Africa Contemporary Record: Annual Survey and Documents, 1971-1972.* London: Rex Collings, 1972.

Malagasy Republic. Commissariat Général au Plan. *Premier Rapport sur l'Exécution du Plan Quinquennal (1964-1968).* Tananarive: n. pub., October 1965.

Malagasy Republic. Institut National de la Statistique et de la Recherche Economique. *Enquête Agricole.* Tananarive: Imprimerie Nationale, 1966.

— —. *Enquête Démographique, Madagascar, 1966.* Tananarive: n. pub., 1967.

— —. *Inventaire Socio-Economique de Madagascar, 1960-65.* I and II. Tananarive: Ministère de Finances et du Commerce, 1966.

— —. *Inventaire Socio-Economique de Madagascar, 1964-68.* Tananarive: Ministère de Finances et du Commerce, 1969.

Massiot, Michel. *L'Organisation Politique, Administrative, Financière et Judiciaire de la République Malgache.* (Série Les Codes Bleus Malgaches.) Tananarive: Editions de la Librairie de Madagascar, 1970.

Ottino, Paul. *Les Economies Paysannes Malgaches du Bas-Mangoky.* (Série L'Homme d'Outre-Mer No. 7.) Paris: Editions Berger-Levrault, 1963.

Pautard, J. "Possibilités de dynamisme interne dans l'agriculture malgache," *Economies et Sociétés* [Paris], I, February 2, 1967, 87-104.

"La production agricole malgache à la fin du 1er plan quinquennal," *Revue du Ministère de l'Agriculture, de l'Expansion Rurale et du Revitaillement* [Tananarive], 3rd year, No. 9, September-October 1969, 2-19.

Production Yearbook, 1970. Rome: Food and Agriculture Organization of the United Nations, 1971.

Rabemananjara, Jacques. "A Unified Madagascar Looks Ahead," *Optima* [Johannesburg], XVIII, No. 4, December 1968, 174-185.

Rakoto, Hervé. "L'économie malgache, ou quatre ans d'exécution du premier plan quinquennal," *Revue Française d'Etudes Politiques Africaines* [Paris], No. 41, May 1969, 66-105.

Rakotonirina, Manandafy. "Transformations sociales et actions de développement rural à Madagascar," *Terre Malgache* [Tananarive], No. 4, July 1968, 85-96.

Rangers, Latimer. "Madagascar: rien n'est joué," *Jeune Afrique* [Paris], No. 605, August 12, 1972, 26-27.

Rouveyran, Jean-Claude. "Dimension des unités de production agricole et politique agricole à Madagascar," *Economie Rurale* [Paris], LXXXVIII, 1971, 59-62.

Stratton, Arthur. *The Great Red Island.* New York: Scribner's, 1964.

Thompson, Virginia, and Adloff, Richard. *The Malagasy Republic: Madagascar Today.* Stanford: Stanford University Press, 1965

U.S. Department of Agriculture. Economic Research Service. *Indices of Agricultural Production in Africa and the Near East.* (ERS-Foreign 265.) Washington: GPO, April 1972.

— —. *Malagasy Republic's Agricultural Economy in Brief,* by Fred de Giorgio. (ERS-Foreign 290.) Washington: GPO, February 1970.

U.S. Department of Commerce. Office of Technical Services. Joint Publications Research Service—JPRS (Washington). The following items are from the JPRS series *Translations on Africa:*

"Agriculture Minister Bars Rice Mill Takeover Now," *Le Courrier de Madagascar,* Tananarive, May 21, 1969. (JPRS: 47,849, Series No. 786, 1969).

"Andriamena Chromium Mine Inaugurated," *Le Courrier de Madagascar,* Tananarive, July 1, 1970. (JPRS: 51,126, Series No. 930, 1970).

"Budget for 1972 Shows Substantial Increase," *Marchés Tropicaux et Méditerranéens,* Paris, February 25, 1972. (JPRS: 44,106, Series No. 284, 1972).

"Cause for Optimism, Concern After 10 Years' Independence," *France Eurafrique,* Paris, July 1970. (JPRS: 51,304, Series No. 938, 1970).

"Critique of National Development Charter," *Réalités Malgaches,* Tananarive, March 1972. (JPRS: 55,668, Series No. 1,137, 1972).

"Development of the Androy Discussed," *Lumière,* Fianarantsoa, April 16, 1972. (JPRS: 55,996, Series No. 1,157, 1972).

"Economic Problems of Southern Madagascar Reviewed," *Lumière,* Fianarantsoa, April 11, 1971. (JPRS: 53,320, Series No. 1,042, 1971).

"Efforts To Place More Malagasies in Economy Discussed," *La République,* Tananarive, March 3, 1972. (JPRS: 55,639, Series No. 1,140, 1972).

"Financial Steps Taken To Improve Development," *Le Moniteur Africain,* Dakar, February 20, 1969. (JPRS: 47,849, Series No. 776, 1969).

"Former Budget Director Discusses National Growth," *Le Courrier de Madagascar,* Tananarive, March 19, 1970. (JPRS: 50,409, Series No. 894, 1970).

"Foundations of Agriculture Seen Shaky," *France Eurafrique,* Paris, July 1970. (JPRS: 51,304, Series No. 938, 1970).

"Government Cooperative Program Discussed," *La Presse Malgache,* Tananarive, January 31, 1972. (JPRS: 55,372, Series No. 1,127, 1972).

"Key National Development Forces Outline Priorities," *Info-Madagascar,* Tananarive, May 16, 1971. (JPRS: 53,556, Series No. 1,050, 1971).

"Madagascar Road Transport System Described," *Info-*

Madagascar, Tananarive, June 14, 1969. (JPRS: 48,449, Series No. 801, 1969).

"Malagasy Economy Can Survive Without French Aid," *Zaire*, Kinshasa, March 10, 1969. (JPRS: 47,793, Series No. 775, 1969.)

"Many Agricultural Development Organs Active," *Lumière*, Fianarantsoa, September 13, 1970. (JPRS: 51,501, Series No. 949, 1970).

"Mining Activity and Exploration Reviewed," *Le Moniteur Africain*, Dakar, May 25, 1972. (JPRS: 56,518, Series No. 1,185, 1972).

"New Projects Approved Under Second FED Program," *Info-Madagascar*, Tananarive, July 19, 1969. (JPRS: 48,725, Series No. 810, 1969).

"Planning Minister Discusses Economic Development," *Le Courrier de Madagascar*, Tananarive, March 11-15, 1970. (JPRS: 50,409, Series No. 894, 1970).

"President Issues Directives for Rural Development," *Le Courrier de Madagascar*, Tananarive, December 5, 1970. (JPRS: 52,269, Series No. 988, 1971).

"Progress of Agriculture Training Program Reported," *Le Courrier de Madagascar*, Tananarive, July 18-20, 1970. (JPRS: 51,204, Series No. 934, 1970).

"Project To Develop the Andapa Region Studies," *Lumière*, Fianarantsoa, February 22, 1970. (JPRS: 50,140, Series No. 879, 1970).

"Report on Development of State Farms," *Lumière*, Fianarantsoa, May 16, 1971. (JPRS: 53,358, Series No. 1,043, 1971).

"Report on Malagasy Business Enterprises," *Lumière*, Fianarantsoa, February 22, 1970. (JPRS: 50,140, Series No. 879, 1970).

"Southern Reforestation Development Seen Feasible," *Info-Madagascar*, Tananarive, March 18, 1972. (JPRS: 55,765, Series No. 1,147, 1972).

"State of Economy Since Independence Studied," *Lumière*, Fianarantsoa, July 5, 1970. (JPRS: 51,097, Series No. 928, 1970).

"Survey of European Aid to Road Construction," *Le Moniteur Africain*, Dakar, January 30, 1969. (JPRS: 47,849, Series No. 776, 1969).

"Ten Years of French-Malagasy Cooperation Reviewed," *Info-Madagascar*, Tananarive, July 11, 1970. (JPRS: 51,204, Series No. 934, 1970).

"Varied Sources of Native Income Analyzed," *Lumière*,

Fianarantsoa, August 23, 1970. (JPRS: 51,378, Series No. 942, 1970).

(Various issues of the following periodicals were also used in the preparation of this section: *Africa: An International Business, Economic and Political Monthly* [London]; *Africa Research Bulletin* [London], January 1969-August 1972; *Economist Intelligence Unit Quarterly Economic Review: Former French Equatorial Africa, Cameroun, Malagasy Republic* [London], No. 1, 1970-No. 2, 1972; *Jeune Afrique* [Paris], January 1971-July 1972; *Marchés Tropicaux et Méditerranéens* [Paris], January 1969-July 1972.)

Section IV. National Security

Bernetel, Paul. "Les Orphelins de Tananarive," *Jeune Afrique* [Paris], No. 595, June 3, 1972, 20-21.

Diallo, Siradiou. "Madagascar: A Change Overdue," *Africa* (London), No. 11, June 1972, 24-25.

Dupuy, Trevor N. *The Almanac of World Military Power*. Dunn Loring, Virginia: T. N. Dupuy Associates, 1970.

Heseltine, Nigel. *Madagascar*. New York: Praeger, 1971.

Jukes, Geoffrey. *The Indian Ocean in Soviet Naval Policy*. (Adelphi Papers No. 87.) London: International Institute for Strategic Studies, May 1972.

"Madagascar—Changes of Government," *Africa Research Bulletin* [London], IX, No. 5, May 1972, 2476-2478.

"Madagascar—Tsirinana Abdicates," *West Africa*]London], No. 2,868, June 2, 1972, 708.

Malagasy Republic. Laws, Statutes, etc. *Code Pénal*. Tananarive: Editions de la Librairie de Madagascar, 1965.

Malagasy Republic. *Madagascar: AN X de la République (1958-1968)*. Tananarive: Ministère de l'Information, 1969.

Masssiot, Michel. *L'Organisation Politique, Administrative, Financière et Judiciaire de la République Malgache*. (Série Les Codes Bleus Malgaches.) Tananarive: Editions de la Librairie de Madagascar, 1970.

The Military Balance, 1971-1972. London: International Institute for Strategic Studies, 1971.

Millar, T. B. *The Indian and Pacific Oceans: Some Strategic Considerations*. (Adelphi Papers No. 57.) London: International Institute for Strategic Studies, May 1969.

Pascal, Roger. *La République Malgache*. Paris: Editions Berger-Levrault, 1965.

"Revue de droits des pays d'Afrique," *Recueil Penant*. [Paris], LXXIV, Nos. 703-704, October-November-December, 1964, 441-451.

"Running from Office," *New York Times*, May 21, 1972.

Salacuse, Jeswald W. *An Introduction to Law in French-Speaking Africa*, I. Charlottesville, Virginia: Michie, 1969.

"Le Service Civique," *Bulletin de Madagascar* [Tananarive], XV, No. 231, August 1965, 731.

"Strife in Madagascar," *New York Times*, May 25, 1972.

Thiout, Michel. *Madagascar et l'Ame Malgache*. Paris: Horizons de France, 1961.

Thompson, Virginia and Adloff, Richard. *The Malagasy Republic:*

Madagascar Today. Stanford: Stanford University Press, 1965.

U.S. Arms Control and Disarmament Agency. *World Military Expenditures, 1969, and Related Data.* Washington: ACDA, 1969.

U.S. Department of Commerce. Office of Technical Services. Joint Publications Research Service—JPRS (Washington). The following items are from the JPRS series *Translations on Africa.*

"Malagasy Foreign Minister Discusses Negritude; An Interview with Jacques Rabemananjara," by Rangers Latimer. *Jeune Afrique,* Paris, July 7-13, 1969. (JPRS: 48,594, Series No. 806, 1969).

"Revision of French Cooperation Accords Urged," by Philippe DeCraene. *Le Monde,* Paris, July 22, 1972. (JPRS: 56,721, Series No. 1,198, 1972).

GLOSSARY

AKFM—Ankoton'ny Kongresi'ny Fahaleovantenan Madagaskara (Party of the Congress for the Independence of Madagascar). The major political opposition party during the 1960-72 period.

baiboho—Malagasy term of the Sakalava people, meaning fertile alluvial deposits of soil left by river floods.

côtiers—Literally, "coastal people." In Madagascar the French term is used in a wider sense to include all peoples not living in the Central Highlands.

extended family—A husband, his wife (or wives), his children, and his married sons and their wives and children.

fady—Malagasy for taboo.

famadihana—Traditional ceremony of exhumation of dead ancestors includes washing, reclothing, and reburial of the remains.

fihavanana—Malagasy term conveying ties of kinship and a sense of friendship, tolerance, and human brotherhood.

fokon'olona.—Historically, the basic unit of local government under early Merina monarchies. Traditionally, an organization or council composed of the heads of all households of the village or hamlet; originally all were members of the same kinship group. In modern times membership often includes people who are not actually kinsmen but who are *mpifakatiavana* (*q.v.*).

French Community—A politicoeconomic association of France and its former overseas possessions. Formed in 1958, it replaced the French Union, which was the successor of the French colonial empire. Initially African members included the autonomous states of Senegal, Mali, Mauritania, Upper Volta, Dahomey, Ivory Coast, Niger, Central African Republic, Gabon, Republic of the Congo, Chad, and Malagasy Republic. After independence, however, only Senegal, Gabon, Congo (Brazzaville), Central African Republic, Chad, and Malagasy Republic maintained membership. Although the association continued to exist in 1972, all of its institutions had ceased to function.

GDP—Gross domestic product. The total value of productive activity occurring within the national borders, theoretically obtained by adding up the estimated value added by each productive sector in the economy. The value added by each producer is identically equivalent to actual or imputed wages, profits, and other incomes payable for factor services. GDP differs from gross national product (GNP), which excludes the value net factor payments to nonresidents (interest, profits, and salary remittances). Monetary GDP excludes the imputed value of subsistence production.

317

Imerina—Traditional homeland of the Merina ethnic group.

KIM—Komity Iombonan'ny Mpitolona (Joint Struggle Committee). Political activist group formed in May 1972 to campaign for social, political, and economic reforms.

Malagasy franc (FMG)—Basic Malagasy monetary unit, which is linked to the French franc (FMG50 equal 1 French franc). First introduced in 1962, the Malagasy franc is divided into 100 centimes. Until August 10, 1969, the rate of exchange was FMG246.8 per US$1. From August 10, 1969, through November 1971, the rate was FMG277.7 per US$1. Beginning in December 1971, the rate became FMG255.8 per US$1.

Merina—Largest Malagasy ethnic group. The term, however, is often used to include other peoples who inhabit the Central Highlands, such as the Betsileo and the Sihanaka, because of their long association with the Merina.

mpifakatiavana—Quasi-kinsmen. Literally, "people who love each other."

nuclear family—A man, his wife, and their unmarried children.

PSD—Parti Social Démocratique (Social Democratic Party). The ruling political party led by President Philibert Tsiranana from 1960 to 1972.

sikidi—Method of divining the future and determing the best course of action. Introduced by Arabs from the Comoro Islands; practiced by the Antaimoro.

tavy—Traditional practice of fertilizing the land by burning off the natural vegetation; slash-and-burn cultivation.

tsiny—Guilt, blame.

vazaha—Malagasy term, denoting Europeans in general and the French in particular.

World Bank Group—Consists of the International Bank for Reconstruction and Development (IBRD) and its two financial affiliates, the International Finance Corporation (IFC), which became operational in 1956, and the International Development Association (IDA), which became operational in 1960. IFC works specifically with the private sector in developing countries, and IDA operates in the same sectors and with the same policies as the IBRD but provides credits only to the poorer developing countries and on easier terms than conventional IBRD loans.

INDEX

Mexico: 196
mica: 42
middle class: 87, 97
migrations: internal, 2, 53, 55-56, 59, 61, 63, 66, 67, 69, 70, 75, 79, 99, 102, 104, 235; with outer islands, 71, 74
mining: 178, 201, 203, 218, 223, 233, 267-268; minerals, 6, 42-44
military academy: 277, 281
ministries: 136
Ministry of Agriculture: 112, 244, 280
Ministry of Agriculture, Rural Expansion and Food Supply: 247
Ministry of Cultural Affairs: 112, 113, 117
Ministry of Finance: 210
Ministry of Information: 159
Ministry of Information, Tourism, and Traditional Arts: 136, 186, 188, 195
Ministry of Interior: 137, 165, 186, 210, 244
Ministry of Justice: 137
Ministry of Labor and Social Affairs: 107
Ministry of Public Works: 208, 287
mixed economy enterprises: 198, 218, 244, 249-253
monopolies, government: 210, 218, 260, 270, 272
Morondava region: xiv, 244, 250, 253
mortality rates: 53
motor vehicles: 98, 230, 232
mountains: vii, 33, 34
museums: 132
music and dance: 120, 123
Muslims: vii, 11, 61, 65, 68, 73, 74, 75, 89, 90, 102, 179
name, official: v
Narinda, Bay of: 220, 231
Natai, Jean Jacques: 156
National Gendarmerie: x, 136, 273, 276, 277, 278-279, 281, 282, 286, 288
National Investment Corporation: 156
National Library: 131
National Malagasy Union: 26, 27
National Movement for the Independence of Malagasy (MONIMA): 151, 152, 161, 162, 163, 165, 286, 287, 290
national security: x, 136, 273-291
Nationalist Youth party: 24
nationalization of the economy: 155, 164, 223
natural disasters (see also.cyclones): 32, 41, 71

Neo-RNM Party: 162
Netherlands: 170, 175, 190, 226
newspapers (see also censorship): ix, 20, 23, 185-187, 190-194, 287; of political parties, 159, 192, 193
Nixon, President Richard: 179
Nosy Be: xiv, 16, 34, 39, 49, 52, 70, 143, 272; agriculture, 260; prison, 285
Nosy Lava: 285, 287
Nosy Mitsio: 34
Ny Antasly Trio: 124
Office of Scientific and Technical Research Overseas (ORSTOM): 130, 131, 132, 166, 286
old age: 87, 92, 93, 108
Olivier, Marcel: 19
Onilahy River: 34
Organization of African Unity (OAU): ix, 7, 172, 181
outrigger canoes: 2, 10, 265
painting: 124
Pangalanes Canal: 34, 48, 49
Party for the Union of the Malagasy People (PUPM): 25, 27
Party of the Congress for the Independence of Madagascar (AKFM): 27, 28, 29, 150, 151, 152, 159, 160, 162, 163, 164, 167, 174, 176, 208, 289; press, 192, 194
Party of the Malagasy Disinherited: 22
Pasteur Institute: 105, 131
penal code: 273, 283
periodicals and journals: 129, 191, 192, 193, 194
petroleum: 44, 222; oil exploration, 267, 268; refinery: 269, 270, 271, 272
Philippines: 180
pirates: 12, 13
Poland: 177
police: x, 136, 273, 279
political organizations (see also.Party of the Congress for the Independence of Madagascar: Social Democratic Party of Madagascar): 19-29 passim,.137, 149-168
polygamy: 83
population: vii, 2, 52-56, 199, 218: density, 49, 51; ethnic composition, 61, 74, 75; growth, 62, 96, 203, 257; homelands of peoples, 60
ports and harbors (see also Diégo-Suarez Province): ix, 20, 31, 32, 49, 210, 227, 229, 230
Portuguese: 11

social values: 92-94, 155
soils: 31, 33, 35, 41, 42, 43, 52, 228, 236
Soucadaux, André: 25
South Africa, Republic of: 7, 169, 171, 178, 220, 231
South Korea: 170, 171
South Vietnam: 181
Soviet Union: x, 7, 160, 161, 177-178
state farms: 156, 239, 244
students: associations, 118, 119; in politics, 118-120, 150, 159, 160, 166, 167, 168, 274, 287, 289
Suez Canal: 224, 231, 275
sugarcane: 218, 226, 228, 234, 237, 255, 263, 272
Switzerland: 170

taboos and sanctions: 79, 91-93, 98, 104
Tamatave Province: 40, 95, 163-164, 191, 232; agriculture, 250; ethnic groups, 64, 75; labor force, 204; population, 53, 55, 56, 83; port, 20, 47, 49, 51, 231; refinery, 271, 272
Tanala people: 60, 61, 64, 67, 77, 241
Tanala Menabe: 67
Tanalana people: 73
Tananarive Province: vii, xiv, 2, 3, 20, 31, 51-52, 95, 97, 102, 107; agriculture, 42, 258, 264; climate, 36, 40; ethnic groups, 64, 75; government, 137, 141, 142; health, 104, 105; housing, 98-99, 101; industry, 47, 232, 272; language, 59; libraries, 131; politics, 163, 164; population, 53, 55, 56; press, 191, 192, 193; radio, 188
Tanzania: 263
tatooing: 126
taxes (see also. cattle tax; head tax): 6, 7, 207, 208, 209; income tax, 212
teacher training: 17, 115, 116, 117, 280
Teheza project: 244, 250, 251
telephone and telegraph system: 232
television: ix, 190, 196
temperatures: 40, 41
textiles: 269, 270, 272
Third Force: 153, 156, 161, 162
tilapia fish: 267
tobacco: 210, 218, 226, 237, 255, 260, 261, 269
tombs (see also. ancestor worship): 101, 125, 127
tourism: 178, 182, 220
tracking station for NASA: 176
trade winds: 36, 49
transportation (see also. ports and

harbors; railroads; roads): 46-50, 98, 227-232
traveler's tree: 44
Tsaratanama massif: 34, 39
Tshombe, Moise: 182
Tsiebo, Calvin: 151
Tsimihety people: 60, 61, 64, 65, 73, 74, 76, 77, 80, 82, 95, 99, 126; marriage, 83; taboos, 104
Tsiranana, Philibert: 1, 4, 6, 7, 25, 26, 27, 28, 29; biography, 65, 118, 134, 172, 176; foreign policy, 177, 178, 179, 182; illness, 149, 157, 164; politics, 152, 154, 163, 165, 166, 167, 206; press and, 185, 186; security, 274, 278, 282, 285, 287, 288, 290
Tsiribihina River: 34
Tsitambala confederation: 13
tuberculosis: viii, 105
Tulear Province: xiv, 3, 13, 39, 40, 44, 45, 49, 95, 231; agriculture, 263, 272; demonstrations, 273, 282, 286, 287, 290, 291; ethnic groups, 64, 73; population, 53, 55, 66
Tunisia: 179

unemployment and underemployment: 54, 149, 205, 280
Union of Independents: 26, 27
Union of Malagasy Intellectuals and Academicians: 26
United Nations: ix, 170, 171, 179; agencies of, 112, 113, 181
United States: 150, 166, 218, 232; foreign aid, 225, 226, 281; relations with, x, 169, 170, 171, 175-176; trade with, 102, 263, 268; USIS library, 132

value added tax: 212-213, 217
vanilla: 182, 207, 209, 218, 226, 227, 228, 234, 237, 255, 262-263
Vaovao:. 191, 194
Varoatangy, Joseph: 20
Vatican: 171
Vazimba people: 14, 62, 63, 76
vegetation: 31, 35, 36, 44; endangered forms, 45
Vezo people: 73, 126
vital statistics registration: 137
vocational training: 115-116
Vohemar: xiv, 263
Vy Vato Sakelika: 18, 19

water supply: 96, 107, 184
welfare: 107-108
West Germany: 155, 196, 221, 225, 226,

PUBLISHED AREA HANDBOOKS

550-65	Afghanistan	550-85	Libya
550-98	Albania	550-163	Malagasy Republic
550-44	Algeria	550-45	Malaysia
550-59	Angola	550-161	Mauritania
550-73	Argentina	550-79	Mexico
550-20	Brazil	550-76	Mongolia
550-61	Burma	550-49	Morocco
550-83	Burundi	550-64	Mozambique
550-50	Cambodia (Khmer Rep.)	550-35	Nepal, Sikkim
550-96	Ceylon		and Bhutan
550-159	Chad	550-88	Nicaragua
550-60	China, People's Rep. of	550-157	Nigeria
550-63	China, Republic of	550-94	Oceania
550-26	Colombia	550-48	Pakistan
550-91	Congo (Brazzaville)	550-46	Panama
550-67	Congo (Kinshasa) Zaire	550-156	Paraguay
550-90	Costa Rica	550-92	Peripheral States of
550-152	Cuba		the Arabian Peninsula
550-22	Cyprus	550-42	Peru
550-158	Czechoslovakia	550-72	Philippines
550-54	Dominican Republic	550-162	Poland
550-155	East Germany	550-160	Romania
550-52	Ecuador	550-84	Rwanda
550-150	El Salvador	550-51	Saudi Arabia
550-28	Ethiopia	550-70	Senegal
550-29	Germany	550-86	Somalia
550-153	Ghana	550-93	South Africa, Rep. of
550-87	Greece	550-95	Soviet Union
550-78	Guatemala	550-27	Sudan
550-82	Guyana	550-47	Syria
550-151	Honduras	550-62	Tanzania
550-21	India	550-53	Thailand
550-154	Indian Ocean Territories	550-89	Tunisia
550-39	Indonesia	550-80	Turkey
550-68	Iran	550-74	Uganda
550-31	Iraq	550-43	United Arab Republic
550-25	Israel	550-97	Uruguay
550-30	Japan	550-71	Venezuela
550-34	Jordan	550-57	Vietnam, North
550-56	Kenya	550-55	Vietnam, South
550-81	Korea, North	550-99	Yugoslavia
550-41	Korea, Republic of	550-75	Zambia
550-58	Laos		
550-24	Lebanon		
550-38	Liberia		